The *New* Children's Encyclopedia

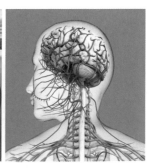

DK

A DORLING KINDERSLEY BOOK

LONDON, NEW YORK, MELBOURNE, MUNICH, and DELHI

Senior editors Carrie Love, Caroline Stamps, Deborah Lock, and Ben Morgan
Senior designers Rachael Smith and Tory Gordon-Harris
Editors Fleur Star, Joe Harris, Wendy Horobin, Lorrie Mack
Designers Clemence Monot, Mary Sandberg, Sadie Thomas, Lauren Rosier, Gemma Fletcher, and Sonia Moore
Packaging services supplied by **Bookwork**

Publishing manager Bridget Giles
Art director Rachael Foster
Production controller Claire Pearson
Production editor Siu Chan
Jacket designer Natalie Godwin
Jacket editor Mariza O'Keeffe
Picture researcher Liz Moore

Consultants Peter Bond, Dr Lynn Dicks, Angus Konstam, Dr Kim Dennis-Bryan, Dr Donald R. Franceschetti, Roger Bridgman MSc, Dr Dena Freeman, and Dr Penny Preston

First published in Great Britain in 2009
This special edition published in 2013 by
Dorling Kindersley Limited,
80 Strand, London, WC2R 0RL

A CIP catalogue record for this book
is available from the British Library

ISBN: 978-1-40934-239-7

Colour reproduction by Media Development
and Printing Limited, United Kingdom
Printed and bound by Hung Hing Printing Group, Hong Kong

Discover more at
www.dk.com

Contents

Introduction

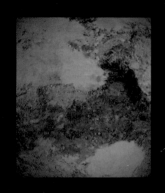

Every child needs a book that answers his or her questions about the world: how it was made, what makes plants grow, why the Sun shines, how the human body works, what happened in the past, and why other countries are different to their own. Properly stimulated, this early thirst for knowledge can become a lifelong process of discovery and understanding. This encyclopedia aims to encourage young readers to make these discoveries for themselves by presenting clear and concise information in an exciting visual manner that draws them in and entices them to read on.

This brand new *Children's Encyclopedia* is divided into thematic chapters. All the major topics are represented: space, earth science, the environment, animals and plants, countries of the world, culture, history, science and technology, and the human body. Stunning photographs and illustrations accompany the text, which is packed with fascinating facts, timelines, and special features. Cross references lead the reader to related topics that help cover the subject in more depth and from new angles. Unique features focus on items of special interest, such as an orchestra or time zones, or collections of bugs or minerals. With so much to look at and find out about, this book will prove to be a valuable reference that young readers will treasure for years to come.

(👁 p110–111) When you see this symbol in the book, turn to the pages listed to find out more about a subject.

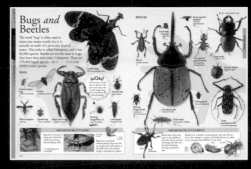

▲COLLECTIONS *look at a particular group of things such as beetles and bugs (* 👁 *p116–117), flags, and mammals.*

▲DETAILED MAPS *accompany features about countries and continents (* 👁 *p128–153). These are packed with facts and figures about the geography, people, and cultures of the region.*

▲GENERAL ARTICLES *focus on particular topics of interest (* 👁 *p196–197). Many have timelines that chronicle key stages in development, fact boxes, and picture features.*

▲ FACT FILES *take an in-depth look at one topic, such as electric cars (* 👁 *p258–259). They detail all you need to know about the subject.*

SPACE

- The Universe was born in a Big Bang about 13.7 billion years ago.

- Space begins 100 km (62 miles) above the Earth.

- There are 8 planets, 5 dwarf planets, and 165 known moons in our solar system.

- The Sun is orbited by billions of asteroids, comets, and Kuiper Belt objects.

- The first artificial satellite, Sputnik, was launched by the Soviet Union in 1957.

? Which star is our nearest star? *Find out on pages 12-13*

? Which planet is the king of the planets? *Find out on pages 16-17*

Definition: **Space** includes the entire Universe – planets, moons, stars, and galaxies. Since its birth in the Big Bang, space has been expanding outwards continuously.

- About 500 people have flown in space since 1961.

- A teaspoonful of material from a neutron star could weigh 5 billion tonnes on the Earth.

- A black hole is a region of space where gravity is so strong that nothing can escape.

- The temperature at the centre of the Sun is 15,000,000°C (27,000,000°F).

- When a dying star explodes, it releases as much energy as the Sun emits in its lifetime.

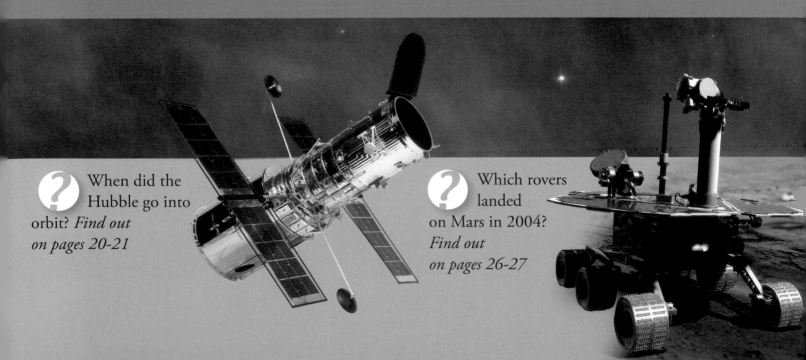

❓ When did the Hubble go into orbit? *Find out on pages 20-21*

❓ Which rovers landed on Mars in 2004? *Find out on pages 26-27*

The Universe

The Universe is unbelievably huge. It is everything we can touch, feel, sense, measure or detect. It includes people, plants, stars, galaxies, dust clouds, light, and even time. Scientists believe our Universe has existed for almost 14 billion years.

EXPANDING UNIVERSE
Across the visible Universe, galaxies are found to be moving away from each other – rather like spots on an inflating balloon. However, it is actually space that is expanding. The further away from us galaxies are, the faster they seem to be moving.

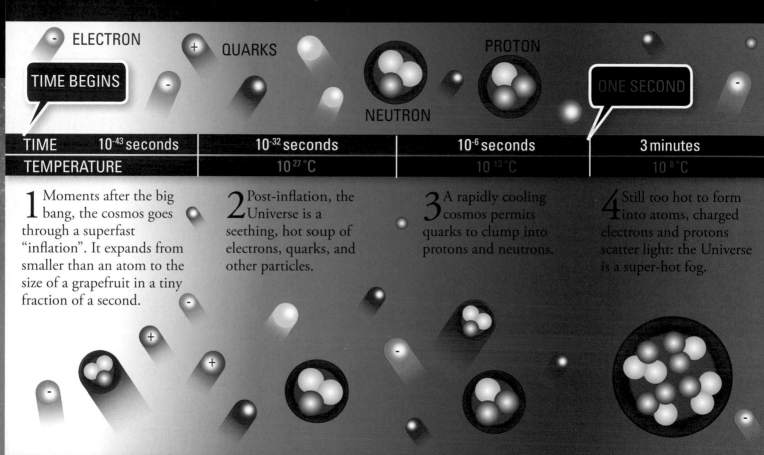

ELECTRON   QUARKS   PROTON

TIME BEGINS   NEUTRON   ONE SECOND

TIME	10^{-43} seconds	10^{-32} seconds	10^{-6} seconds	3 minutes
TEMPERATURE		10^{27} °C	10^{13} °C	10^{8} °C

1 Moments after the big bang, the cosmos goes through a superfast "inflation". It expands from smaller than an atom to the size of a grapefruit in a tiny fraction of a second.

2 Post-inflation, the Universe is a seething, hot soup of electrons, quarks, and other particles.

3 A rapidly cooling cosmos permits quarks to clump into protons and neutrons.

4 Still too hot to form into atoms, charged electrons and protons scatter light: the Universe is a super-hot fog.

SPACE FACTFILE

■ Light from distant galaxies has taken more than 12 billion years to arrive – so we see them as they were before the Earth was born.

■ There are more stars in the Universe than there are grains of sand on all of Earth's beaches.

■ In its first second, the Universe grew from smaller than an atom to about 1,000 times the size of our solar system today.

Astronomers measure distance in light years. One light year is the distance light travels in one year. Visible light travels at 300,000 km/second (186,282 miles/second) in space. It takes a long time for light to reach us from distant stars and planets. Telescopes are like time machines, allowing us to see what things looked like in the past.

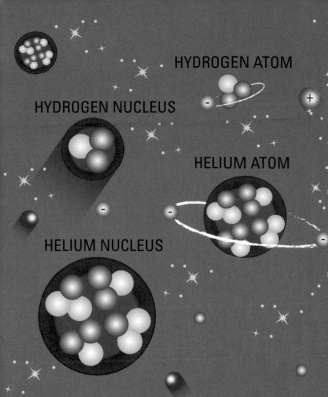

HYDROGEN ATOM

HYDROGEN NUCLEUS

HELIUM ATOM

HELIUM NUCLEUS

PROTOGALAXY

PRESENT DAY

300,000 years	1 billion years	13 billion years	
10,000 °C	-200 °C	-270 °C	

5 Electrons combine with protons and neutrons to form atoms, mostly hydrogen and helium. Light can finally travel long distances across the Universe.

6 Gravity makes hydrogen and helium gas come together to form clouds where the first stars are born. Larger clouds and groups of young stars form the first galaxies.

7 As galaxies cluster together under gravity, the first stars die and spew heavy elements into space: these will eventually form into new stars and planets.

◄ *In 1974, a coded radio message (right) was sent towards the M13 star cluster from the huge Arecibo radio telescope (left). The message will take about 25,000 years to get there, so we may get a reply 50,000 years from now!*

▶ *From the top the symbols represent the numbers from one to ten, some atoms, molecules, DNA, a human, the basics of our solar system, and information about the sending telescope.*

WOW!

Does **ET** really exist? The only place known to support life is Earth. But scientists believe that life could exist on other worlds if they possess liquid water and the right temperature. As telescopes become more powerful, scientists expect to find huge numbers of Earth-like planets. Some may support life.

Galaxies

Scattered across the Universe are billions of galaxies, each containing millions or even billions of stars. They come in many different shapes and sizes. Modern telescopes can now see very old galaxies that were born not long after the birth of the Universe.

SHAPES AND SIZES

Some galaxies are "elliptical" or almost round, like huge balls. Some are spirals, with long, curved arms. Many small galaxies are "irregular", with no special shape. Small galaxies may contain a few million stars and measure less than 3,000 light years across. The galactic supergiants contain billions of Suns and are more than 150,000 light years across.

GALAXY SHAPES

■ **Spiral galaxy** Spinning spiral galaxies have long, curved arms. Young stars, pink nebulas and dust are found in the arms.

■ **Barred spiral** Barred spirals have long, trailing arms and a central bar. The most recent stars form at the ends of the bar.

■ **Elliptical galaxy** These galaxies are round and made up of older stars. Many are found in galaxy clusters. Most are thought to hold supermassive black holes.

■ **Irregular galaxy** Galaxies with no recognisable shape are irregular. They are small with lots of young stars and bright nebulas.

◀ THE WHIRLPOOL GALAXY
This is a huge, well defined spiral galaxy, 31 million light years away. Its smaller satellite galaxy can be seen. There are thought to be supermassive black holes at the centre of most spiral galaxies.

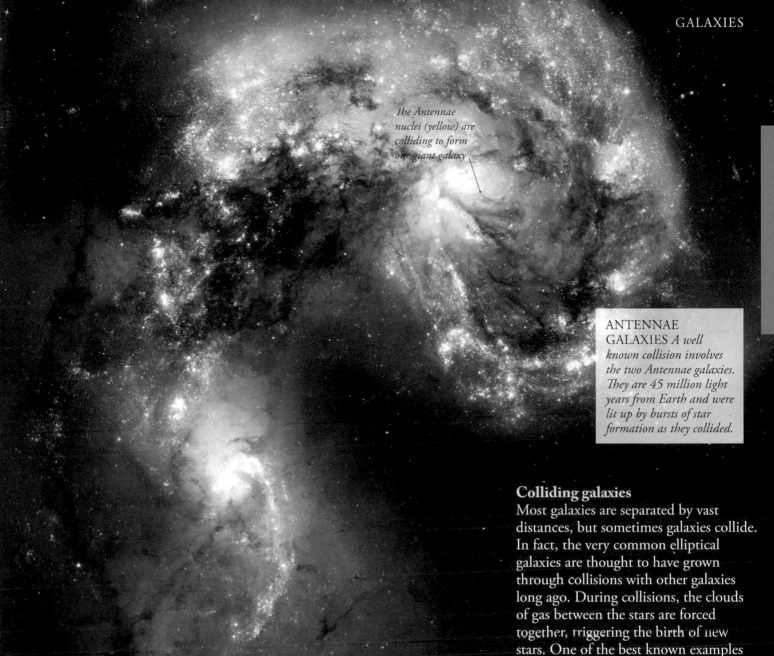

The Antennae nuclei (yellow) are colliding to form one giant galaxy

ANTENNAE GALAXIES *A well known collision involves the two Antennae galaxies. They are 45 million light years from Earth and were lit up by bursts of star formation as they collided.*

Colliding galaxies

Most galaxies are separated by vast distances, but sometimes galaxies collide. In fact, the very common elliptical galaxies are thought to have grown through collisions with other galaxies long ago. During collisions, the clouds of gas between the stars are forced together, triggering the birth of new stars. One of the best known examples is the Antennae galaxies.

GALAXY FACTFILE

▲ SATELLITE GALAXIES *Most large galaxies have smaller, satellite galaxies in orbit around them. The Andromeda galaxy has many satellite galaxies, two are shown in this photo. The Milky Way has several dozen.*

▲ GALAXY CLUSTER *Galaxies form clusters because of their huge gravitational pull. They often pull each other out of shape and may collide.*

▲ BLACK HOLE *Most galaxies have supermassive black holes at their centre. Their gravity is so strong that not even light can escape. We can only see the hot gas, dust, and stars getting pulled in.*

Balls of gas

A star is a huge, glowing ball of hydrogen gas which shines because of nuclear reactions in its core. The hottest stars die within a few million years. Red dwarf stars are the coolest and live the longest.

SPACE

TAKE A LOOK

■ **Constellations** Only a few thousand stars can be seen without a telescope. All of these are in our own galaxy. Ancient people saw patterns and shapes (constellations) in them and named them after mythological creatures or people. The most famous are the 12 zodiac constellations. They form a belt across the sky.

▼ URSA MAJOR *The seven brightest stars, located in the Bear's hindquarters and tail, form the well-known Big Dipper.*

The small orange dots are stars that are still forming.

There are four young, massive stars at the centre of the Orion Nebula.

The clouds are many different colours because they are made up of different gases and dust particles.

Orion Nebula
This galaxy is 15,000 light years away from Earth.

STAR BIRTH

■ **Most stars are born** inside giant dust clouds called nebulas. Parts of these clouds collapse and as they shrink, the gas and dust get hotter and forms a star. When nuclear reactions begin in its core, radiation makes the surrounding material glow. Eventually this is blown away and the star appears.

GHOST HEAD NEBULA

An extremely hot, newborn star lights up the nearby gas and dust.

◀ *The Ghost Head Nebula is a star-forming region in the Large Magellanic Cloud, a satellite galaxy of the Milky Way. The "eyes of the ghost" are two very hot, glowing blobs of gas that are heated by nearby, massive stars.*

12

The Sun

- **Diameter** 1,390,000 km (863,746 miles)
- **Mass (Earth=1)** 330,000
- **Core temperature** 15,000,000 °C (27,000,032 °F)
- **Distance from Earth** 150,000,000 km (93,205,679 miles)

The Sun is our nearest star. Without the Sun, Earth would be frozen and lifeless. The Sun was born in a cloud of gas and dust about 4.6 billion years ago and is now half way through its life.

FACTFILE

- Betelgeuse, a red supergiant, is about 700 times the size of the Sun.
- Neutron stars are only about 20 km (12 miles) across, but so heavy that one teaspoonful could weigh 5 billion tonnes.
- Brown dwarfs are stars that weren't hot enough for nuclear reactions to begin.

Brown dwarf (right) with a nearby orbiting object (red).

THE SUN

The Sun is a yellow dwarf, a fairly ordinary star made mainly of hydrogen. Hydrogen is changed to hclium at its centre (the core). When this happens, huge amounts of radiation are released.

WOW!

The colour of a star is a guide to its surface temperature. The hottest stars are blue or white, stars like the Sun are yellow, and cool stars are orange or red.

Huge plumes of hot gas sometimes stream away from the Sun. They are called prominences.

STAR DEATH

- **Planetary nebulas** Small stars expand to become red giants. When they run out of fuel they collapse. Their outer layers are puffed out in rings called planetary nebulas. Each star creates a different shape, such as a cat's eye (below), a butterfly, or a ring. The central star shrinks to a tiny, hot white dwarf.

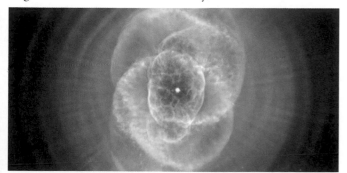

▲ *The Cat's Eye Nebula is made up of many gas clouds ejected by a dying star.*

Before

After

- **Supernovas** When big stars run out of fuel, they collapse. Their outer layers explode into space in a supernova (right). These can briefly outshine an entire galaxy, but are rare events. The photograph on the left shows the same star ten days before a supernova. Medium-sized stars become neutron stars. Massive stars create black holes.

The solar system

The solar system is our local area of space. As its centre is the Sun, our nearest star, which accounts for almost all (99.9 per cent) of the solar system's mass. The Sun's gravity keeps the planets in their orbits.

MERCURY   EARTH

THE SUN   VENUS   MARS

DISTANCE FROM THE SUN

The red line to the right shows the distance of each planet from the Sun in millions of kilometres. Mercury is closest and Neptune is furthest away. Earth is about 150 million kilometres from the Sun.

All of the planets and asteroids go around the Sun in near-circular orbits in the same direction (west to east).

SUN   Mercury   Venus   Earth   Mars

0   250

INNER PLANETS

The four planets nearest the Sun are called the inner planets. They are also known as the rocky planets because they are balls of rock and metal. They are dense and have central cores made of iron.

LUNAR AND SOLAR ECLIPSES

In any year there can be up to seven solar or lunar eclipses, when light from the Sun or Moon is blocked for a short time. Solar eclipses are more common, but are seen only in a narrow area. Lunar eclipses can be seen anywhere on Earth where the Moon is shining in the sky.

A "diamond ring effect" appears just before or just after an eclipse of the sun. Then the Sun's corona (atmosphere) can be seen around the Moon.

People at the centre of the Moon's shadow experience a total solar eclipse

The Sun

The Moon

SOLAR ECLIPSE   The Earth

■ A lunar eclipse happens when the Earth passes between the Sun and the Moon, so that the Earth casts a shadow on the Moon.

■ A solar eclipse happens when the Moon passes between the Earth and the Sun, casting a shadow on the Earth. A total eclipse lasts for up to eight minutes.

JUPITER

SATURN

URANUS

NEPTUNE

▼ SCALE OF THE PLANETS
The Sun is thousands of times bigger than all of the planets rolled into one. Jupiter is by far the largest planet. It is so big that all of the other planets will easily fit inside it.

SPACE

Jupiter   Saturn   Uranus   Neptune

1,000   1,500   2,000   2,500   3,000   3,500   4,000   4,500

OUTER PLANETS

The four planets furthest away from the Sun are called the outer planets. They are huge balls of gas (mainly hydrogen and helium) and liquid and are known as the gas giants. Uranus and Neptune are also known as the ice giants.

FAST FACTS ▶▶▶

■ Only six planets were known before telescopes were first used to look at the sky in 1609.

■ The planets were born in a huge cloud of gas and dust about 4.5 billion years ago.

■ About 4 billion years ago the Sun was 25 per cent dimmer than it is today.

■ Halley's comet doesn't orbit the Sun in the normal clockwise direction. It travels from beyond Neptune to inside the orbit of Venus.

■ Excluding the Sun, Jupiter and Saturn contain 90 per cent of the solar system's mass.

▶ ASTEROID
BELT *Between Mars and Jupiter is the asteroid belt. It separates the inner planets from the outer planets. About 15,000 asteroids have been found and named. They are thought to be rocks that never clumped together to form planets.*

ORBITING THE SUN

The solar system includes eight planets, five dwarf planets, more than 150 moons, and millions more comets and asteroids. These bodies are all orbiting the Sun.

Mercury
Messenger of the Roman gods

- **Earth days to orbit Sun** 88
- **Discovery date** Unknown (but known since ancient times)
- **Number of moons** None
- **Location** First planet from the Sun

The solar system's smallest planet, and the densest, temperatures on Mercury range from a freezing -173°C (279°F) to a blistering 427°C (801°F.) Unlike Earth, Mercury has no atmosphere, so the planet cannot retain heat.

Saturn
Roman god of agriculture

- **Earth years to orbit Sun** 29½
- **Discovery date** Unknown (but known since ancient times)
- **Number of moons** 62
- **Location** Sixth planet from the Sun

Saturn is an enormous gas giant, made mainly of hydrogen gas. It is so light that it would float – if you could find a big enough ocean! Its rings are made of billions of small, icy chunks orbiting the planet. They are the remains of a moon which got too close to Saturn and broke apart.

Venus
Roman goddess of love

- **Earth days to orbit Sun** 224.7
- **Discovery date** Unknown (but known since ancient times)
- **Number of moons** 0
- **Location** Second planet from the Sun

Venus is almost the same size as Earth, but you wouldn't want to visit Venus. Its atmosphere is incredibly dense and the temperature is so high you would be fried to a crisp. The planet is covered in acid clouds that trap heat.

Neptune
Roman god of the sea

- **Earth years to orbit Sun** 165
- **Discovery date** 1846
- **Number of moons** 13
- **Location** Eighth planet from the Sun

This is an icy planet. That's because it is 30 times further away from the Sun than Earth. A day on Neptune lasts 16 hours and 7 minutes. Neptune has huge storms and very strong winds. It also has six dark, thin rings.

Jupiter
King of the Roman gods

- **Earth years to orbit Sun** 12
- **Discovery date** Unknown (but known since ancient times)
- **Number of moons** 66
- **Location** Fifth planet from the Sun

The solar system's largest planet, Jupiter is a gas giant made mainly of hydrogen. It has many storms in its deep, cloudy atmosphere. The largest of these, which has been blowing for at least 300 years, is called the Great Red Spot. Jupiter has more moons than any other planet.

Uranus
Greek god of the sky

- **Earth years to orbit Sun** just over 84
- **Discovery date** 1781
- **Number of moons** 27
- **Location** Seventh planet from the Sun

Uranus was discovered in 1781 by William Herschel. Much of the planet is thought to be made of water and ice. It has 11 thin, dark rings. The planet spins on its side, like a top that has fallen over. This is probably the result of a huge impact long ago.

Mars
Roman god of war

- **Earth days to orbit Sun** 687
- **Discovery date** Unknown (but known since ancient times)
- **Number of moons** 2
- **Location** Fourth planet from the Sun

Mars is one of the closest planets to us in space. It is barren and mainly covered with dust and rocks. Two ice caps cover the poles. It is about half the size of Earth, but has no flowing water, which means there is no life.

Earth

- **Earth days to orbit Sun** 365.2
- **Number of moons** 1
- **Location** Third planet from the Sun

Earth is the only planet known to support life. It has the right temperature for life because it's neither too close to the Sun, nor too far from it. Earth is the only planet with oceans on its surface. It is also the only planet with lots of oxygen – the gas that keeps us alive.

Moon
Luna

- **Days to orbit Earth** 27.3
- **Discovery date** Unknown (but known since ancient times)
- **Location** Only moon of the Earth

The Moon orbits Earth at an average distance of 384,400 km (238,855 miles) – a journey of three days by spacecraft. It was born when a huge Mars-sized object crashed into the young Earth. The dark patches on its surface that make up the face of "the man in the Moon" are old seas of lava. The Moon has no atmosphere.

TAKE A LOOK: PHASES OF THE MOON

As the Moon orbits Earth, it seems to change shape night after night. We say it goes through phases. This is because we see different amounts of the Moon's sunlit side. At new moon it is dark and cannot be seen (except during a solar eclipse). At full moon the entire Earth-facing side is lit up by the Sun. (👁 p31)

▶ MOONS *The period from full moon to full moon lasts 29½ days.*

SPACE

◀ HIDDEN FAR SIDE *The Moon always keeps the same side pointing towards Earth. We never see the "far side".*

WOW!

Earth and Mars have had many ice ages in the past. When they get colder, ice sheets spread out from the poles and cover large areas. Most of the Earth may have been covered in ice 600 million years ago. Ice ages happen because of changes in the orbits and tilt of the planets.

THE OCEAN PLANET

Earth is the only planet with oceans of water on its surface. This water turns to gas, then forms clouds and rain (or snow). It is also the only planet we know with lots of oxygen – the gas that keeps us alive. Its powerful magnetic field shields Earth from harmful particles and radiation from the Sun.

▶ LIFE ON EARTH *Life is thought to have existed on Earth for almost four billion years.*

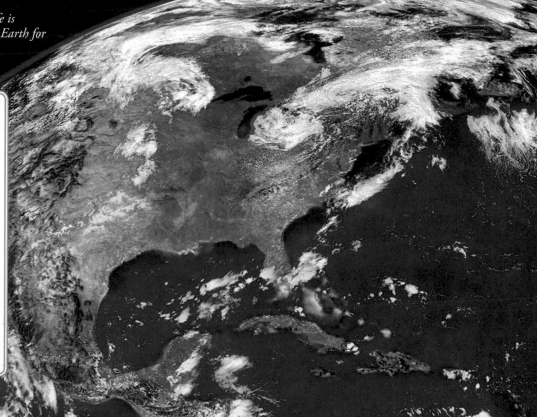

FAST FACTS

- The planets of our solar system orbit the Sun in nearly perfect circles.
- Our nearest neighbour, Venus, is only 38 million km (23½ million miles) away during close approaches.
- Use this simple sentence to remember the order of the planets: **M**y **V**ery **E**ducated **M**other **J**ust **S**erved **U**s **N**oodles (My = Mercury, Mother = Mars).
- Even today, comets and small asteroids crash into the planets (including Earth). One impact 65 million years may have wiped out the dinosaurs.

Flying rocks

There are billions of rocks in the Milky Way that never became big enough to be planets. They orbit the Sun and sometimes crash into each other and the planets. They can create spectacular light shows in the sky or even devastate whole planets.

ASTEROIDS are small, rocky bodies that orbit the Sun. Most of them are found between the orbits of Mars and Jupiter. They are left-overs from the birth of the planets 4.5 billion years ago. The main asteroid belt contains tens of thousands of asteroids. The first asteroid, Ceres, was discovered in 1801.

Pluto
The Roman god of the underworld

- **Diameter** 2,320 km (1,441 miles)
- **Mass (Earth=1)** 0.002
- **Year to orbit Sun** 248
- **Number of moons** 5

Pluto was discovered in 1930. In 2006, astronomers decided it should be classed as a dwarf planet. It is smaller and lighter than the Moon and its egg-shaped orbit means that it sometimes comes closer to the Sun than Neptune. Pluto is very cold because it is so far away from the Sun.

DWARF PLANETS
Other than Pluto, there are four dwarf planets – Haumea, Eris, Makemake, and Ceres. Ceres is the only asteroid big enough to be classed as a dwarf planet. The other dwarf planets are much like Pluto and are found in the outer solar system beyond the orbit of Neptune.

WOW!

Most meteorites are too small to cause much damage. However, 65 million years ago, a 10 km (6 mile) wide asteroid hit the Earth, causing massive earthquakes and tidal waves. A cloud of dust from the impact entered the atmosphere and blocked sunlight, causing plants and animals to die. This impact may have ended the age of the dinosaurs.

► COMETS *orbit the Sun in the outer solar system and sometimes appear in our skies. They have two tails – of gas and dust – and a solid nucleus made of ice. The Hale-Bopp comet passed near our Earth in 1997. It was one of the brightest comets of the 20th century.*

TAKE A LOOK: METEORS

Look up at the sky on a cloudless night and you will eventually see a meteor, or "shooting star". Meteors are particles of dust and rock that burn up as they enter Earth's atmosphere.

It's strange to think that the Willamette meteorite (above), now found in a museum, was once a brilliant fireball shooting towards the Earth. It's made of iron and nickel.

Meteor showers occur at the same time each year, when the Earth passes through trails of dust left by passing comets. Very rarely, a shower may produce thousands of shooting stars that light up the sky.

METEORITES

Meteorites are small chunks of rock that have come from space and landed on the Earth's surface. Most of them are pieces which have broken off asteroids. A few have come from the Moon and Mars.

► METEOR CRATER
One of the youngest and best-preserved craters on Earth is in Arizona, USA. It is 50,000 years old and 180 m (600 ft) deep.

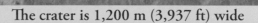

The crater is 1,200 m (3,937 ft) wide

Eye spy space

People have been staring at the heavens since prehistoric times. They measured the positions of the stars and watched the movement of the Sun, Moon, and planets across the sky. But there was a limit to what could be learned with the naked eye.

LICK TELESCOPE *The James Lick Telescope is an antique refracting telescope built in 1888. It is the third largest example of this type of telescope in the world. It is in California and is 4,209 ft (1,283 m) above sea level.*

WOW!

In order to avoid becoming ill with altitude sickness, people visiting mountain-top observatories, such as Keck I and II, have to stop and wait halfway up the mountain. This allows their bodies to adapt to the decrease in oxygen in the air.

TAKE A LOOK

Optical telescopes can obtain images of far away planets and stars. Other telescopes study the Universe by capturing radio waves, X-rays, and other types of radiation.

▲ MARS FROM HUBBLE *This picture of Mars was taken with the Hubble Space Telescope. It shows the southern polar cap, the orange deserts, and sheets of ice cloud.*

SPACE

Keck I and II
Largest optical telescopes today

- **Overall height** 24.6 m (81 ft)
- **Total moving weight** 274 tonnes (270 tons)
- **Total weight of glass** 14.6 tonnes (14⅖ tons)
- **Location** 4,200 m (13,780 ft) above sea level on Mauna Kea, Hawaii

The largest optical telescopes today are the identical Keck I and II, each with 10 m (33 ft) wide mirrors. They are on an extinct volcano in Hawaii. Their telescopes are linked so that the light they collect can be combined. Giant air conditioners run constantly during the day, keeping the dome temperatures at or below freezing.

Each main mirror is made of 36 segments that act like a single piece of glass.

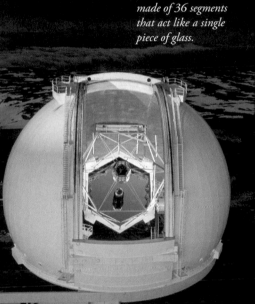

James Webb
Largest space telescope

- **Length** 22 m (72 ft)
- **Weight** 6,500 kg (14,300 lb)
- **Mission length** 5–10 years
- **Location** 1.5 million km (1 million miles) from Earth

In 2013, the James Webb Space Telescope will replace the Hubble Space telescope. It will have a 6.5 m (21 ft) mirror (nearly three times bigger than Hubble's).

Chandra
Most powerful X-ray observatory

- **Length** 13.8 m (45³⁄₁₀ ft)
- **Weight** 4,800 kg (10,560 lb)
- **Mission length** 10 years
- **Location** Earth orbit

Today, large space observatories, like Chandra, are used to study very hot, X-ray objects such as supernovas, white dwarfs and active galaxies. X-rays are captured by four pairs of cylindrical mirrors.

Hubble space observatory
Famous NASA-ESA observatory

- **Height** 13.3 m (43³⁄₅ ft)
- **Weight** 10,843 kg (23,855 lb)
- **Mission length** 23 years
- **Location** Earth orbit

Launched in 1990, the world's most famous space telescope has a 2.4 m (7½ ft) mirror. It is named after American astronomer, Edwin Hubble, who showed that the Universe is expanding.

Very Large Array
27-dish radio telescope

- **Size** 27 dishes, each 25 m (82 ft) across
- **Length of each railway arm** 21 km (13 miles)
- **Location** Socorro, New Mexico, USA

The Very Large Array is currently the world's largest radio telescope array, consisting of 27 dish antennae. The dishes can be moved along the arms of a Y-shaped railway network.

Allen Telescope Array
350-dish radio telescope

- **Size** 350 dishes, each 6.1 m (20 ft) across
- **Location** Hat Creek, California, USA

Under construction, this array is planned to contain 350 dishes inside a 1 km- (⅗ mile-) wide circle. They will be linked and act as a single dish to study the distant Universe and search for alien life.

Giant Magellan
7 mirror optical giant

- **Height** Seven 8.4 m (27½ ft) mirrors
- **Total moving weight** more than 1,000 tonnes (more than 1,000 tons)
- **Location** Cerro Las Campanas, Chile

Due to be completed in 2017, the Giant Magellan will produce images ten times sharper than the Hubble Space Telescope.

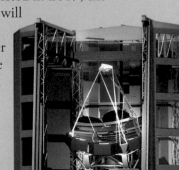

The Apollo programme

In the early 1960s, Russia was ahead in the space race, so President Kennedy announced that American astronauts would land on the Moon before 1970. In July 1969, after spending 25 billion dollars on the *Apollo* programme, they did.

GETTING THERE

■ The astronauts' journey to the Moon would not have been possible without the *Saturn V*, the most powerful rocket ever built. The huge, three stage rocket towered 110 m (361 ft) above the Florida launch pad. After the first two stages ran out of fuel, they were released and the third stage was used to boost the *Apollo* spacecraft and its crew towards the Moon.

First man on the moon *Apollo 11* was the first manned mission to land on the Moon. On 20 July 1969, the lunar module *Eagle* landed and Neil Armstrong made the first lunar footprint.

APOLLO TIMELINE

1966	1967	1968	1969
26 February First unmanned test flight of *Saturn* 1B rocket. It eventually carried the first manned *Apollo* test flight to orbit Earth.	**27 January** Gus Grissom, Edward White, and Roger Chaffee were killed on the launch pad by a fire in their *Apollo* spacecraft during a launch test.	**11 October** First manned *Apollo* flight tests the Command Module in Earth orbit. **21 December** First manned flight around the Moon.	**20 July** *Apollo 11* makes the first manned landing on the Moon.

22

APOLLO SPACECRAFT

For the three-day trip between Earth and the Moon, the *Apollo* crew spent most of their time in the cone-shaped Command Module (CM). The crew also returned to Earth in the Command Module and landed by parachuting into the ocean.

🔍 **TAKE A LOOK**

■ Scientists wanted to learn more about the Moon, so astronauts collected lots of soil and rock samples.

▶ Bending in spacesuits wasn't easy, so tools were designed to pick things up. Altogether, 380 kg (838 lb) of rocks were brought to Earth and stored in a special room.

SPACE

▼ **COMMAND MODULE** One astronaut stayed in the CM in orbit around the Moon. The others went down to the Moon's surface.

◀ **LUNAR MODULE** *The Moon lander was officially called the lunar module. The crew lived in the upper of the two sections. It was this section that blasted off from the Moon and carried them back to the CM.*

Dish antenna for communications with Earth.

A camera took pictures and sent them back to Earth.

The wheels were solid and made of wire mesh.

The moon buggy Walking and carrying samples was hard work, even in the Moon's low gravity (everything weighs one sixth of what it does on Earth). So NASA gave the last three *Apollo* crews a lunar rover to drive. Crews travelled further and could carry more.

1970

13 April An oxygen tank exploded on *Apollo 13* cancelling its Moon landing.

1971

26 July Launch of *Apollo 15*, the first mission with a rover.

1972

19 December Splashdown of Apollo 17, the last manned mission to the Moon.

1975

17 July *Apollo-Soyuz* docking: first joint US-Russian manned mission.

Exploring space

The Space Age began in 1957, with the launch of *Sputnik*, the world's first artificial satellite, by the Soviet Union. In 1961, Yuri Gagarin became the first person to fly in space.

The International Space Station is the most expensive and ambitious space project ever flown. The 450 tonne (443 ton), station is being built in Earth orbit by the USA, Russia, Japan, Canada, and 11 European countries.

International Space Station (ISS)

▶ LARGEST OBJECT *The International Space Station is the largest object ever to orbit the Earth.*

FAST FACTS

- Valeri Poliakov holds the record for the longest space mission – 437 days.
- Mir flew more than 3 billion km (1⁹⁄₁₀ billion miles) in its lifetime.
- Mir space station was home to 111 people (1986–2001).
- The shuttle *Challenger* blew up in 1986, 71 seconds after launch.
- The shuttle *Columbia* broke apart during its return to Earth in 2003.
- More than 90 per cent of the world's population can see the International Space Station when it flies overhead.
- The International Space Station orbits Earth every 90 minutes.

THE FIRST SPACE STATIONS

Space stations are places where people can live and work in space for long periods of time. The first space station, Salyut (Salute) 1, was launched by the Soviet Union on 19 April 1971. Six more *Salyuts* were launched until 1986 – two of them mainly for taking spy photographs.

▶ SALYUT 7 SPACE STATION
The 20 tonne (19½ ton) Salyut 7 space station was launched in 1982 and burned up during re-entry in 1991.

FOOTBALL FIELD ▶
When it is finished in 2010, the ISS will be about the size of a football field.

TIMELINE OF SPACE EXPLORATION

1950s

1957
First man-made satellite, *Sputnik*, in space.

1959
First pictures of the far side of the Moon (*Luna 3*).

1960s

1961
First human in space, Yuri Gagarin.

1963
First woman in space, Valentina Tereshkova.

1965
Alexei Leonov makes first spacewalk.

1969
First man to walk on the Moon, Neil Armstrong.

Space shuttle In 1981, a new space age began when the first reusable spacecraft blasted off from Cape Canaveral, Florida. Five US space shuttle orbiters have been built. They come back to Earth like giant gliders.

▼ SPACE SHUTTLE LANDING
The shuttle lands on a runway at a speed of 345 km/h (215 mph). If it misses the runway it go round and try again. A tail parachute helps to slow it down.

BACK TO THE MOON

The USA, Russia, Europe, and Japan are planning to send people back to the Moon by 2020. The USA is developing the *Ares I* and V rockets. *Ares I* will carry a crewed spacecraft called *Orion,* which will carry six people to the International Space Station and eventually on to the Moon.

▲ THE SPACECRAFT ORION *will dock with the International Space Station.*

Space tourism Almost all of the astronaut and cosmonaut flights have been funded by tax payers. However, space tourism is becoming increasingly popular. The first real space tourist was millionaire businessman Dennis Tito, who paid 20 million US dollars for a week on board the ISS.

Dennis Tito

WOW!

Just 12 astronauts have walked on the Moon. They are the only people ever to have set foot on another world. Nearly 500 people have flown around the Earth since Gagarin's historic flight. Most have come from Russia or the United States.

▼ VIRGIN GALACTIC *is selling tickets for suborbital flights to an altitude of 68 km (42 miles).*

1970s	1980s	1990s	2000s
1973 *Skylab* launch – the first US space station.	**1986** *First* section of Mir space station launched.	**1998** First part of the ISS launched.	**2004** *Cassini-Huygens* in orbit around Saturn.

1977 *Voyager* 2, then 1 are launched to Jupiter, Saturn, and beyond.

The red planet

Apart from Earth, Mars is the most suitable planet for humans to live on. It looks red because iron minerals in its surface rocks have rusted. In the past, it was much more like Earth than it is today.

GIANT CANYONS

The Valles Marineris are more than 4,000 km (2,500 miles) long – 10 times the length of the Grand Canyon – and extend a fifth of the way around Mars. The canyon is about 7 km (5 miles) deep and more than 600 km (375 miles) wide in the centre.

These dark circles are volcanoes.

VALLES MARINERIS
The canyon system was discovered by the Mariner 9 orbiter (after which it was named).

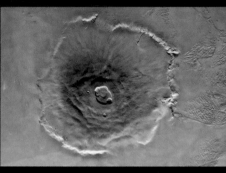

Volcanoes Mars has the largest volcanoes in the solar system. The most impressive is Olympus Mons, which is 600 km (375 miles) across and 26 km (more than 16 miles) high. The volcano hasn't erupted for millions of years.

POLAR ICE CAPS

■ There are ice caps at both Martian poles, but they are much smaller than Earth's. Each pole is different. The northern sheet is about 3 km (2 miles) thick and mainly water ice. The southern polar cap is colder but thicker, and made of water ice with a coating of carbon dioxide ice. The polar caps melt and shrink in summer, then grow in winter when the temperature drops.

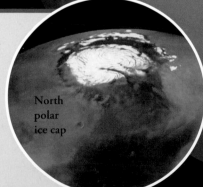

North polar ice cap

TIMELINE OF MARS EXPLORATION

1960s

1960
Korabl 4 (USSR) did not reach Earth orbit.

1962
Mars 1 (USSR) lost contact on way to Mars.

1964
Mariner 4 (US) the first success returned 21 images.

1969
Mariner 7 (US) was a success and returned 126 images.

1970s

1971
Mariner 9 (US) the first successful Mars orbiter.

1973
Mars 5 (USSR) Orbiter got 22 days of data.

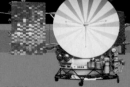

1976
Viking 1 (US) made the first successful landing on Mars.

WHERE IS THE WATER?

Today, Mars is very cold and the air is too thin for liquid water to exist on the surface. However, huge, winding channels suggest that large rivers raged over the surface long ago. The water was probably released in sudden floods, possibly when underground ice melted. These river channels have been dry for billions of years.

Northern plains

WOW!

Mars has two small moons, Phobos and Deimos. They are thought to be asteroids that were captured by Mars long ago. Phobos is no more than 27 km (17 miles) across with large craters on its surface. Deimos is just 12 km (7 miles) across and has a smoother surface.

Phobos

Mars Explorers Many robotic spacecraft have been sent to Mars but failed. The successful *Viking* missions in the 1970s included two orbiters and two landers. The first rover was part of the *Mars Pathfinder* mission of 1997. Today there are three large rovers on Mars (*Spirit*, *Opportunity*, and *Curiosity*) which are still returning images and data to Earth.

Southern highlands

▶ SPIRIT AND OPPORTUNITY ROVERS *Two American automated (robotic) rovers landed on Mars in January 2004 to search for evidence of water.*

1980s		1990s	2000s	
1988-89 *Phobos 1 and 2* (USSR) were both lost on route to Mars.	**1997** *Mars Pathfinder* (US) delivers first successful rover to Mars.	**1998** *Nozomi* Japan's first Mars explorer failed with fuel problems.	**2003** Europe's *Mars Express* orbiter began taking detailed pictures of Mars.	**2008** *Phoenix* (US) landed in Martian Arctic and operated for over 5 months (before its batteries went flat).

EARTH

- The Earth formed from the gas and dust of a nebula 4.5 billion years ago.

- Earth's inner core is as hot as the surface of the Sun.

- It spins on its axis at about 1,600 km/h (1,000 mph).

- Seventy per cent of Earth's surface is covered in water. Most of this is salt water.

- At the moment, Earth is the only planet in the Universe known to support life.

? How does
water shape
a coastline?
Find out on page 45

? How hard is
fluorite?
Find out on page 41

Definition: **Earth** is the planet on which we live. Unlike other planets in our solar system, it is covered with liquid water, which makes it look blue.

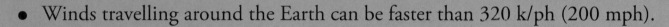

- Winds travelling around the Earth can be faster than 320 k/ph (200 mph).

- The highest tsunami on record was 525 metres (1,720 feet) tall.

- A manned submersible has reached an ocean depth of about 11 km (7 miles).

- Stromboli volcano (off the coast of Sicily) has erupted continuously for 2,000 years.

- Earth is surrounded by a thick atmosphere, largely composed of the gas nitrogen.

? How can wind create huge rock sculptures?
Find out on page 44

? What causes Earth's seasons to change?
Find out on page 53

Our unique world

Among all the planets in the solar system, Earth is the only one known to support life. It is a perfect distance from the Sun, has a breathable atmosphere, and is bathed in life-giving water.

The atmosphere gives us our weather, provides us with oxygen, and protects us from harmful solar energy.

EARTH'S STRUCTURE

Earth may look like a solid ball of rock, but if you slice through it you can see it is made up of different layers. At the centre is a hot metallic core. It is surrounded by the stony mantle, which is like sticky toffee. On top is a thin crust that forms the continents and ocean floor.

The crust shapes the continents and sea floor.

The outer mantle is fused to the crust.

The inner mantle has a temperature of about 3,000ºC (5,400ºF).

The outer core is made of molten metal.

The temperature of the inner core is about 6,000ºC (10,800ºF).

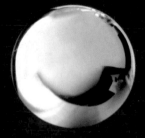

▲ EARTH'S CORE
The core is a mixture of iron and nickel mixed with lighter elements. The pressure at the centre is so high that the inner core remains solid.

TIMELINE OF LIFE ON EARTH

EARLY EARTH

4.5 billion years ago: Earth forms into a red-hot ball of liquid rock.

4.2 billion years ago: Earth develops a crust, and oceans form.

FIRST LIFE

3.5 billion years ago: first living cells.

630 million years ago: complex (multicellular) animals evolve.

EXPLOSION OF LIFE

540 million years ago: the Cambrian explosion – sudden appearance of many new species with teeth, feet, intestines, spines, and hard shells.

416 million years ago: first land animals appear.

500 million years ago: Earth's atmosphere becomes breathable.

Magnetic field Our Earth acts like a huge bar magnet, which is why it has north and south poles. The magnetic field is thought to be produced by movement in the liquid outer core. The molten metal carries an electrical charge, which generates an electromagnetic field as it swirls around.

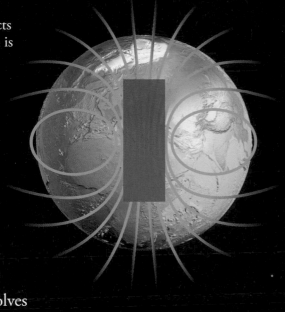

 TAKE A PICTURE

Auroras are created when high-energy particles are drawn in at the poles by the magnetic field. This energizes atoms in the atmosphere, which show as curtains of light.

DAY AND NIGHT

Our planet doesn't stand still. Every 24 hours it revolves once around its axis, so that half the planet is in sunlight and the other half is in darkness. If it didn't rotate, one side would have permanent day and the other, permanent night.

Phases of the moon If you look at the night sky you will see that the appearance of the Moon changes over the course of a month. As the Moon orbits Earth, the angle between it and the Sun shifts, so that the amount of the Moon's face that is lit by the Sun changes. It is difficult to see a new Moon as the light is shining on the side we cannot see. A slender crescent then appears and gradually increases (waxes) until the full face is lit. It then starts to decrease (wane) back into darkness.

WAXING GIBBOUS

FIRST QUARTER

FULL MOON

WANING GIBBOUS

WAXING CRESCENT

EARTH

LAST QUARTER

NEW MOON

SUN

WANING CRESCENT

We only ever see the same face of the Moon because for every orbit it makes around Earth it spins once on its axis.

PANGAEA

225 million years ago: all land joined into one continent, Pangaea.

AGE OF THE DINOSAURS

145 million years ago: the modern continents begin to take shape.

225 million years ago: the age of the dinosaurs begins.

65 million years ago: mass extinction of species, including the dinosaurs.

HUMANKIND

250,000 years ago, modern humans appeared.

Today

Dynamic planet

Earth's surface is constantly changing. The rocks it is made from have been recycled many times. Even though we rarely feel it moving, the signs that our planet is active are all around us.

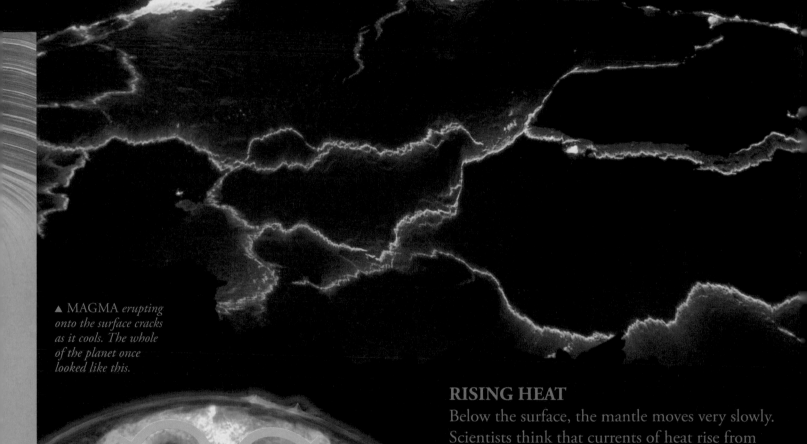

▲ MAGMA *erupting onto the surface cracks as it cools. The whole of the planet once looked like this.*

RISING HEAT

Below the surface, the mantle moves very slowly. Scientists think that currents of heat rise from the lower mantle, cool as they near the surface, and then sink back down again. This has a dragging effect on the surface layers, carrying them along like a conveyor belt.

Earth's metal core provides the heat. It contains radioactive elements that give out heat as they become more stable. Even though the inner core is very hot, the huge pressure keeps it solid. The slightly cooler outer core is liquid.

EARTH'S CRUST

The uppermost surface of Earth is called the crust. It has two layers: a light top layer and a slightly thinner but denser bottom layer. The crust is broken into pieces that fit together like a jigsaw. These plates float on the mantle. As the mantle moves, the plates go with it.

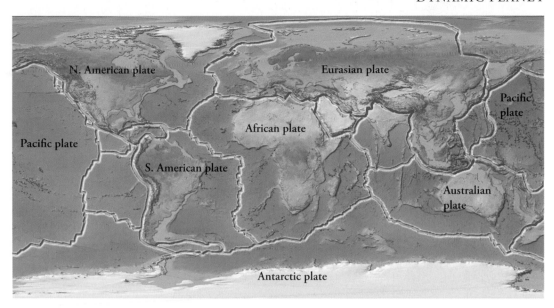

N. American plate

Eurasian plate

Pacific plate

African plate

Pacific plate

S. American plate

Australian plate

Antarctic plate

EARTH

Divergent boundaries At the points where the mantle currents rise upwards, the plates above them get pulled apart (diverge). Some of the mantle melts to form magma and fills the gap between the plates. Each time this happens the plates move apart. Sometimes the plates simply slide past each other without any volcanic activity. These are called transform boundaries.

Plates moving in opposite directions.

Plates slide past each other at transform boundaries.

Oceanic crust forms as the magma cools and solidifies.

Magma rises up from the mantle.

Ridge forms along divergent boundary.

Volcanoes form where the land is pushed up.

Direction of continental plate.

The oceanic plate starts to melt and rises to the surface as magma.

The oceanic plate is pulled under the continental plate.

Direction of oceanic plate.

Convergent boundaries When two plates meet (converge), one of the plates is pulled under the other. If a continental plate meets an oceanic plate, the denser oceanic plate gives way. If two oceanic plates meet, the cooler, older plate is dragged under. Should two continental plates collide, the rocks on both sides bend and fold to form mountains.

TAKE A LOOK: PLATE MOVEMENTS

The continents have not always been in the positions they are today. Since Earth's crust cooled they have split, collided, rotated, and reformed. They are still moving about 15 cm (6 in) a year.

N. America

▲ *About 225 million years ago all the continents were joined together.*

N. America

▲ *Over time, the plates beneath began to pull the continents apart.*

N. America

▲ *Today, the continents look like this, but they are still on the move.*

Volcanoes and earthquakes

People have always been terrified by the fiery power of volcanoes and earthquakes shaking the ground. Although these are just the natural movements of our planet, they can be highly destructive.

VOLCANOES

Volcanoes form when molten rock pushes up through Earth's crust. When molten rock is underground it is called magma, but when it flows onto the surface it is called lava. Some volcanoes erupt gently but others can be explosive, blasting gas, ash, and rock into the air. Volcanoes may erupt at regular intervals, while others lie dormant for centuries.

▲ MOLTEN LAVA
Lava that does not contain much gas flows over longer distances.

Parasitic cones form over fractures in the crust.

Vent

Sills are formed when magma pushes between existing rock strata.

Side vent

Lava erupting from a side vent.

Underground magma chamber

Dykes form in fissures in the rock.

▲ SHIELD VOLCANO *These are broad, low-profile cones. They are formed when runny lava flows over a long distance before it cools and hardens.*

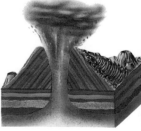

▲ CINDER CONE *Most volcanoes are cinder cones. They are made of ash and lava blown into fragments by escaping gas.*

Ash clouds blast fine particles high up into Earth's atmosphere where they can affect the world's weather for months.

EARTHQUAKES

Earthquakes occur when two blocks of Earth's crust slip past each other. The place where this happens is called a fault. Because the blocks do not slide easily, a large amount of energy is released when they move. This ripples away like waves on a pond, shaking the ground above.

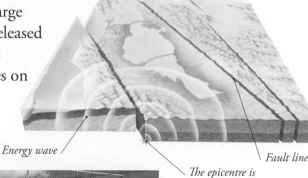

Energy wave

Fault line

The epicentre is the source of the earthquake.

◄ ON SHAKY GROUND
When the ground shakes, buildings and other structures may collapse. The strength of an earthquake is measured using the Richter scale. This earthquake in Kobe, Japan, measured 7.3. It lasted for 20 seconds, and made 200,000 buildings fall down. An even bigger earthquake hit Japan in 2011.

RING OF FIRE

■ The "ring of fire" lies around the rim of the Pacific Ocean. It is an area where a number of crustal plates meet, resulting in frequent volcanic and earthquake activity. There are 452 volcanoes in the ring, and 80 per cent of the world's largest earthquakes occur in this area.

▲ COMPOSITE VOLCANO *These cones rise steeply towards the summit. They are the most deadly type because they usually erupt explosively.*

TSUNAMI

■ **Tsunamis** are giant ocean waves caused by a sudden movement of the ocean floor. Sometimes colliding plates get stuck. When they finally release, it can trigger an earthquake, which gives the overlying water a huge shove. The waves grow stronger as they cross the ocean, and cause devastation when they hit land.

Bangladesh 2.5 hours

India 2 hours

Sri Lanka 1.5 hours

Malaysia 30 minutes

Epicentre

Indonesia 15 minutes

▲ WORLD-WIDE WAVE *The tsunami of 2004 began with an earthquake off the coast of Indonesia. The wave was eventually felt as far away as Iceland and Chile.*

▲ BEFORE *Banda Aceh in Indonesia was close to the epicentre of the 2004 earthquake and was the first place the tsunami struck.*

▲ AFTER *Most of the northern shore was submerged by the tsunami. An estimated 230,000 people in eleven countries died when the waves hit land.*

Making mountains

Mountain ranges cover about a fifth of Earth's land surface. They have built up over millions of years, as massive tectonic plates crash into one another. Many ranges, such as the Himalayas, are still being pushed upwards.

LIFT AND FOLD

Most mountains are fold mountains, which have been created by the movement of tectonic plates across Earth's surface. When two tectonic plates push against each other, the rock of Earth's crust lifts up and folds over on itself. The folds get bigger and bigger over time.

Shifting sand This experiment below uses layers of sand on a sheet of paper to show how rock strata buckle and double over as a mountain forms. Each layer of sand represents a layer of Earth's crust. The paper is pulled along slowly, at a rate of 1 cm (½ inch) per 100 seconds. As the paper moves, it drags the sand with it. This is similar to the way the Earth's slowly flowing upper mantle pulls along the crust.

▲ MOUNTAIN MACHINE *The paper and sand are held between fixed wooden blocks inside a tank.*

▼ SEDIMENTS *Layers of sediment are laid down evenly on top of the paper.*

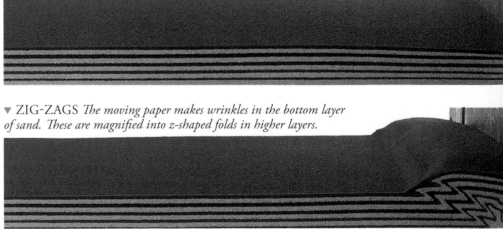

▼ ZIG-ZAGS *The moving paper makes wrinkles in the bottom layer of sand. These are magnified into z-shaped folds in higher layers.*

▼ HIGHER AND HIGHER *The sand folds build up on top of each other, making large loops.*

▲ CROSS SECTION *This cliff face in Dorset, England shows how rock strata twisted and folded over as the African and European plates collided millions of years ago. This same collision gave birth to the Alps.*

TYPES OF MOUNTAINS

Not all mountains are fold mountains. Some are formed by eruptions from volcanoes, and others are made up of massive blocks of rock pushed up as Earth's crust cracks. Mountains are given their jagged appearance by heavy erosion, which strips the rock away from their sides.

Going up The higher you climb, the air becomes thinner and the temperature gets colder. The tree line marks the cut-off point beyond which it is too cold for trees to grow.

TAKE A PICTURE

The Matterhorn is an easily recognisable peak in the Alps. It was first climbed in 1865 by an English mountaineer, Edward Whymper.

FAMOUS MOUNTAINEERS

■ **Sir Edmund Hillary** and **Tenzing Norgay** were the first climbers to reach the summit of Mount Everest. They did so on 29th May 1953. Hillary was a New Zealander, and Norgay was Nepalese.
■ **Lino Lacedelli** and **Achille Compagnoni** were Italian mountaineers, and the first people to conquer K2. They reached its peak on July 31st, 1954.
■ **Richard Bass** was the first person to climb the "Seven Summits" – the tallest mountains on each of the world's seven continents. He finished on 30th April, 1985.

EARTH

MT EVEREST
(SAGARMATHA)
Nepal–China
8,848 m (29,029 ft)

K2
(MT GODWIN AUSTEN)
Pakistan–China
8,611 m (28,251 ft)

A SAVAGE MOUNTAIN *One in four people die when they try to reach the summit of K2.*

ACONCAGUA
Argentina
6,960 m (22,835 ft)

KILIMANJARO
Tanzania
5,895 m (19,341 ft)

MT MCKINLEY
United States
6,194 m (20,322 ft)

MELTING ICE-CAP
It is estimated that the ice-caps on Mount Kilimanjaro will have melted by 2020.

MATTERHORN
(CERVINO)
Italy–Switzerland
4,478 m (14,692 ft)

MT FUJI
Japan
3,776 m (12,388 ft)

MONT BLANC
France–Italy
4,807 m (15,770 ft)

MT COOK
(AORAKI)
New Zealand
3,764 m (12,349 ft)

NAMED BY AN EXPLORER
Mount Cook was named by the explorer Captain James Cook. Its original, Maori name is Aoraki.

AN ACTIVE VOLCANO *The last eruption of Mount Fuji was in 1707–1708, when it erupted for 16 days. Some scientists believe that it may erupt again soon.*

VESUVIUS
Italy
1,277 m (4,190 ft)

OTHER NAMES *Mountains often have different names in different languages. The Matterhorn is so-called in English and German, but in Italian it is called Cervino and in French, Mont Cervin.*

Rocks

Our planet is a big ball of rock. Rock is what gives Earth its features – mountains, canyons, and plains. Rocks can be massive, or as small as a grain of sand. All of them started life deep inside the mantle.

WHAT IS A ROCK?

Rocks are usually made up of several different minerals. Looking closely at a rock can tell you a lot about its history. The shapes of crystals or grains in the rock and how they fit together reveal whether the rock is one of three types: igneous, metamorphic, or sedimentary.

▼ STONE CYCLE
Earth's rocks are endlessly recycled, but it takes millions of years for rocks to form and change.

Igneous rocks

Sedimentary rocks

Metamorphic rocks

Igneous rocks began as molten rock deep inside Earth. They are the commonest rocks in Earth's crust. Some were erupted onto the surface as lava, others solidified underground. The speed at which they cooled is shown by the crystals they contain – big crystals indicate slow cooling.

Metamorphic rocks These began as other types of rocks but have been altered by great heat, pressure, or both, deep inside Earth's crust. Most of the minerals in the original rock have changed. These rocks often show folded or squashed bands.

Most sedimentary rocks are made of small particles of other rocks, transported by water, wind, or ice. The particles may all be the same size or a jumble of sizes. These build up in layers, and pressure from new layers above squashes them into hard rock.

Minerals

When Earth first formed, it inherited many different chemical elements. Over billions of years, these elements combined to form thousands of different chemical compounds.

WHAT IS A MINERAL?

Minerals are the building blocks of every type of rock. They consist of a single chemical element or a compound of mixed elements. There are about 4,000 different minerals, but only 100 occur in any great quantity.

Types of minerals The common minerals that make up Earth's crust are called "rock-forming minerals". They are mostly compounds of the elements silicon and oxygen. Other minerals are "ore minerals" – they contain large amounts of mainly metallic elements that are very useful to us.

How minerals form Most minerals form when molten rock or a hot solution cools and forms crystals. The crystals that form are affected by pressure and temperature, so a mineral can look different depending on how it crystallizes. However, some minerals, such as coal and chalk, start off as living organisms.

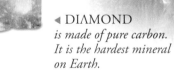

◄ DIAMOND
is made of pure carbon. It is the hardest mineral on Earth.

◄ CHALCOPYRITE
is a copper and iron sulphide ore seen here mixed with clear quartz crystals.

WHAT USE IS A MINERAL?

Minerals have a huge range of practical uses…

■ They can be mined to extract metals (for example, copper, gold, or silver).
■ Minerals like potash and apatite can be used as plant fertilizers.
■ Crystals can be cut and polished into gemstones (diamond, ruby, emerald).
■ Coloured minerals are used as pigments.
■ Some minerals are used in bath or beauty products.

CRYSTALS

Most minerals are crystals. The atoms in the minerals are arranged in regular patterns, which give crystals their simple geometrical shapes. The crystal structure affects many of the mineral's physical properties, such as hardness, and how the crystal fractures.

▲ CINNABAR *is a sulphide of mercury that forms hexagonal crystals.*

▲ GALENA *is the name given to lead sulphide. Its crystals are cubic in shape. If it is hit with a hammer, the crystals break off into smaller cubes.*

Rock and mineral guide

Collecting rocks and minerals can be a rewarding hobby. Rocks are identified by features like colour, texture, and mineral content. Minerals are classified by crystal structure, hardness, and how they break.

KEY

Rocks are graded by the size of their grains, as either fine, medium, or coarse. The size limits for each category vary depending on whether rocks are igneous, metamorphic, or sedimentary (p28).

(F) = fine
(M) = medium
(C) = coarse

IGNEOUS ROCKS

(F) Obsidian

(F) Pumice

(F) (M) (C) Anorthosite

(M) (C) Kimberlite

(C) Granite

(C) Peridotite

(C) Pegmatite

SEDIMENTARY ROCKS

(F) Chalk

(F) (M) Siltstone

(F) (M) (C) Limestone

(C) Tillite

(C) Conglomerate

METAMORPHIC ROCKS

(F) Slate

(F) (M) Quartzite

(F) (M) (C) Marble

(F) (M) (C) Serpentinite

(M) (C) Schist

(M) (C) Gneiss

EARTH

40

EARTH

MOHS' SCALE

One way of telling the difference between similar looking minerals is to test their hardness. This is measured by scratching minerals against each other. A hard mineral can always scratch a softer one. The hardest mineral is diamond.

1. Talc 2. Gypsum 3. Calcite 4. Fluorite 5. Apatite 6. Feldspar 7. Quartz 8. Topaz 9. Corundum 10. Diamond

Softest → *Hardest*

ORES

Sulphur: 1.5–2.5 on Mohs' scale

Gold: 2.5–3

Silver: 2.5–3

Malachite *(contains copper)*: 3.5–4

Illmenite *(contains titanium)*: 5–6

Magnetite *(contains iron)*: 5–6

Cobaltite *(contains cobalt)*: 5.5

Rhodonite *(contains manganese)*: 5.5–6.5

SEMI-PRECIOUS STONES

Lapis lazuli: 3–5.5

Jade: 6–7

Olivine: 6.5–7

Agate: 7

Amethyst: 7

Tormaline: 7

Zircon: 7.5

PRECIOUS STONES

■ Gemstones are divided into precious and semi-precious stones based on value. The four that qualify as precious are diamond, emerald, sapphire, and ruby.

Diamond

Emerald

Sapphire

Ruby

Riches from the Earth

Many useful materials are hidden away below Earth's surface. Some of these rich resources, such as precious metals and gemstones, have been used since ancient times. Others, such as fossil fuels, are more recent discoveries but equally important.

▲ DRILLING FOR GOLD *A miner drills for deposits of gold at a mine in South Africa. The rock face lies deep underground, and the work is physically demanding and very dangerous.*

MINING

People need to dig up the resources from Earth's crust before they can use them. This is called mining. There are two main techniques, depending on the types of minerals being extracted. They are surface mining, or quarrying, and underground mining.

Underground mining Any minerals buried deep beneath Earth's surface must be extracted using underground mining techniques. Miners use heavy machinery to drill deep shafts under the ground. They lay rails to carry the minerals, drilling gear, waste material and the miners themselves to and from the rock face. Underground mining is dangerous work and much more expensive than surface mining.

▼ IRON MINE
Iron ore mines in Brazil are some of the most productive in the world.

◀ HEMATITE, *the mineral form of iron oxide, is identified by its rusty red streaks.*

Surface mining The largest mines are open-cast mines, which extract minerals on or near Earth's surface. Miners use explosives, diggers, and heavy machinery to dig huge holes in the ground. Most of the world's mining output comes from surface mining, which is much safer than underground mining.

FOSSIL FUELS

Coal, oil, and natural gas are fossil fuels. These vital resources formed from the remains of animals and plants that lived millions of years ago. Over time, the vast pressure and temperature under the ground changed the remains into coal, oil, and natural gas. Fossil fuels now provide most of the world's power.

ENVIRONMENTAL CONCERNS

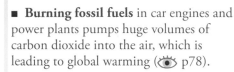

- **Oil spills** from tankers spread over vast distances in ocean currents. These environmental disasters devastate marine wildlife such as fish and seabirds.

- **Burning fossil fuels** in car engines and power plants pumps huge volumes of carbon dioxide into the air, which is leading to global warming ( p78).

- **Oil exploration** destroys habitats in wilderness areas, decimating local populations of animals and plants.

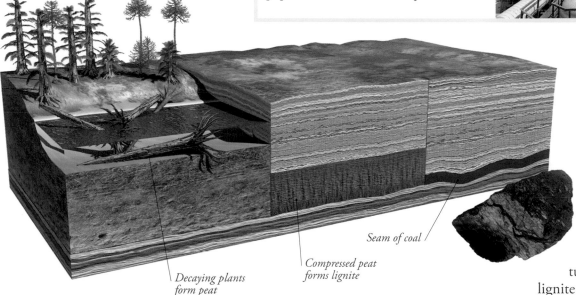

Coal This hard black solid forms when peat deposits become buried underground. Peat is a rich type of soil formed from plants and their decaying remains. Over millions of years, the weight of the top layers of peat pushes down on the lower levels. This squeezes the peat, which first turns into a mineral called lignite and eventually into coal.

Decaying plants form peat

Compressed peat forms lignite

Seam of coal

Oil This thick black liquid forms from the remains of marine animals and plants that lived millions of years ago. The dead bodies were buried under the sea floor and then slowly transformed into crude oil, which became trapped in layers of rock.

Oil rig

▲ STRIKE IT LUCKY *An oil worker guides a giant hydraulic pump into position to extract the crude oil from an oil well.*

Decaying remains of marine life

Rock layer traps the decaying remains

Oil reservoir

43

Erosion

Earth's landscape is constantly changing, as rock and soil are worn away by the destructive effects of water, wind, ice, and gravity. Erosion can be sudden, such as when a landslide happens. But gradual erosion can be just as dramatic, for example as rivers carve deep valleys into the Earth's surface.

WIND EROSION

As wind flows across the land, it lifts up and carries countless grains of sand and other tiny particles. These particles, called sediment, may be blown against rocks at high speeds, grinding away at their surfaces. Over many years wind erosion has the effect of wearing rock into new shapes, and resculpting the landscape. Wind erosion happens most in dry, desert regions.

TELL ME MORE...

What happens to the sediment transported by erosion? Much of it mixes with organic remains and becomes soil. Rivers drop sediment as they lose speed. In time, sediment may become buried and harden into new rock.

LANDSLIDE!

Huge amounts of rock, soil, and mud can suddenly slip down hillsides under the effects of gravity, tearing down trees and burying homes. Landslides may be caused by activities such as tree-felling. Trees' roots hold soil in place, so when forests are cut down, landslides become more likely.

▼ WIND SCULPTURES
Wind erosion wears down soft rock faster than hard rock. As the soft rock disappears, strange shapes are revealed.

The caprock at the top of this pillar is harder than the mudstone underneath.

Wind erosion will eventually wear away the mudstone to the point where the caprock falls off.

WATER EROSION

As rainwater flows downhill, it picks up small fragments of rock. These fragments wear channels into the earth, gradually carving out the beds of rivers. In the same way, ocean waves and tides grind down the rocks of the shoreline, creating bays, headlands, cliffs, and rock pillars called stacks.

TAKE A LOOK: THE POWER OF WATER

Rivers constantly erode away the rock of their own beds, which gradually changes their courses. This can create features such as oxbow lakes.

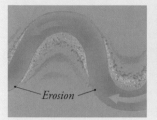

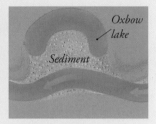

▲ STEP 1 *As a river flows round a meander, it erodes the outside of each bend.*

▲ STEP 2 *The bends gradually change shape, until a shortcut is created.*

▲ STEP 3 *Sediment deposited by the river cuts off the meander.*

Oxbow lake

Sediment

Erosion

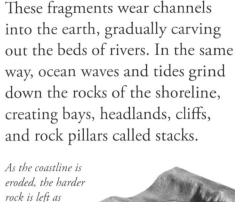

As the coastline is eroded, the harder rock is left as headlands.

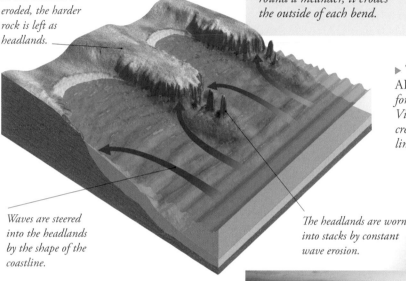

Waves are steered into the headlands by the shape of the coastline.

The headlands are worn into stacks by constant wave erosion.

▶ TWELVE APOSTLES *These rock formations off the coast of Victoria, Australia, were created by the sea eroding limestone headlands.*

ICE EROSION

About 10 per cent of Earth's land surface is covered by slow-moving masses of ice called glaciers. As glaciers move, rocks trapped in the ice scour the land, wearing it smooth. Water can also split rocks as it freezes, since water in cracks expands as it turns to ice.

▲ DEPOSITION *The sediments transported by rivers and by ocean tides can be deposited in large quantities, creating new land features such as this spit.*

A look at time

What time is it right now? The answer depends on where you are. If it's midday in Santiago, Chile it will be midnight in Perth, Australia. To make sense of this, the world is divided into 24 time zones, and clocks in each zone are set to the same time.

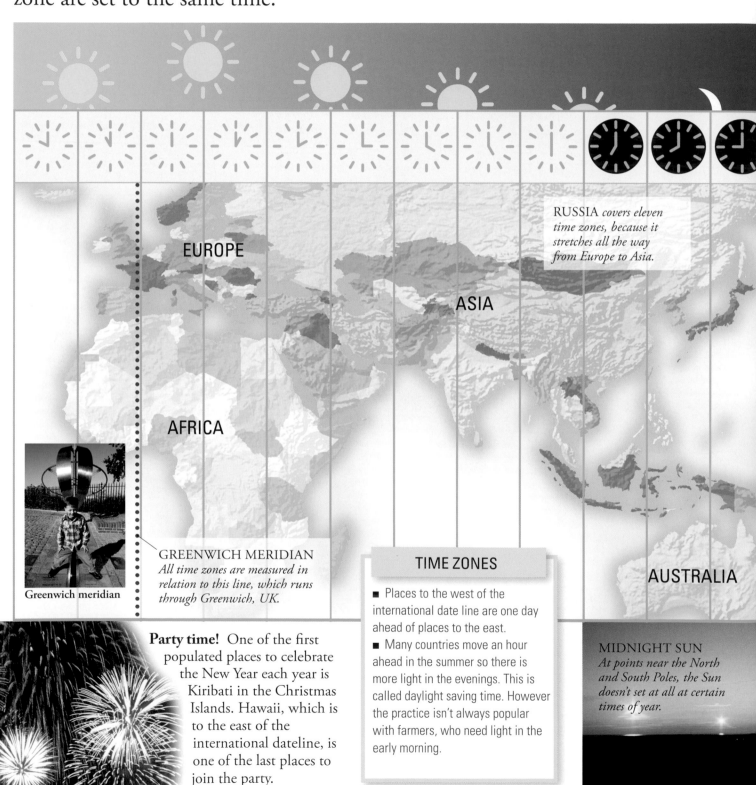

RUSSIA *covers eleven time zones, because it stretches all the way from Europe to Asia.*

EUROPE

ASIA

AFRICA

Greenwich meridian

GREENWICH MERIDIAN
All time zones are measured in relation to this line, which runs through Greenwich, UK.

AUSTRALIA

TIME ZONES

■ Places to the west of the international date line are one day ahead of places to the east.
■ Many countries move an hour ahead in the summer so there is more light in the evenings. This is called daylight saving time. However the practice isn't always popular with farmers, who need light in the early morning.

MIDNIGHT SUN
At points near the North and South Poles, the Sun doesn't set at all at certain times of year.

Party time! One of the first populated places to celebrate the New Year each year is Kiribati in the Christmas Islands. Hawaii, which is to the east of the international dateline, is one of the last places to join the party.

THE TIME BELOW IS...

Some countries are split into several time zones, whereas others lie in just one. If you fly from one side of the United States to the other, you'll find a time zone difference of four hours. In contrast, China has just one official time across the whole country, despite its size.

WOW!

Your internal body clock tells you when to wake and sleep. Plane passengers who cross several time zones may experience jet lag, which makes them tired during the day, but restless at night.

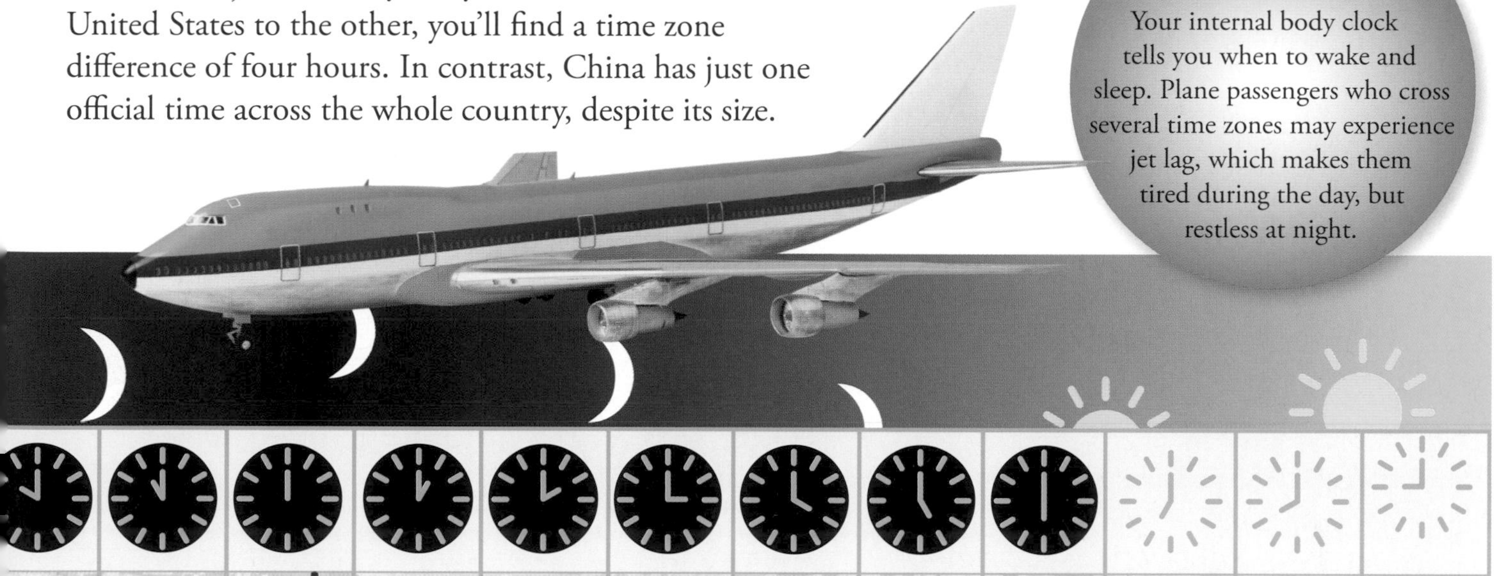

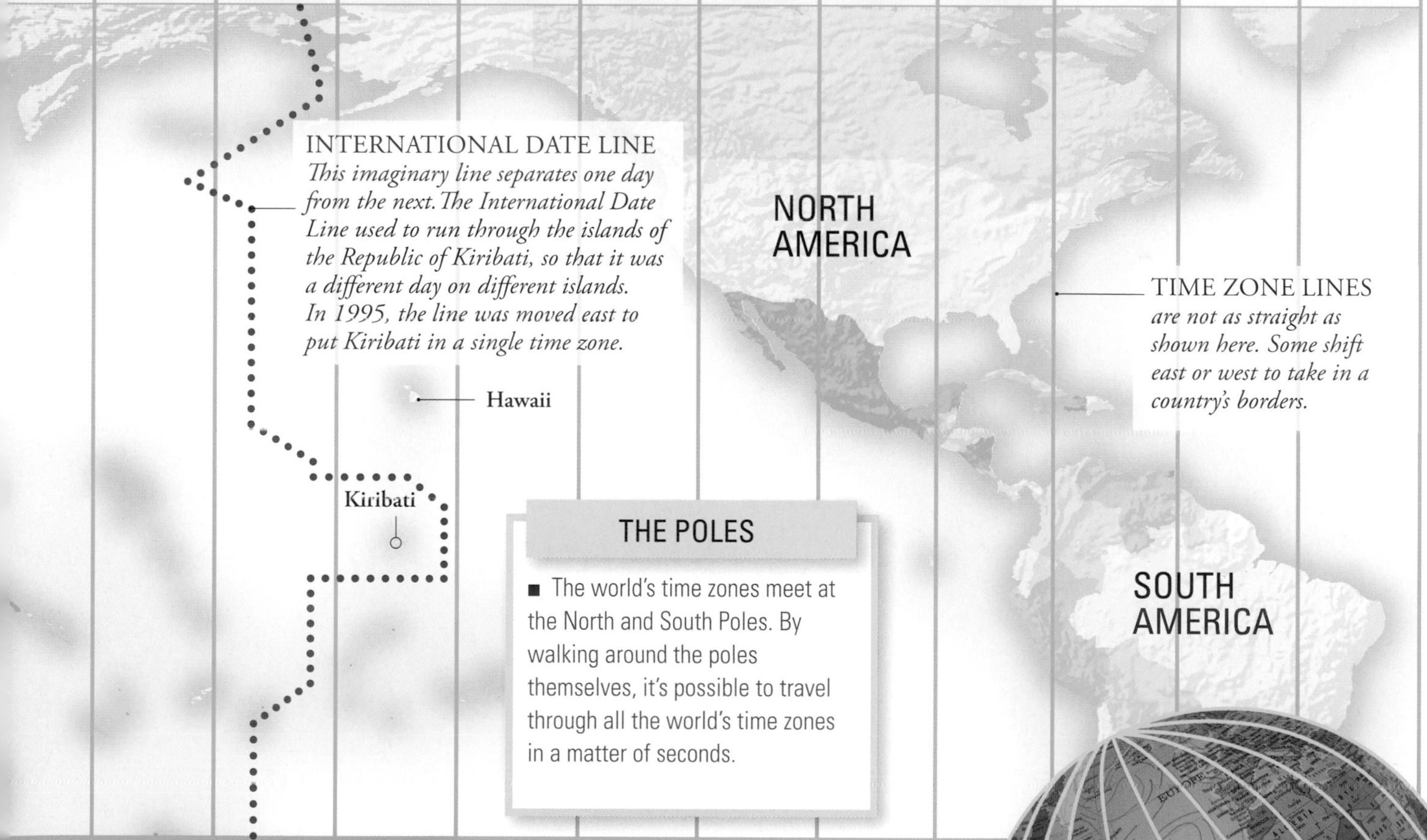

INTERNATIONAL DATE LINE
This imaginary line separates one day from the next. The International Date Line used to run through the islands of the Republic of Kiribati, so that it was a different day on different islands. In 1995, the line was moved east to put Kiribati in a single time zone.

— Hawaii

NORTH AMERICA

TIME ZONE LINES *are not as straight as shown here. Some shift east or west to take in a country's borders.*

Kiribati

THE POLES

■ The world's time zones meet at the North and South Poles. By walking around the poles themselves, it's possible to travel through all the world's time zones in a matter of seconds.

SOUTH AMERICA

Time traveller The system of worldwide, standardized time zones was first proposed by Canadian Sir Sandford Fleming in 1878. He pointed out that the world is divided into 360 degrees of longitude (imaginary lines running from north to south), and that these could be split into 24 time zones of 15 degrees each.

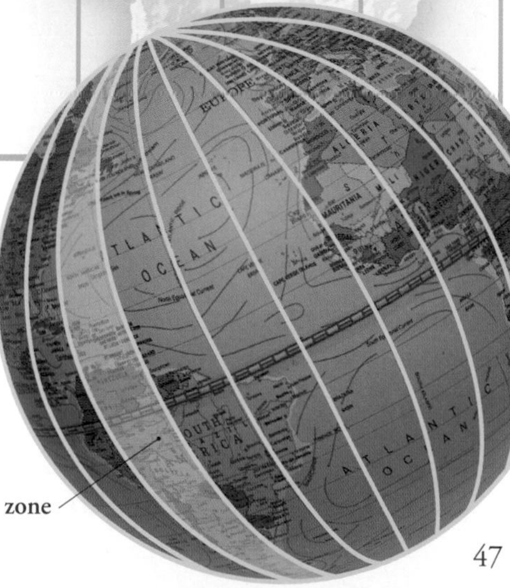

One time zone

47

Precious water

Without water, life on Earth could not exist. This vital resource fills the world's oceans, lakes, and rivers or soaks into the earth to form ground water. A small fraction of the world's water exists as ice or water vapour in the air, or is held inside the bodies of animals and plants.

FRESH WATER

The salty seas and oceans make up 97 per cent of the world's water. The rest is fresh water, and most of it is locked away in the polar ice caps and glaciers. The fresh water we drink comes from lakes, ponds, and rivers and accounts for just 0.6 per cent of the world's water supply.

WOW!

The Earth's oceans contain 1.36 billion cubic kilometres (324 million cubic miles) of water.

Only 3 per cent of Earth's water is fresh water.

Water cycle Water moves through a continuous cycle between the oceans, the atmosphere, and the land. The water cycle provides fresh water, which is essential to life on Earth.

As the air rises and cools over land, the water condenses in clouds

Water runs down the slopes to form streams and rivers

The clouds release water as precipitation (rain or snow)

Plants release water into the air by a process called transpiration

The Sun warms the ocean, and fresh water evaporates into the air

Some water soaks through the soil to form ground water

The reservoir that forms behind a dam supplies people with water

Most of the world's water is held in the oceans

Rivers channel the water back toward the ocean

A dam interrupts the water cycle by delaying the return of water to the ocean

WORLD'S LONGEST RIVERS

▲ *The River Nile was the lifeblood of the ancient Egyptians, providing the water to grow their crops.*

The world's longest rivers (by continent) are:

■ **Nile:** Africa's longest river, at 6,650 km (4,135 miles).

■ **Amazon:** At 6,400 km (4,000 miles), the longest river in South America.

■ **Yangtze:** Asia's longest river, at 6,300 km (3,915 miles).

■ **Mississippi:** At 6,275 km (3,902 miles), the longest river in North America.

■ **Volga:** Europe's longest river, at 3,692 km (2,294 miles).

■ **Murray–Darling:** At 2,739 km (1,701 miles), the longest river in Australia.

Underground water Some of the water that falls as rain seeps into the soil and into the rocks below to become ground water. Some rocks soak up water and form a saturated layer called the water table. But water can also leak through cracks in rocks and form pools in underground caves.

▶ BLIND CAVEFISH
These fish live in deep caves and rely on touch, rather than sight, to sense their surroundings.

Solid water Some water falls from clouds as snow. In the polar regions, and high in the mountains, the snow builds up in layers that push down to form an icy mass called a glacier. The glacier flows to the sea and breaks up into icebergs, which gradually melt, and the water cycle starts all over again.

WATER

■ There are approximately 75,000 dams in the United States alone.

■ Las Vegas gets 85 per cent of its water from Lake Mead—the vast reservoir behind the Hoover Dam.

■ At 300 metres (990 feet) tall, Nurek Dam in Tajikistan is the world's tallest dam.

▲ WATER SUPPLY *Lucky Peak Dam traps water from the Boise River in Idaho, USA.*

⚠ SAVE FRESH WATER

■ Running taps uses up a lot of water so turn them off when you have finished.

■ Only flush the toilet when you have to.

■ Take a shower instead of a bath because it uses up much less water.

■ Keep waste water from sinks and baths and use it to water plants in the garden.

The world's oceans

Earth is known as the "blue planet", after the oceans that cover two-thirds of its surface. Much of the ocean remains mysterious because the dark, cold conditions make its deep waters difficult to explore.

MIGHTY OCEANS

Our oceans are in constant motion. They are driven by flowing currents that mix warm and cold water, which in turn affect our climate. There are five great oceans. In order of size, these are the Pacific, Atlantic, Indian, Southern, and Arctic oceans. Smaller areas are called seas.

▼ WAVE POWER *Waves contain a huge amount of energy. This energy can be captured and turned into electricity.*

TELL ME MORE...

Twice a day the sea level rises and falls. This movement is called a tide. It is caused by the gravitational effects of the Moon, Sun, and Earth. When these combine, a bulge of water forms on either side of Earth causing a high tide. When it passes, the tide goes out.

North Sea
Average depth 94 m (308 ft)

Arctic Ocean
Average depth 990 m (3,248 ft)

Mediterranean Sea
Average depth 1,500 m (4,921 ft)

World oceans

The depth of the ocean varies enormously. On average, the Southern Ocean is the deepest, but many oceans have submarine canyons running through them. The deepest of these is the Mariana Trench in the Pacific. At 10,920 m (35,829 ft) deep, you could fit in Mount Everest with room to spare.

Caribbean Sea
Average depth 1,512 m (4,960 ft)

Atlantic Ocean
Average depth 3,330 m (10,925 ft)

Indian Ocean
Average depth 3,890 m (12,762 ft)

Pacific Ocean
Average depth 4,280 m (14,041 ft)

Southern Ocean
Average depth 4,500 m (14,763 ft)

Ocean circulation The circulation of the ocean partly controls climate, because warm or cold air masses move with ocean currents. The Gulf Stream takes warm, salty water from the Caribbean to the Nordic seas, and brings mild weather to northern Europe. Without the Gulf Stream, winters in Lisbon, Portugal, would be more like winters in New York, which is a similar distance from the North Pole. Around Iceland, the Gulf Stream's salty water gets cold and heavy, and sinks down, sucking more warm water from further south to replace it. That deep cold water flows from the Arctic to the Southern Ocean, where it meets an even deeper cold current flowing eastwards around Antarctica. Similar processes take place in the Indian and Pacific Oceans.

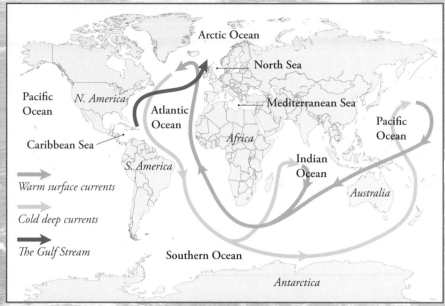

Arctic Ocean

North Sea

Pacific Ocean

N. America

Atlantic Ocean

Mediterranean Sea

Pacific Ocean

Caribbean Sea

Africa

S. America

Indian Ocean

Australia

→ Warm surface currents

→ Cold deep currents

→ The Gulf Stream

Southern Ocean

Antarctica

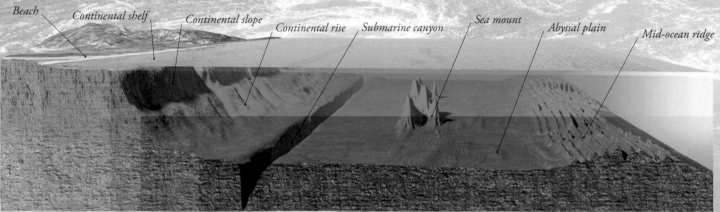

Beach   Continental shelf   Continental slope   Continental rise   Submarine canyon   Sea mount   Abyssal plain   Mid-ocean ridge

Continental margins The land does not stop when it meets the sea. The continental shelf extends out for about 200 m (660 ft) then slopes sharply down to the ocean floor. Although large areas of the floor, or abyssal plain, are flat, it is not featureless. There are deep canyons and trenches, volcanic sea mounts, and spreading ocean ridges.

Breaking wave crashes onto beach.

Waves pile up as they near land.

Ocean swell

Waves Waves are caused by winds blowing over the sea. These produce smooth, large waves called swells. As they get closer to shore they begin to pile up. The depth between the wave and the sea floor becomes shallower, causing the wave to break into a foamy crest that crashes onto the beach.

▼ BUOYED UP *Some "seas" are actually salty lakes. The Dead Sea is so salty you can float without making any effort.*

DEEP, BLUE SEA

Life at the bottom of the **deep ocean** is hard. The weight of water above is so heavy it can crush organisms that use lungs to breathe. It is very dark because light cannot reach very far, which also makes it very cold. Animals that live here need special adaptations to help them survive.

Salt water As everyone knows, sea water tastes salty, and will make you thirsty if you try to drink it. Not only is common salt (sodium chloride) found in sea water, but many other minerals as well. There is even a little dissolved gold. Scientists estimate there could be as much as 50 million billion tonnes of dissolved salts in the sea. If this was spread on the land it would measure 150 m (500 ft) deep.

Atmosphere

Life on Earth could not exist without the thick blanket of gases that surrounds the planet. This "atmosphere" is a complex, dynamic system that interacts with the oceans, land, and the Sun to create our weather and climate.

PROTECTING EARTH

The atmosphere plays a vital role in protecting life on Earth. It absorbs much of the Sun's harmful rays but allows enough through to warm up the planet. It protects the planet from meteor showers. The atmosphere also holds oxygen and water, which are essential for life.

Other gases

Oxygen

Nitrogen

◄ WHAT'S IN THE AIR? *Around 20 per cent of the atmosphere consists of oxygen, which we need to breathe. Most of the rest is nitrogen, but a tiny fraction is made up of other gases, such as carbon dioxide and methane.*

TAKE A LOOK

The atmosphere consists of five layers – the troposphere, stratosphere, mesosphere, ionosphere and exosphere.

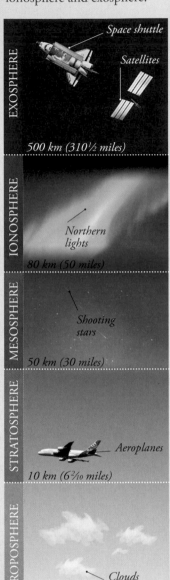

EXOSPHERE

Space shuttle

Satellites

500 km (310½ miles)

IONOSPHERE

Northern lights

80 km (50 miles)

MESOSPHERE

Shooting stars

50 km (30 miles)

STRATOSPHERE

Aeroplanes

10 km (6³/₁₀ miles)

TROPOSPHERE

Clouds

WOW!

A satellite orbiting Earth at an altitude of roughly 20,000 km (12,500 miles) will be travelling at an amazing 14,000 km/h (8,500 mph).

◄ TIGHT SQUEEZE *Gravity squeezes 99 per cent of the gases in the atmosphere into the first 40 km (25 miles) above Earth's surface. The rest extends 1,000 km (600 miles) out into space.*

OZONE LAYER

■ **Ozone forms** a thin layer around Earth, about 25 km (15 miles) above the surface.

■ **The ozone layer** protects life from the harmful ultraviolet (UV) radiation in sunlight.

■ **Harmful gases** in aerosols and other systems destroy ozone, creating holes in the ozone layer over the polar regions.

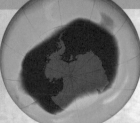

▲ HOLE *A satellite image reveals the ozone hole (purple).*

Climate

The climate of a particular area is the different patterns of weather and temperature over time. Factors that influence climate include distance from the equator and the sea, height above sea level, and the surrounding landscape.

SEASONS

The seasons are annual changes in climate that occur in the northern and southern hemispheres. There are four seasons in temperate regions – spring, summer, autumn, and winter. They are due to the differences in day length and the strength of the sunlight as Earth orbits the Sun. In many tropical and subtropical areas, there are two seasons – dry and wet.

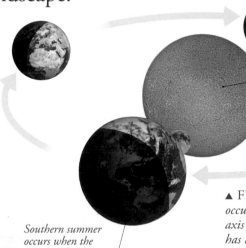

Northern summer occurs when the North Pole tilts towards the Sun.

Sun

Southern summer occurs when the North Pole tilts away from the Sun.

▲ FULL TILT *The seasons occur since Earth tilts on its axis as it orbits the Sun. This has little effect at the equator, where there is only one season.*

WEATHER MACHINE

The Sun heats Earth's surface, which warms the atmosphere. Warm air rises, and cool air moves in to replace it, causing winds. Warm air rises in the tropics. Cool air moves in from the north and south. Since Earth rotates on its axis, the winds bend, creating huge swirling weather patterns.

Warm air rises at the equator until it hits the top of the troposphere and can rise no further.

Dry air sinks over the world's deserts.

Westerlies

Trade winds

Doldrums

Doldrums

Trade winds

Westerlies

Very cold air sinks at the poles and flows outward, creating winds called easterlies.

The circulating air patterns are called "cells".

The area where the trade winds die out is known as the doldrums. Sailing ships may become stranded here.

◄ TEMPERATE *This zone experiences changes in temperature and rainfall during the year, but none are too extreme.*

◄ POLAR *The Arctic and Antarctic polar regions experience freezing conditions and little*

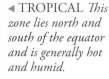

◄ TROPICAL *This zone lies north and south of the equator and is generally hot and humid.*

Extreme weather

These days we can watch the weather from space and even forecast it, but the one thing we cannot do is control it. Weather is one of the great powers on our Earth and in its extreme form is an awesome, deadly natural force.

EARTH

HURRICANE

Also known as cyclones and typhoons, these enormous swirling storms rip away buildings, and wash away roads. In 2005 the 280 km/h (175 mph) winds of Hurricane Katrina caused catastrophic flooding in New Orleans, USA, killing more than 1,500 people.

▲ THUNDERSTORMS *Huge storms form when warm air rises and cools causing huge clouds to grow higher and higher. As the water vapour cools, it falls down as heavy rain.*

▲ LIGHTNING *High up in a thundercloud icy raindrops collide and create an electric charge. The bottom of the cloud is negatively charged and the top is positive. Electricity jumps between them and that's lightning.*

▲ FLOODS *cause more damage and kills more people than any other catastrophe caused by extreme weather. In 1997 more than 250,000 people were driven from their homes in Bangladesh.*

54

PREDICTING WEATHER

Weather can be very unpredictable, but most of the time forecasts warn us of extreme weather and can help save lives. Weather satellites orbit the Earth continuously taking photographs. There are about 10,000 weather stations all over the world, on land and at sea, gathering data on clouds, temperature, air pressure, wind direction and speed, and so on. They pass the information to huge computers allowing meteorologists to predict how the weather will change.

▲ FIRE *All it takes is dry, parched earth and a bolt of lightning for a devastating forest fire to rage across miles and miles of land. If a fire hits urban areas it can destroy homes and claim many lives.*

▲ SNOW *A snowstorm can be great fun but can also be deadly. A blizzard can bury cars and even houses. In 1999 a heavy snowfall caused an avalanche and buried the town of Galtür, Austria under 10 m (33 ft) of snow.*

▶▶ FAST FACTS ▶▶

■ There are about 2,000 thunderstorms happening in the world right now.
■ Lightning kills 100 people every year.
■ Australia suffers from about 15,000 bushfires each year.
■ Arica, Chile is one of the driest places on Earth. From 1903 to 1918 it had no rain.
■ A tidal wave, or tsunami, hit Indian Ocean shorelines in 2004. It killed an estimated 230,000 people (👁 p35).

▶ HAILSTONES
Hail forms inside huge cumulonimbus clouds and often falls during a storm. Most of the time hailstones are no bigger than marbles, but in June 2003 a hailstone measuring 17.8 cm (7 in) wide fell in the USA. That's the size of a football!

◀ TORNADO *A tornado is a whirling funnel of air that moves across the ground and destroys everything in its way. The USA suffers from more tornadoes than any other country.*

ENVIRONMENT AND ECOLOGY

- Only simple organisms, such as algae, can survive in the Dead Sea as it is so salty.

- Bacteria live in the mud of the Mariana Trench, 11 km (6⅘ miles) under the sea.

- Tropical rainforests get more than 180 cm (70 in) of rain a year.

- Antarctica is the driest and coldest desert in the world.

- Grassland covers more than half of Earth's land surface, but most is used for farming.

What is the greatest threat to Australia's **coral reef**?
Find out on pages 76–77

What important role do **fungi** play in a forest?
Find out on pages 66–67

Definition: **Environment** is the natural surroundings or conditions in which a plant, organism, or animal is found. **Ecology** is the study of species in their environment.

- Only 3 per cent of the world's water is fresh water. More than 65 per cent of this is ice.

- The volume of water in the Pacific Ocean is the same size as the Moon.

- The biggest hot desert is the Sahara. It covers one-third of the area of Africa.

- The Aral Sea has almost dried up because the rivers that supplied it have been diverted.

- Eighty per cent of forests have been cut down by humans in the past 10,000 years.

How do **cacti** survive in the desert without water?
Find out on pages 62–63

Why do **zebras** prefer to live in herds?
Find out on pages 64–65

WHAT IS ECOLOGY?

■ Ecology is the study of the relationships between animals and plants and the environment they live in. Ecologists divide the world up into a series of environmental regions called biomes that are based on climate and inhabited by similar types of animals and plants. Within these biomes are smaller areas called ecosystems that have their own groups of animals and plants that have adapted to the particular conditions found there.

A shared planet

Humans are not the only species on the planet. We share it with at least 1.6 million other types of animals and plants. The way that living things interact is highly complex, but vital for survival.

LIVING WORLD

There are very few places on Earth where life does not exist. Even extreme places, such as the icy poles or hot volcanoes, are populated by organisms. Scientists describe the whole of the living world as the biosphere.

JUST THE JOB

Animals and plants have adopted different strategies to survive in their environment. Some have specialized to live in one particular habitat, others can survive in many. Often, they have changed physically or adapted their lifestyle to suit the conditions.

Habitat Thorny devils change the colour of their skin when they are cold or alarmed.

Migration Some birds and animals travel great distances every year to find food or to breed.

Population The number of lemmings changes according to food availability.

FOOD CHAINS

All animals eat other living things to get the nutrients they need for energy and to build their bodies. This energy starts with sunlight, which is used by plants and phytoplankton. This is the start of a food chain, where energy is transferred from plants to a series of bigger and more predatory animals.

▼ SUN *The energy that shines down from the Sun is absorbed by phytoplankton.*

▼ KRILL *Billions of these shrimp-like creatures feed on plankton in the cold polar seas.*

▼ COD *Fish eat krill and plankton in the upper layers of the ocean.*

▼ SEAL *Hungry seals chase schools of fish, such as herring and young cod.*

▼ KILLER WHALE *These large predatory mammals eat seals.*

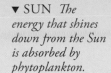     

▲ THE CRABS *of Christmas Island will cross roads, tennis courts, and golf courses to get to the sea during the breeding season.*

THE CARBON CYCLE

Carbon is a vital element to all life on Earth. Its atoms move in a natural cycle between land, water, and the atmosphere. Animals and plants are part of that cycle. Many systems on Earth work in a similar way, recycling vital ingredients such as nutrients, water, and oxygen.

Plants take in CO_2 during the day and emit it at night.

Burning gas from oil deposits releases CO_2

Animals give off CO_2 and methane.

Volcanoes emit CO_2

Marine algae and phytoplankton absorb and release CO_2

CO_2 in rain washes carbonates out of rock.

Carbon is washed into lakes.

Carbon accumulates in sediments when plankton die.

Carbon in the form of oil and coal gives off CO_2 when it is burned.

Dead plants can be slowly compressed under rock and turn into coal.

Pumping oil and gas releases stored carbon.

Marine animals breathe out CO_2 and release carbon when they die.

Lifestyle Pandas are only found in small areas of China where their main food, bamboo, grows.

Numbers Small plants grow quickly and produce lots of seeds so they have more chance of survival.

Cooperation Many plants need insects to pollinate them. The insect benefits from their nectar.

Dominance Trees put more effort into growing tall so they can get more light and nutrients than other plants.

Habitats

All living things need a place where they can live and breed successfully. This place is called a habitat. Habitats can be as big as a prairie or as small as a puddle. There can be many different habitats in a single area of land or sea.

Mountains Near cold and rocky mountain tops animals need a warm coat and nimble feet to survive.

Forests These are home to a wide variety of plants and animals that live at different levels among the trees.

Coasts Animals that live here have to cope with the sea coming in and out twice a day, and constant battering by waves.

A home of their own Every animal and plant needs particular conditions for it to thrive. Plants need the right temperature, rainfall, and soil to grow in. Animals need shelter, food, and space to roam around. An organism will often adapt its lifestyle or even how it looks and behaves to suit its surroundings. This process is called evolution.

Mangroves The roots of mangrove trees are surrounded by salty water, but they make good hiding places for fish.

Coral reefs Reefs provide homes for hundreds of species. They are created by the skeletons of small marine animals.

FRAGMENTATION OF HABITAT

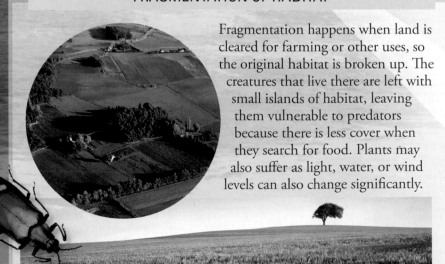

Fragmentation happens when land is cleared for farming or other uses, so the original habitat is broken up. The creatures that live there are left with small islands of habitat, leaving them vulnerable to predators because there is less cover when they search for food. Plants may also suffer as light, water, or wind levels can also change significantly.

BIOMES OF THE WORLD

Ecologists group similar types of ecosystems into areas called biomes. Each type of biome, such as a tropical rainforest, has the same sort of climate and habitat as other rainforests around the world, but the species it contains may be different. Hot, wet, tropical biomes have many more species than cold or dry ones.

Boreal forest	Coral reef	Rainforest	Mountain	Freshwater
Desert	Temperate forest		Polar	Grassland

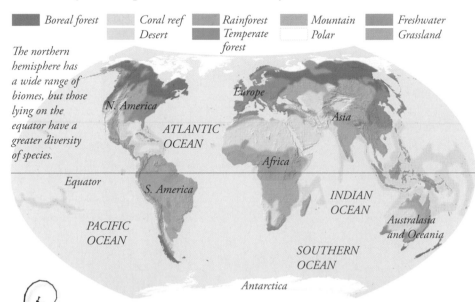

The northern hemisphere has a wide range of biomes, but those lying on the equator have a greater diversity of species.

N. America

Europe

Asia

ATLANTIC OCEAN

Africa

Equator

S. America

INDIAN OCEAN

Australasia and Oceania

PACIFIC OCEAN

SOUTHERN OCEAN

Antarctica

Evolution Every part of the world has species that do not live anywhere else. These are called native species and have evolved to suit the local conditions. These tree ferns only grow wild in New Zealand.

Invaders When new species are introduced to an area they can have a devastating effect on the ecosystem. Cane toads (right) were brought in to eat beetles in Australian sugar fields, but have become a pest because they also eat other animals.

BIODIVERSITY

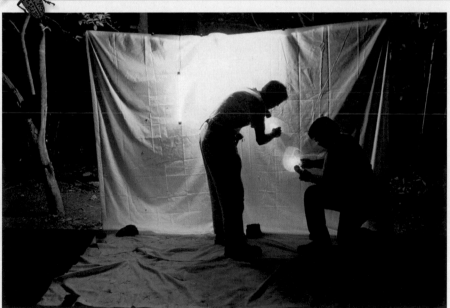

Biodiversity is a measure of the variety of species in an ecosystem. All species have a role to play in the ecosystem. To understand an ecosystem properly, scientists have to identify all the organisms living there and find out how they interact. These researchers are collecting moths. Then they can protect any species or groups of species that are important to that ecosystem.

►► FAST FACTS ►►

- Nearly 1.65 million species of plants and animals are known to exist.
- Almost 1 million of those species are insects.
- More amphibians face extinction than any other animal group.
- About 5,000 new species are discovered every year, mostly insects.
- Rainforests are the most biodiverse regions on Earth.

Many species face extinction. These groups are the most threatened.

| Mammals 21% | Birds 12% | Amphibians 30% | Corals 11% | Woody plants 33% |

Percentages of threatened species

TELL ME MORE...

The Saguaro cactus is one of the tallest in the world – it can grow as high as 12 m (40 ft) and live for up to 200 years. Only found in Arizona, California, and northern Mexico, it needs more water than some cacti, but it's fairly tolerant of frost.

Deserts

We think of deserts as being hot, but some of them are very cold. What deserts ARE is dry. Any place that gets less than 25 cm (10 in) of rain or snow per year (such as the Antarctic ice sheet) is a desert.

WARM DESERTS

The thing about hot deserts is that they're hot all the time – cold deserts can be frosty in winter and boiling in summer. There is not much moisture, so there are very few clouds. At night, with no cloud "blanket", the temperature can drop dramatically.

This is the **Sonoran Desert** in the southwestern United States.

CACTI – FIT FOR PURPOSE

The "body" of a cactus plant is actually a swollen, water-storing stem. The "prickles" are a kind of leaf that allows very little water to evaporate. In some desert plants, it's the leaves that swell and store water – these are called succulents.

Golden barrel cactus

DESERT IN BLOOM

Once in a while, there is a rare and precious shower of rain, and the desert bursts into bloom. (See above, Anza-Borrego State Park, California, USA.) This is because seeds lie dormant – sometimes for years. When water falls, they germinate, flower, and create new seeds.

LOOK CLOSER: DESERT FEATURES

■ Deserts have formed in many different landscapes, wherever water is in short supply. Because there aren't many plants on the surface, deserts are vulnerable to weathering and erosion. Also, the huge variation in temperature can cause massive rocks to crack.

▲ DUNES *form large "sand seas" called ergs. The wind sculpts their graceful shapes.*

▲ ARCHES *Erosion and sandstorms can puncture a rocky ridge to form an arch.*

▲ EARTH *Natural salts can cement rocks together into "desert pavement".*

▲ BUTTES *form when a plateau has been eroded to leave a flat hill with steep sides.*

COLD DESERTS

The coldest and most northern of all the world's deserts, the Gobi Desert (shown here) stretches across China and Mongolia. Like many cold deserts, it sits on a high plateau, where the temperature is naturally lower than at sea level.

SANDSTORMS

Strong, dry winds blow across the desert, carrying clouds of sand that reduce visibility to almost zero. Roads and wells are often covered completely, and a violent storm can dehydrate – or even suffocate – animals and people. Sandstorms last for hours, and some can even go on for days.

DESERT ANIMALS

From insects and reptiles to huge mammals, most desert animals have highly specialized characteristics that are precisely suited to their extreme conditions. Some get their water from the food they eat, for example, while others sleep during the hot days.

▲ FENNEC FOXES *use their huge ears to help them locate prey. The large surface area also allows heat to escape.*

▲ JERBOAS *keep cool by sealing themselves in an underground den.*

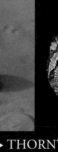
▶ THORNY DEVILS *have skin that absorbs water like blotting paper.*

Grasslands

Grasslands spring up in places that are too dry for forests to grow but get enough water to stop them becoming deserts. Almost half of Earth's land surface is covered by grasslands. They support a wide variety of animals, but the wide open spaces offer little protection from predators for larger animals.

TROPICAL GRASSLANDS

Also called savannas, tropical grasslands have distinct wet and dry seasons. Although it is warm all year round, rain only falls for six to eight months of the year. During a drought the grass can catch fire, but this is good for regenerating the savanna.

SAVANNA TREES
The leaves and small branches of savanna trees provide important food for browsing animals such as giraffes.

CHEETAHS *are perfectly camouflaged against the savanna grass.*

TEMPERATE GRASSLANDS

Temperate grasslands (called prairies in America) have hot summers and cold winters. Although they get rain throughout the year, there is too little for trees or shrubs to survive. However, the rich soil is good for the hundreds of wild flower species that grow among the grasses.

WILD BISON
have been replaced by cattle as farmers have turned prairie into land for agricultural grazing and cereal crops.

FACTFILE

- Elephant grass can grow to 8 m (26 ft) high – tall enough for an elephant to hide in!
- Cheetahs probably evolved in Asia. Until about 20,000 years ago, their relatives were commonplace in Europe, India, China, and North America, not just in Africa. They disappeared from many areas after the last ice age.
- The lack of trees mean that many birds have to build their nests in burrows.
- Grasslands are found on every continent except for Antarctica.

LIFE ON THE PLAIN

The huge quantities of grass out on the prairie support some of the worlds biggest herbivores, such as elephants, rhinos, and giraffes. It also offers a hiding place for smaller animals and cover for predators to stalk their victims.

Meerkat

Burrowers Many small animals live in burrows. These protect them from the hot sun and cold nights, and help them escape from predators. Some animals live in burrows dug by other species.

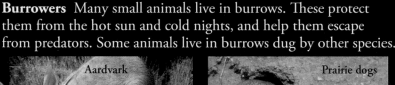

Aardvark

Prairie dogs

Grazers Most grazing animals live in herds that offer protection from predators. They have long legs for running and strong teeth for chewing. They have to migrate to find fresh grass in the dry season.

Kangaroo

Bison

Zebra

Predators These rely on stealth to obtain food. They frequently hunt in packs to isolate an animal from a herd or to scare other predators from a kill.

Lion

Jackal

Wolf

Hyena

TURKEY VULTURES *soar over the American prairies, sniffing the wind for dead animals to eat.*

LOOK CLOSER: AMAZING GRASS

- Grasses are one of the biggest families of flowering plants. They are well suited to dry conditions as they can store food in their roots. Because their leaves grow from below ground, grasses can survive being nibbled by animals as long as their roots are not disturbed. Their tiny flowers are pollinated by the wind rather than insects.

▲ FOXTAILS *These grasses have spiky seeds that attach to passing animals for dispersal.*

▲ BUFFALO GRASS *This short, hardy grass is found on the plains of North America.*

▲ SPINIFEX *Properly known as* Triodia, *this hummock grass covers the Australian bush.*

▲ WHEAT *Cereal crops were originally wild grasses cultivated for food by humans.*

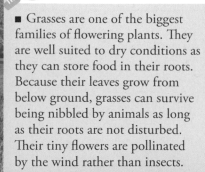

Forests

Trees are the biggest plants on the planet. Forests of them cover large areas of land and provide shelter for other plants and animals. They will flourish anywhere that is warm and wet enough during their growing season.

TELL ME MORE...

The Amazon rainforest in South America covers an area almost as big as Australia. A single hectare (2.5 acres) may contain more than 750 types of trees and 1,500 other plants. Almost a sixth of all flowering plants and one-seventh of all bird species live there. The trees keep their leaves all year long.

RAINFOREST

There are two types of rainforests – temperate and tropical. Both are found in areas of very high rainfall, which helps the trees grow tall and fast. Rainforests are full of animals and plants. In fact, about half of all species on the planet live in rainforests. Despite all the plant material, the soils in these regions are thin and poor in nutrients.

BOREAL FOREST

Boreal forests are found in northern countries that have long, snowy winters. Most of the trees that grow here are conifers, such as pine, spruce, and larch. Instead of flat leaves they have thin needles that help them save water and resist strong winds. Their branches slope downwards so that snow slides off.

▼ DYING LEAVES *turn brown in autumn.*

▲ LEAVES *fall from deciduous trees in autumn when light levels and the temperature drop. This allows trees to save energy and conserve water over the winter.*

TEMPERATE FOREST

Mixed, mainly broadleaf woodlands grow in regions that have long, warm summers and cool, frosty winters. They drop their leaves in winter, which allows flowering plants such as bluebells and aconites to grow in early spring before it gets too shady. The leaves break down to form a deep, rich soil. Many of these forests have been cleared for farming.

▼ BUTTERFLIES *are important pollinators of rainforest flowers high up in the canopy. The caterpillars of this postman butterfly feed on passion flower vine leaves.*

UNDER THREAT: DEFORESTATION

■ Forests face a number of threats. Large areas of the Amazon rainforest are being cleared to provide land for cattle ranching and soya bean production. Other forests are logged for their valuable timber or for fuel. This can have a devastating effect on the forest ecosystem. Animals lose their homes and food supply, and the changing conditions affect plant growth. Some forests are planted to produce wood, but these lack much of the native wildlife of natural forest.

RAINFOREST LAYERS

■ EMERGENTS – the tallest trees are home to butterflies, eagles, and bats.

■ CANOPY – this layer is full of animals, birds, climbing plants, and orchids.

■ UNDERSTOREY – provides homes for snakes and lizards and cover for predators.

■ SHRUB LAYER – consists of saplings and broad-leaved shrubs.

■ FOREST FLOOR – receives little light and is covered in decaying plant material.

▼ CONIFERS *protect their seeds in cones.*

Cone

Seeds

▲ SQUIRRELS *are experts at breaking open cones. Their sharp teeth can gnaw through the woody casing to expose the seeds.*

◄ FUNGI *are useful in forests. They break down rotting trees and leaves and provide food for animals and insects.*

Mountains

No other place on Earth shows such a dramatic variation in habitats as you can find on the slopes of a mountain. The warm, sheltered valleys abound with animal and plant life, but freezing winds batter the exposed peaks. Only the hardiest of species can survive in this extreme environment.

RICH RESOURCES

Almost 25 per cent of Earth's land surface area is covered by mountains. They feed most of the world's river systems and are rich in mineral resources. Few people live high up in the mountains, but many use them for activities such as climbing and skiing.

MOUNTAIN HIGHS AND LOWS

- Standing at a height of 8,848 m (29,029 ft), Mount Everest is the tallest mountain on the land. It is part of the enormous range called the Himalayas in Central Asia.
- Mauna Kea, in Hawaii, is the world's highest mountain, rising up 10,203 m (33,474 ft) from the ocean floor. Only 4,205 m (13,796 ft) is visible above sea level.
- Oxygen levels drop sharply with increasing altitude. Many animals produce more red blood cells, or have larger hearts, to carry more oxygen around their bodies.
- A "dead zone" occurs above 6,000 m (19,600 ft). Few animals can survive in the dead zone due to the high winds and freezing temperatures.
- The Himalayan pika lives at an altitude of 5,250 m (16,800 ft) – the highest of any known mammal in the world.

◄ THE HIGH LIFE *Hardy birds, such as the colourful ptarmigan, can withstand the harsh environment on the upper slopes of the mountain.*

◄ FLOWER SLOPES
Highland vegetation such as bell heather supports a range of herbivores which, in turn, are food for predators such as the grey wolf.

◄ RIVER VALLEY *Mountain streams trickle down through the valley floor, forming a rich habitat for bank voles and other animals.*

MOUNTAIN MAMMALS

Despite the rugged terrain and cold air, many mammals make their home in the mountains. They must adapt to survive, so many grow thick winter coats to keep warm. Others migrate up and down the slopes through the year to avoid the worst weather.

▲ MOUNTAIN GOAT *Thick winter coats protect these agile, muscular herbivores as they scramble up steep mountain slopes.*

▲ SNOW LEOPARD *The predatory snow leopard has thick fur and small, rounded ears to conserve body heat.*

TELL ME MORE...

Mountains contain a rich range of habitats. Lush alpine meadows give way to conifer forests, while the snow-capped peaks dominate above. The main reason for the variation is the sharp drop in temperature with altitude – about 6°C (11°F) for every 1 km (⅗ mile) in winter.

BUILDING MOUNTAINS

Mountains form when vast sheets of rock, called tectonic plates, collide beneath Earth's surface. Depending on which plates collide, the land is either pushed up to form mountains or molten rock rises to the surface to form volcanoes ( p32–33, p34–35). Volcanoes are more regularly shaped than mountains that have been folded and bent. Mountains tend to have poor, rocky soils and little grows near their peaks. Despite the danger of volcanoes, their ash turns into fertile soil for growing crops.

Polar regions

Imagine living in a place where for six months of the year, there is no day, and the other six months, there is no night. Add to this freezing cold temperatures and you have two of the most inhospitable places on Earth – the North and South Poles. Surprisingly, they are teeming with life.

NORTH POLE

THE ARCTIC

The Arctic is a huge raft of floating ice surrounded by land. At the North Pole the ice remains frozen all year, but further south the ice breaks up and melts in summer. There are concerns that climate change may melt the sea ice permanently.

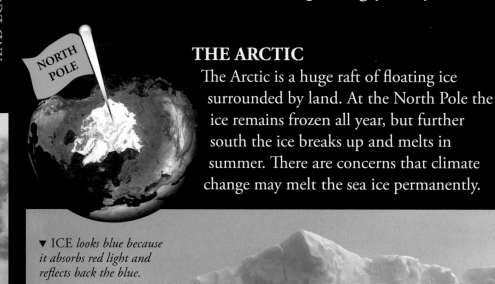

▼ ICE *looks blue because it absorbs red light and reflects back the blue.*

Walking on top of the world

More animals live in the Arctic than Antarctica. This is because the winter ice provides a bridge to Russia and North America and more varied food sources. Land predators, including polar bears and humans, also take advantage of the seals and fish that live beneath the ice.

HUMAN INFLUENCES

People have lived in the Arctic for thousands of years. Natives, such as the Inuit and Yupik, have learned to survive the cold and live on a diet of mainly fish and meat. However, there is oil beneath the surface of the Arctic and Antarctica, which makes them a target for prospectors. Antarctica is protected from exploitation by treaty, but the shrinking ice of the Arctic is opening it up for exploration. Oil and gas pipelines already cross Alaska and Siberia, which has led to oil spills and environmental damage.

THE ANTARCTIC

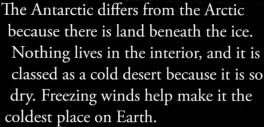

The Antarctic differs from the Arctic because there is land beneath the ice. Nothing lives in the interior, and it is classed as a cold desert because it is so dry. Freezing winds help make it the coldest place on Earth.

A safe refuge
There are no predatory land mammals on Antarctica, which makes it an ideal place for colonies of seals, penguins, and seabirds to breed. Despite it being so cold, the water is full of plankton, krill, and fish to feed their young.

THE TUNDRA

Tundra is the name given to cold, windy regions where the soil is frozen most of the year. The plants that grow here are low and stunted, but mosses, lichens, and small shrubs can survive the freezing conditions.

▼ CARIBOU *scrape away snow in search of lichen and moss.*

Migration Every summer huge herds of elk and caribou cross the tundra in search of food. Arctic foxes and hares stay all year.

Winter coats Some animals that live on the tundra change their coat from brown to white to hide them when it snows.

Fresh water

Fresh water covers less than one per cent of Earth's surface. Falling rain flows back to the ocean in streams and rivers, or gathers to form ponds, lakes, and wetlands.

FRESHWATER HABITATS are challenging for the creatures that live in them. They can flood or shrink to almost nothing, silt up with mud, or be choked by pollutants. Many animals have adaptations that help them cope. Salmon (right) spend part of their lives at sea and have a special mechanism that allows them to change from fresh to salt water and back again when they return to their home river to breed.

FOOD CHAINS

Food chains in rivers depend on inputs from the land around. This can be nutrients from farm land or fallen leaves, which provide food for algae and bacteria. These are eaten by insect larvae and snails, which are then eaten by fish and frogs.

▲POND LIFE
A sample of water from a pond shows how many species live there, such as insects, snails, tadpoles, and pond weed.

Water snail

FISH HAVENS

Nearly 40 per cent of fish species live in fresh water. Many fresh waters contain unique species, such as this African cichlid, because rivers and lakes rarely connect for species to colonize new areas.

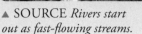

▲ SOURCE *Rivers start out as fast-flowing streams.*

▲ MOUTH *When they reach the sea, rivers are slow and wide.*

The ecology of a river changes as it runs from the hills to the sea. At its source, the water is too fast for plants to take root, but invertebrates and fish thrive in the well-oxygenated conditions. As it slows, a wider variety of plants take root in mud brought down from the hills. Animals make homes and hunt along its banks.

Wetlands

Wetlands are among the richest habitats on Earth. They include permanently wet swamps and marshes, and bogs and fens that have waterlogged soils. The water can be fresh or salty.

WATERY ROOTS

Wetland plants have adapted to cope with the wet conditions. Many can float, or have waxy leaves that resist water. Their leaves also transport oxygen to submerged roots to keep them alive. Some roots can survive being exposed to the air, or changes from fresh to salt water.

▶ HERONS *stalk wetlands for fish hiding among plant roots.*

SWIMMERS

Capybaras are rodents that live in the Pantanal, a large wetland in South America. Like most semi-aquatic mammals their ears, eyes, and nostrils are on top of their heads so they can stay alert while swimming.

WOW!

Archerfish (below) live in mangrove swamps around Indonesia. They prey on insects that land on the leaves and roots of mangrove trees. After selecting a target from under the water, the fish sticks its snout out and blasts the insect with a jet of water. The insect falls into the water and is gobbled up by the fish.

TAKE A LOOK: LIFE IN THE WETLANDS

Wetlands are home to many species of insects, amphibians, and reptiles that need water to feed or reproduce in. This in turn attracts hungry birds and larger animals that prey on them. Many mammals have also adapted to wetland life, including beavers, hippos, and water buffalo.

▲ PITCHER PLANTS *These trap insects to obtain nutrients they can't get from the soil.*

▲ MAMMALS *The Okavango Delta in Africa is an ideal home for water-loving hippos.*

▲ REPTILES *Caimans and alligators are the chief predators in many swamps.*

▲ BIRDS *Still, wetland waters make ideal fishing grounds for waterbirds.*

Oceans and sea life

Not only do oceans cover more than 70 per cent of Earth's surface, but they're also incredibly deep – easily the biggest habitat on the planet. What's more, they offer their residents a fairly stable temperature – and plenty of water!

WOW!

The biggest fish in the ocean is the whale shark. This monster can grow up to 18 m (60 ft) long – bigger than a bus!

⊘ TAKE A LOOK: INGENIOUS FEEDERS

Earth's oceans accommodate a wide variety of exotic creatures. Many of these have developed unique adaptations that allow them to search for food and devour prey in their watery environment.

▲ SQUID *grab prey using the suckers at the end of their two long tentacles.*

OCEAN ZONES AND HABITATS

In fact, the ocean is not just one habitat, but many. The first metre (3 ft) from the top – the surface layer – is the richest in both nutrients and vital gases from the atmosphere. But the surface layer is also vulnerable to pollution and floating litter, which can damage ocean life. Below this lie five more layers:

THE SUNLIT ZONE *gets enough sunlight for photosynthesis to take place. If the water is clear, it can extend to 200 m (650 ft), but it's often much shallower. The base of all food chains is here.*

THE TWILIGHT ZONE *gets just enough light so that ocean creatures can hunt, but not enough for photosynthesis.*

THE DARK ZONE *gets virtually no light, and the only food is fallout or "snow" from above. Temperatures are low (2–4°C), and pressure is high.*

THE ABYSSAL ZONE *contains the vast, muddy, seabed plains (abyssal plains) after which it's named, but very little life of any kind.*

THE HADAL ZONE *extends below the abyssal zone over less than two per cent of the ocean floor. Only two human beings have ever been there, and we know little about it.*

MAN THE DESTROYER

Modern, intensive fishing boats can inflict serious harm on ocean ecosystems. Often, they take too many of one, popular fish, or scoop up endangered species unintentionally with their catch.

▲ SEA ANEMONES *cling to rocks, and kill their prey with venomous barbs.*

▲ SEA SLUGS *scrape algae off hard surfaces using sharp, tooth-like scales called denticles.*

▲ ANGLER FISH *use the dorsal spine on their head like a fishing rod.*

COASTS

Coastlines provide many different habitats. High up on rocky shores, tough creatures such as barnacles survive crashing waves and exposure at low tide. In coastal mud, buried bivalves such as clams filter food from the water.

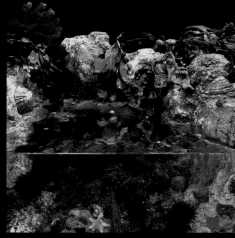

▲ ROCKPOOL *ecosystems contain algae and seaweed. Limpets feed on algae, and starfish feed on limpets, mussels, and other shellfish.*

▼ FISHING *is difficult to control because no one owns the open sea, and its vast waters are hard to police.*

BLACK SMOKERS

At hydrothermal vents, water heated under the sea dissolves minerals from the rocks. When it erupts through the ocean floor, it forms crusty "chimneys" that can reach several metres (yards) in height.

Coral reefs

Sometimes called "rainforests of the sea", coral reefs are spectacular marine ecosystems that thrive in warm, clear, shallow waters. Ecotourists love to visit the reefs to see the colourful and amazing variety of animals that live and hunt here.

RICH PICKINGS
Ocean predators such as dolphins (left) and sharks (right) lurk in coral reefs. They feed on the small creatures who live there.

FAST FACTS

- Corals are actually simple animals with tiny plant-like cells living inside them.
- The Great Barrier Reef, off northeastern Australia, is about 2,300 kilometres (1,430 miles) long.
- Excess CO_2 in the atmosphere is making the ocean more acidic, which could damage coral.
- Fossil reefs have been discovered dating from more than 500 million years ago.

THREATS TO CORAL

A reef can be damaged by anchors scraping its surface, and explosives thrown into the water to kill fish. Coastal developments release harmful sediment into the water, and stress, such as higher temperature, can cause coral to expel the algae in their body, so they turn white.

TAKE A LOOK

The main reef-forming organisms are known as hard or stony corals. Each one, called a coral polyp (right), secretes limestone from its gut cavity, and this builds up on the rock underneath. Some corals exist as single, large polyps, but most live in large colonies.

ALL SHAPES AND SIZES

Coral reefs come in different forms. The most common is the fringing reef (such as this one in the Indo-Pacific Ocean), which grows off many tropical coasts. Corals can't grow above water, so the reef's flat top usually lies just below the surface. Barrier reefs grow parallel to a coastline, but further out, while atolls (see right) form coral rings in the middle of the sea.

BIRTH OF AN ATOLL

An atoll starts life as a fringing reef around a volcanic island. As the volcano weakens and sinks (or sea levels rise), the coral grows and turns into a barrier reef. Eventually, the volcano disappears, leaving an atoll – a ring of established coral reef around a central lagoon.

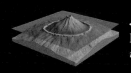

◄ FRINGING REEF *forms around volcanic island.*

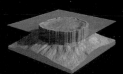

◄ BARRIER REEF *grows around the sinking volcano.*

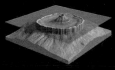

◄ VOLCANO DISAPPEARS *leaving atoll with central lagoon.*

CROWN OF THORNS

The world's largest starfish (it has a leg span of 30–40 cm/ 12–16 in), the crown of thorns feeds mainly on corals. Because of this, it can cause serious harm to coral reefs. The Great Barrier Reef off the coast of Australia, for example, has been severely damaged by hungry crown of thorns. These prickly creatures hurt people too – their spines are poisonous, so stepping on one can cause severe pain and sickness.

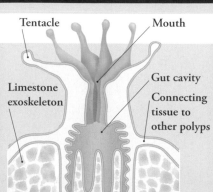

Tentacle — Mouth

Limestone exoskeleton

Gut cavity

Connecting tissue to other polyps

▲ BRAIN CORAL *is arranged in wiggly lines that look like the surface of a brain.*

▲ FAN CORAL *feathers into delicate shapes and provides a home for tiny creatures.*

▲ STAGHORN *coral grows in the shape of branches, which look like tiny antlers.*

▲ SOFT CORALS *have tiny, individual polyps, and can look like branching bushes.*

Climate change

One of the biggest concerns facing our planet is the possibility of climate change. Although Earth has swung between extreme heat and cold throughout its existence, human activity, especially the burning of fossil fuels, may be interfering with the natural cycle and heating up the atmosphere.

IMPACT OF CLIMATE CHANGE

Trying to predict what will happen as our planet warms up is not easy. We know that ice at the poles is melting and this is making sea levels rise. Warmer temperatures are likely to change other aspects of the weather. Some countries, such as those in North Africa, may become hotter and drier, while other areas, such as Northern Europe, may become colder and wetter. There will probably be more intense storms, droughts, and flooding.

◄ IF GLOBAL warming makes the glaciers melt, all the water locked in them will enter the sea. Sea levels will rise, and many areas will be submerged.

GLOBAL WARMING

Earth is getting warmer. Scientists have been measuring the temperature and have noticed that the global average is slowly increasing. This coincides with the increase of carbon dioxide in the atmosphere over the last 200 years. It is set to keep climbing.

Carbon dioxide levels (parts per million)

PPM
360
340
320
300
280
260

YEAR
1000   1200   1400   1600   1800   2000

(°C)

Temperature levels (°C)

14.5
14
13.5
13

YEAR
1000   1200   1400   1600   1800   2000

GREENHOUSE GASES

■ The atmosphere helps keep Earth warm. Gases such as water vapour, carbon dioxide, and methane trap heat from the Sun and keep the surface warm enough to support life. However, if these gases increase, Earth could turn into a giant greenhouse.

Heat from the Sun enters the atmosphere. Some is reflected back from the surface, but most of it is trapped by the gases in the atmosphere.

Burning fossil fuels is adding more "greenhouse" gases to the atmosphere. If we add too much it could have a huge impact on the climate.

Beware of the burps!

One of the most worrying greenhouse gases is methane. Huge quantities of it are produced in rice paddies and also by cows, which belch it out as a by-product of eating grass. Methane is 21 times better at warming Earth than carbon dioxide. Each cow can produce up to 200 litres (53 gallons) of methane a day – that's a lot of gas.

UNDER THREAT

■ Climate change is not just a threat to humans. Many animals and plants will also suffer through changes to their environment. For example, reduced rainfall can be serious for trees or wetland habitats. The most vulnerable species are those that live only in one small area, or are unable to move quickly. This includes some of the world's rarest species.

▶ THE COSTA RICAN *golden toad is thought to have been driven to extinction by climate change, even though it lived on a nature reserve.*

SAVING ENERGY

Almost everything humans do in everyday life requires energy. Most of our energy comes from burning coal, gas, or oil, but these produce greenhouse gases. To prevent this happening, scientists are looking at new ways to save energy and cleaner ways of making it.

Preventative measures We can all do our bit to prevent global warming by using energy saving devices, switching off lights, and turning the heating down a few degrees.

▼ WIND-UP *radios save on batteries and electricity.*

▼ FLUORESCENT *bulbs use less energy than ordinary bulbs.*

Alternative fuels Transport is one of the biggest sources of greenhouse gases. Scientists are trying to develop new vehicles that use hydrogen, biofuels, and electricity instead of polluting petrol.

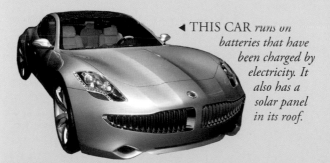

◀ THIS CAR *runs on batteries that have been charged by electricity. It also has a solar panel in its roof.*

Eco living Houses can be built that need less energy to run them. This one is kept warm by the soil around it, and is lit by special tubes that reflect and magnify sunlight. Solar panels and windmills can be used to provide electricity.

Looking to the future

Humans are the dominant species on the planet. We make use of all Earth's resources, but there is a limit to how long these will last if we carry on using them up at our current rate. It is in our own best interests to find ways of living that do not harm the environment, and protect the animals and plants that live here too.

TELL ME MORE...

Human population changes

The number of people on Earth has been growing rapidly. There are currently around 6.7 billion, but there could be more than 9 billion by 2050. All these people will need food, water, and places to live, which could put a huge strain on resources.

POPULATION (BILLIONS)

YEAR

1980 1990 2000 2010 2020 2030 2040 2050

POLLUTION PREVENTION

For years, humans have been dumping the waste products of industrial processes on the ground, in rivers, or into the air. By using new and cleaner technologies we can reduce the amount of toxic substances produced and find ways to make them less damaging to the environment.

Recycling Humans use and waste an enormous amount of Earth's resources. Most rubbish is put in large holes in the ground, but we are rapidly running out of space. A better way to save resources is recycling. Paper, plastics, metal, glass, and textiles can all be recycled and used again.

WOW!
An increasing number of people live in cities. Since 2008, at least half of the world's population have been living in cities rather than in the countryside. By 2030 it is expected that two-thirds will be city dwellers.

Earth is getting warmer. Scientists have been measuring the temperature and have noticed that the global average is slowly increasing. This coincides with the increase of carbon dioxide in the atmosphere over the last 200 years. It is set to keep climbing.

PROTECTING SEEDS

■ More than one-third of all flowering plants are vulnerable to extinction. Many of these species could be valuable to humans, but are being wiped out before their uses can be discovered. Scientists are now going around the world looking for plants and taking their seeds for storage in seed banks. This way, they can grow new plants if their original habitat is destroyed.

CONSERVATION

Wild areas are important, but many are being destroyed or raided for their resources. Organizations around the world are trying to protect wildlife and habitats by building sanctuaries for endangered species, such as the orang-utan, and preserving key areas, including wetlands and forests.

TAKE A PICTURE

Tourists bring wealth to an area. When wildlife itself is a tourist attraction, local businesses are likely to look after the habitat.

Ecotourism Travelling to a new place is fun, but tourism has an impact on the people, animals, and plants that live there. Ecotourism helps protect the future of national parks and other protected areas by encouraging operators to plan resorts in a way that looks after the local wildlife and environment.

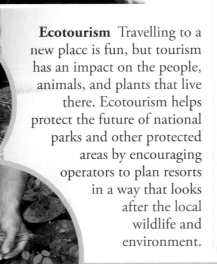

Reforestation Many of the world's original forests have been cut down. Forests are a vital ecosystem, so in some areas new woodlands are being developed using native trees. If managed sustainably they will provide an income for local people and a safe home for wildlife.

LIVING WORLD

KEY TO SYMBOLS

The following symbols are used in this chapter:

Habitat The type of place where the animal is typically found in the wild.

Lifespan The average maximum age of the species in the wild, which might be different to specimens kept in captivity. A question mark is used when there is no data available.

Status These triangles show if the animal is endangered, as listed on the IUCN Red List (p85 for more information). A purple triangle shows there is not enough data to assess the animal.

See how large (or small) an animal is compared to an adult human.

? What features make carnivores such efficient predators? *Find out on pages 96–97*

? How many types of feather do birds have? *Find out on pages 104–105*

Definition: Animals, plants, fungi, protists, and bacteria are the five main groups – or kingdoms – of life on Earth. These life forms make up the **living world**.

 Tropical forest and rainforest

 Temperate forest, including woodland

 Coniferous forest, including woodland

 Grassland habitats: moor, savanna, fields, scrubland

 Desert and semi-desert

 Seas and oceans

 Coastal areas, including beaches and cliffs

 Coral reefs and waters immediately round them

 Rivers, streams and all flowing water

 Wetlands and still water: lakes, ponds, marshes, bogs, and swamps

 Polar regions and tundra

 Mountains, highlands, scree slopes

 Caves

 Urban

 Parasite

 Animal lifespan in the wild

 Animal not endangered

 Animal numbers are declining

 Animal endangered

 Animal status unknown

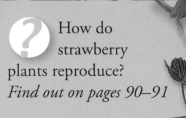
How do strawberry plants reproduce? *Find out on pages 90–91*

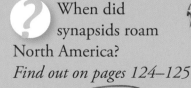
When did synapsids roam North America? *Find out on pages 124–125*

Life on Earth

Life on Earth is hugely varied. Sunflowers and sharks look like they have nothing in common, but all living things share certain features: they are made up of cells; they need energy to survive; they have a life cycle; and they can reproduce.

Animals are living things that are made up of many cells (multi-celled). They get energy by eating food.

Plants are also multi-celled. The cell walls are made of cellulose. Plants make their own food through a process called photosynthesis.

Fungi are multi-celled organisms that do not need sunlight to grow. Many fungi live underground – all that can be seen above ground are the parts that make spores for reproduction, which are called mushrooms.

PHYLUM: *Chordates* – *Animals with some form of spine.*

CLASS: *Mammals* – *These are chordates that nurse their young with milk. Most give birth to live young.*

ORDER: *Carnivores* – *These mammals have powerful jaws and specialized teeth for killing and eating meat.*

FAMILY: *Felids* – *These are carnivores that have extending claws. The common name for Felids is "cat".*

GENUS: **Panthera** – *These are large cats that can roar as well as purr.*

SPECIES: **Panthera pardus** – *This name identifies the roaring cat as a leopard.*

LIFE CYCLE

All living things have a time when they grow and a time when they die. They also reproduce, which ensures the survival of the species. Animals lay eggs or give birth to live young, plants and fungi produce seeds or spores, and bacteria and protists usually divide in two to reproduce.

DUCKLING

EGG

ADULT DUCK

FOOD CHAINS

Desert shrub
Fagonia sp.

Gerbil
Meriones sp.

Fennec fox
Vulpes zerda

Striped hyena
Hyaena hyaena

▲ PRODUCERS *such as plants are the first stage in a food chain. Plants need energy from sunlight, nutrients from the soil, and water to grow.*

▲ PRIMARY CONSUMERS, *such as gerbils, are the first animals in a chain. They are herbivores – animals that eat only plants.*

▲ SECONDARY CONSUMERS *are carnivores – animals that eat meat.*

▲ SCAVENGERS AND DECOMPOSERS *Scavengers eat dead animals, helping to break down organic matter. Maggots, fungi, and bacteria are major decomposers.*

Protists are basic life forms. Most protists are single-celled and are microscopic, but some group together and are more easily seen, such as algae on a pond.

Bacteria are the simplest form of life. They are single-celled organisms that are too small to see without a microscope. Bacteria can live in the air, in water, and even inside bodies.

FAST FACTS

■ The word "organism" refers to any living thing.

■ There are different ways of classifying organisms. They change as more information is discovered about species.

■ All living things are linked to others. This is how a food chain works: if parts are missing, the chain may collapse. This could lead to species dying out.

■ Bacteria can be harmful or helpful: *E. coli* bacteria cause disease, but penicillin can cure some illnesses.

■ The organism that makes bread go mouldy is a fungus.

THREATENED SPECIES

In every kingdom, there are species that are under threat of extinction.
There are many reasons why a species fails to continue, from habitat loss to disease to poaching (👁 p80–81).

The International Union for the Conservation of Animals (IUCN) has researched more than 1.5 million animal and plant species to create their Red List of Threatened Species. They found that:

■ in 2008 nearly 1,000 animals and plants became extinct or extinct in the wild;

■ more than 16,000 other species are under threat of extinction.

◄ More than one out of every five mammal species are threatened with extinction, including the Père David deer.

▼ Plants are also at risk, with more than 8,000 species under threat, including the lady's slipper orchid.

◄ Nearly 30 per cent of amphibians are under threat. Poison dart frogs are being wiped out along with their forest habitat.

Which species are at risk?

Most of the animals in this chapter appear on the IUCN Red List. Those with red triangles are at risk of extinction, and may already be extinct in the wild. Yellow triangles show species that are vulnerable – they risk becoming endangered in the near future. Green triangles mean there is little or no risk of them becoming endangered at present.

Plant life

There are 400,000 identified species of plants in the world. From the tallest redwood tree to the smallest duckweed, and the plainest moss to the most exotic orchid, plants all play a vital role in sustaining life on Earth.

WHAT IS A PLANT?

A plant is an organism made up of many cells that is able to manufacture its own food. Most plants do this using sunlight, carbon dioxide, and water to make carbohydrates.

LARGEST AND SMALLEST

■ The world's largest plant is the **giant redwood** tree, at up to 84 m (275 ft) tall with a trunk 11 m (36 ft) in diameter. The largest flower head is that of the titan arum from Sumatra, which grows to about 3m (10 ft) tall.

■ Some plants are too small to see clearly without a magnifying lens. The tiniest flowering plant is a duckweed known as **watermeal**. A whole plant is about 1 mm ($^1/_{32}$ in) long.

*The **flower** contains the reproductive parts of flowering plants.*

*The **stem** provides support for the leaves and flower head and carries water, minerals, and food to all parts of the plant.*

*The main **root**, or taproot, anchors the plant in the ground. Together with the side roots, it absorbs water and minerals from the soil.*

Leaves collect sunlight and contain the tiny structures that make food for the plant.

*Some plants, such as daisies, have **simple** leaves: a leaf that has just one flat blade.*

*Other plants have **compound leaves,** made up of smaller leaflets.*

PLANTS ARE ESSENTIAL FOR LIFE...

■ Without plants there would be very little oxygen in the air for us to breathe. Plants help reduce the Greenhouse Effect (👁 p78–79) by using up some of the extra carbon dioxide we produce.

■ Plants and algae form the base of most food chains. Nearly everything we eat comes from plants, or from animals that eat plants. Animals that eat only plants are called herbivores.

■ Plants have many other uses. Without them there would be no timber for building or burning, and no cotton, coal, paper, or rubber. Many medicines, toiletries, and dyes also come from plants.

Photosynthesis

All living things need food for energy but, unlike animals, plants make their own food. The plant's leaves absorb sunlight and a gas called carbon dioxide from the air, while the roots take up water. Inside the leaf, energy from the sunlight is used to turn the carbon dioxide and water into sugary food for the plant. The process is called photosynthesis, which means "making things with light". The plant also creates oxygen as a by-product of photosynthesis, which it releases through its leaves.

At night the plant takes some of the **oxygen** back in to help it burn its own sugars for energy.

The plant's leaves absorb **carbon dioxide** from the air and use it in photosynthesis.

CARBON DIOXIDE

OXYGEN

▲ INSIDE A LEAF
Photosynthesis takes place within tiny structures called chloroplasts, inside leaf cells. Chloroplasts are green because they contain a pigment called chlorophyll.

Plants need **water** to stay strong and healthy. Water is carried round a tree in minute tubes called xylem.

Tree **roots** can take up as much space underground as branches do above it. They give the tree stability and take up water and minerals.

WATER

TAKE A LOOK: TRANSPIRATION

The surface of a leaf is covered in microscopic pores called stomata. When a stoma opens it allows carbon dioxide into the leaf for photosynthesis, and also water vapour to escape in a process called transpiration. The lost moisture is replaced by water drawn up through the roots. Water from the soil contains many of the minerals that the plant needs.

Guard cell   Stoma

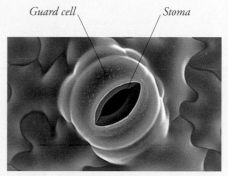

▲ OPEN STOMA Each stoma or pore is flanked by a pair of guard cells, which open and close to control the amount of gas and water vapour passing in and out of the leaf.

Leaf colours

Leaves contain a variety of pigments. In spring and summer the green pigment chlorophyll masks the colours of the others. In winter, lack of sunlight forces deciduous trees to stop photosynthesis. The chlorophyll in their leaves is broken down, allowing other colours – yellow, red, and brown – to show.

Types of plant

There are two main groups of plants: those that make seeds in order to reproduce, and those that are seedless. Seedless plants reproduce from spores.

SPORES

Spores are tiny cells that can divide to form a many-celled body. This body contains sex cells that can be fertilized and grow into a new plant.

Ferns store spores in capsules on the underside of their leaves.

SEEDLESS PLANTS

■ **Mosses** *12,000 species*
Mosses do not have roots. Instead, they take in water through their leaves, which means they can grow without soil. They attach to bare ground, trees, and rock using root-like hairs called rhizoids.

■ **Liverworts** *6,000–8,000 species* Liverworts are the earliest known form of plant life. They are generally small, leafy-looking plants that grow in damp places, and sometimes in water. The umbrella-like structures are reproductive bodies.

■ **Horsetails** *20–30 species*
We can tell from fossils that today's horsetails look very similar to those living 300 million years ago. Modern horsetails are small plants but the ancient ones grew up to 45 m (150 ft) high and formed great forests.

■ **Ferns** *around 12,000 species*
Ferns are typically found in damp, shaded places. They come in a great variety of shapes and sizes, from dainty miniatures to great tree ferns with fronds (leaves) up to 5 m (16 ft) long.

PLANT EVOLUTION

Seedless plants are the oldest plants on the planet, first appearing about 475 million years ago. Flowering plants are the youngest, a mere 130 million years old.

WOW!

I'M A SURVIVOR

Ginkgo biloba is the sole surviving species of a group of plants that once grew all over the world, but today grow wild only in China. Ginkgo fossils have been found that are 160 million years old – and they show that the plant has not changed in all that time.

TIMELINE OF PLANT EVOLUTION

475 Million Years Ago	390–360 MYA	360–290 MYA	135 MYA
Liverworts and mosses – the first seedless plants	Ferns	Conifers – the first seeded plants	

Flowering Plants

CONIFERS

The group of trees known as conifers produce seeds on cones rather than in flowers. Most conifers are "evergreen" plants, which don't drop their leaves in the winter. There are 630 species of conifer, including cypresses, firs, pines, larches, and the tallest trees in the world, coastal redwoods. Yew trees are unusual, coneless conifers.

Cypress
Cupressus macrocarpa

Korean fir
Abies koreana

Norway spruce
Pinus abies

Yew
Taxus baccata

BROADLEAF TREES

Trees that produce their seeds in flowers rather than cones tend to have broad leaves. Most broadleaf trees are "deciduous" – they lose their leaves in winter to save energy.

FLOWERING PLANTS

Three-quarters of all known plant species are flowering plants, also known as angiosperms. This group includes a huge range of plants, from trees and grasses to garden flowers, and from cacti to carnivorous plants.

Types of flower
Flowers contain the organs that a plant uses to make seeds and pollen.

▶ SIMPLE *Tulips have simple flowers. They are built around a circle, and all the petals look the same.*

▶ COMPLEX *Orchid flowers are complex. They have the same parts as simple flowers, but they develop into all kinds of unusual forms to attract the right kind of pollinating insect.*

▶ COMPOSITE *Gerberas produce composite flowers. The head is not one flower, but made up of hundreds of little florets.*

▶ SPIRE *Gladioli flowers grow in tall spires or inflorescences. The flowers open one at a time, starting from the bottom.*

TOUGH FLOWERING PLANTS

Some flowering plants have extraordinary abilities to survive in harsh environments.

■ No soil
Parasitic plants such as mistletoe can grow without soil, because they tap into a host plant and steal its nutrients instead. Epiphytes such as bromeliads also grow on other plants, usually to help them reach sunlight, but do not damage their hosts.

■ Poor soil
Carnivorous plants cannot get all their nutrients from the soil, so they supplement their diet with meat. When a fly lands on a Venus flytrap, the leaves close up and the plant releases juices that help it digest the fly's body.

■ No water
Cacti grow in very dry places. After rain, the cactus absorbs and stores enough water in its thick stem to survive the next dry spell.

Plant reproduction

Flowering plants and cone-bearing plants (such as conifers) are seed-producers. Most flowering plants reproduce through seeds, although some have vegetative reproduction too. In order to produce seeds, a flower must first be pollinated.

WOW!

Pollinators such as insects and bats may be attracted to flowers by their scent – but that doesn't mean the flower smells nice to us. Rafflesia flowers fill the air with the smell of rotting meat to attract flies. Yuck!

WHAT IS A FLOWER?

Flowers contain a plant's sexual organs. Flowers are often brightly coloured or scented to attract pollinators.

*In a simple plant, **petals** grow in a circle, or whorl.*

*The filaments and anthers together are called **stamens**. They are the male parts of the plant.*

*The **anther** is where pollen is produced.*

Sepals grow on the outer whorl. In some flowers, they look the same as the petals.

*The **filament** supports the anther.*

*The stigma, style, and ovary together are called the **carpel**. They are the female parts of the plant.*

*The **stigma** receives pollen.*

*The **ovary** is where seeds are produced.*

*The **style** connects the stigma to the ovary.*

TAKE A LOOK: GERMINATION

■ Seeds contain everything a plant needs to grow: an embryo and a food supply, which are protected inside a hard coat called a testa.

■ In the right conditions – usually a dark, damp, and warm place, such as in soil – the seed will germinate. First, the seed absorbs water. Then the embryo starts to grow, using its food store. A root appears, followed by a shoot. Seed leaves are attached to this shoot; the first true leaves don't appear until later.

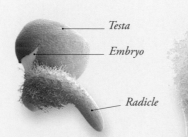

Testa

Embryo

Radicle

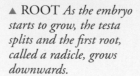

Plumule

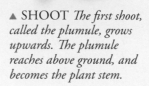

Seed leaf

▲ ROOT *As the embryo starts to grow, the testa splits and the first root, called a radicle, grows downwards.*

▲ SHOOT *The first shoot, called the plumule, grows upwards. The plumule reaches above ground, and becomes the plant stem.*

▲ SEED LEAF *Some plants have just one seed leaf, but others have two. They contain the remains of the seed's food store.*

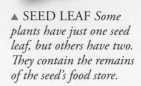

PLANT REPRODUCTION

■ Flowers attract insects, birds, and mammals, which come to feed on nectar. Bees also collect pollen. Once a plant is fertilized, the flower is no longer needed. The petals die and fall off.

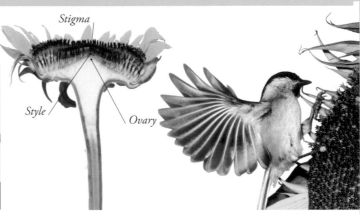

Stigma

Style

Ovary

▲ POLLINATION *When a bee visits a flower to drink nectar, it picks up pollen from the flower's anthers.*

▲ FERTILIZATION *The bee visits a second sunflower, and transfers the pollen to the stigmas. This fertilizes the plant.*

▲ SEEDS *The pollen grows down the style to the ovary, where it fertilizes an egg cell. A new plant starts to form. This is the seed.*

▲ DISPERSAL *In order to grow, seeds need to leave the plant. Birds eat the tasty seeds and pass them through, dispersing them.*

SEED DISPERSAL

■ Many plants produce fruit that encourage animals to eat and disperse their seeds, but not all...

▲ HITCHING A RIDE *Burrs become hooked onto animal fur. Their host carries them away, then they fall off to the ground.*

▲ FORCE *When the seeds are ready, Himalayan balsam flowers burst open. The force sends the seeds flying out.*

▲ WATER *Coconut palms use the sea to disperse their seeds. Coconuts have been known to drift for huge distances.*

▲ WIND *Dandelion seeds are light and fluffy. Like tiny parachutes, they catch the wind to disperse far and wide.*

VEGETATIVE REPRODUCTION

■ Some flowering plants don't only reproduce through seeds. Instead, they form plantlets that are genetically identical to the parent plant.

▲ STOLONS *Strawberries have stolons – stems that grow along the ground. New plants grow from leaf nodes along the stolon.*

▲ TUBERS *such as Jerusalem artichokes are food stores for the parent plant, but they can also sprout and grow into new plants.*

▲ RHIZOMES *Irises spread through underground stems called rhizomes. The rhizome divides and forms new plants.*

▲ BULB *Onions and tulips grow from bulbs, which are buds that are surrounded by very swollen leaves.*

Animal life

There are more than 1.2 million identified species of animal, making this the largest kingdom of living things.

WHO'S WHO?

Most animals are invertebrates: they have no backbone. Animals with backbones are known as vertebrates, and they can be divided up into different classes.

▲ THOSE ARE ANIMALS?
It's usually easy to tell an animal from a plant – animals are the ones that move about. But this isn't always the case. Corals look like plants and have limited movement. However, they take in food to get energy and they have nerves that control their reactions (such as shrinking away from danger). These things are what make them animals.

Vertebrates

Invertebrates

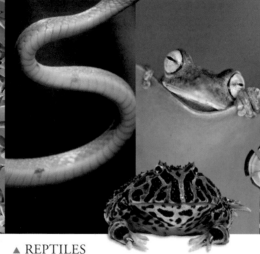

▲ MAMMALS
There are more than 5,000 species of mammal. What makes this class unique is that the young feed on milk from their mother. Mammals are warm-blooded, most have a hairy body, and most give birth to live young.

▲ BIRDS *There are about 9,500 species of bird. They are warm-blooded, have wings and a bill, and a body covered in feathers. All birds lay eggs and most can fly.*

Leopard tortoise

▲ REPTILES
The 8,000 species of reptile are recognized by their scaly skin. They are cold-blooded, and lay eggs to reproduce.

▲ AMPHIBIANS
Most of the 6,000 species of amphibian live part of their life in water and part on land. They are cold-blooded.

▲ FISH *This is an informal group of three different classes, which together have 29,000 species. All fish are cold-blooded and live in water.*

Rhinoceros beetle

▲ INVERTEBRATES
An informal grouping of about 29 major groups (phyla), the invertebrates include all those animals that do not have a backbone. Worms, insects, shrimps, jellyfish, and octopuses are all invertebrates.

RECORD BREAKERS

BIGGEST, HEAVIEST, LOUDEST
At up to 30 m (98 ft) long, the blue whale is easily the biggest animal on Earth. It's also the heaviest, weighing 120 tonnes (118 tons), and the loudest. At 188 decibels its calls are louder than a jet engine. A blue whale's heart is the size of a small car and its largest blood vessel is wide enough for a small person to crawl inside. Blue whales are threatened with extinction due to over-hunting in the past.

▲ SMALLEST VERTEBRATE
Australia's infantfish is less than 1 cm (½ in) long.

▲ STRONGEST
The rhinoceros beetle can lift 850 times its own weight. If the beetle weighed as much as a human it could lift at least two fully laden doubledecker buses.

The bodies of vertebrates, such as apes, are supported by an internal skeleton made of bone or cartilage. Invertebrates may have a hard external skeleton, a shell, or a soft body (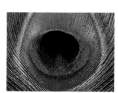 p110–111).

TELL ME MORE...

Animals need oxygen to survive. Many species that live on land have lungs to breathe air; those that live underwater, such as fish, have gills to filter oxygen from the water. Aquatic birds and mammals have lungs and must surface to breathe air.

ON THE OUTSIDE

Animals have different body coverings that protect them from heat and cold, from waterlogging or drying out, and from all kinds of attack. Birds are the only animals to have feathers; reptiles and most fish have scales; and mammals are the only animals to have hair on their body.

Bright colours and patterns can be used to attract mates...

... as a warning that the animal is foul-tasting or poisonous...

... or as camouflage so the animal blends in with its surroundings.

THE INSIDE STORY

Animals come in an enormous variety of forms. Yet on the inside, most of them share certain features. Apart from the simplest creatures, all animals have a body made up of many cells. These cells are organized into tissues. In complex animals, these tissues form organs that perform particular jobs that help keep the whole body functioning.

▲ SOCIAL Elephants live in large herds

▶ SOLITARY Pandas live alone

Solitary or social?

Some animals are solitary: they hunt, eat, sleep, and live alone and only seek out other members of their species to mate and produce offspring. Other animals live in pairs or groups, which increases their chance of survival. Members of a group may work together to find food, defend a territory, rear young, or keep watch for predators.

Body heat

Mammals and birds are warm-blooded, or endothermic – they generate their own body heat using energy from food, and can control their body temperature. Most other animals are ectothermic, which means they cannot control their temperature naturally. When they want to warm up they sunbathe, and if they are too hot they seek shade to cool down.

Ectothermic animals such as lizards can be seen basking in the morning sunlight in order to warm their body.

◀ FASTEST The peregrine falcon can swoop at a breathtaking 360 km/h (220 mph) in unpowered flight. The fastest creature on land is the cheetah, and in water is the sailfish. Both can reach 110 km/h (68 mph)

▲ MOST DEADLY A single sea wasp jellyfish has enough venom to kill 60 men. The venom of cone snails and some fish is even more toxic.

▲ BIGGEST KILLER Female Anopheles mosquitoes kill more than a million people each year by infecting them with malaria.

▲ LONGEST LIFESPAN A Madagascan radiated tortoise like this one is known to have lived at least 188 years. Bowhead whales may survive even longer, maybe as long as 250 years.

Mammals

Mammals are vertebrates that feed their young on milk produced by the mother. The milk is made in her mammary glands, which is why the group is called "mammals". Most mammals give birth to live young.

WHAT IS A MAMMAL?

All mammals have a lower jaw made up of just one bone. This is how scientists identify mammal fossils, long after mammary glands and hair have disappeared.

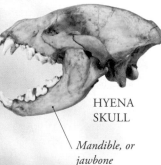

HYENA SKULL

Mandible, or jawbone

▲ ALL EARS *Grazing impala must live in the open where their food grows. They are wary animals with large eyes and mobile ears tuned to signs of danger.*

Browsers and grazers

Nearly all hoofed mammals are herbivores – they eat only plants. Some are browsers, which means they nibble leaves and shoots from trees and shrubs; others are grazers that eat mainly grass. Plant matter, especially grass, is hard to digest, so many of these animals ruminate, or chew the cud. After swallowing a meal, they lie down to rest while bacteria in their stomach weaken the tough plant cell walls. Then the animal regurgitates its food (now called cud) and chews it again to help release nutrients.

HAIR

Mammals are the only animals to have hair. Hair is made from keratin, the same material found in fingernails, fish scales, and bird feathers. A dense coat of hair is called fur; its main purpose is to keep the animal warm. Hair also appears in other forms, such as protective spines (as in hedgehogs and echidnas) and the sensitive facial whiskers of other mammals.

Short-beaked echidna
Tachyglossus aculeatus

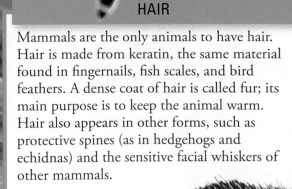

ORDER, ORDER!

There are more than 5,000 species of mammal, arranged into 28 orders. The members of an order tend to be descended from a shared ancestor, and are united by similar anatomy or lifestyle. For example, camels, deer, hippopotamuses, giraffes, cattle, whales, and dolphins are all families within the order Cetartiodactyla.

MONOTREMES

There are five species of mammal that don't give birth to live young, but instead lay eggs. They are called monotremes, and include the duck-billed platypus. Once hatched, young monotremes feed on their mother's milk, just like other mammals.

BATS

Bats are the only mammals that can truly fly (not just glide). All bats have wings, which are in fact delicate webbed hands. Hearing is very important to bats: they can find prey and avoid obstacles in total darkness by listening to the way their calls echo off nearby objects.

POUCHED MAMMALS

There are more than 330 species of pouched mammal in seven orders, including kangaroos, opossums, and the koala. Commonly called marsupials, these mammals give birth to very tiny young. The newborns crawl inside their mother's pouch, where they feed on milk and continue to grow.

▶ SAFE INSIDE
A joey in its mother's pouch.

PRIMATES

Monkeys, lemurs, apes, and humans are all primates. Primates have grasping hands and forward-facing eyes. The great apes (including chimpanzees, gorillas, and the orangutan) are humans' closest relatives.

CARNIVORES

◀ LESSON TIME
Polar bear cubs learn to hunt by watching their mother.

There are 12 families of meat-eating mammals grouped into one order called carnivores. They have bodies that are adapted to hunting and eating flesh.

Leopard
Panthera pardalis

Mammal record breakers

Mammals come in a staggering variety of forms and have mastered almost every habitat on Earth. They walk, run, swim, burrow, and fly, and one species, our own, has even been to the Moon.

Human beings

Humans (species *Homo sapiens*) are mammals from the great ape family. We can live to around 125 years, but the worldwide average is 66 years. We inhabit every continent except Antarctica, making us the most widespread mammals.

Hog-nosed bat
Craseonycteris thonglongyai
■ **Length** 30 mm (1¼ in)

The world's **smallest mammal** is also known as the bumblebee bat. It weighs about half as much as a cube of sugar.

The **biggest mammal on land** reaches full size at about 20 years of age, but its tusks keep on growing.

African savanna elephant
Loxodonta africana
■ **Weight** 6 tonnes (6½ tons)

Blue whale
Balaenoptera musculus
■ **Length** 30 m (98 ft)

Giraffe
Giraffa sp.
■ **Height** 5.3 m (17½ ft)

The **tallest** mammal's long legs and neck allow it to reach leaves on high branches.

Mountain gorilla
Gorilla beringei
■ **Weight** 200 kg (440 lb)

Compared to the size of its body, a male gorilla has the **longest arms** of any mammal.

With a body that is 50% fat after feeding on its mother's fatty milk, a ringed seal pup is the **fattest** wild mammal.

Ringed seal
Phoca hispida
■ **Length** 1.3 m (4¼ ft)

Sea otter
Enhydra lutris
- **Length** 1.3 m (4¼ ft)

With 125,000 hairs per cm² (800,000 hairs per square inch), sea otter fur is waterproof, warm, and the **densest fur** of any mammal.

Striped skunk
Mephitis mephitis
- **Length** 68 cm (2¼ ft)

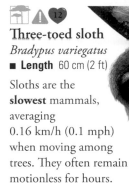

The stinking spray from a skunk is used as a defence against predators – and makes it the **smelliest** mammal.

Three-toed sloth
Bradypus variegatus
- **Length** 60 cm (2 ft)

Sloths are the **slowest** mammals, averaging 0.16 km/h (0.1 mph) when moving among trees. They often remain motionless for hours.

Cheetah
Acinonyx jubatus
- **Length** 1.35 m (4½ ft)

Over short distances, a cheetah can sprint at up to 95 km/h (62 mph) in pursuit of prey, making it the **fastest** mammal.

Camels are the **biggest drinkers**. Bactrians can drink 57 litres (120 pints) in one session.

Bactrian camel
Camelus bactrianus
- **Height** 2.3 m (7½ ft)

The blue whale is the **largest living animal** on Earth. Its voice carries up to 800 km (500 miles) through the ocean.

Scimitar-horned oryx
Oryx dammah
- **Length** 1./ m (5½ ft)

These antelope have been hunted to extinction in the wild, making them among the **rarest** mammals.

Grey whale
Eschrichtius robustus
- **Length** Up to 15 m (49 ft)

Grey whales make the **longest migration**: an annual round-trip of 20,000 km (12,500 miles) from the Arctic to breeding grounds off Mexico.

White rhinoceros
Ceratotherium simum
- **Length** 4 m (14 ft)

Rhinos have the **thickest skin**, which acts as armour. In vulnerable places like the shoulders it can be almost 5 cm (2 in) thick.

Killer carnivores

Many animals are described as carnivorous: it means that they eat meat. But there is also an order of mammals called carnivores, which have unique features such as sharp cheek teeth. Many can kill prey bigger than themselves.

BUILT TO HUNT

A typical carnivore has a body that is adapted to hunting. It has good eyesight, hearing, and sense of smell to locate prey, and can run fast or for long distances to give chase. Cats have sharp claws to grab prey and bring it down, while powerful jaws and teeth bite to kill.

ON THE MENU

- **Carnivores** Different carnivore species eat different prey. Lions hunt in prides to kill large animals such as wildebeest; otters hunt alone, feeding on fish and shellfish.
- **Herbivorous carnivores** Pandas are largely herbivorous – they rarely eat meat at all, but fill up on bamboo. They have flat cheek teeth for chewing plants, rather than sharp teeth for tearing meat.
- **Omnivorous carnivores** Many carnivores, including foxes and skunks, are omnivorous – they eat all kinds of food, from plants to birds' eggs to frogs… In fact, almost anything they can find.

Scavengers Not all carnivores are predators. Hyenas are very good at hunting, but they will also scavenge – eat an animal that is already dead, killed by others or by natural causes.

TAKE A LOOK: JAWS AND CLAWS

Killer carnivores have four sharp cheek teeth, called carnassial teeth, which can cut through hide, meat, and bone. A huge muscle called the temporalis muscle gives enough power for the teeth to break bones or suffocate prey. Sharp claws are equally important for some carnivores. Lions and other cats use their claws to hold onto prey, in defence, for climbing, and for grip when running.

Lion's sharp claws

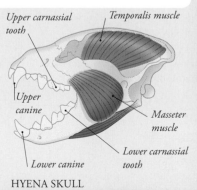

Upper carnassial tooth

Temporalis muscle

Upper canine

Masseter muscle

Lower canine

Lower carnassial tooth

HYENA SKULL

Snow leopard
Panthera uncia

- **Length** 1–1.3 m (3¼–4¼ ft)
- **Weight** 25–75 kg (55–165 lb)
- **Location** Central, southern, and eastern Asia

The endangered snow leopard has a thick tail that's around the same length as its body. This gives the cat balance when climbing mountain slopes and hunting for prey such as wild sheep.

Red panda
Ailurus fulgens

- **Length** 50–64 cm (20–25 in)
- **Weight** 3–6 kg (6½–13 lb)
- **Location** Southern and south eastern Asia

Red pandas are not pandas, nor any other type of bear. They are more closely related to raccoons. However, like giant pandas, they mostly eat bamboo. Red pandas are rare and solitary (they live alone). They are known for being shy, and spend most of the time hidden up in trees, where they find food, hide from predators, and even sunbathe in the winter. It can get very cold in the pandas' natural habitat – temperate mountain forests.

Least weasel
Mustela nivalis

- **Length** 24 cm (9½ in)
- **Weight** 250 g (9 oz)
- **Location** North America, Europe, and northern, central, and eastern Asia

Weasels eat mostly mice and voles. They can track their prey through thick grass and under snow, and are small enough to squeeze into mouse burrows. Weasels are usually brown and white, but those that live in the far north turn completely white in the winter, so they are camouflaged in snow.

Lion
Panthera leo

- **Length** 1.7–2.5 m (5½–8¼ ft)
- **Weight** 150–250 kg (330–550 lb)
- **Location** Sub-Saharan Africa and South Asia

Lions are the only big cats to live in groups, called prides. There may be up to 10 lionesses and their cubs in a pride, with two or three male lions. Lionesses often work together to hunt and kill prey for the pride.

Eurasian badger
Meles meles

- **Length** 90 cm (35 in)
- **Weight** 34 kg (75 lb)
- **Location** Europe and eastern Asia

Badgers live in groups in setts – underground dens and tunnels they dig out with their strong claws. Badgers are nocturnal (active at night), but have poor eyesight, so hunt mainly by smell. Their main diet is earthworms.

Giant panda
Ailuropoda melanoleuca

- **Length** 1.5–2 m (5¼–6¾ ft)
- **Weight** 70–160 kg (155–350 lb)
- **Location** Central China

Giant pandas are easily recognized, but rarely seen: there are thought to be fewer than 1,600 left in the wild. They are also known as bamboo bears, after their main source of food.

Grey wolf
Canis lupus

- **Length** 150–200 cm (4¼–6½ ft)
- **Weight** 20–60 kg (44–130 lb)
- **Location** North America, eastern Europe, and Asia

All domestic dogs have evolved from the grey wolf, the largest member of the dog family. Grey wolves hunt in packs to kill large animals. Each pack has a territory where it lives and hunts, and wolves will howl to stop other packs straying into their patch.

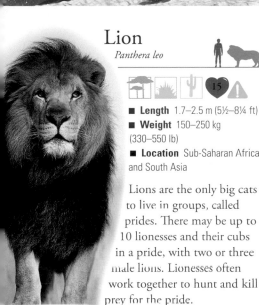

Tiger
Panthera tigris

- **Length** 2.8 m (9¼ ft)
- **Weight** 260 kg (573 lb)
- **Location** Southern and eastern Asia

Tigers ambush their prey, which includes deer and cattle. They silently prowl in tall grasses, camouflaged by their stripes. With a sudden pounce, the tiger leaps onto its prey, bringing it down and killing it by breaking its neck or biting its throat, suffocating it.

Brown bear
Ursus arctos

- **Height** 3 m (10 ft)
- **Weight** 780 kg (1,720 lb)
- **Location** Northern North America, northern and eastern Europe, and northern Asia

Brown bears feed on forest fodder: nuts, berries, and small animals, such as river salmon. The bears can become aggressive when protecting their cubs.

Amphibians

Most amphibians begin life in water breathing with gills, and then venture onto land as adults, where they breathe using lungs and through their skin. They live in damp places, and most return to the water to breed. There are three groups of amphibians: frogs and toads, newts and salamanders, and caecilians.

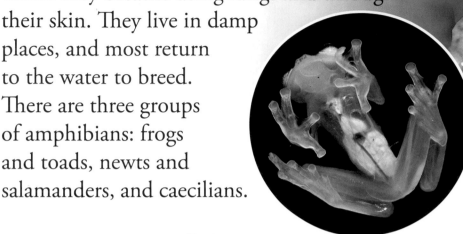

▲ SEE-THROUGH SKIN *Frogs have delicate skin. A glass frog's skin lacks strong pigment and is almost transparent.*

Gills, lungs, and skin
Some salamanders spend their whole life in water, and may keep their tadpole gills even as adults (although they do have lungs as well). Others live entirely on land, where some manage without lungs. They absorb oxygen directly into their bloodstream through their thin skin. Keeping the skin moist helps the oxygen pass through.

FROM EGG TO ADULT

Young amphibians such as this frog hatch as larvae (tadpoles) that look nothing like their parents. The series of changes that take place as a larva grows into an adult is called metamorphosis.

▶ 1. SPAWN
Frog and toad eggs are laid in clusters or strings, protected by a special jelly.

▼ 2. TADPOLE *This young tadpole has yet to develop external gills. The gills become internal as the limbs develop.*

▼ 3. FROGLET
The tadpole first grows back legs, then front limbs. The tail begins to shrink until the youngster resembles a tiny version of the adult.

▶ 4. FROG
The adult lives mostly on land but is also happy in water. It breathes using lungs and through its skin.

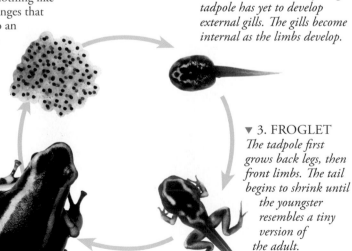

Bright colours warn predators

▲ POISON! *Amphibians have glands in their skin that ooze toxins. The foul taste deters potential predators and may kill them. Some tree frog toxins are used to make deadly poison-tipped darts.*

Golden poison dart frog

Phyllobates terribilis

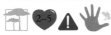

- **Length** 3–4.5 cm (1⅕–1⅘ in)
- **Weight** 3–5 g (1⁄10–⅕ oz)
- **Location** Colombia, South America

This frog's striking colours carry a serious warning. The toxin that secretes from glands in its skin is the most deadly poison produced by any vertebrate animal, and predators will avoid contact with the frog at all costs. There are three varieties of poison dart frog – gold (like this one), green, and orange.

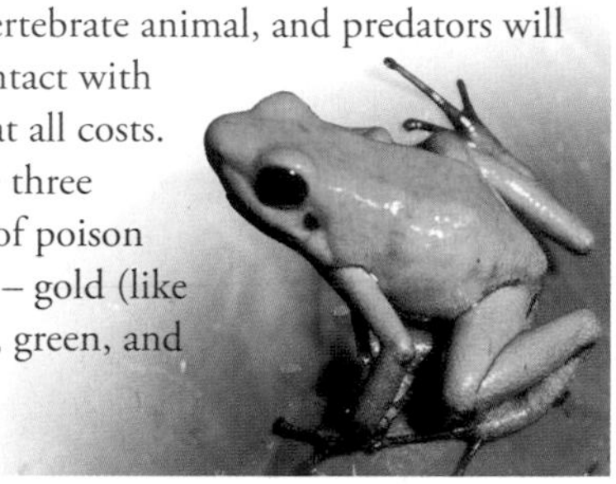

European common frog

Rana temporaria

- **Length** 6–9 cm (2⅖–3½ in)
- **Weight** 25–35 g (9⁄10–1⅕ oz)
- **Location** Europe

A familiar animal in Europe, the common frog lives and breeds in pools and damp places. In climates with harsh winters it may hibernate for several months in a moist burrow or in mud at the bottom of a pool. Prey, including slugs, worms, and insects, are whipped into the frog's large mouth with its sticky tongue.

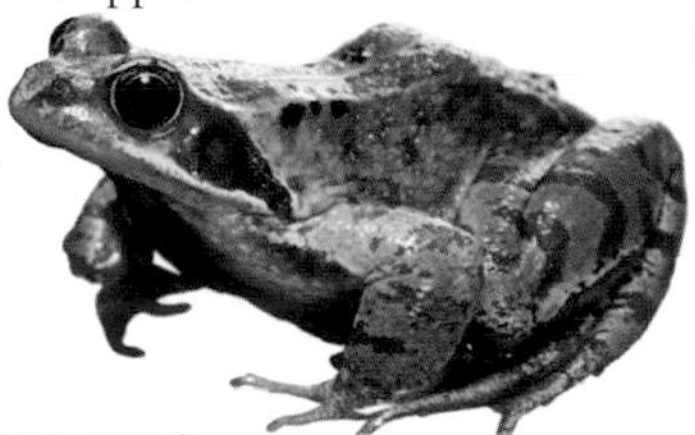

Tiger salamander

Ambystoma tigrinum

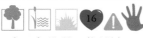

- **Length** 15–30 cm (6–12 in)
- **Weight** 100–150 g (4–6 oz)
- **Location** Most of North America

Like most amphibians, this large salamander begins life in water. Most metamorphose into land-living adults but some manage to mature and breed without ever leaving the water. On land, tiger salamanders live in grasslands or woodland edges, where they hunt insects, worms, and even mice and frogs.

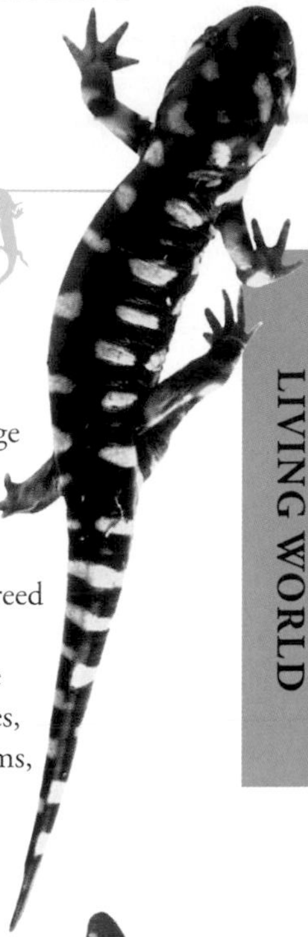

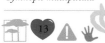

Oriental fire-bellied frog

Bombina orientalis

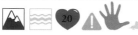

- **Length** 4–8 cm (1⅗–3⅕ in)
- **Weight** 20–30 g (¾–1 oz)
- **Location** China, Russia, and Korea

The magnificent colours of the fire-bellied frog give this species its name – and warns predators about the poison glands in its skin. The frogs live in humid forests and spend most of their time wallowing in shallow water. Their vision is limited to detecting movement, so potential prey that does not move may be lucky and get away.

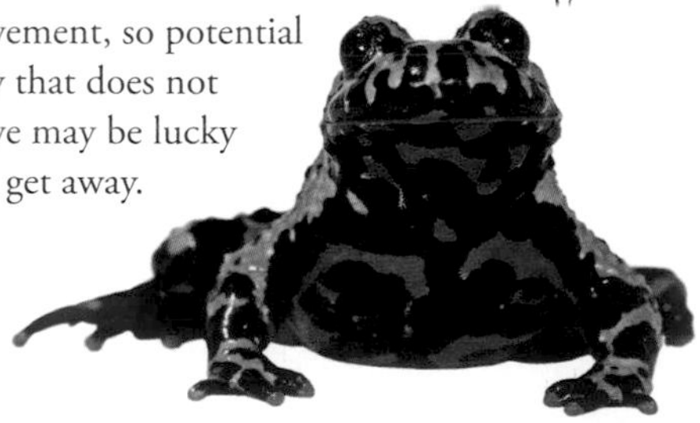

Emperor newt

Tylototriton shanjing

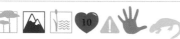

- **Length** 17 cm (20 in)
- **Weight** Exact weight unknown
- **Location** Yunnan Province, China

This handsome newt is at risk in its native China where it is collected for food, the pet trade, and for use in traditional medicine. Adults live on land most of the year, but return to the shallow pool where they were born to find a mate and lay eggs, which are deposited carefully on water weeds. The name shanjing means "mountain spirit" in Mandarin.

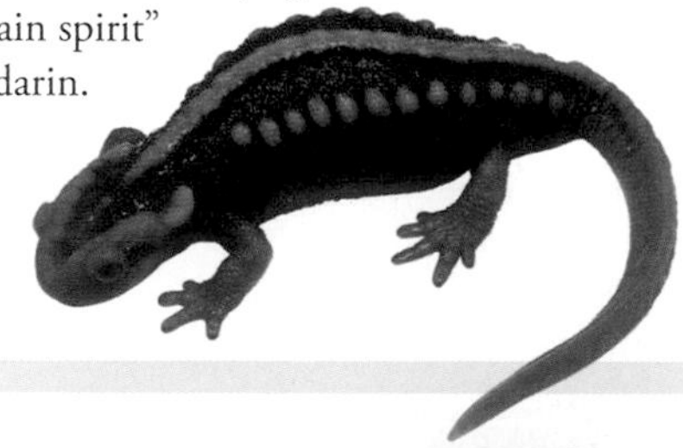

Caecilian

Gymnopis multiplicata

- **Length** 50 cm (20 in)
- **Weight** Exact weight unknown
- **Location** Tropical forests

This strange legless and eyeless creature belongs to the smallest group of amphibians, the caecilians. They spend their lives burrowing through the warm, damp leaf litter or soil of tropical forests. Earthworms happen to be the caecilian's favourite prey, which they hunt by smell, using short tentacles to pick up the earthworm's faint chemical signals. Rather than spawning eggs, this species gives birth to live young that look like miniature adults.

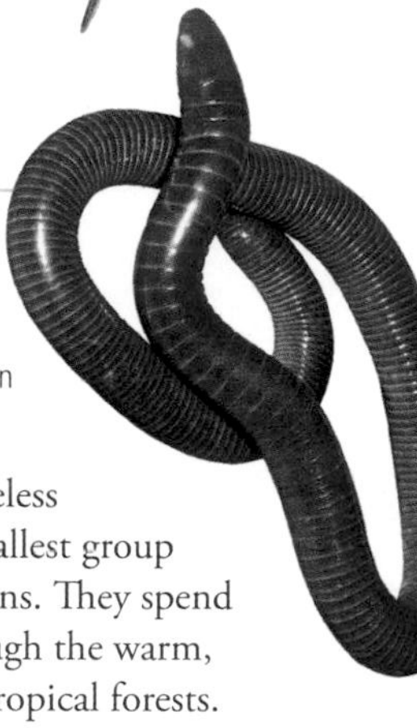

TAKE A LOOK: FROG FEET

Amphibians usually live in damp, humid, or sheltered places, which helps them keep their skin moist. Their ability to swim, walk, hop, climb, and even glide means they are able to live a wide variety of lifestyles. The frogs shown here have feet adapted to very different habitats.

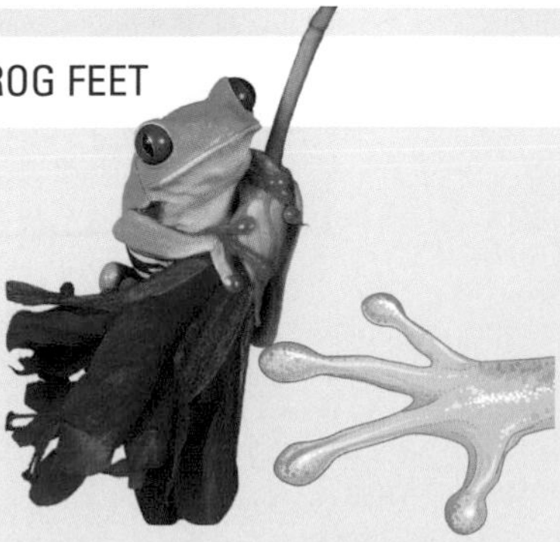

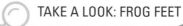

▲ STICKY FEET *Tree frogs have sticky toe pads to provide extra grip.*

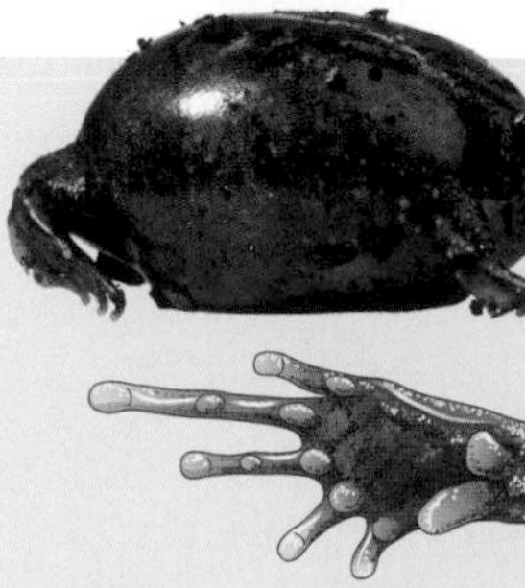

▲ DIRTY FEET *Burrowing frogs have strong feet for loosening and shovelling soil.*

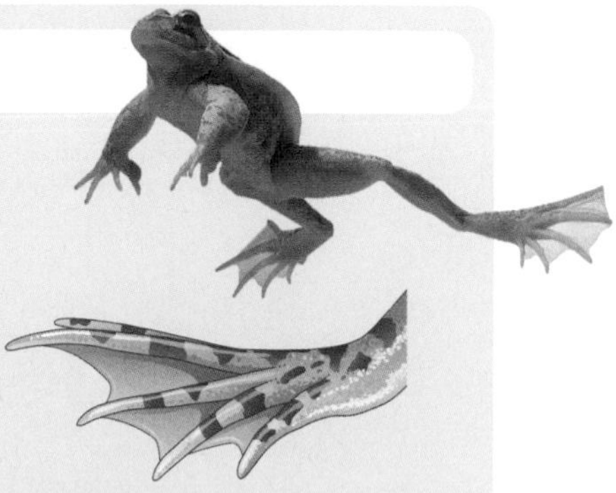

▲ WEBBED FEET *Common frogs have webbed, flipper-like hind feet to help them swim.*

Reptiles

Reptiles are cold-blooded vertebrates that have tough skin covered in scales. The scales are made of keratin – the same material as mammal hair and bird feathers. There are nearly 8,000 species of reptile, grouped in four orders. The biggest order is snakes and lizards.

Panther chameleon
Furcifer paradalis

FEARSOME FANGS

Some snakes have venom glands just behind their fangs. Venom is used to kill prey, and sometimes in defence. Baring fangs is a warning to attackers to back off.

Western diamondbacked rattlesnake
Crotalus atrox

TAKE A PICTURE

A dione ratsnake (Elaphe dione) begins "sloughing" its skin. Snakes shed their skin up to eight times a year.

Emerald tree boa (juvenile)
Corallus caninus

BENDY BACKBONE

A snake's backbone is incredibly flexible. Tree boas coil around branches to rest and to spot prey. Desert vipers squeeze under rocks for shade. Sidewinding snakes zip across the ground in S-shape waves.

Thorny devil
Moloch horridus

REPTILE EGGS

Although some snakes and lizards give birth to live young, most reptiles reproduce by laying eggs. Some look like birds' eggs – they have hard, rounded shells – but most eggs have softer, leathery shells. The hatchlings break through their shells using a sharp "egg tooth", which then falls out.

◄ SNAKE *Young snakes coil up tightly inside a shell. Some can be up to seven times longer than their egg.*

▲ LIZARD *Leopard geckos lay a clutch of two long, sticky eggs in their underground burrows.*

◄ TORTOISE *Large tortoises and turtles, such as leopard tortoises, lay almost perfectly round eggs.*

TAKING A STAND

A reptile's legs stick out at right angles to its body (unlike mammals' and birds', which do not). This gives them a very sturdy frame for walking on uneven land.

SNAKES

Despite having no limbs, snakes are incredible predators. There are around 2,900 species of snake, and 300 of these are venomous. Other snakes are constrictors: they coil around their prey and squeeze until it suffocates.

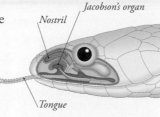

Nostril

Jacobson's organ

Tongue

▲ JACOBSON'S ORGAN *A snake often hunts by smell and by tasting the air – picking up scents with its tongue. It uses its Jacobson's organ to analyze the scent for signs of prey.*

◄ DEADLY GRIP *A rock python kills a gazelle.*

LIZARDS

There are 4,500 species of lizard, from the enormous komodo dragon to the tiny pygmy chameleon. Most of them have long tails. Some lizards, mostly skinks, have an interesting defence technique: if a predator catches their tail, it can break off so the lizard can run free. Eventually the tail will grow back.

◄ SMALLEST & LARGEST ► *At up to 3 m (10 ft) long, the komodo dragon is 60 times the length of the 5 cm (2 in) pygmy chameleon.*

CROCODILES AND ALLIGATORS

There are 23 species of crocodilian, which have flat, wide bodies, powerful tails, and menacing jaws. They have eyes on the tops of their heads and nostrils on the tops of their noses so they can see and breathe while lying submerged in water, which is where they wait to ambush prey. Fish, and mammals that come down to a lake or river to drink, are the main targets: caught in the crocodile's immense jaws, mammals are dragged into the water and drowned. The crocodile can safely open its mouth underwater: it has a flap of skin that it closes across the back of its throat.

▲ CAUGHT *Crocodiles that live in the Grumeti River, Africa, take advantage of the wildebeeste migration that crosses the river.*

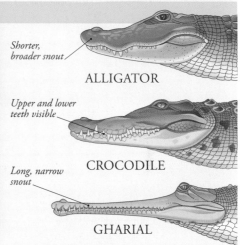

Shorter, broader snout

ALLIGATOR

Upper and lower teeth visible

CROCODILE

Long, narrow snout

GHARIAL

▲ SNOUTS *Alligators have shorter, wider snouts than crocodiles; gharial snouts are the narrowest. Only the alligator's top teeth can be seen when its mouth is shut.*

TORTOISES AND TURTLES

The 255 species of tortoises, turtles, and terrapins are easily recognized by their hard shells. They move slowly, and so most are herbivorous (eat plants) as they are too slow to catch prey. Turtles are more likely to be carnivorous (eat meat): they lie in wait for fish to swim past, then snap their jaws around the prey.

▲ LAND AND SEA *Tortoises live on land, but turtles are water-based.*

◄ LONG NECK *The common snake-necked turtle uses its long neck to lunge at prey.*

TUATARAS

There are just two species of tuatara. They look a lot like iguanas (which are lizards), but tuataras are found only on islands off the coast of New Zealand, coming out of their burrows at night to hunt insects. Tuataras have changed little in the 100 million years since their prehistoric ancestors died out.

Tuatara
Sphenodon punctatus

Birds

There are around 9,700 species of bird. Like mammals, they are warm-blooded vertebrates, but unlike most mammals, they lay eggs, their bodies are covered in feathers, and most can fly.

FEATHERS FOR FLIGHT

A bird's feathers not only help to keep the bird warm, but also play an important role in flight by giving the wings and tail the correct shape. Feathers are made of a substance called keratin – the same protein found in your hair and fingernails.

Chisel-shaped bill

Woodpecker

Barbet

Conical bill

Puff bird

Sharp, slim bill

Bill shapes

Birds have no teeth or jaws. Instead they have a bill made of tough, horny keratin. The bill serves many purposes: it can be a deadly weapon for stabbing and tearing, a tool for probing, crushing, or drilling, and a delicate filter. Most birds also use their bill for grooming.

*Long, stiff **flight feathers** give wings the shape needed to create lift.*

*Smaller than flight feathers, **contour feathers** give the bird its streamlined body shape in flight.*

*Under the contour feathers on the bird's body, a layer of short, fluffy **down feathers** keeps the bird warm.*

*The bird uses its **tail feathers** as both brake and rudder.*

Red-tailed hawk
Buteo jamaicensis

*Most birds have excellent **eyesight**. Hawks such as this one can spy prey from great distances.*

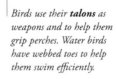

*Birds use their **talons** as weapons and to help them grip perches. Water birds have webbed toes to help them swim efficiently.*

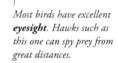

Bird bones

Most animal bones are filled with squidgy marrow, but bird bones are hollow, which makes them light. They are also strong, thanks to the supporting struts inside.

FLIGHTLESS BIRDS

Not all birds fly. Flightlessness can be a feature of birds that have few natural predators, such as the New Zealand kiwi. Flying would use a vast amount of energy in very large birds such as ostriches, rheas, emus, and cassowaries. Instead, they invest their energy in running fast. They also grow too large for most predators to tackle.

Male common ostriches
Struthio camelus

WOW!

All birds lay eggs. One reason why is that the female would struggle to fly with a brood of heavy chicks developing inside her. Most birds incubate their eggs by sitting on them. Mother birds usually lay a single egg at a sitting.

KEEPING ORDER

There are 29 orders of birds, including:

- **Swifts and hummingbirds** These fast flyers have tiny legs and feet.
- **Parrots** There are 352 parrot species, including macaws and budgerigars.
- **Rheas** Flightless rheas have large wings, but weak flight muscles.
- **Waders, gulls, and auks** Puffins are one of 344 species in this varied order.
- **Gamebirds** Peafowl are part of this ground-dwelling order.
- **Flamingos** The only birds that feed with their head upside-down.
- **Waterfowl** Webbed feet help ducks and other waterfowl to swim.
- **Owls** There are 194 owl species.

Ruby-throated hummingbird

Archilochus colubris

- **Length** 7–9 cm (2¾–3½ in)
- **Wingspan** 8–11 cm (3–4 in)
- **Weight** 2–6 g (1/15–1/5 oz)
- **Location** North and Central America

This tiny jewel of a bird uses its specially adapted bill to sip nectar from tube-shaped flowers, while it hovers on wings that beat about 50 times per second. Hummingbirds are among the smallest warm-blooded animals on Earth.

Hyacinth macaw

Anodorhynchus hyacinthinus

- **Length** 100 cm (3¼ ft)
- **Wingspan** 130 cm (4 ft)
- **Weight** 1.5–2 kg (3⅓–4⅖ lb)
- **Location** Central South America

This is the world's largest parrot, though the flightless kakapo from New Zealand is heavier. Sadly it is also one of the rarest of its kind, as it suffered greatly from over-collection for the pet trade. Its habitat has shrunk as loggers and farmers fell its native forests.

Rhea

Pterocnemia pennata

- **Height** up to 100 cm (39½ in)
- **Weight** 20 kg (44 lb)
- **Location** South America

Rheas are South America's version of the ostrich. They favour open habitats where they can see trouble coming. A male will mate with several females and care for all the resulting eggs himself, in one large nest.

Atlantic puffin

Fratercula arctica

- **Length** 30 cm (12 in)
- **Wingspan** 60 cm (24 in)
- **Weight** 450 g (16 oz)
- **Location** High Arctic to the Mediterranean

Puffins are not the best flyers, and are awkward on land too – but they are expert swimmers, hunting fish under water. Outside the breeding season they spend all their time at sea.

Common peafowl

Pavo cristatus

- **Length** Male 1.8–2.3 m (6–7½ ft) Female 1 m (3¼ ft)
- **Wingspan** 1.4–1.6 m (4½–5¼ ft)
- **Weight** 4–6 kg (8¾–13 lb)
- **Location** India and Pakistan

The male peafowl (a peacock) is famous for his magnificent tail, which he displays to show off his health and vigour. The female (peahen) has dowdy brown plumage and a short tail. Peafowl eat a varied diet of seeds, flowers, and insects.

Lesser flamingo

Phoenicopterus minor

- **Height** 80–90 cm (31½–35⅖ in)
- **Wingspan** 100 cm (3¼ ft)
- **Weight** 2 kg (4½ lb)
- **Location** Africa

Colonies of lesser flamingos form a spectacle when they gather in their thousands to breed in the alkaline lakes of the Rift Valley. Each pair produce one egg in a nest of baked mud. Flamingos feed on blue-green algae, which they filter from the water using a specially adapted bill.

Plumed whistling duck

Dendrocygna eytoni

- **Length** 40–50 cm (16–23½ in)
- **Weight** 0.5–1.5 kg (1–3¼ lb)
- **Location** Australia, Indonesia, and Papua New Guinea

The plumed whistling duck is named for the ornate plumage on its flanks (sides), and its distinctive call, which resembles the noise created by blowing air past a blade of grass trapped between two thumbs. It eats grass and weeds.

Sokoke Scops owl

Otus ireneae

- **Height** 16–18 cm (6⅓–7 in)
- **Weight** 50 g (1¾ oz)
- **Location** Kenya and Tanzania

One of the world's smallest owls, the Sokoke Scops owl specializes in catching beetles and other insects. It hunts by night and hides by day in thickets of scrub. Loss of this habitat means the owl is threatened with extinction.

Penguins

Agile and speedy in the water, penguins more than make up for their inability to fly. These birds hunt fish, krill, and squid in the waters of the southern hemisphere. In the warmer months, they come onto land to breed in large colonies.

Swimming

Emperor penguins have sleek, streamlined bodies and flattened wings, or flippers, to cut through the water. Dense feathers and a thick layer of blubber keep them warm in the icy Antarctic waters.

Adélie penguin
Pygoscelis adeliae

   16

- **Height** 40–75 cm (16–30 in)
- **Weight** 4–5.5 kg (10–12 lb)
- **Location** Antarctica

One of the smallest and most abundant of all penguins, the Adélie spends most of the winter at sea but then comes ashore in the summer to breed. Mating pairs build nests in large colonies, which offers protection from egg thieves such as skuas (seabirds).

Huddling

When they are seven weeks old, emperor penguin chicks huddle together in a "creche" to keep warm. The fluffy grey down feathers of the chicks also trap body heat, insulating them from the cold Antarctic winds.

Yellow-eyed penguin
Megadyptes antipodes

 **23**

- **Height** 66–70 cm (26–28 in)
- **Weight** 5.5 kg (12 lb)
- **Location** New Zealand

Fewer than 4,000 of these rare penguins live on the islands of southern New Zealand. The striking yellow eye-stripe gives them their common name.

Rockhopper penguin
Eudyptes chrysocome

  10

- **Height** 50 cm (19$\frac{7}{10}$ in)
- **Weight** 2.5 kg (5½ lb)
- **Location** Sub-Antarctic

These small, crested penguins take their common name from the way they hop as they move around their rocky colonies on the islands of the sub-Antarctic.

Emperor penguin
Aptenodytes forsteri

  20

- **Height** 110 cm (43 in)
- **Weight** 35–40 kg (77–88 lb)
- **Location** Antarctica

Emperor penguins breed in the winter. The female lays a single egg and leaves it with the male. The male rests the egg on his feet, under his belly, and incubates it for about 2½ months.

Birds of prey

These spectacular birds are some of the most efficient predators of the animal world. Most have large eyes, excellent hearing, and a keen sense of smell, which they use to good effect when hunting. The smallest species hunt insects, but large raptors, such as eagles, can kill a young deer.

MASTER FISHER
The osprey is a skilled hunter, perfectly adapted for catching fish.

1. EYE IN THE SKY *The osprey patrols a stretch of water in search of fish, hovering and gliding 70 m (230 ft) or more above the surface.*

2. GOTCHA! *The osprey spots a fish near the surface and plunges down into the water, grabbing both sides of its prey with long, curved talons.*

3. DINNER TIME *The osprey returns to the nest to feed its young. The male is the main provider of food for the female and her chicks.*

Osprey
Pandion haliaetus

- **Height** 50–60 cm (19$\frac{7}{10}$–23$\frac{6}{10}$ in)
- **Weight** 1.5 kg (3¾ lb)
- **Diet** Fish
- **Location** Worldwide (except Antarctica)

This spectacular bird of prey lives near freshwater rivers and lakes and coastal waters, where it has a plentiful supply of its favourite food: fish.

Peregrine falcon
Falco peregrinus

- **Length** 34–50 cm (13–20 in)
- **Weight** 0.5–1.5 kg (1–3¼ lb)
- **Diet** Small birds
- **Location** Worldwide (except Antarctica)

The fastest bird of prey hunts at high speed, reaching a dizzying 360 km/h (220 mph) in a "stoop" (dive).

Griffon vulture
Gyps fulvus

- **Length** 94–109 cm (37–43 in)
- **Weight** 6–10 kg (13¼–22 lb)
- **Diet** Carrion
- **Location** North Africa, southern Europe, and Asia

The Griffon vulture does not kill. It is a scavenger, feeding on carrion (dead animals) – often the leftovers of predatory animals.

Bald eagle
Haliaeetus leucocephalus

- **Length** 71–96 cm (28–38 in)
- **Weight** 3–6.5 kg (6½–14 lb)
- **Diet** Fish, small mammals, birds, and carrion
- **Location** North America

Bald eagles are expert fishers, swooping down to grab fish from the water. They may also steal the catch of another eagle.

Fish

Fish are the biggest and oldest group of vertebrates. They were the first animals to have backbones, evolving 500 million years ago. There are around 25,000 species of fish, all of which are cold-blooded and have bodies that are adapted to living in water.

Also called the tail fin, the **caudal fin** acts as a paddle, providing "thrust" to propel the fish forward.

Dorsal fins give the fish stability, helping it to make sudden changes in direction and stopping it rolling from side to side. This fish has two dorsal fins, but other fish might have three separate dorsal fins or just one.

The gas-filled **swim bladder** helps the fish control its buoyancy. By inflating or deflating its swim bladder, a fish can rise up or sink in the water.

The **trunk**, or back end, of the fish is packed with swimming muscles. It's these muscle blocks that make many fish good to eat.

The **skeleton** of a bony fish comprises a backbone made up of vertebrae, fine rays to support the fins, and a skull.

Horny **scales** grow from the skin, providing a flexible protective covering.

The **anal fin** provides stability as the fish swims.

The **gills** contain a great many blood vessels. Oxygen and other gases are exchanged here.

There are two sets of paired fins. The **pelvic fins** (shown) help "steer" the fish up and down in the water, while the pectoral fins (not shown) may be used for steering and propulsion or even for "walking" along the sea bed.

REPRODUCTION

◄ MALE MUM *Seahorses are unusual in that the female lays her eggs in the male's pouch and he carries the young until they hatch.*

While some fish mate and give birth to live young, most reproduce by releasing eggs into the water. This is called spawning. Often fish will gather at special spawning sites where their young will have the best chance of survival.

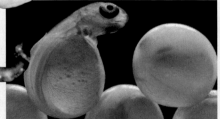

▲ LARVAE *Some species hatch as small, fully formed fish, but others hatch as larvae and will change as they grow.*

▲ SPAWNING *Many species release vast amounts of eggs at a time, to increase the chances of some surviving.*

TAKE A LOOK: GILLS

Fish obtain oxygen using their gills. Water is taken in through the mouth, flows over the gills, and out under the gill covers on the sides of the head. Most cartilaginous fish do not have gill covers.

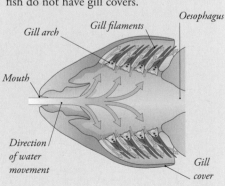

Gill arch

Gill filaments

Oesophagus

Mouth

Direction of water movement

Gill cover

Blue spotted stingray
Taeniura lymma

- **Length** 70 cm (27 in); up to 2 m (6 ½ ft) incl. tail
- **Weight** Up to 30 kg (65 lb)
- **Depth** Shallow water to 20 m (65 ft)
- **Location** Indian Ocean, western Pacific, Red Sea

This relatively common fish lives around tropical coasts and reefs, where it feeds on molluscs and crustaceans hidden on the sandy sea floor. Like most rays, it "flies" through the water using wave-like movements of its large pectoral fins, which give the body its disc shape. The long tail bears a sting, used in self-defence.

Common fangtooth
Anoplogaster cornuta

- **Length** 15–18 cm (6–7 in)
- **Weight** Unknown
- **Depth** 500–5,000 m (1,600–16,000 ft)
- **Location** Oceans worldwide

Also known as the ogrefish, this ugly-looking fish usually lives at great depths. It detects prey, mainly other fish, using its lateral line organs – lines of pressure-sensitive cells on the sides of its body that pick up vibrations in the water.

Giant sea bass
Stereolepis gigas

- **Length** 2.5 m (8¼ ft)
- **Weight** 400 kg (882 lb)
- **Depth** 5–45 m (15–150 ft)
- **Location** Eastern Pacific, from California to Mexico, and Japan

These huge fish lurk close to kelp-fringed drop offs on the rocky coasts of California, Mexico, and Japan. An individual may live to the great age of 100 years, but the species breed so slowly that losses due to over-fishing take decades to make up.

Clown anemonefish
Amphiprion ocellaris

- **Length** 8–11 cm (3–4 in)
- **Depth** Up to 15 m (50 ft)
- **Location** Seas around southeast Asia and northern Australia

These brightly coloured little fish live in the shallow sheltered lagoons created by coral reefs. They gain protection from predators by hiding among the tentacles of anemones, which other fish avoid because of their deadly stings. No one knows for sure how anemonefish avoid being stung. Anemonefish begin life as males and change into females once they have reached a certain size.

Puffer fish
Diodon sp.

- **Length** 90 cm (36 in)
- **Weight** Exact weight unknown
- **Depth** 2–50 m (6–160 ft)
- **Location** Tropical and subtropical Atlantic, Pacific, and Indian Oceans

Inflated

Deflated

When threatened, the puffer fish inflates its body into a spiky ball, making it impossible for all but the largest predators to swallow. But even large predators may avoid eating puffer fish: they not only taste awful, but some are also poisonous.

Banded moray eel
Gymnothorax rueppellii

- **Length** 80 cm (31½ in)
- **Weight** Exact weight unknown
- **Depth** 1–40 m (3–130 ft)
- **Location** Tropical Indian and Pacific Oceans

Like other morays, this species is an aggressive ambush hunter. By day it hides in dark crevices on shallow reefs and at night lurks in the entrance to its lair, waiting to strike at passing fish or shrimp.

African lungfish
Protopterus annectens

- **Length** Up to 2 m (6½ ft)
- **Weight** Up to 17 kg (37½ lb)
- **Location** West and Central Africa

Lungfish live in the swamps and backwaters of sluggish rivers, which often dry up completely in the dry season. When this happens, the fish survives up to a year in a cocoon of mud, breathing air with primitive lungs and waiting to emerge with the next rains.

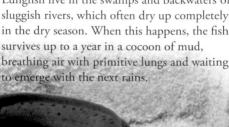

Red-bellied piranha
Pygocentrus nattereri

- **Length** 33 cm (13 in)
- **Weight** 1 kg (2 lb)
- **Location** South America

Famed for their powerful bite and wickedly sharp teeth, these ferocious freshwater fish live in large schools. Their usual prey includes other fish and aquatic invertebrates, though they will attack other animals. Their sensitive hearing and lateral line organ allow them to home in on disturbances caused by struggling prey. Piranhas in turn are hunted and eaten by people.

Great white shark
Carcharodon carcharias

- **Length** Up to 7 m (23 ft)
- **Weight** Can reach over 3,000 kg (6,600 lb)
- **Depth** 0–1,300 m (0–4,300 ft)
- **Location** Oceans worldwide

Probably the most feared fish in the seas, the great white is a predator of large fish, squid, and seals. Great white sharks are protected as they were over-fished in the past.

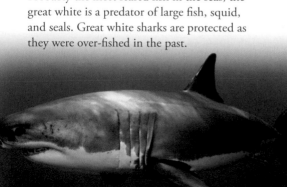

Invertebrates

There are thought to be 5 million species of invertebrates roaming the planet – that's 95 per cent of all animal life on Earth. They are the world's most successful animals, and can be found on land, in the sea, in the air, and even inside your body!

There is a huge variety of invertebrates.
The differences lie not just in the way they look, but also in their behaviour and even the way they move.

TAKE A LOOK: INVERTEBRATES

As well as no backbone, invertebrates also have no true jaws.

Earthworm

Garden snail

Tenebrionid beetle

WHAT IS AN INVERTEBRATE?
Animals without a backbone are called invertebrates. They have no internal skeleton; instead, some have an exoskeleton (a hard outer cover, like a crab or a beetle), some live inside a shell (such as snails and clams), and some are divided into soft segments (such as worms).

▲ SPONGES are invertebrates of the simplest kind: they haven't even got a head or a brain…

… Yet octopuses are very intelligent. A female in captivity learned to open jars by copying her keeper.

▲ ANTS are social animals that work together for survival…

… But tarantulas live and hunt alone.

▲ CORAL looks like a plant and barely moves, rooted to the seabed…

… But monarch butterflies can fly 4,000 km (2,500 miles) on migration every year.

New clothes please!
Exoskeletons don't grow even when the body inside them does. So as an invertebrate gets bigger, it needs to shed its shell and make a new one.

Crab with pincers raised

INVERTEBRATE GROUPS

In a classification tree of the animal kingdom (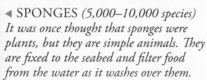 p84–85), there is no group called invertebrates. There is one called vertebrates (it is part of the chordates phylum, and is split into mammals, birds, etc.) – but there are more than 30 different main groups of invertebrates, including:

◄ MOLLUSCS – *squid, snails, bivalves (50,000 species)* Squid, slugs, and oysters are all molluscs. Most molluscs have a shell, and a radula – a ribbon-like "tongue" covered in scaly denticles.

◄ ECHINODERMS – *starfish, sea urchins, sea cucumbers (7,000 species)* Nearly all echinoderms live on the sea floor. They have spiny bodies, which are usually divided into five equal parts.

◄ ANNELIDS – *earthworms, leeches, polychaetes (12,000 species)* Annelid worms have bodies that are divided into segments.

◄ CNIDARIANS – *jellyfish, corals, hydras (8,000–9,000 species)* All cnidarians have basic bodies with stinging tentacles, a very simple nervous system, and just one opening: the mouth.

◄ ARTHROPODS – *insects, arachnids, crustaceans (1,000,000 species)* Arthropods, such as this beetle, have an exoskeleton – a hard outer cover. Their exoskeleton and body are divided into parts.

◄ SPONGES *(5,000–10,000 species)* It was once thought that sponges were plants, but they are simple animals. They are fixed to the seabed and filter food from the water as it washes over them.

Making sense
Simple invertebrates, such as sea anemones, have simple senses: they can detect food and reach towards it, and they can sense danger and shrink from it. More advanced invertebrates have superior senses. Flies see lots of images through compound eyes, so they can notice the slightest movement; and grasshoppers have eardrums in their abdomen.

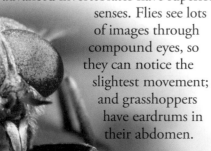

▼ BUTTERFLIES *can taste with their feet. Chemical sensors on the insect's feet "taste" what it lands on, so it knows if it's standing on something it can drink, such as nectar.*

WITHOUT INVERTEBRATES, the planet would not survive. Krill (a type of crustacean) form the basis of the food chain in polar seas. Insects such as ants and beetles, and their larvae, help clean up the planet. Other insects, such as bees, are essential for pollination (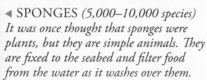 p90-91).

▲ KRILL
Without krill, entire species of fish would disappear. These tiny creatures form the main part of many marine animals' diets, including the whale shark, the world's biggest fish.

▶ ANTS
Decomposers such as ants break up dead animals and plants. The bits that aren't eaten are more easily absorbed into the ground, releasing nutrients for plants.

▼ DUNG BEETLE
Without dung beetles rolling away animal poo, all sorts of places from African savannas to Australian farmland would be knee-deep in dung. Less dung means fewer places for flies to breed, so there are fewer fly-borne diseases.

Amazing arthropods

With more than a million species, arthropods make up the largest phylum (main group) in the animal kingdom. They were the first creatures to walk on land, more than 400 million years ago.

WOW!

There are as many arthropods on Earth as all other animals put together.

INSECTS

Insects have three pairs of legs, and a body made up of three parts: a head, a thorax, and an abdomen. This is the biggest group of arthropods; in fact, 90% of *all* animal species are insects. Bugs, butterflies, bees, and beetles are all insects.

▶ WING PATTERNS *help some species to hide and evade predators.*

ARACHNIDS

Arachnid bodies are made up of two parts. They have four pairs of legs, and two pairs of mouthparts: one set look like legs or claws for grabbing prey, while the other set form pincers or fangs for stabbing and killing. They have no antennae. Spiders, scorpions, ticks, and mites are all arachnids.

▲ THE IMPERIAL SCORPION *uses its sting in defence, and its claws to catch prey.*

CENTIPEDES AND MILLIPEDES

These arthropods have a long body divided into many segments. Centipedes have one pair of legs per segment and millipedes have two pairs per segment. *Centipede* means "100 feet" and *millipede* means "1,000 feet", but different species can have between a dozen and 750 legs.

◀ THE GIANT DESERT *centipede has a painful, venomous bite.*

CRUSTACEANS

Most crustaceans live in water – including crabs, lobsters, shrimps, and barnacles – although woodlice live on land. The species can look very different: a blue lobster grows to 1 m (3 ft) long, but acorn barnacles are a tiny 15 mm (½ in) across.

▶ LIVE LOBSTERS *range in colour, but most are bluish-brown. They turn orangey red when they are cooked.*

HORSESHOE CRABS

While they look like crustaceans, horseshoe crabs are actually related to arachnids: they have four pairs of legs, two pairs of mouthparts, and no antennae. These animals have scarcely changed in the 300 million years they have existed.

▲ HORSESHOE CRABS *are close relatives to extinct trilobites.*

SEA SPIDERS

Sea spiders are not spiders at all, although they do have long, spider-like legs. Most have four pairs of legs, but some have five or six pairs. They have two pairs of eyes.

▶ SEA SPIDERS *live deep below the waves.*

SPIDER ATTACK

There are more than 40,000 species of spider, and all of them are venomous. Most are harmless to people – their venom is deadly only to their prey.

BEWARE OF THE SPIDER

Trapped! Many spiders do not hunt, but wait for prey to come to them. Using sticky silk spun from a gland in its abdomen, the orb weaver spider creates a web to trap passing insects. The victim is then killed with a deadly bite.

Do not disturb Spiders don't usually attack people, but some are dangerous if they are disturbed and bite in self-defence. Mediterranean black widow spiders have enough venom to kill a human. Females usually have the deadliest bite.

Red-kneed tarantula
Euathlus smithi

30

- **Length** 10 cm (4 in)
- **Legspan** 18 cm (7 in)
- **Prey** Insects, small mammals, and lizards
- **Location** western central Mexico

The red-kneed tarantula hunts at night. It can sense smells, tastes, and vibrations through the ends of its legs. Females live to 30 years, whereas males live 3–6 years.

▲ FATAL FANGS *Tarantulas bite into their prey with hollow fangs, injecting potent venom to paralyse their victim.*

Four-spot orb weaver
Araneus quadratus

- **Length** 8–17 mm (¼–¾ in)
- **Legspan** Up to 7 cm (2¾ in)
- **Prey** Small flying insects
- **Location** Europe and Asia

Orb weavers spin webs in grasses or scrub. Females can change colour over several days to camouflage themselves.

Peacock parachute spider
Poecilotheria metallica

- **Length** 6 cm (2½ in)
- **Legspan** 18 cm (7 in)
- **Prey** Insects, baby birds, lizards
- **Location** Southern India

This spider is also known as the Gooty sapphire because of its blue colouring. While females live to 12 years, males live only 3–4 years. It is very rare, and faces extinction because of habitat loss.

Fen raft spider
Dolomedes plantarius

- **Length** Females 17–22 mm (⁶⁄₁₀–⁹⁄₁₀ in) Males 13–18 mm (½–⁷⁄₁₀ in)
- **Legspan** Up to 9 cm (3½ in)
- **Location** Europe

This spider uses its feet to sense the movement of prey in pools of water – then it runs across the water to catch it.

Incredible insects

Insects are the most successful animals on Earth. There are more than one million known species, but scientists think there may be millions more still to be discovered. Many other life forms rely on insects: most plants use them as pollinators, and lots of animals are insect-eaters.

An insect's body is made up of three parts: the head, thorax, and abdomen. These parts are linked by the exoskeleton, the circulatory system, soft tissue, and nerves, which control the insect's body functions.

The **thorax** is packed with muscle to power the legs and wings.

Head

Thorax

The **head** contains sense organs such as eyes and antennae.

The **abdomen** contains most of the digestive system and the reproductive system.

Abdomen

Insects have one pair of **antennae**, or feelers, which they use to explore their environment. Insects use their feelers in many different ways: to touch, smell, taste, and even hear (by picking up vibrations in the air).

Most insects have two pairs of **wings**. In this wasp the front and hind wings are linked. In beetles and many bugs the front wings form hard cases called elytra, which protect the softer hindwings below.

Adult insects respire (breathe) by taking in air through **spiracles** — openings along the thorax and abdomen.

TAKE A LOOK: INSECT MOUTHS

Different types of insects eat very different foods, and so the mouthparts of each species are suited to different styles of feeding. Some insects have jaws shaped into pincers to kill their prey, or tiny clippers for cutting plant leaves. In many other insects the jaws are replaced by other specialized mouthparts.

Labium

Sponge-like labellum

▲ SPONGER *Flies soak up liquid foods through a spongy tube.*

Proboscis

▲ SUCKER *Butterflies uncurl their long, thin proboscis to use as a straw for sucking up nectar.*

Piercing stylet

▲ STABBER *Mosquitoes have needle-sharp stabbing mouthparts for piercing skin and sucking up blood.*

Ladybird Lifecycle

1. EGG LAYING *Insects reproduce by laying eggs. After mating, a female ladybird lays her eggs on a leaf. About a week later, the larvae emerge.*

2. HATCHING *The larvae look nothing like their parents! They have a soft body covering, called a cuticle, which soon hardens and turns dark.*

3. GROWING *The larva must eat lots of food to grow. Over about four weeks it will kill and eat hundreds of sap-sucking aphids.*

4. PUPATING *When the larva is ready to pupate, it fixes itself to the underside of a leaf and sheds its skin, revealing a soft cuticle underneath. This "pupal cuticle" takes about a week to turn hard and dark. The larva does not move during this time.*

5. EMERGENCE *A week later, the pupal cuticle splits open and a new adult ladybird crawls out. To begin with, its body and wing cases are soft and lack the typical bright colour and spots.*

6. ADULT *The new adult's wing cases expand and harden into a protective shield. The colour darkens and the distinctive ladybird spots appear. The cycle can now begin again.*

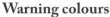

Warning colours

Many insects protect themselves from predators by storing toxins in their body. They then warn predators by displaying bright colours, usually red, orange, or yellow. Monarch and viceroy butterflies, which look similar, both benefit from a colour and pattern that say "I taste *really* bad!"

Monarch *Danaus plexippus*

Viceroy *Limenitis archippus*

Rustic sphinx moth *Manduca rustica*

Insect camouflage

Another great way of avoiding being eaten is to make yourself invisible. Many insects are masters of disguise, able to hide in full view of predators by blending in perfectly with their background. Can you spot this moth?

IS IT A BEE OR WASP?

There are many differences between these similar-looking insects.

- There are about 20,000 bee species.
- Social bees live in colonies in nests made of beeswax.
- Bees feed on nectar and pollen from plants.
- Bees have hairier bodies than wasps.
- A bee can sting only once – the sting is ripped out of the bee's abdomen and left behind in the victim. The bee will die soon after.

- There are around 75,000 species of wasp.
- Social wasps live in nests made out of paper, which they make by chewing wood.
- Wasps eat other insects.
- Wasps are more brightly coloured than bees.
- A wasp's sting can be used many times. Like bees, only females have a stinger. It is adapted from her ovipositor – the tube through which she lays her eggs.

Bees feed on nectar...

... but wasps eat other insects.

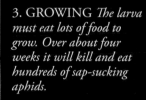

Bugs *and* Beetles

The word "bug" is often used to mean any creepy-crawly, but it is actually an order of a particular kind of insect. This order is called Hemiptera, and it has 82,000 species. Beetles are not the same as bugs: they have their own order, Coleoptera. There are 370,000 beetle species – that's one-third of all known insect species.

Lantern bug
Phrictus quinquepartitus

BUGS

Cotton stainer bug
Dysdercus decussatus

Cicada
Angamiana aetherea

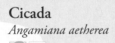

WOW!

All the insects you see here are life-size. The giant water bug is the world's longest bug, but it's dwarfed by the Hercules beetle.

Assassin bug
Eulyes illustris

Water scorpion
Nepa sp.

Squash bug
Coreus marginatus

Giant water bug
Lethocerus grandis

Bed bug (magnified x 2)
Cimex lectularius

Leaf hopper
Cicadella viridis

HOW CAN YOU TELL IF IT'S A BUG?

Bugs have two pairs of wings and a beak-like mouth for piercing and sucking up food.

◀ *A stink bug preys on a caterpillar.*

Lacewing nymph

Adult lacewing

Bugs have incomplete metamorphosis: they start life as nymphs that look similar to the adult form, but without wings or reproductive organs.

BEETLES

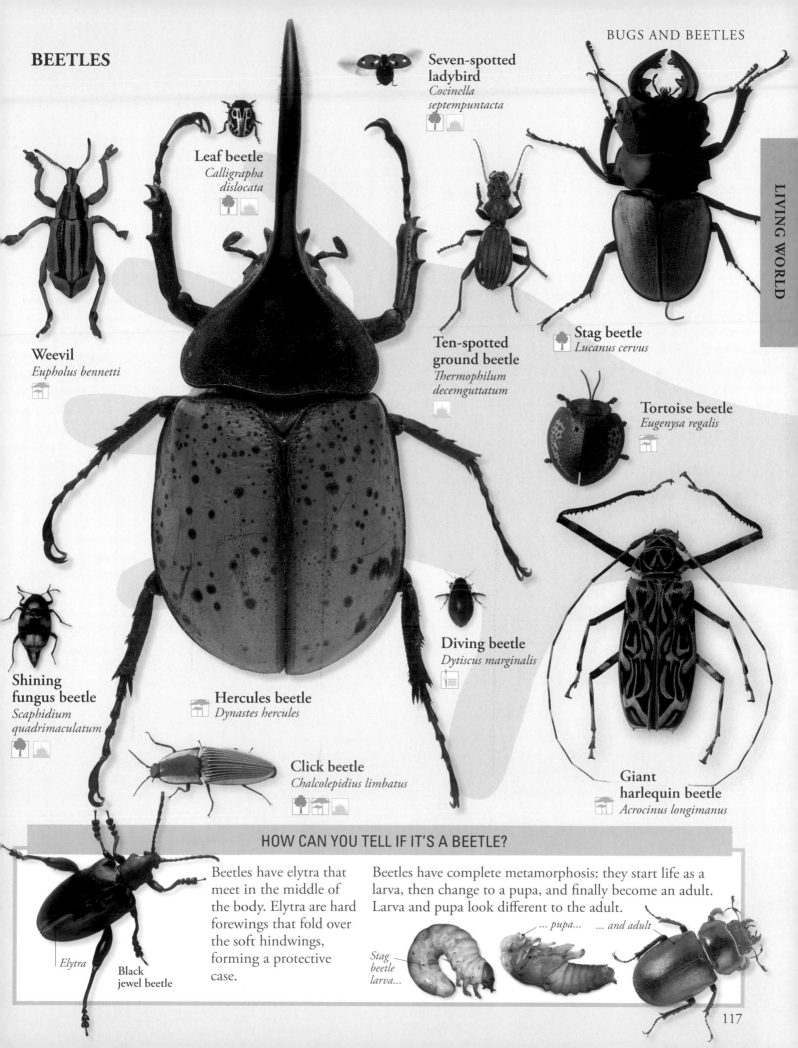

Leaf beetle
Calligrapha dislocata

Seven-spotted ladybird
Cocinella septempuntacta

Weevil
Eupholus bennetti

Ten-spotted ground beetle
Thermophilum decemguttatum

Stag beetle
Lucanus cervus

Tortoise beetle
Eugenysa regalis

Shining fungus beetle
Scaphidium quadrimaculatum

Hercules beetle
Dynastes hercules

Diving beetle
Dytiscus marginalis

Click beetle
Chalcolepidius limbatus

Giant harlequin beetle
Acrocinus longimanus

HOW CAN YOU TELL IF IT'S A BEETLE?

Beetles have elytra that meet in the middle of the body. Elytra are hard forewings that fold over the soft hindwings, forming a protective case.

Beetles have complete metamorphosis: they start life as a larva, then change to a pupa, and finally become an adult. Larva and pupa look different to the adult.

Elytra

Black jewel beetle

Stag beetle larva...

... pupa...

... and adult

117

Marine invertebrates

Huge numbers of invertebrates live in the sea. Some, such as corals and sponges, live fixed to the spot, but others, including jellyfish and squid, drift in mid-water. Starfish and crabs creep and scuttle on the seabed everywhere from sunlit shallows to pitch black depths.

OCTOPUS ANATOMY

Octopuses belong to a group of molluscs called cephalopods, thought to be the smartest of all invertebrates. Some cephalopods have an external shell, but in others the shell is internal. Most of an octopus's organs are inside its head, including its digestive system and gills.

Day octopus
Octopus cyanea

- **Size** Body: 16 cm (6¼ in); arms 80 cm (32 in)
- **Location** Indo-pacific region

Unlike most other octopuses this animal hunts by day, using changing body patterns to disguise itself. Its preferred foods include clams, shrimps, crabs, and fish.

The octopus's eight arms bear rows of suckers that grip onto rocks – and also onto prey.

▶ OCTOPUSES *generally crawl on the seabed, but also use arm movements and a form of jet propulsion to swim in open water.*

TAKE A LOOK: COLOURFUL CHARACTERS

Octopuses can change colour rapidly, adopting different patterns to communicate emotions and to camouflage themselves on the sea floor to avoid predators. If the camouflage doesn't work, they squirt out a jet of ink. Hidden in the cloud, they can escape from danger.

▲ ESCAPE *An octopus releases ink over a potential threat.*

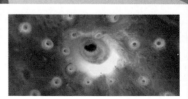

▲ MOUTH *The octopus's mouth is a stretchy circular opening. Inside is a sharp beak made of horn, used for tearing up prey.*

Red general starfish
Protoreaster linckii

- **Diameter** Up to 30 cm (12 in)
- **Location** Indian Ocean

Like most starfish, the red general is a slow-moving predator. It creeps over reefs and rocks on hundreds of tiny, suckered, tube feet, hunting small clams, tubeworms, sponges, and other fixed invertebrates. It feeds by covering the prey with its body and pushing its stomach out through its mouth (in the middle of the star).

Horned ghost crab
Ocypode ceratophthalmus

- **Width** 6–8 cm (2½-3 in)
- **Location** Indian and Pacific Oceans

Ghost crabs live on sandy beaches, where they feed on organic matter washed up by the tide. They scuttle and burrow at such speed that they sometimes seem to disappear.

Yellow tube sponge
Aplysina fistularis

- **Height** Up to 61 cm (24 in)
- **Location** Tropical seas

Sponges are among the simplest of animals. Yellow tube sponges have a chimney-shaped body supported by a flexible skeleton made of protein. Some other species may have more rigid skeletal parts. Water is drawn in through pores in the tube.

Sea slug
Chromodoris kuniei

- **Length** 5 cm (2 in)
- **Location** Western Pacific Ocean

Sea slugs, also known as nudibranchs, are shell-less relatives of snails. They are carnivorous, and hunt by gliding through coral reefs in search of prey that cannot escape, such as sponges, barnacles, and corals.

European lobster
Homarus gammarus

- **Length** 60–100 cm (24–40 in)
- **Location** European coasts

This powerful cousin of shrimps and crabs lurks in rocky lairs by day, emerging at night to hunt smaller invertebrates and fish using its sensitive antennae and large claws. Like other crustaceans, lobsters must shed their rigid body armour in order to grow.

Elkhorn coral
Acropora palmata

- **Size** Up to 3 m (10 ft) across
- **Location** Caribbean Sea

This brittle structure is not a single animal, but a colony of thousands, all growing on a stony base which they build themselves. Each tiny coral animal, or polyp, has a simple bag shape, with a mouth at the top surrounded by tiny tentacles.

Dahlia anemone
Urticina felina

- **Width** 25–35 cm (10–14 in)
- **Location** Northern hemisphere coastal waters

The dahlia anemone's colourful, flower-like body grows attached to a rock or other hard surface. The tentacles bear tiny stinging cells that paralyse small animals. Food caught this way is passed to the mouth.

Lion's mane jellyfish
Cyanea capillata

- **Width** Up to 2 m (6½ ft)
- **Location** Cool northern seas

Named for the mass of brown frills on its central arms, the lion's mane jelly is common in northern seas and is often washed ashore in storms. Jellyfish lack any kind of brain, but their simple design has been successful for 500 million years.

What are you doing here?

Birds that can't fly and reptiles that appear to; snakes that live in the sea and fish out of water... Sometimes animals just don't seem to behave how you might expect them to!

AIR

Only birds, bats and insects are capable of true flight, but several other kinds of animal have developed the ability to control long glides through the air.

▼ FLYING GECKO
Flaps of skin, webbed feet, and a flat tail help the gecko control glides from tree to tree.

▲ GOLDEN TREESNAKE
By spreading its ribcage this amazing snake turns its whole body into a ribbon-like glider.

LAND

Sometimes life on land is the best option even for animals you would normally expect to see in the air or under water.

◄ EMU
The Australian emu has huge, powerful legs, but no wings.

SURFACE OF WATER

The surface of water is an important barrier for most animals, but some species use it to their advantage to escape predators or to surprise unwary prey.

▲ FLYING FISH
Flying fish skim over the waves at up to 60 km/h (37 mph), but predators cannot follow.

◄ BASILISK LIZARD
Big feet and an amazing turn of speed allow this reptile to sprint over still water.

UNDERWATER

Many air-breathing animals visit the underwater realm, which is a great place to find food. Some, such as penguins, must return to land to breed, but others manage this in water too.

▼ PENGUINS
Penguins gave up flight but have perfected the art of swimming underwater.

TAKE A LOOK: FROM SEA TO TREE

The coconut crab is the largest arthropod on land. It it a confident but careful climber and can shin up palm trees to collect fresh coconuts. It will crack these open with its huge claws to get to the flesh inside.

Coconut crab *Birgus latro*

A DIFFERENT APPROACH

We're used to seeing certain animals in particular places, but in the struggle for life, many animals find that they can gain an advantage by exploiting a completely different environment. They may have developed their extraordinary behaviour as a way of finding food, of escaping predators, or simply to stay alive.

◄ FLYING SQUIRREL
A flap of skin along the squirrel's flanks acts as a controllable parachute.

◄ FLYING FROG
Long, strong toes support webs of skin on the flying frog's umbrella-like feet.

◄ CASSOWARY
The forest-dwelling cassowary uses its big feet for running and fighting.

◄ MUDSKIPPER
The mudskipper crosses mud flats using its fins to drag its body over the sand.

UNDERGROUND

Many animals spend at least part of their lives underground, where there are few predators. Some animals survive unfavourable conditions such as droughts by hibernating underground.

◄ PERIODICAL CICADA
Periodical cicada larvae spend their early lives underground before emerging all together after 13 or 17 years.

► AFRICAN LUNGFISH
When tropical rivers dry up, these amazing fish burrow and survive by breathing air in small damp chambers in the hard baked mud.

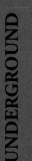

◄ WATER SPIDER
Hairs on the water spider's body trap air, which the spider breathes while under water. It's just like diving with an air tank.

► MANATEE
These gentle vegetarians live and breed in shallow tropical seas.

◄ SEA SNAKE
Sea snakes spend their whole life in water, and are often seen hundreds of miles from land.

Microlife

Some living things, such as elephants and oak trees, are difficult to miss if you're standing next to one, but others are much harder to see. There are thousands of species of microscopic organisms living in the air, on land, and in water all around you, and on your body too!

WHAT'S IN THE WATER?

As well as fish and other marine creatures, our oceans, rivers, and lakes are teeming with plankton – microscopic life that drifts with the current. Plankton includes tiny animals (zooplankton) and plant-like life forms (phytoplankton). Many creatures eat plankton, and in this way whole aquatic ecosystems depend on it.

◄ KRILL *are tiny crustaceans that eat plankton. Large marine animals, including whales, feed on the krill, making them a vital link in the food chain.*

◄ ALGAE *Most phytoplankton is made up of algae. Many algae are made up of just one cell, like these diatoms.*

TAKE A LOOK: ALGAE

Single-celled algae belong to a group of organisms known as protists. Like plants, these algae make food from sunlight, using a process called photosynthesis (👁 p87).

◄ BLOOMING
Algal blooms are a sign of nature out of balance. The bloom blocks sunlight, uses up nutrients, and starves or poisons other plants and animals.

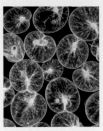

◄ GLOWING
Several algae are bioluminescent: they give out light when they are disturbed. This alga, Noctiluca, can make the sea glow an eerie green.

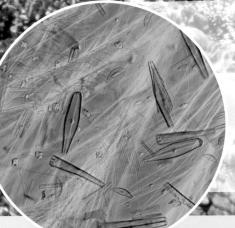

BRILLIANT BACTERIA

Bacteria are an essential part of life on Earth. Some types live in soil and release nitrates, without which plants would not grow and the food chain would collapse. Other types live in your gut, helping you digest your food. But bacteria can also be harmful, causing dangerous diseases in all kinds of plants and animals, including people.

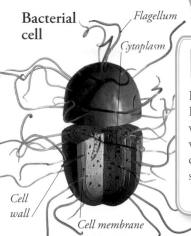

Bacterial cell

Flagellum

Cytoplasm

Penicillin colony

Cell wall

Cell membrane

TELL ME MORE...

In 1862, French scientist Louis Pasteur created a way of killing bacteria with heat. This process, called pasteurization, is still used today.

▲ POWERFUL PENICILLIN
If you have an illness, your doctor might give you penicillin. This is an antibiotic – a medicine that kills bacteria. In 1928, scientist Alexander Fleming found a dish of bacteria with a type of mould growing on it. Where the mould grew, the bacteria had died. From this discovery, Fleming developed penicillin.

MINI MONSTERS

Ticks and mites belong to the same class of invertebrate as spiders, the arachnids. They are parasites, living and feeding on plants or other animals, known as hosts. Some species destroy crops, while others pass on diseases.

WOW!

There are around 30,000 species of ticks and mites, most of which are less than 1mm ($\frac{1}{32}$ in) long. They can be found in stored food such as flour and cheese; in animal dung; and skin, hair, and fur. They feed on plants, and on the skin and blood of host animals.

▼ CRAB LARVA *Many animals start life as microscopic larvae. Crab larvae find a place to settle as a tiny crab where they can then grow to be an adult.*

▶ MEAL MITE
Many of the foods you eat probably contain the remains of mites like this one, which feeds on stored cereal products such as flour and oatmeal.

◀ GROWING
Noctiluca *algae are also responsible for "red tides". These are usually caused, for example, by sewage or fertilizer. Algae growing in this way can kill other life forms.*

Eyelash mites
You won't be able to see them or feel them, but living on your face are tiny, 0.2 mm- ($\frac{7}{1000}$ in-) long mites called *Demodex folliculorum*. The mites cling to eyelashes, to feed on dead skin cells at the eyelash roots – but don't worry, they are harmless.

▼ A DUST MITE
can fit on the tip of a needle. This tiny creature eats fragments of dead skin and hair found in house dust.

Animals of the past

The most famous prehistoric animals have got to be the dinosaurs – but they lived many hundreds of thousands of years after the first life forms appeared on Earth. It is thought that life first appeared on Earth around 3.8 billion years ago. They were small, single-celled organisms called prokaryotes. Some prokaryotes survive today in the form of cyanobacteria.

WHAT WAS A DINOSAUR?
The word "dinosaur" means "terrible lizard". These reptiles ruled the Earth for more than 160 million years until around 65 million years ago. But not all dinosaurs were terrible: many were herbivorous, not carnivorous, and while many were huge and ferocious, there were also some that were no bigger than a chicken.

▶ DINKY DINOSAUR
The plant-eating Lesothosaurus *is thought to be the smallest dinosaur.*

WOW!
In Precambrian times, prokaryotes grew in colonies that spread out like mats, absorbing sunlight so they could photosynthesize. Billions of years later, their fossilized remains still exist. These stony platforms are called stromatolites, and some can be found off the coast of northwest Australia.

TIMELINE OF PREHISTORIC LIFE
History is divided into different periods of time.   MYA = million years ago.

PRECAMBRIAN 4,600–545 MYA	**CAMBRIAN** 545–490 MYA	**ORDOVICIAN** 490–445 MYA	**SILURIAN** 445–415 MYA	**DEVONIAN** 415–355 MYA	**CARBONIFEROUS** 355–290 MYA
The first forms of life appeared on Earth: simple, single-celled prokaryotes.	The first multi-celled and hard-bodied life developed, including molluscs and arthropods such as trilobites.	The first crustaceans and jawless fish evolve.	Evolution of the first fish with jaws, and giant sea scorpions – the ancestors of modern arachnids.	The "Age of Fishes", when fish diversified rapidly. The first amphibians evolved from fish, becoming the first vertebrates to live on land.	Flying insects and amphibians lived in swampy forests during this warm period, but reptiles ruled the land.

HIP, HIP

There were two types of dinosaurs, classified by the shape of their hip bones: bird-hipped (ornithischians), and lizard-hipped (saurischians). Birds actually evolved from the lizard-hipped dinosaurs (👁 p244).

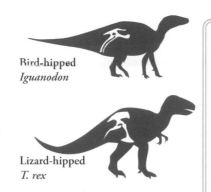

Bird-hipped
Iguanodon

Lizard-hipped
T. rex

(see p244)

FAST FACTS

- Scientists that study the history of life on Earth are called palaeontologists.
- The term "dinosaur" only refers to a certain type of land-based reptile. Those that flew or lived in the sea are not dinosaurs, but different reptiles.
- There are about 700 named dinosaur species.
- The first dinosaur fossils were *Iguanodon* teeth and bones, found in England in the 1820s.
- The first complete dinosaur skeletons were of 32 *Iguanodons*, found in a coal mine in Belgium in 1878.
- The first dinosaur to be named was the *Megalosaurus*, in 1824.
- The oldest dinosaur fossils discovered to date are 230 million years old.

What is a fossil?

Palaeontologists use fossils to work out what early life forms would have looked like. Most fossils form when the remains of an animal or plant get buried in sediment (sand or mud). Over time, the remains are replaced by minerals in the sediment, which keep the shape of the animal or plant.

Fossil of a *Pterodactylus*

Tyrannosaurus rex
"King of the tyrant lizards"

- **Length** 12 m (39 ft)
- **Time** Late Cretaceous
- **Fossil location** North America

Like all life forms, dinosaur species have scientific names, which are written in Latin. The name may reflect what the species looks like, or one of its characteristics – as with *T. rex*, one of the largest and fiercest meat-eating dinosaurs.

Dimorphodon
"Two-form tooth"

- **Wingspan** 1.2–2.5 m (4–8 ft)
- **Time** Early Jurassic
- **Fossil location** Europe and North America

Dimorphodon was not a dinosaur, but a pterosaur – a flying reptile. It had an enormous skull and differently sized teeth in its bill – large, pointy teeth at the front, and small teeth at the back. It ate fish, insects, and small animals, but no one knows if it caught its prey while flying or standing on all fours.

Dimetrodon
"Two types of teeth"

- **Length** up to 3.5 m (11.5 ft)
- **Time** Early Permian
- **Fossil location** Europe and North America

Dimetrodon was a sail-backed synapsid. The sail probably helped it warm up and cool down. Synapsids were cold-blooded and scaly like reptiles, but they are actually the ancestors of mammals.

PERMIAN 290–250 MYA	TRIASSIC 250–200 MYA	JURASSIC 200–140 MYA	CRETACEOUS 140–65 MYA	TERTIARY 65–1.6 MYA	QUATERNARY 1.6 MYA to present
Sail-back synapsids appeared.	The first dinosaurs, early mammals, turtles, and frogs appeared.	The first bird, *Archaeopteryx*, evolved from the dinosaurs.	Dinosaurs die out. The first modern mammals take over.	The first appearance of many of today's creatures, from dogs and cats to apes and elephants.	The first modern human.

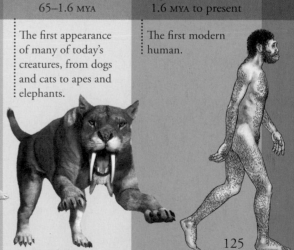

CONTINENTS of the WORLD

- People naturally inhabit all continents except one: Antarctica.

- The Arctic is not a continent because it is not solid land – it is mostly frozen sea.

- Asia, the biggest continent, stretches from the Arctic circle to the Equator.

- North and South America were named after the Italian explorer Amerigo Vespucci.

- Africa contains 54 countries (including islands) – more than any other continent.

At what event does a cowboy test his skills?
Find out on pages 132-133

Which countries are the richest in the world?
Find out on pages 144-145

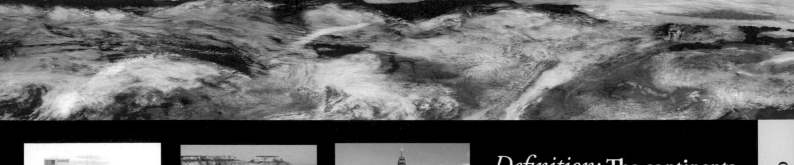

Definition: **The continents** are Earth's major landmasses. There are seven continents: North America, South America, Africa, Europe, Asia, Australasia, and Antarctica.

- Europe holds the world's smallest country: Vatican City, Italy, is .44 sq km (⅕ sq mile).

- South America's largest country, Brazil, covers more than half the continent's area.

- About 250 million years ago, all of Earth's continents were joined into one big one.

- There are areas of desert on all seven of Earth's continents.

- Apart from Antarctica, Australasia is the most sparsely populated continent.

? In what mountain range would you find llamas?
Find out on pages 136-137

? Where in the world does classical dancing look like this?
Find out on pages 148-149

Our world

Just one-third of Earth's surface is land, the rest is covered by water. The land is divided into seven vast landmasses (continents): North America, South America, Europe, Asia, Africa, Australasia, and Antarctica.

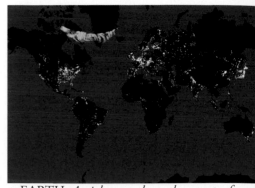

▲ EARTH *A night map shows those parts of the world with plentiful electricity supplies.*

EUROPE

ASIA

AFRICA

ATLANTIC

OCEAN

INDIAN

OCEAN

SOUTHERN OCEAN

ANTARCTICA

30°W · 0° · 30°E · 60°E · 90°E · 120°E

Arctic Circle
60°N
30°N
Tropic of Cancer
Equator
Tropic of Capricorn
30°S
60°S
Antarctic Circle

FAST FACTS

- World population 6,756 million (January 2009)
- Independent countries 196
- Dependent territories 50
- Continents 7
- Oceans 5
- Largest continent Asia
- Smallest continent Australasia

KEY TO MAPS

- ■ Capital city
- ● State city
- State border
- — Coast line
- ⋯⋯ River
- △ Mountain

- **N** North compass

Scale

0 km — 500
0 miles — 500

Note: Only main languages are given.

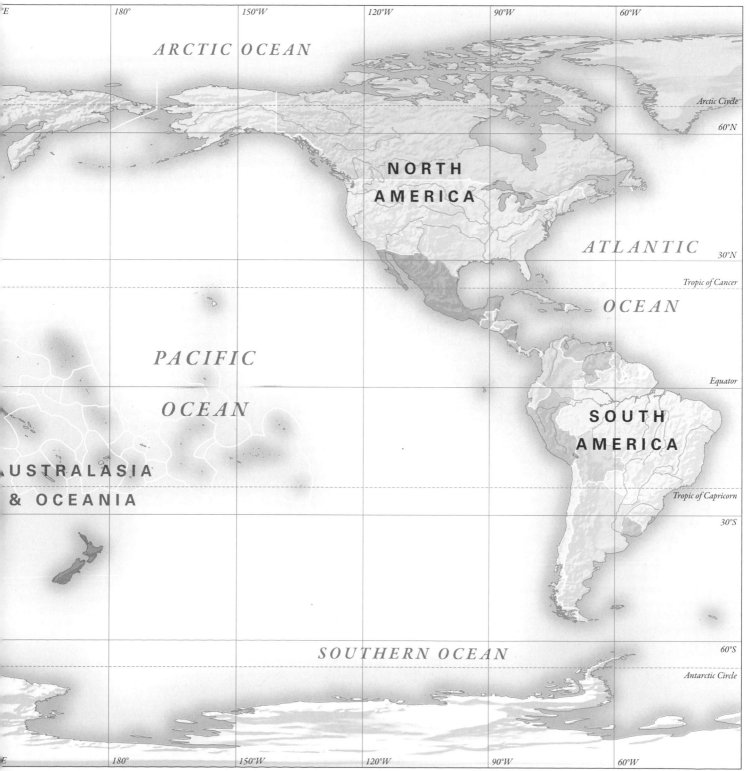

ARCTIC OCEAN

NORTH AMERICA

ATLANTIC OCEAN

PACIFIC OCEAN

AUSTRALASIA & OCEANIA

SOUTH AMERICA

SOUTHERN OCEAN

Arctic Circle
60°N
30°N
Tropic of Cancer
Equator
Tropic of Capricorn
30°S
60°S
Antarctic Circle

180°   150°W   120°W   90°W   60°W

North America

Stretching from the Arctic Circle to the tropics, North America is the third-largest continent. Two countries, Canada and the USA, take up three-quarters of the continent, which also contains Mexico, seven Central American countries, and the Caribbean Islands.

ASIA

Bering Strait

Aleutian Islands

Bering Sea

UNITED STATES OF AMERICA

ALASKA
Mt. McKinley 6194m

Anchorage

Gulf of Alaska

NORTH AMERICAN FACTS

- **Covers** approximately 16.5 per cent of Earth's land area
- **Number of countries** 23
- **Biggest country** Canada
- **Smallest country** St Kitts and Nevis
- **Languages** English, Spanish, French
- **Population of continent** Estimated at 529 million
- **Largest North American city** Mexico City, Mexico
- **Highest point** Mount McKinley (Denali) in Alaska, USA at 6,194 m (20,320 ft)
- **Longest river** the Mississippi-Missouri in the USA is 6,019 km (3,740 miles) long
- **Biggest lake** Lake Superior, situated between the USA and Canada, is the world's largest freshwater lake by surface area

How many people?

About 529 million people live in North America, more than half of them in the USA. Barbados is the most densely populated country, with 640 people per kilometre^2 (1,658 per mile^2).

Population density
People per km^2 (0.39 mi^2)

	below 50
	50-90
	100-149
	150-199
	200-299
	above 300

▼ HAWAII *The Hawaiian Islands lie in the mid Pacific Ocean but are part of the USA.*

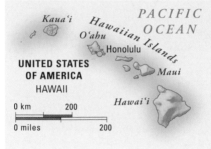

Kaua'i

Hawaiian Islands

PACIFIC OCEAN

O'ahu
Honolulu

UNITED STATES OF AMERICA
HAWAII

Maui

0 km   200
0 miles   200

Hawai'i

▼ INUIT PEOPLE *have lived in the Arctic for centuries, surviving by hunting fish, seals, walruses, and whales. Today, most Inuit live in towns or small settlements.*

THE POLAR REGION

The climate in the Arctic is harsh – average winter temperatures can be as low as -40 °C (-40 °F), and in mid-winter the Sun never rises. Parts of the region are permanently covered by ice. Despite this, the Arctic is home to many animals, including polar bears and seals.

EXTENT OF THE ARCTIC

The Arctic region includes Greenland, northern Canada and Alaska, as well as the northernmost parts of Europe and Asia, and a huge area of frozen ocean around the North Pole.

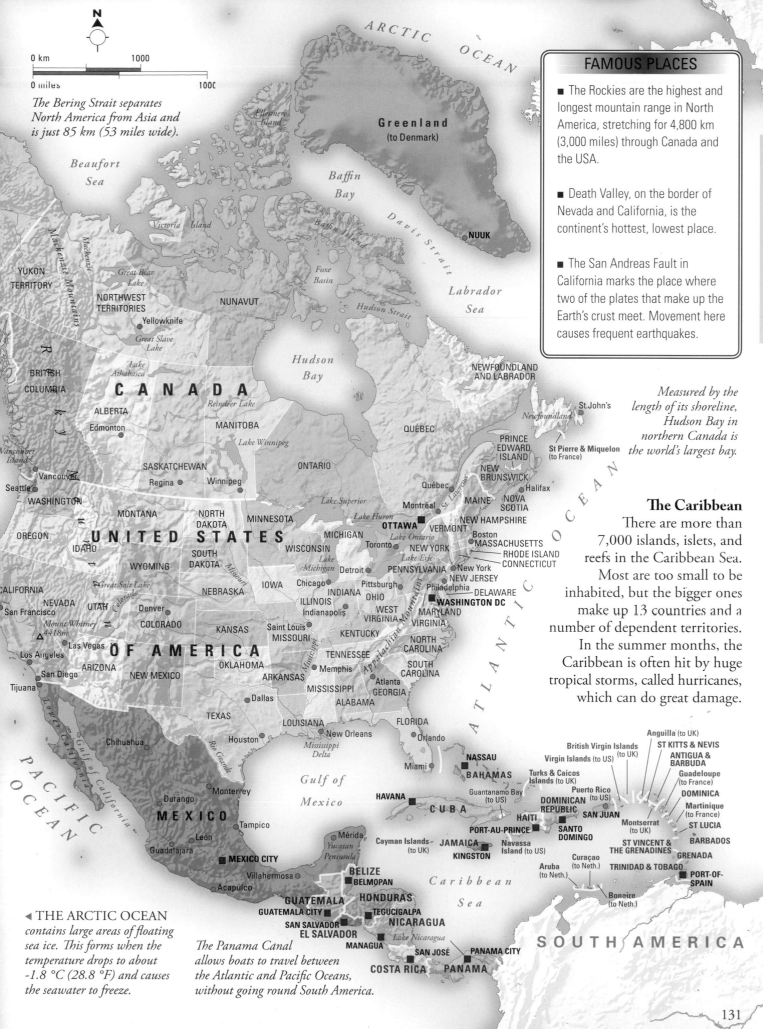

The Bering Strait separates North America from Asia and is just 85 km (53 miles wide).

FAMOUS PLACES

- The Rockies are the highest and longest mountain range in North America, stretching for 4,800 km (3,000 miles) through Canada and the USA.

- Death Valley, on the border of Nevada and California, is the continent's hottest, lowest place.

- The San Andreas Fault in California marks the place where two of the plates that make up the Earth's crust meet. Movement here causes frequent earthquakes.

Measured by the length of its shoreline, Hudson Bay in northern Canada is the world's largest bay.

The Caribbean

There are more than 7,000 islands, islets, and reefs in the Caribbean Sea. Most are too small to be inhabited, but the bigger ones make up 13 countries and a number of dependent territories. In the summer months, the Caribbean is often hit by huge tropical storms, called hurricanes, which can do great damage.

◀ THE ARCTIC OCEAN contains large areas of floating sea ice. This forms when the temperature drops to about -1.8 °C (28.8 °F) and causes the seawater to freeze.

The Panama Canal allows boats to travel between the Atlantic and Pacific Oceans, without going round South America.

131

Life in North America

The first people crossed from Asia to modern-day Alaska thousands of years ago. Today's North Americans include the descendants of native peoples, European settlers, and African slaves.

Cattle ranching

The cowboys made famous in films were farm hands employed to round up and drive the large herds of cattle that once roamed free in the American west. Cattle are still raised for their meat in the USA and Canada.

▲ RANCH *Cattle are now raised on large farms, called ranches, like this one in Alberta, Canada.*

◀ RODEO *A rodeo is a series of events, such as riding a bucking horse or bull, which are designed to test the skill of a cowboy.*

INDUSTRY

North American companies have been responsible for the invention of the silicon chip, the microprocessor, the iPod, and many other advances in computer technology.

LANDSCAPE

North America contains a huge variety of landscapes. Many areas are popular tourist destinations.

FAMOUS NORTH AMERICANS

■ **Barack Obama** (born 1961) The first African-American President of the USA, elected in 2008 after promising to bring change to the country.
■ **Amelia Earhart** (1897–1937) American pioneer of flying, and the first woman to fly solo across the Atlantic (in 1928).
■ **Frida Kahlo** (1907–54) Mexican artist who is famous for her self-portraits, painted in vibrant colours.
■ **Sir Frederick Banting** (1891–1941) and **Charles Best** (1899–1978) Canadian scientists who discovered insulin, since used to treat millions of people who suffer from diabetes.

TAKE A PICTURE

The Grand Canyon is a steep-sided gorge in Arizona, USA. It has been cut out of the rock by the Colorado River.

TAKE A PICTURE

Each year, about 20 million people visit Niagara Falls, a massive group of waterfalls on the US-Canada border.

▼ MANHATTAN *New York is the biggest city in the USA.*

MUSIC

The USA is the birthplace of some of the world's most popular styles of music, including jazz, rock and roll, blues, hip-hop, and country music. Jazz, blues, and rock all evolved from the blending of African and European musical styles that started in communities in the southern USA.

In basketball, two teams of five players try to score goals by shooting the ball through a hoop 3 m (10 ft) high.

SPORT

The most popular spectator sports in North America are basketball, baseball, American football, and ice hockey. American football follows different rules to European football and is popular in the USA, while Mexico favours the European game. Canadian football is similar to the American version.

American football is a contact sport in which tackling is essential, so players wear helmets and pads to protect themselves from injury.

CAR CULTURE

People in the United States and Canada own a lot of cars – 19 million new ones were sold in 2007 and in the USA there is more than one car on the road for every licensed driver. Many of these vehicles are built in Detroit, Michigan, although the US car industry has lost ground to foreign competitors in recent years.

American towns are designed around the car, with streets laid out in a grid pattern.

NATIVE AMERICANS

Native Americans are the descendants of the original inhabitants of North America. There are about two million native people living in the USA today and one million in Canada.

When Europeans first arrived in North America in the 1500s, they thought they were in Asia and called the native people Indians. The term "American Indian" was born.

DID YOU KNOW? FASCINATING FACTS

1 Canada's 243,000-km (151,000-mile) coastline is the longest of any country in the world.

243,000 km

2 Alaska used to belong to Russia. The United States bought it from the Russians in 1867 for a bargain price of just two cents per acre (0.004 km²).

2 cents 2 cents

3 America is named after the Italian Amerigo Vespucci, who was one of the first European explorers to travel to the New World.

4 The five Great Lakes, on the US-Canadian border are the largest group of freshwater lakes in the world. They cover an area about the same size as the UK.

5 Chocolate first appeared in Mexico and Central America at least 1,600 years ago, as a bitter tasting drink called xocolatl.

South America

South America is the fourth-largest continent. It contains the world's longest mountain range, biggest rainforest, driest desert, and highest waterfall. It is also home to a vast range of plants and animals, and to 382 million people.

Population density
People per km² (0.39mi²)

- below 50
- 50-90
- 100-149
- 150-199
- 200-299
- above 300

SOUTH AMERICAN FACTS

- **Covers** approximately 12 per cent of Earth's land area
- **Number of countries** 12
- **Biggest country** Brazil
- **Smallest independent country** Surinam
- **Languages** Spanish, Portuguese, French, Dutch, and many native Indian languages
- **Population of continent** Estimated at 382 million
- **Largest South American city** Sao Paulo, Brazil
- **Highest point** Cerro Aconcagua in Argentina at 6,959 m (22,833 ft)
- **Longest river** the Amazon is approximately 6,437 km (4,000 miles) long
- **Biggest lake** Lake Titicaca, situated between Peru and Bolivia

THE AMAZON

The Amazon is the world's second-longest river and the largest by volume. It pours so much water into the Atlantic that drinkable water can be drawn out of the ocean more than a kilometre (¾ mile) from the river mouth.

How many people?

About six per cent of the total world population live in South America. Brazil is the largest country and has the biggest population, while Colombia and Ecuador are the most densely populated countries.

▲ FOREST *The Amazon is surrounded by the biggest tropical rainforest on Earth, home to a huge variety of wildlife and groups of native peoples.*

▲ CATTLE RANCHING *Vast areas of forest are being cut down each year to clear land for cattle ranches, threatening the area's delicate ecosystem.*

THREATENED ZONES

The total area lost to forest clearance in the Amazon is at least 587,000 km² (227,000 miles²) – that's bigger than France.

▶ HABITAT *The weather in the rainforest is hot and humid all year round.*

ANIMALS IN THE AMAZON

One in ten of the world's known species of plants and animals live in the Amazon rainforest, including:

- 40,000 species of plants
- 3,000 species of fish
- 1,294 species of birds
- 427 species of mammals
- 428 species of amphibians
- 378 species of reptiles

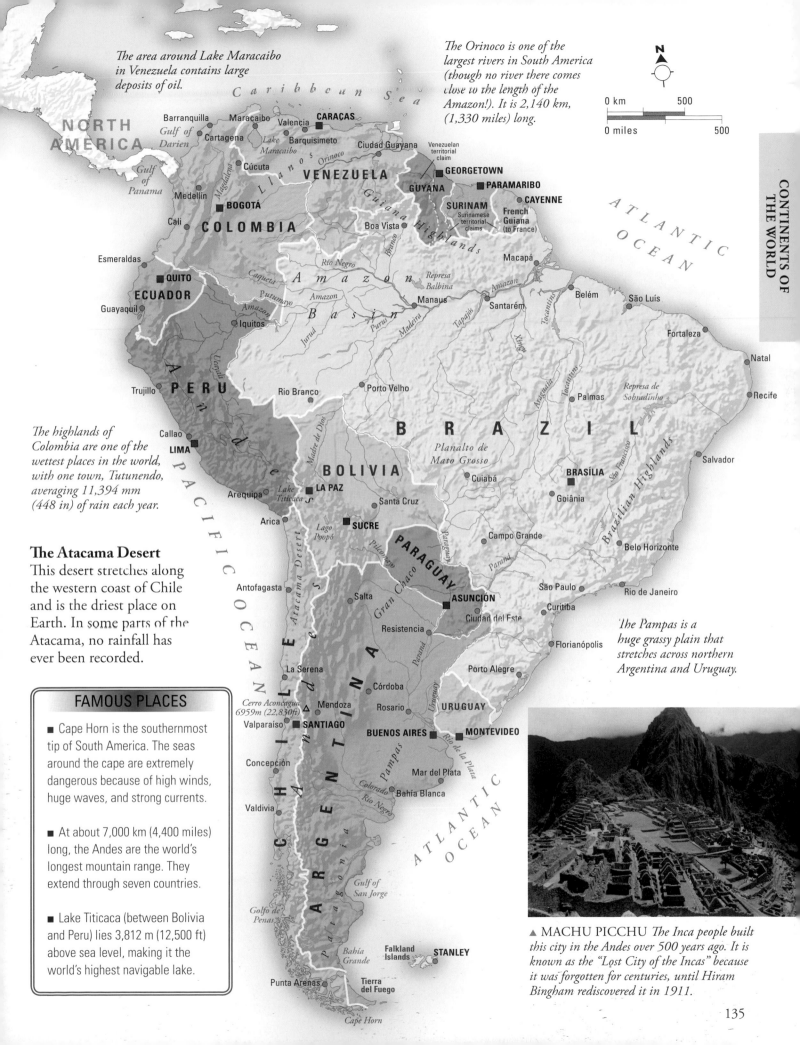

The area around Lake Maracaibo in Venezuela contains large deposits of oil.

The Orinoco is one of the largest rivers in South America (though no river there comes close to the length of the Amazon!). It is 2,140 km, (1,330 miles) long.

0 km   500
0 miles   500

NORTH AMERICA

Caribbean Sea

Barranquilla   Maracaibo   Valencia   **CARACAS**
Gulf of Darien   Cartagena   Lake Maracaibo   Barquisimeto
Cúcuta   Ciudad Guayana   Venezuelan territorial claim
Medellín   *Llanos*   *Orinoco*   **GEORGETOWN**
BOGOTÁ   VENEZUELA   GUYANA   **PARAMARIBO**
Cali   SURINAM   **CAYENNE**
COLOMBIA   Boa Vista   *Guiana Highlands*   French Guiana (to France)
Surinamese territorial claims
Gulf of Panama

Esmeraldas   *Río Negro*   *Branco*   Macapá
QUITO   *Caquetá*   *Amazon*   *Amazon*
ECUADOR   *Putumayo*   *Amazon*   Belém   São Luís
Guayaquil   *Amazon*   Manaus   Santarém
Iquitos   *Basin*   Fortaleza
Jurúa   *Purus*   *Madeira*   *Tapajós*   *Xingu*   *Tocantins*   Natal

A   Trujillo   P E R U   Rio Branco   Porto Velho   Palmas   *Represa de Sobradinho*   Recife
n
Callao   *d*   *Madre de Dios*   B R A Z I L   Salvador
LIMA   *e*   *Planalto de Mato Grosso*   *São Francisco*   *Brazilian Highlands*
s   BOLIVIA   **BRASÍLIA**
Arequipa   Lake Titicaca   Cuiabá   Goiânia
LA PAZ   Santa Cruz
Arica   *Lago Poopó*   **SUCRE**   Campo Grande   Belo Horizonte
Pilcomayo   *Paraguay*   *Paraná*

Antofagasta   *Atacama Desert*   Salta   PARAGUAY   São Paulo   Rio de Janeiro
Gran Chaco   **ASUNCIÓN**   Curitiba
C   Resistencia   Ciudad del Este
H   *Paraná*   Florianópolis
I   La Serena   Córdoba   URUGUAY   Porto Alegre
L   *Cerro Aconcagua 6959m (22,830ft)*   Mendoza   Rosario
E   Valparaíso   **SANTIAGO**   *Uruguay*   **MONTEVIDEO**
BUENOS AIRES   *Río de la Plata*
Concepción   A   *Pampas*   Mar del Plata
R   *Colorado*   Bahía Blanca
Valdivia   G   *Río Negro*
E
N   ATLANTIC OCEAN
T
I
P A C I F I C   O C E A N   N
A   *Gulf of San Jorge*

Golfo de Penas   *P*   Falkland Islands   **STANLEY**
a
t
Bahía Grande   *g*
Punta Arenas   Tierra del Fuego   *o*
n
Cape Horn   *i*
a   ATLANTIC OCEAN

The highlands of Colombia are one of the wettest places in the world, with one town, Tutunendo, averaging 11,394 mm (448 in) of rain each year.

The Atacama Desert

This desert stretches along the western coast of Chile and is the driest place on Earth. In some parts of the Atacama, no rainfall has ever been recorded.

The Pampas is a huge grassy plain that stretches across northern Argentina and Uruguay.

FAMOUS PLACES

- Cape Horn is the southernmost tip of South America. The seas around the cape are extremely dangerous because of high winds, huge waves, and strong currents.

- At about 7,000 km (4,400 miles) long, the Andes are the world's longest mountain range. They extend through seven countries.

- Lake Titicaca (between Bolivia and Peru) lies 3,812 m (12,500 ft) above sea level, making it the world's highest navigable lake.

▲ MACHU PICCHU *The Inca people built this city in the Andes over 500 years ago. It is known as the "Lost City of the Incas" because it was forgotten for centuries, until Hiram Bingham rediscovered it in 1911.*

135

Life in South America

Dramatic landscapes, including the Andes mountains, lively cities, music, dancing, exuberant carnivals, and passionate football crowds are just some of the things to see in South America.

▶ MANED WOLF *This long-legged wolf lives in Uruguay.*

▲ LLAMA *People who live in the Andes keep llamas for their wool and use them to carry heavy loads.*

LANDSCAPE
South America contains almost every kind of landscape, including rainforest, grassland, desert, and mountain.

📷 **TAKE A PICTURE**

At 979 m (3,212 ft), Angel Falls in Venezuela is the world's highest waterfall. It was named after an American pilot, Jimmy Angel, in 1933.

WILDLIFE
This continent is home to a huge variety of animals: tropical parrots and snakes in the rainforest, bears and condors in the Andes, and anteaters and cavies on the Pampas grasslands.

👤 FAMOUS SOUTH AMERICANS

- **Eva Peron** (1919–1952), often known as Evita, was married to the Argentinian president, Juan Perón. She helped many poor people and campaigned for better conditions for workers.
- **Pele** (born 1940) Brazilian former football player, considered by many to be the greatest footballer of all time.
- **Gabriel Garcia Marquez** (born 1927) Colombian novel writer who was awarded the Nobel Prize for literature in 1982.
- **Simón Bolívar** (1783-1830), born in Venezuela, was a key leader in the successful struggle for independence of much of South America, including Peru, Venezuela, Colombia, Ecuador, and Bolivia.

▲ FAVELA *Rio is not all beaches and skyscrapers. Many of its inhabitants live in poverty in shantytowns called favelas.*

◀ RIO DE JANEIRO *Famous for its dramatic setting on the Atlantic coast, Brazil's second-largest city is overlooked by a giant statue of Christ the Redeemer.*

FOOD

Meat forms an important part of the South American diet. One traditional dish in Paraguay, Uruguay, and Argentina is a barbecue of sausages, steaks, and chicken, called asado. A tea called "mate" is popular in Southern Brazil and is drunk from a gourd through a silver straw.

PANAMA HAT

Despite their name, these brimmed straw hats do not actually come from Panama – they are made in Ecuador.

FARMING

Almost a third of all the world's coffee is grown in Brazil. Other important South American crops include bananas, cocoa, and sugarcane. Chile and Argentina are important wine producers.

TOURISM

Many people visit Rio to see the carnival or to relax on the famous beaches. Other popular tourist attractions include Iguacu Falls and the ancient Inca city of Machu Picchu in Peru.

INDUSTRY

Venezuela has some of the world's largest oil and gas reserves, and the petroleum industry accounts for 80 per cent of its exports. In Brazil, many cars run on ethanol, which is a fuel made from sugar cane.

FOOTBALL

Football is a passion for people in many South American countries – from children playing football in the streets up to fanatical support for the big teams. Brazilian football is famous for its fast-flowing and attacking style of play. The national team has won the football World Cup a record five times.

MUSIC

The samba, tango, and bossa nova are just some of the famous dances that come from South America. This couple is dancing the tango, a dramatic dance that originated in the slums of Buenos Aires in Argentina. Tango music is played on a type of concertina called a bandoneon, accompanied by a piano and violin.

DID YOU KNOW? FASCINATING FACTS

1 Chile is the longest and thinnest country in the world. It is 4,200 km (2,610 miles) long but only 180 km (112 miles) at its widest point.

2 The city of Ushuaia is the southernmost city in the world. It is situated on the island of Tierra del Fuego at the southern tip of Argentina.

3 There are nearly 137 million Roman Catholics in Brazil – more than in any other country in the world.

4 La Paz in Bolivia is the world's highest capital city at 3,640 m (11,942 ft) above sea level.

5 Argentina was named by the first Spanish settlers, who went there in search of silver and gold. The name comes from the Latin word for silver, *argentum*.

Africa

Africa is often called the "birthplace of humankind". That's because human beings originated from Africa several million years ago, although humans as we would recognize them only emerged about 200,000 years ago. Today, about 1 in 8 of the world's population live in Africa.

AFRICAN FACTS

- **Covers** approximately 20 per cent of Earth's land area
- **Number of countries** 54 +dependencies
- **Biggest country** Algeria
- **Smallest country** The Seychelles
- **Languages** 1,000s
- **Population of continent** Estimated at 778 million
- **Largest African city** Egypt's capital, Cairo
- **Highest point** Kilimanjaro in Tanzania at 5,895 m (19,341 ft)
- **Longest river** Nile, running through Uganda, Sudan, South Sudan and Egypt into the Mediterranean Sea, at 6,671 km (4,145 miles)
- **Biggest lake** Lake Victoria, bordering Tanzania, Uganda, Kenya. The lake contains more than 3,000 islands, many inhabited.

How many people?

The population of Africa is thought to be around 14 per cent of the total world population. Nigeria is the most populated African country.

Population density
People per km² (0.39 mi²)

- below 50
- 50-90
- 100-149
- 150-199
- 200-299
- above 300

Madeira
(to Portugal)

Canary Islands
(to Spain)

LAÂYOUNE

WESTERN SAHARA
(disputed)

Nouâdhibou

MAURITANIA

CAPE VERDE   NOUAKCHOTT

Senegal

PRAIA   DAKAR   **SENEGAL**

BANJUL   **GAMBIA**

BISSAU

GUINEA-BISSAU   **GUINEA**

CONAKRY   SIERRA LEONE

FREETOWN   LIBERIA

N

MONROVIA

0 km   1000

0 miles   1000

◄ OASIS *There are about 90 big oases scattered across the Sahara. These are places where underground water comes to the surface, allowing plants to grow.*

▲ DESERT MAMMAL *This fennec fox keeps cool by losing heat through its huge ears.*

THE SAHARA

"Sahara" comes from the Arabic word for "desert". The Sahara stretches across North Africa and covers parts of 11 countries. Much of it consists of vast seas of sand, with dunes up to 180 m (600 ft) high.

A VARIED LANDSCAPE

Africa's varied landscapes include three deserts – the Sahara (Earth's largest desert) in North Africa, and the Kalahari and Namib in the south. There are also large areas of forest and grassland.

SAHARA

Kalahari
Namib

- Desert*
- Dry grassland
- Tropical grassland
- Tropical forest
- Mediterranean
- Mountain

*Red areas indicate the extent of the named deserts.

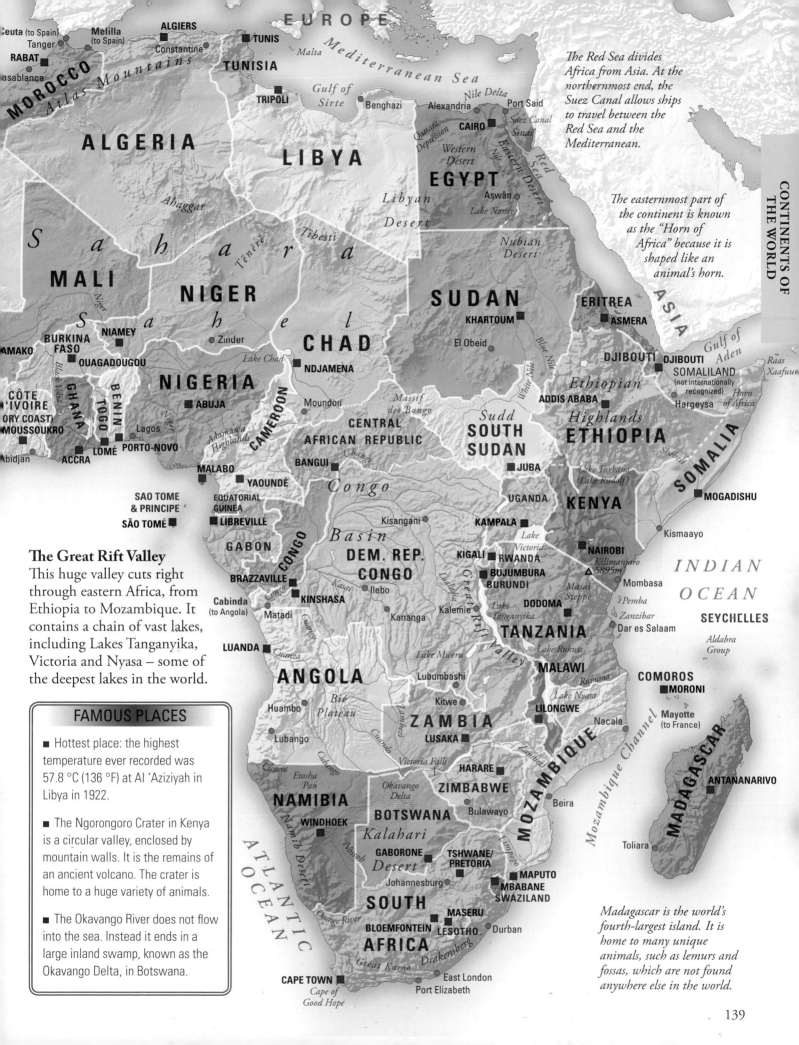

Ceuta (to Spain)
Tanger
Melilla (to Spain)
RABAT
Casablanca
MOROCCO
Atlas Mountains
ALGIERS
Constantine
TUNIS
TUNISIA
TRIPOLI
Malta
Mediterranean Sea
EUROPE
Gulf of Sirte
Benghazi
Alexandria
Port Said
CAIRO
Nile Delta
Suez Canal
Sinai

The Red Sea divides Africa from Asia. At the northernmost end, the Suez Canal allows ships to travel between the Red Sea and the Mediterranean.

ALGERIA
LIBYA
EGYPT
Aswân
Qattara Depression
Western Desert
Eastern Desert
Nile
Red Sea
Lake Nasser
Libyan Desert
Nubian Desert

The easternmost part of the continent is known as the "Horn of Africa" because it is shaped like an animal's horn.

ASIA

Ahaggar
Tibesti
Ténéré
MALI
NIGER
CHAD
SUDAN
KHARTOUM
El Obeid
ERITREA
ASMERA
Gulf of Aden
Raas Xaafuun

S   a   h   a   r   a
S   a   h   e   l
Niger
Zinder
Lake Chad
NDJAMENA
Blue Nile
DJIBOUTI
DJIBOUTI
SOMALILAND (not internationally recognized)
Hargeysa
Horn of Africa

BURKINA FASO
NIAMEY
BAMAKO
OUAGADOUGOU
NIGERIA
ABUJA
Moundou
Massif des Bongo
White Nile
Sudd
SOUTH SUDAN
ADDIS ABABA
Ethiopian Highlands
ETHIOPIA
Shebeli

CÔTE D'IVOIRE (IVORY COAST)
YAMOUSSOUKRO
Abidjan
GHANA
TOGO
BENIN
ACCRA
LOMÉ
PORTO-NOVO
Lagos
Black Volta
Niger
CAMEROON
Adamawa Highlands
CENTRAL AFRICAN REPUBLIC
BANGUI
Ubangi
JUBA
Lake Turkana (Lake Rudolf)
SOMALIA
MOGADISHU

MALABO
YAOUNDÉ
EQUATORIAL GUINEA
SAO TOME & PRINCIPE
SÃO TOMÉ
LIBREVILLE
GABON
Congo
Basin
Kisangani
DEM. REP. CONGO
UGANDA
KAMPALA
KENYA
Lake Victoria
NAIROBI
Kismaayo

The Great Rift Valley

This huge valley cuts right through eastern Africa, from Ethiopia to Mozambique. It contains a chain of vast lakes, including Lakes Tanganyika, Victoria and Nyasa – some of the deepest lakes in the world.

INDIAN OCEAN

CONGO
BRAZZAVILLE
Cabinda (to Angola)
KINSHASA
Matadi
Congo
Kasai
Ilebo
Kananga
KIGALI
RWANDA
BUJUMBURA
BURUNDI
Lualaba
Kalemie
DODOMA
Great Rift Valley
Lake Tanganyika
Masai Steppe
△ Kilimanjaro 5895m
Mombasa
Pemba
Zanzibar
Dar es Salaam

SEYCHELLES

LUANDA
Cuango
Cuanza
ANGOLA
Huambo
Lubango
Bié Plateau
Lubumbashi
Kitwe
ZAMBIA
LUSAKA
Lake Mweru
Lake Rukwa
TANZANIA
Lake Nyasa
MALAWI
LILONGWE
Ruvuma
COMOROS
MORONI
Mayotte (to France)
Aldabra Group

Zambezi
Victoria Falls
HARARE
ZIMBABWE
Bulawayo
MOZAMBIQUE
Nacala
Beira
Mozambique Channel
ANTANANARIVO
MADAGASCAR

Cuando
Cubango
Cunene
Etosha Pan
Okavango Delta
NAMIBIA
WINDHOEK
Kalahari Desert
BOTSWANA
GABORONE
TSHWANE/ PRETORIA
Johannesburg
MAPUTO
MBABANE
SWAZILAND
Limpopo

Namib Desert
Nossob
MASERU
LESOTHO
ATLANTIC OCEAN
Orange River
SOUTH AFRICA
BLOEMFONTEIN
Durban
Toliara

Madagascar is the world's fourth-largest island. It is home to many unique animals, such as lemurs and fossas, which are not found anywhere else in the world.

CAPE TOWN
Cape of Good Hope
East London
Port Elizabeth
Great Karoo
Drakensberg

Life in Africa

Home to the world's longest river and the biggest desert, to one of the oldest tourist attractions and to some of the most dramatic wildlife on the planet, Africa is a fascinating continent.

LANDSCAPE

Africa contains a huge variety of landscapes, from snow-capped mountains to baking deserts. Northern Africa is mostly desert, while further south are grassy plains, called savanna, and dense rainforest.

📷 **TAKE A PICTURE**

Africa's highest mountain is Mount Kilimanjaro in Tanzania at 5,895 m (19,340 ft). Its peak is always covered in snow.

📷 **TAKE A PICTURE**

Lake Victoria is the largest lake in Africa and the second largest freshwater lake in the world.

FAMOUS AFRICANS

- **Nelson Mandela** (born 1918) Former political prisoner who became South Africa's first fully democratically elected president in 1994.
- **Kofi Annan** (born 1938) Secretary General of the United Nations (1997–2007). Winner of the Nobel Peace Prize in 2001.
- **Desmond Tutu** (born 1931) Former archbishop of Cape Town in South Africa, and an anti-apartheid campaigner.
- **Haile Gebreselassie** (born 1973) Ethiopian long-distance runner who has broken numerous world records.

Traditional African villages

Most Africans live in the countryside, often in small villages. Many homes, such as these in a Shona village, are made from mud. People live very simply with no access to electricity.

► MANY *Africans make their living from farming or herding. This Samburu man in Kenya is herding his goats.*

▼ NAIROBI *Only around one out of every five Africans lives in a big city like Nairobi, the capital of Kenya.*

FARMING

About 60 per cent of African workers are subsistence farmers, farming their own land and growing crops such as barley, cassava, corn, sorghum, and sweet potatoes to feed their families. Many also produce "cash crops", such as coffee, which are sold to make money. Larger farms usually grow cotton, cocoa, or rubber as cash crops.

Some places in Africa use wind pumps to pump water from the ground, because many areas are not connected to a national electricity supply.

FOOD

The main ingredients of most African dishes are the staple crops grown on local farms – maize, cassava, yams, rice, beans – along with various green vegetables. One popular dish eaten across West Africa is Jollof rice. It is made from rice with tomatoes, onions, spices, and chilli, all cooked in one pot, and is often served with cooked meat or fish.

WILDLIFE

Africa is famous for its zebra, giraffes, lions, and other large animals. But it is also home to many other creatures, from the 500 different species of fish that live in Lake Malawi to colonies of penguins in South Africa.

INDUSTRY

The main African industries are mining for gold, diamonds, and copper, as well as oil production. The biggest oil producers are Nigeria and Libya.

TOURISM

Each year, about 3 million people visit the ancient pyramids at Giza in Egypt, making them Africa's number one tourist attraction. Many people also travel to Africa to see the continent's spectacular wildlife.

Diamonds About half of all diamonds come from southern Africa, especially South Africa and Botswana. The largest diamond ever found, the Cullinan, was mined in South Africa in 1905.

MUSIC

Most African music features complex rhythms, created through patterns of drumbeats. African musicians also play flutes, xylophones, and stringed instruments.

▶ MBIRA *This African instrument is made of metal keys set on a wooden soundboard. The musician plucks the keys with his fingers.*

DID YOU KNOW? FASCINATING FACTS

1 One of the toughest races on Earth is the *Marathon des Sables* (Marathon of the Sands), which takes place each year in Morocco. Entrants run 254 km (156 miles) across the desert in six days.

2 Malaria is a huge killer in Africa. Many people die as a result of mosquito bites passing this disease.

3 Many African children don't get the chance to go to school. In Mali in West Africa, for example, only one out of every three children goes to primary school.

4 At 6,695 km (4,184 miles), the Nile is the longest river in the world. It flows north through 10 African countries.

5 The world's five fastest land animals are the cheetah, pronghorn antelope, wildebeest, lion, and Thomson's gazelle. Four are found in Africa. The pronghorn is native to North America.

Europe

Unlike many of the other continents, Europe is not a separate landmass – it is joined to Asia. Europe's eastern boundary is formed by the Ural mountains and the Caspian Sea. Russia falls into both Europe and Asia.

EUROPEAN FACTS

- **Covers** approximately 7 per cent of Earth's land area
- **Number of countries** More than 50
- **Biggest country** Russia (note that part of Russia also lies in Asia)
- **Smallest country** Vatican City
- **Languages** More than 50
- **Population of continent** Estimated at 731 million
- **Largest European city** Moscow
- **Highest point** Mount Elbrus in Russia at 5,642 m (18,510 feet) high
- **Longest river** the Volga in Russia is 3,688 km (2,292 miles) long
- **Biggest lake** Lake Ladoga in Russia

How many people?

The 731 million Europeans make up about 11 per cent of the total world population. Russia has the largest population, while the most densely populated country is the Netherlands.

Population density
People per km² (0.39 mi²)

- below 50
- 50-90
- 100-149
- 150-199
- 200-299
- above 300

▲ ST BASIL'S CATHEDRAL
This beautiful cathedral, with its onion-shaped domes, stands in Red Square in Moscow, Russia.

THE ALPS

Extending through seven countries, the Alps are the largest mountain system in Europe. They are a popular holiday destination in both summer and winter for skiing, mountaineering, and walking.

▼ ALPS *Mont Blanc is the highest peak in the Alps at 4,808 m (15,774 ft).*

A Coruña
Porto
Vallad
Tagus
LISBON
PORTUGAL
S
Seville
Gibraltar (to UK)
Mála

RESCUE DOG
Specially trained German shepherd dogs are used in the Alps to find missing people. They can smell a person buried under snow.

FAMOUS PLACES

- Surtsey, a small island off Iceland, was formed by the eruption of an underwater volcano. It rose above sea level in 1963–68, making it one of the world's youngest islands.

- The Low Countries – Belgium and the Netherlands – are so low that some of the land actually lies below sea level and has to be protected by huge dykes (sea walls).

The island of Iceland is extremely volcanically active. It is home to several volcanoes and many geysers.

The northeastern part of Europe, known as Scandinavia, includes the countries of Norway, Sweden, Denmark, and Finland.

Mount Etna, on the island of Sicily, is the largest active volcano in Europe. Etna erupts almost continuously, making it one of the world's most active volcanoes.

Istanbul, the largest city in Turkey, is the only city to span two continents. Part is in Europe, and part in Asia.

The Mediterranean Sea
Europe is divided from Africa by the Mediterranean, a sea that is almost completely surrounded by land. The only way in and out to the Atlantic Ocean is through the Strait of Gibraltar, which is just 14 km (9 miles) wide.

Map labels

Svalbard (to Norway)
Novaya Zemlya
Kara Sea
Denmark Strait
REYKJAVÍK ICELAND
Barents Sea
Murmansk
RUSSIAN FEDERATION
ASIA
Faeroe Islands (to Denmark)
Norwegian Sea
Arkhangel'sk
Northern Dvina
White Sea
Shetland Islands
ATLANTIC OCEAN
Trondheim
FINLAND
Lake Onega
Bergen
Tampere
Lake Ladoga
Outer Hebrides
Stavanger
OSLO
HELSINKI
St Petersburg
SWEDEN
NORWAY
North Sea
STOCKHOLM
Åland
Vänern
ESTONIA
TALLINN
Nizhniy Novgorod
Kazan'
Ufa
SCOTLAND
Glasgow
Gothenburg
Vättern
Gotland
RIGA
Samara
Orenburg
NORTHERN IRELAND
Edinburgh
Aalborg
LATVIA
MOSCOW
Belfast
DENMARK
Baltic Sea
LITHUANIA
Saratov
ISLE of Man (to UK)
DUBLIN
IRELAND
UNITED
Manchester
COPENHAGEN
Kaliningrad
VILNIUS
MINSK
Voronezh
WALES
KINGDOM
Birmingham
Hamburg
Gdansk
RUSS. FED. (Kaliningrad)
Vitsyebsk
Cardiff
ENGLAND
NETHERLANDS
Elbe
Oder
BELARUS
Volga
LONDON
AMSTERDAM
BERLIN
Poznan
WARSAW
Channel Islands (to UK)
English Channel
THE HAGUE
Vistula
Astrakhan'
Lille
BELGIUM
GERMANY
POLAND
KIEV
Kharkiv
Volgograd
le Havre
BRUSSELS
Wroclaw
Rostov-na-Donu
Seine
PARIS
LUXEMBOURG
Frankfurt am Main
Krakow
UKRAINE
Caspian Sea
Nantes
LUXEMBOURG
PRAGUE
L'viv
Dnieper
Loire
Strasbourg
CZECH REPUBLIC
Dnipropetrovs'k
Donets'k
FRANCE
Munich
SLOVAKIA
Dniester
Clermont-Ferrand
BERN
SWITZERLAND
LIECHTENSTEIN
VIENNA
BRATISLAVA
MOLDOVA
Rostov-na-Donu
Mont Blanc 4807m (15,771ft)
AUSTRIA
BUDAPEST
CHISINAU
Bay of Biscay
Lyon
Milan
LJUBLJANA
HUNGARY
Odesa
Sea of Azov
Bilbao
Turin
Po
SLOVENIA
ZAGREB
ROMANIA
Simferopol'
Caucasus
Bordeaux
Venice
CROATIA
BELGRADE
BUCHAREST
Groznyy
Toulouse
Pyrenees
MONACO
SAN MARINO
BOSNIA & HERZEGOVINA
SERBIA
Danube
Elbrus 5642m (18,510ft)
Zaragoza
Marseille
SARAJEVO
SOFIA
Black Sea
ANDORRA LA VELLA
ANDORRA
Corsica
MONTENEGRO
KOSOVO (disputed)
BULGARIA
Barcelona
ITALY
PODGORICA
PRISTINA
Istanbul
VATICAN CITY
ROME
TIRANA
SKOPJE
MACEDONIA
Ibiza
Mallorca
Menorca
Sardinia
Tyrrhenian Sea
ALBANIA
Salonica
Turkey
Palma
Balearic Islands
Naples
Lárisa
Aegean Sea
AFRICA
Palermo
Cagliari
Sicily
Ionian Sea
GREECE
ASIA
Mediterranean
ATHENS
MALTA
VALLETTA
Crete
Irákleio

Life in Europe

Europe is only slightly bigger than the USA, but has more than twice the US population. It is also crowded with countries – around 50 are crammed into the tiny continent.

EUROPEAN UNION

The European Union (EU) is a political and economic union of 27 countries, that operate as a single market. This means that people, goods, and money can move freely between the various countries. Sixteen of the member states share a common currency, the Euro. The EU has its own parliament, court of justice, and central bank.

The circle of stars on the EU flag represent unity among the members.

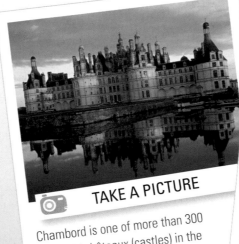

TAKE A PICTURE

Chambord is one of more than 300 beautiful châteaux (castles) in the Loire Valley in France.

TAKE A PICTURE

Stonehenge is a circle of standing stones, built in prehistoric times, that stands on Salisbury Plain in Britain.

▼ ROME'S *mix of old and new buildings shows how the city has evolved over centuries.*

FOOD

Pasta, pizza, croissants, moussaka, goulash, and profiteroles are just some of the foods that originated in Europe and are now popular worldwide.

Cheese from France

Sausages from Germany

Tapas from Spain

Pasta from Italy

SPORT

Football, tennis, cricket, golf, and rugby are played around the world, but were all invented in Europe. Rugby, for example, was a variant of football invented at a school in the UK in the early 19th century.

WEALTH

All the European countries have high standards of living, and even poorer Europeans are well off compared to people in the developing world. According to World Bank statistics, the three richest countries in the world are Luxembourg, Norway, and Switzerland – all in Europe.

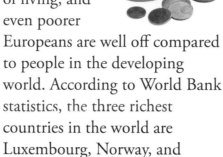

MUSIC

Europe is the birthplace of classical music, opera, and the modern orchestra. These styles of music were performed in concert halls or opera houses, many of them extremely grand buildings, with audiences paying to attend. Europe's famous composers include Mozart, Haydn, Bach, Beethoven, Verdi, and Puccini.

▲ MOZART
(1756-1791)

CROWDED CONTINENT

Europe is densely populated. Overall, there are about 70 people per square kilometre (181 per square mile), compared to just 23 people per square kilometre (59 per square mile) in North America. About three-quarters of its population live in towns and cities.

London, UK

TOURISM

France is the most visited country in the world, with almost 82 million visitors in 2011. Tourists travel to Europe to see the many historic buildings and cities, and to relax on the Mediterranean beaches.

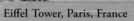
Eiffel Tower, Paris, France

DID YOU KNOW? FASCINATING FACTS

1 The River Danube flows through 10 European countries, and four European capital cities (Vienna, Bratislava, Budapest, and Belgrade).

2 Europe's population is shrinking. The average number of births per woman is just 1.52. Experts estimate that by 2050 Europeans will make up just 7 per cent of the world's population (currently 11 per cent).

3 Europe is named after Europa, a character in Greek myth. She was a princess, abducted by the god Zeus, who had disguised himself as a white bull.

4 Swiss people eat more chocolate than any other nation. Each of them munches through an average of 11.6 kg (25½ lb) of chocolate in a year.

5 The three smallest states in Europe are: San Marino (25,000 residents), Vatican City (900 residents), and Monaco (30,000 residents). Vatican City is just 0.44 km² (0.17 miles²).

Asia

Asia is the biggest continent, covering about a third of Earth's land area. It has the biggest population, and it contains the world's biggest country, highest mountain, and largest lake.

ASIAN FACTS

■ **Covers** approx 30 per cent of Earth's land area
■ **Number of countries** circa 48
■ **Biggest country** Russia (though part of Russia also lies in Europe)
■ **Smallest country** the Maldive Islands
■ **Languages** Unknown, but more than 200
■ **Population of continent** In excess of 4 billion (more than 60 per cent of the world's population)
■ **Largest Asian city** Tokyo, Japan
■ **Highest point** Mount Everest, on the border of Nepal and China, at 8,848 m (29,029 ft)
■ **Longest river** the Yangtze River (Chang Jiang) in China is 6,300 km (3,915 miles) long
■ **Biggest lake** the Caspian Sea is the world's largest lake

How many people?
More than 4 billion people live in Asia – that's about two out of every three people in the world. China has the biggest population with 1.3 billion people.

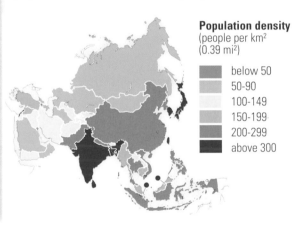

Population density
(people per km² (0.39 mi²)

below 50
50-90
100-149
150-199
200-299
above 300

Ural

Black Sea
Caspian Sea
Istanbul
GEORGIA
T'BILISI
Akt...
AZERBAIJA...
ANKARA
ARMENIA
YEREVAN
BAKU
TURKEY
Mosul
CYPRUS
NICOSIA
SYRIA
TEHRAN
BEIRUT
DAMASCUS
Qon...
LEBANON
BAGHDAD
ISRAEL
AMMAN
IRA...
JERUSALEM
JORDAN
IRAQ
Shiraz
KUWAIT
KUWAIT
The Gulf
SAUDI
BAHRAIN
ARABIA
MANAMA
QATA...
RIYADH
DOHA
AB...
DHA...
AFRICA
Red Sea
Jedda
Arabian
Peninsula
UAE
OMA...
SANA
YEMEN
Aden
Gulf of Aden
Socotra
(to Yemer...

▼ BATHING
in the Ganges is said to wash away sins.

THE GANGES
The Ganges is the longest river in the Indian Subcontinent and a sacred river for Hindus. Each year, thousands of pilgrims visit Varanasi and other holy cities along its banks.

THE DELTA
This satellite picture shows the Ganges delta in Bangladesh. This area is very low lying and often floods.

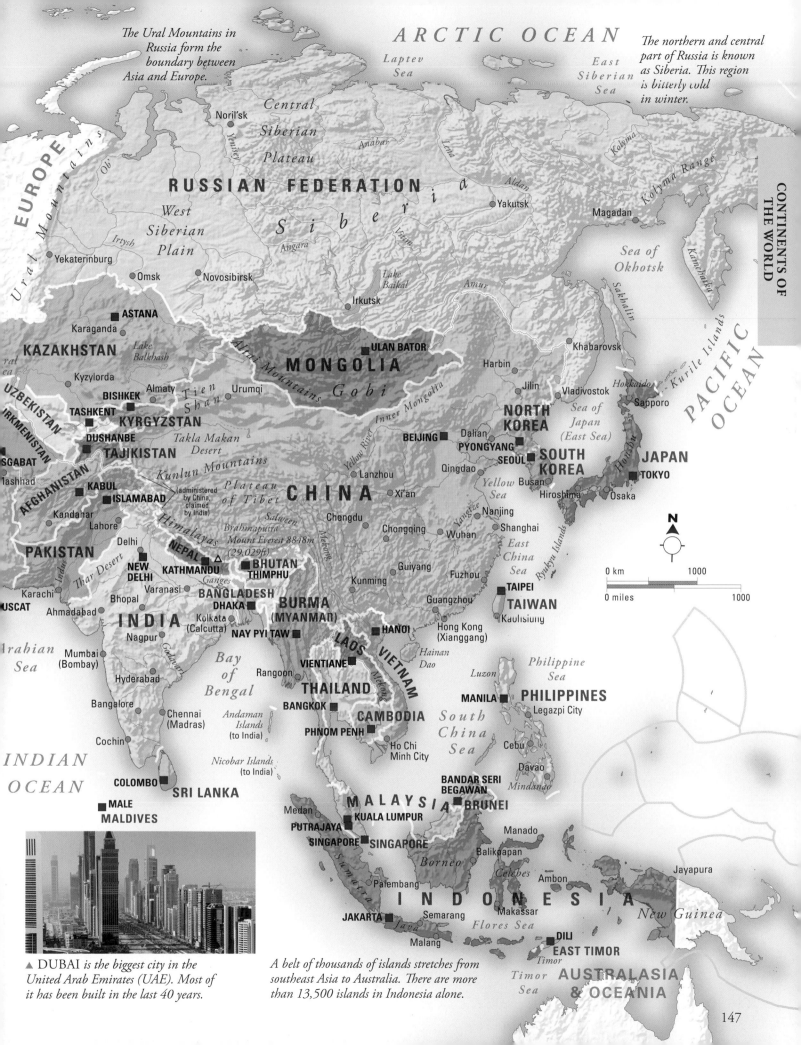

The Ural Mountains in Russia form the boundary between Asia and Europe.

The northern and central part of Russia is known as Siberia. This region is bitterly cold in winter.

Laptev Sea

East Siberian Sea

EUROPE

Noril'sk

Central Siberian Plateau

Ob

Yenisey

Anabar

Lena

Kolyma

Kolyma Range

RUSSIAN FEDERATION   S i b e r i a

Yakutsk

Magadan

West Siberian Plain

Irtysh

Omsk

Novosibirsk

Angara

Lake Baikal

Irkutsk

Vilyuy

Aldan

Amur

Sea of Okhotsk

Sakhalin

Kamchatka

Khabarovsk

Kurile Islands

PACIFIC OCEAN

Yekaterinburg

Ural Mountains

ASTANA

Karaganda

KAZAKHSTAN

Lake Balkhash

Kyzylorda

ral ea

UZBEKISTAN

TASHKENT

BISHKEK

Almaty

Tien Shan

Urumqi

Altai Mountains

MONGOLIA

Gobi

ULAN BATOR

Harbin

Jilin

Vladivostok

Hokkaido

Sapporo

KYRGYZSTAN

RKMENISTAN

DUSHANBE

TAJIKISTAN

Takla Makan Desert

Inner Mongolia

NORTH KOREA

Sea of Japan (East Sea)

JAPAN

SGABAT

ashhad

KABUL

AFGHANISTAN

ISLAMABAD

Kunlun Mountains

(administered by China, claimed by India)

Plateau of Tibet

CHINA

Yellow River

BEIJING

Dalian

PYONGYANG

SEOUL

Qingdao

SOUTH KOREA

Busan

Lanzhou

Xi'an

Yellow Sea

Hiroshima

Osaka

TOKYO

Honshu

Kandahar

Lahore

Himalayas

Brahmaputra

Mount Everest 8848m (29,029ft)

Chengdu

Chongqing

Yangtze

Nanjing

Shanghai

Wuhan

East China Sea

PAKISTAN

Delhi

NEPAL

KATHMANDU

Ganges

BHUTAN

THIMPHU

Salween

Mekong

Guiyang

Ryukyu Islands

Thar Desert

Indus

NEW DELHI

Varanasi

BANGLADESH

DHAKA

BURMA (MYANMAR)

Kunming

Fuzhou

TAIPEI

TAIWAN

Karachi

Bhopal

NAY PYI TAW

Guangzhou

Kaohsiung

USCAT

Ahmadabad

Nagpur

INDIA

Kolkata (Calcutta)

HANOI

Hong Kong (Xianggang)

Hainan Dao

Arabian Sea

Mumbai (Bombay)

Hyderabad

Godavari

Bay of Bengal

Rangoon

LAOS

VIENTIANE

VIETNAM

Luzon

Philippine Sea

Bangalore

Chennai (Madras)

Andaman Islands (to India)

THAILAND

BANGKOK

CAMBODIA

MANILA

PHILIPPINES

Legazpi City

South China Sea

INDIAN OCEAN

Cochin

Nicobar Islands (to India)

PHNOM PENH

Ho Chi Minh City

Cebu

Davao

COLOMBO

SRI LANKA

Mindanao

MALE

MALDIVES

MALAYSIA

BANDAR SERI BEGAWAN

BRUNEI

Medan

KUALA LUMPUR

Manado

PUTRAJAYA

SINGAPORE

SINGAPORE

Balikpapan

Borneo

Celebes

Ambon

Jayapura

Sumatra

Palembang

I N D O N E S I A

New Guinea

JAKARTA

Semarang

Makassar

Flores Sea

Java

Malang

DILI

EAST TIMOR

Timor

Timor Sea

AUSTRALASIA & OCEANIA

N

0 km   1000
0 miles   1000

▲ DUBAI is the biggest city in the United Arab Emirates (UAE). Most of it has been built in the last 40 years.

A belt of thousands of islands stretches from southeast Asia to Australia. There are more than 13,500 islands in Indonesia alone.

Life in Asia

Asia contains just about everything – great wealth and extreme poverty, modern ways and ancient traditions, empty deserts and overcrowded cities, small-scale farming and high-tech industry.

TAKE A PICTURE

These limestone pinnacles near Yangshou in China were formed by rainwater, which has gradually worn away all the surrounding rock.

TAKE A PICTURE

Mount Fuji is a volcano near Tokyo in Japan. The Japanese consider it a sacred mountain and it often appears in Japanese paintings.

TOURISM

Asia's most-visited tourist attractions are the Great Wall of China and the Taj Mahal in India. There are more modern attractions in Dubai, famous for its shops and nightlife, and home to the world's tallest hotel.

▼ MUMBAI *is the biggest city in India. It is the country's business centre and home to the Bollywood film industry.*

OIL

About 80 per cent of the world's easily accessible oil is in the Middle East, and money from oil has made some of the countries in this region extremely rich.

MANUFACTURING

From clothes to cars, lots of the goods sold in western countries are made in Asia. Many companies have factories in Asia because it is cheaper to employ workers there than in the west.

MUSIC AND DANCE

This girl is performing a classical Indian dance. These are often inspired by traditional Hindu stories and poems. The dancer's moves and hand gestures tell the story.

FOOD

Rice is the staple (main) food for many people in Asia. It is served with many Chinese, Thai, and Indian dishes, such as curry or stir-fried foods.

ANCIENT AND MODERN

There are huge differences in people's lifestyles around the continent. Many Asians live in big modern cities such as Tokyo and Beijing. But in other areas, people such as the Bedouin are living much as their ancestors did hundreds of years ago. Many Bedouin still live in tents and move from place to place.

In parts of Mongolia, nomadic farmers live in traditional felt tents, called yurts.

In Japan, many people live in modern blocks of flats.

WILDLIFE

Tigers are only found in eastern and southern Asia. The tiger is now an endangered animal, because large areas of its habitat have been destroyed and it is often hunted for its skin.

TECHNOLOGY

Japan is a world leader in manufacturing televisions, music players, game consoles, cameras, and other electronics. India is one of the world's largest exporters of software and other computer services.

FARMING

About half of all Asians make their living from farming, and rice is the continent's biggest crop. It has to be grown in wet conditions, often in a flooded paddy field.

DID YOU KNOW? FASCINATING FACTS

1 The Himalayas contain 14 peaks that are over 8,000m (26,000 ft) high – there are no other mountains this high elsewhere in the world.

2 Asia was the birthplace of all the world's major religions, including Judaism, Christianity, Islam, Hinduism, and Buddhism.

3 The world's deepest lake is Lake Baikal in Russia, at 1,637 m (5,371 ft). It contains more water than the five North American Great Lakes.

4 Japan is home to 10 per cent of all the active volcanoes in the world. It has about 40 active volcanoes, while another 148 are dormant.

5 The Indian railway system is one of the world's largest employers, with more than 1.6 million members of staff.

Australasia and Oceania

The region known as Australasia includes the countries of Australia, New Zealand, and Papua New Guinea. Australia is so big that it is a continent in its own right. To the east lie thousands of tiny Pacific Islands, known as Oceania.

FACTS ABOUT THE REGION

- **Covers** approximately 6 per cent of Earth's land area
- **Number of countries** 14 independent countries and 16 dependencies
- **Biggest country** Australia, which is also a continent
- **Languages** there are 25 official languages in the region
- **Population of the region** estimated at around 30 million
- **Largest city** 4.3 million people live in Sydney, Australia
- **Highest point** Mt Wilhelm in Papua New Guinea is 4,509 m (14,793 ft) high
- **Longest river** the Murray-Darling in Australia is 3,750 km (2,330 miles) long
- **Biggest lake** Lake Eyre in Australia

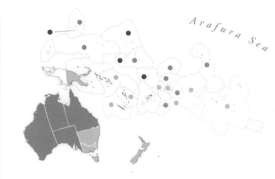

Population density
People per km² (0.39mi²)

- below 50
- 50-90
- 100-149
- 150-199
- 200-299
- above 300

How many people?

About 30 million people live in Australasia and Oceania. This is just 0.5 per cent of the total world population. The vast majority of people live in Australia, which has a population of 21 million.

THE OUTBACK

Away from the coasts, Australia is mostly a hot, dry, desert-like plain, known as the outback. Very few people live there, but it is home to many animals, including kangaroos, dingoes, wombats, and emus, and to huge sheep and cattle farms.

▼ ULURU *or Ayers Rock, is a large outcrop of sandstone rock in the centre of Australia. Local Aboriginal people consider it a sacred site.*

Philippine Sea

NGERULMUD
Babeldaob ■
PALAU

Arafura Sea

ASIA

Arafura

INDIAN OCEAN

Timor Sea

Darwin

Arnhem Land

Broome

NORTHERN TERRIT

Great Sandy Desert

Alice Spr

WESTERN AUSTRALIA

AUST

Geraldton

Great Victoria Desert

SOUTH AUSTRA

Kalgoorlie

Nullarbor Plain

Perth

N

Albany

Great Australian Bight

0 km   1000
0 miles   1000

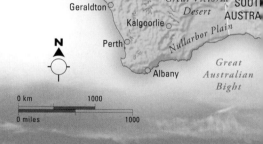

PACIFIC OCEAN

Huahine Tahiti, Polynesia

MICRONESIA *means "small islands". The islands in this group are coral reefs or atolls.*

The Pacific Islands

The thousands of islands scattered across the Pacific are divided into three main groups: Melanesia, Micronesia, and Polynesia. Some of these islands were formed by underwater volcanoes, others are the tips of circular coral reefs, called atolls.

FAMOUS PLACES

- The Great Barrier Reef, off Australia's north-east coast, is the world's largest coral reef (👁 p76). It has built up over thousands of years.
- The town of Rotorua on New Zealand's North Island is famous for its geysers and bubbling pools of hot mud, caused by volcanic activity under the ground.

POLYNESIA *means "many islands" – there are more than 1,000 of them.*

Map labels:

Northern Mariana Islands (to US) · Mariana Islands · Saipan · Guam (to US) · HAGÅTÑA · Micronesia · Caroline Islands · Chuuk · Pohnpei · PALIKIR · Kosrae · MICRONESIA · Melanesia · MARSHALL ISLANDS · Bikini Atoll · Ralik Chain · Ratak Chain · Tarawa · NAURU · Tunga-'u · KIRIBATI · KIRIBATI · TUVALU · FONGAFALE · Tokelau (to NZ) · KIRIBATI · Kiritimati · Line Islands · Penrhyn · Northern Cook Islands · Millennium Island · Marquesas Islands

PAPUA NEW GUINEA · New Guinea · Rabaul · Madang · Mount Wilhelm 4509m (14,793ft) · Lae · New Britain · Solomon Islands · Solomon Sea · HONIARA · Guadalcanal · PORT MORESBY · Torres Strait · SOLOMON ISLANDS · VANUATU · Banks Islands · PORT-VILA · New Caledonia (to France) · Îles Loyauté · NOUMÉA · Vanua Levu · Wallis & Futuna (to France) · SAMOA · APIA · American Samoa (to US) · PAGO PAGO · Cook Islands (to NZ) · Society Islands · PAPEETE · Tahiti · Tuamotu Islands · Viti Levu · SUVA · TONGA · Niue (to NZ) · Southern Cook Islands · AVARUA · Rarotonga · French Polynesia (to France) · Îles Gambier · Pitcairn Islands (to UK) · FIJI · NUKU'ALOFA · Polynesia

PACIFIC OCEAN

Gulf of Carpentaria · Cairns · Great Barrier Reef · Coral Sea · Mount Isa · Townsville · Great Dividing Range · Rockhampton · QUEENSLAND · Brisbane · AUSTRALIA · Lake Eyre North · NEW SOUTH WALES · Newcastle · Darling · Murray · Port Augusta · CANBERRA · AUSTRALIAN CAPITAL TERRITORY · Sydney · Adelaide · VICTORIA · Geelong · Melbourne · Bass Strait · Tasmania · TASMANIA · Hobart

Tasman Sea · Auckland · Hamilton · North Island · WELLINGTON · Cook Strait · South Island · Southern Alps · Christchurch · Dunedin · NEW ZEALAND · Stewart Island

▶ THE ABORIGINAL PEOPLE *were the first inhabitants of Australia. Today in outback communities the traditions are handed on.*

NEW ZEALAND *is one of the most isolated countries in the world. It is about 2,000 km (1,250 miles) away from its nearest neighbour, Australia.*

▶ WILDLIFE
Kangaroos live in the bush, surviving on grasses. They are most active in the early morning and evening, when it is cooler.

▶ DINGOES *are wild dogs. They come from domestic dogs that people brought to Australia.*

Life in Australasia and Oceania

This region was one of the last parts of the world to be settled by people. The Maori, for example, arrived in New Zealand only a thousand years ago. The region is still sparsely populated, with an average of just 4 people per square kilometre (10 per square mile).

▲ KOALA *These marsupials rarely drink, obtaining moisture from the leaves they eat.*

WILDLIFE

The region's unique wildlife includes marsupials (pouched mammals) such as kangaroos and koalas, and flightless birds such as emus and kiwis.

Kiwi

TAKE A PICTURE

The Great Barrier Reef is home to more than 1,500 species of fish and 400 species of coral, as well as thousands of plants.

TAKE A PICTURE

New Zealand's southwest coast is punctured by many long, narrow inlets, known as fjords. The most famous is Milford Sound.

▼ SYDNEY *Australia's biggest city is built around a large harbour. The Harbour Bridge is one of the country's most famous landmarks.*

MUSIC

This traditional Australian wind instrument, called a didgeridoo, is made from a hollow tree trunk. It makes a droning sound.

▲ DIDGERIDOOS *are traditionally made from Eucalyptus trees.*

SPORT

The most popular spectator sports in Australia and New Zealand are cricket and rugby. New Zealand is also famous for extreme sports, such as bungee jumping, white water rafting, and snowboarding.

▲ ALL BLACKS *The New Zealand rugby team is known as the All Blacks. They perform a fierce Maori dance, called a "haka", before each match.*

TOURISM

Many people visit Australasia to take part in outdoor activities, such as snorkelling on the Barrier Reef, surfing and windsurfing off Australia's beaches, and trekking in New Zealand.

FARMING

Sheep farming is important in both Australia and New Zealand – in fact, there are about five times as many sheep as people in Australia. Wool and meat are among the countries' biggest exports.

DID YOU KNOW? FASCINATING FACTS

1 Australia is the flattest of all the continents. Its highest point, Mount Kosciuszko, is only 2,228 metres (7,310 ft) high – just a quarter of the height of Mount Everest.

2 No one knows exactly how many islands there are in the Pacific Ocean. Estimates vary from 20,000 to 30,000.

3 New Zealand is the home of bungee jumping. One of the pioneers of this extreme sport was a New Zealander called A J Hackett, who demonstrated it in 1987 by bungee jumping off the Eiffel Tower in Paris, France.

4 One of the world's most deadly spiders, the Sydney funnel-web, lives in Australia. Its bite could kill you, but luckily an anti-venom was invented in the 1980s, so there is a cure as long as you get to hospital quickly.

5 About 820 different languages are spoken in Papua New Guinea.

▼ PAPUA NEW GUINEA *tribesmen during a festival.*

World Flags

Every country in the world has its own flag. Countries use flags to highlight their identity.

CONTINENTS OF THE WORLD

NORTH AND SOUTH AMERICA

 Antigua & Barbuda

 Argentina

 Bahamas

 Barbados

 Belize

 Bolivia

 Brazil

 Canada

 Grenada

 Guatemala

 Guyana

 Haiti

 Honduras

 Jamaica

 Mexico

Nicaragua

 United States of America

 Uruguay

 Venezuela

AFRICA

 Algeria

 Angola

 Benin

 Botswana

Burkina Faso

 Djibouti

 Egypt

 Equatorial Guinea

 Eritrea

 Ethiopia

 Gabon

The Gambia

 Ghana

 Malawi

 Mali

 Mauritania

 Morocco

 Mozambique

 Namibia

 Niger

 Nigeria

EUROPE

 Swaziland

 Tanzania

 Togo

 Tunisia

 Uganda

 Zambia

 Zimbabwe

Albania

 Denmark

Estonia

Finland

France

Germany

Greece

Hungary

Iceland

 Malta

 Moldova

Monaco

 Montenegro

The Netherlands

 Norway

Poland

 Portugal

Romania

RUSSIA AND CENTRAL ASIA

 Vatican City

Armenia

 Azerbaijan

 Georgia

Kazakhstan

 Kyrgyzstan

Russian Federation

 Tajikistan

 Cambodia

 China

 East Timor

India

Indonesia

 Iran

 Iraq

 Israel

 Mongolia

 Nepal

 North Korea

 Oman

 Pakistan

 Philippines

Qatar

 Turkey

 Saudi Arabia

AUSTRALIA AND THE PACIFIC

Vietnam

Yemen

Australia

 Fiji

Kiribati

 Marshall Islands

Micronesia

 Nauru

■ **Religion:** the flags of many European countries feature the Christian cross; the flags of many Islamic countries are based around the four traditional Arab colours – red, white, green, and black.

■ **Regions:** some countries that are made up of different regions show this in their flags. The crosses of St George, St Patrick, and St Andrew in the UK flag represent England, Ireland, and Scotland respectively.

■ **Tricolours:** many flags consist of three coloured vertical stripes, known as a tricolour. These flags are inspired by the red, white, and blue French flag, adopted during the French Revolution.

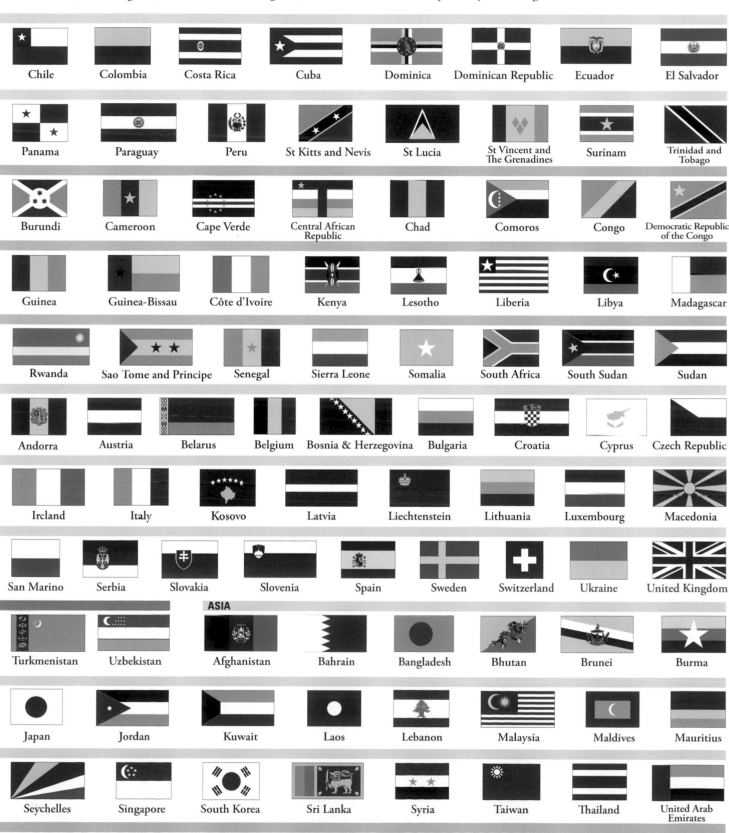

Chile · Colombia · Costa Rica · Cuba · Dominica · Dominican Republic · Ecuador · El Salvador

Panama · Paraguay · Peru · St Kitts and Nevis · St Lucia · St Vincent and The Grenadines · Surinam · Trinidad and Tobago

Burundi · Cameroon · Cape Verde · Central African Republic · Chad · Comoros · Congo · Democratic Republic of the Congo

Guinea · Guinea-Bissau · Côte d'Ivoire · Kenya · Lesotho · Liberia · Libya · Madagascar

Rwanda · Sao Tome and Principe · Senegal · Sierra Leone · Somalia · South Africa · South Sudan · Sudan

Andorra · Austria · Belarus · Belgium · Bosnia & Herzegovina · Bulgaria · Croatia · Cyprus · Czech Republic

Ireland · Italy · Kosovo · Latvia · Liechtenstein · Lithuania · Luxembourg · Macedonia

San Marino · Serbia · Slovakia · Slovenia · Spain · Sweden · Switzerland · Ukraine · United Kingdom

ASIA

Turkmenistan · Uzbekistan · Afghanistan · Bahrain · Bangladesh · Bhutan · Brunei · Burma

Japan · Jordan · Kuwait · Laos · Lebanon · Malaysia · Maldives · Mauritius

Seychelles · Singapore · South Korea · Sri Lanka · Syria · Taiwan · Thailand · United Arab Emirates

New Zealand · Palau · Papua New Guinea · Samoa · Solomon Islands · Tonga · Tuvalu · Vanuatu

CULTURE

- The world's most popular religion, Christianity, has more than 2.1 billion followers.

- The Lascaux cave paintings in France have survived more than 30,000 years.

- The most expensive painting sold to date was bought in 2011 for $250 million.

- While 230 different languages are spoken across Europe, in Asia there are 2,197.

- Classical composer Mozart started writing music when he was just 5 years old.

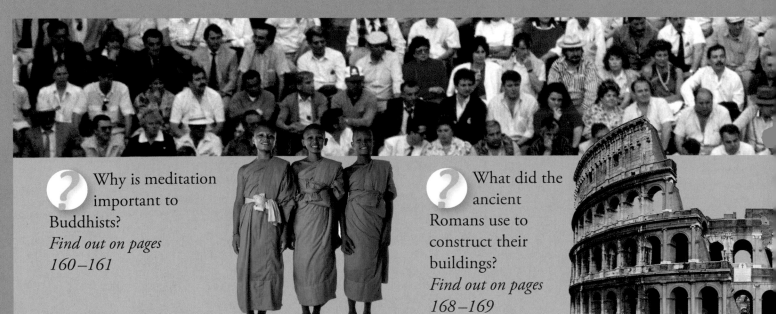

? Why is meditation important to Buddhists? *Find out on pages 160–161*

? What did the ancient Romans use to construct their buildings? *Find out on pages 168–169*

Definition: What makes one group of people different to another? Whether it's their religious beliefs or the music they listen to, **culture** reflects the way in which people live.

- The first Hollywood film studio was set up in an old tavern in 1911.

- The world's oldest dance form is bellydancing.

- The idea of writing and performing plays started in ancient Greece…

- … as did the original Olympic Games, in 776 BCE.

- The Olympic motto is *Citius, Altius, Fortius*. It means "Swifter, Higher, Stronger".

When and where did salsa dancing first appear? *Find out on pages 176–177*

How many musicians are there in an orchestra? *Find out on pages 174–175*

World religions

A religion is a set of beliefs that explain where the world came from, what happens after death, and how we should live our lives. Religious people come together to worship and take part in festivals. They believe in an unseen, spiritual world that cannot be explained by science.

Abrahamic religions
Judaism, Islam, and Christianity are part of the same "family" of religions, known as the Abrahamic religions. All three consider Abraham as one of the forefathers of their faith. Islam and Christianity have been spread throughout the world by immigrants and missionaries.

▲ THE ABRAHAM ICON *in the Church of the Holy Sepulchre, Jerusalem.*

The six religions with the most followers in the world are:

Christianity

Islam

JUDAISM

Judaism emerged more than 3,500 years ago in the Middle East, among a tribe called the Israelites. Jews believe that there is only one God, who created the world and continues to care for it.

▶ *MENORAH The candles on this nine-branched holder are lit during* Chanukah, *the Jewish festival of light. The central candle is used to light the eight outer candles – one for each day of* Chanukah.

▼ THE *KIPPA*
Some Jewish men wear a skullcap – called a kippa *– to show their respect for God.*

▲ THE *TORAH is the sacred text that Jews believe God dictated to Moses on Mount Sinai. It includes the Ten Commandments, which show the Jewish people the right way to live. Together with other sacred texts it makes up the Tanakh.*

TAKE A LOOK: PASSOVER

▲ SEDER
This is a special meal in which symbolic foods are placed on a special platter in the middle of the table, including bitter herbs to signify suffering and an egg to represent rebirth.

Passover is a festival that celebrates the release of the Israelites from Egypt, where they were held in slavery. Jews believe that God sent ten plagues against the Egyptians, the last of which killed all first-born children and animals. The Israelites marked their houses with lamb's blood and God "passed over" without harming them. After this, the Pharaoh released the Israelites.

CHRISTIANITY

Christians believe that Jesus Christ, a Jewish holy man born in Bethlehem, around 0 CE, was God in human form. According to Christian tradition he was put to death by the authorities, but returned to life three days later. The Christian Bible is made up of the Jewish Tanakh – the Old Testament – and a new set of scriptures – the New Testament.

◄ THE CHALICE
Holy Communion is a Christian ritual in which bread is eaten and wine is drunk to remember Jesus' sacrifice. The wine may be served in a chalice.

▲ THE SUPPER AT EMMAUS
This stained glass window shows Jesus, having risen from the dead, sharing a meal with two disciples.

Catholicism There are many different branches of Christianity, the largest of which is Roman Catholicism. The leader of the Roman Catholic Church is the Pope. Catholics believe that the Pope is the successor to Saint Peter, who Jesus appointed as the first head of the Church.

▲ THE CROSS
Jesus Christ died on a cross. Christians believe that because of this sacrifice, his followers will have eternal life with God in heaven.

Saints are people who lived especially holy lives. Some saints are linked with specific countries or causes. For example, Saint Andrew is the patron saint of Russia and Scotland.

 Hinduism **Buddhism**  **Sikhism** **Judaism**

ISLAM

Islam was founded in Arabia in the 7th century CE by the prophet Muhammad. Muslims believe in one God, Allah, who sent 25 prophets down to Earth, the last one being Muhammad. Earlier prophets included Abraham, Moses, and Jesus.

The *Qur'an* Allah's teachings, as dictated to Muhammad, were recorded in a book called the *Qur'an*. Muslims try to live by rules set down in the *Qur'an*. The most important duties are known as the Five Pillars:
- praying five times a day
- giving to the needy
- fasting during *Ramadan*
- making a pilgrimage to Mecca
- proclaiming your beliefs

Ramadan is the ninth month of the Islamic calendar, during which the *Qur'an* was revealed to Muhammad. Throughout *Ramadan* Muslims neither eat nor drink between dawn and sunset. This helps them to understand poverty, and to focus their minds on prayer and reading the *Qur'an*. *Ramadan* ends with *Eid ul-Fitr*, the Fast-Breaking Festival. Believers visit the mosque and eat traditional foods with family.

► MECCA, *in Saudi Arabia, is the most holy city in Islam, and the birthplace of Muhammad. Muslims must face Mecca whenever they pray, wherever they are in the world.*

159

Religions such as Hinduism, Buddhism, and Jainism have their roots in South and East Asia. However, during the 20th century they spread across the world as a result of migration, and today they are practised in both East and West. In many parts of the world smaller, traditional religions are still practised alongside larger, world religions.

HINDUISM

Hinduism originated in India in about 2,500 BCE. Hindus believe that souls are born again after death, and that good or bad deeds in this life result in a good or bad rebirth. The greatest goal of Hinduism is to find perfect peace and liberation by escaping the cycle of rebirth.

▲ WORSHIP
Hindus believe in a multitude of gods, each with a different role. Elephant-headed Ganesh (above) is identified with wisdom. But most Hindus single out one God, such as Vishnu or Shiva, as creator and saviour of the world.

▲ THE SACRED COW *is greatly revered by Hindus. Killing cows is banned in India, and cows are allowed to wander wherever they like, even through busy traffic.*

▲ *DIWALI*
Diwali *is the Hindu festival of lights. It marks the beginning of the Hindu new year. Families light oil lamps to invite Lakshmi, the goddess of wealth and purity, into their homes.*

SIKHISM

Sikhism was founded in the 15th century by Guru Nanak, in what is now Pakistan. Sikhs believe in one all-powerful God, who is best understood through meditation. The holy book of the Sikhs is the *Guru Granth Sahib*, which is the teachings of the first leaders of the Sikh faith, the ten Gurus.

▶ THE WORD OF GOD
This Indian Sikh man is working on a hand-written version of the Guru Granth Sahib. This holy book is treated with utmost respect: it is placed on a throne, and a sacred whisk is waved over it as it is read.

◀ THE GOLDEN TEMPLE
in Amritsar, Punjab, India is the most important holy place of the Sikh religion.

▼ THE FIVE Ks
Followers of Sikhism outwardly show their devotion by keeping five symbolic objects starting with the letter K.

- Kesh *(uncut hair). Sikhs do not cut their hair, and allow their beards to grow.*
- Kara *(a steel bracelet)*
- Kanga *(a wooden comb)*
- Kacch *(a cotton undergarment)*
- Kirpan *(a steel dagger)*

BUDDHISM

Buddhism was founded in India in about 500 BCE. Buddhists do not worship a god, but instead follow the teachings of a man called the Buddha, who realised the true nature of reality. Like Hindus, Buddhists believe in rebirth. The Buddha showed his followers how to escape rebirth and suffering through good deeds and meditation.

▼ BUDDHA STATUES
Statues of the Buddha often show him meditating in a cross-legged position. The Big Buddha on the island of Koh Samaui, Thailand, was built in 1972 and is 15 metres tall. It can be seen from several kilometres away.

▲ PRAYER WHEELS
Tibetan Buddhists use prayer wheels printed with mantras, *which are verses that bring about spiritual understanding. As the wheel is turned, the* mantra *repeats itself over and over again.*

▲ BUDDHIST TEMPLES
Buddhist temples are home to monks and nuns who have chosen to follow a life of good deeds and meditation. The temples are designed to symbolize the five elements: earth, air, fire, water, and wisdom, which is respresented by the pinnacle at the top.

Traditional religions

SHAMANISM

Shamanism is the ancient, widespread belief that an invisible world of good and evil spirits exists all around us. Specially trained people called shamans can perform rituals which allow them to communicate with the spirit world. The Chukchi people of Eastern Siberia, for example, have shamans in their community who use drums to contact the spirit world.

CONFUCIANISM

Confucius was a Chinese philosopher (551–479 BCE) who stressed the importance of respecting elders, acting dutifully towards the family and state, and honouring ancestors. His writings include the *I Ching*, which is used for telling the future.

ABORIGINAL RELIGION

Australian Aborigines traditionally believe that the land, the sea, animals and plants were created by ancestor spirits. These spirits, which live in a hidden world called the Dreamtime or the Dreaming, continue to give life to our world. Stories and songs about the Dreamtime have been passed down from generation to generation for thousands of years.

Celebrations

Celebrations are an incredibly important part of religious, public, and family life. They bring people together, give people something to look forward to, and are generally a time for enjoying oneself.

■ Family is an important part of human life, and families all over the world get together to celebrate events such as new babies, birthdays, or weddings.

TELL ME MORE...

Chinese calendar In the Chinese calendar, each year is named after one of the 12 animals of the Chinese zodiac: rat, ox, tiger, rabbit, dragon, snake, horse, goat, monkey, rooster, dog, or pig.

LENT

■ Lent is a Christian festival that lasts 40 days and 40 nights and leads up to Easter. Traditionally it is a time for fasting and praying as they remember the 40 days Jesus spent in the wilderness.

CHINESE NEW YEAR

■ **Where** China and Chinese communities across the world.
■ **When** It begins with the new moon on the first day of the new year, which falls in January-February, and ends on the full moon 15 days later.
■ **What happens** Everyone hangs lanterns in their windows and dragon dances are performed in the streets. Families celebrate with a special meal and honour their ancestors. Red clothes are worn, which represent happiness.
■ **What it's celebrating** New beginnings and the sowing of new crops.

DIWALI

■ **Where** India, and celebrated by Hindus all over the world.
■ **When** Within the months of Asvina and Kartika (October/November).
■ **What happens** Diwali is the Festival of Lights. People light small lamps (diyas) and put them around their houses and gardens. They give each other gifts of sweets and let off fireworks.
■ **What it's celebrating** The return of Lord Ram from exile and his crowning as king. According to legend people lit lamps to light his way in the darkness. The lights also show the "inner light" or soul within a person.

RIO CARNIVAL

■ **Where** Rio de Janeiro, Brazil
■ **When** Carnival goes on for four nights in February, just before the beginning of Lent.
■ **What happens** Everyone takes to the streets in carnival clothes, they dance or ride on huge floats. The highlights of the carnival are a competition between samba schools and parading in amazing costumes in the sambadrome.
■ **What it's celebrating** Pre-Lent fun

FASNACHT (CARNIVAL)

■ **Where** Austria, Germany, Alsace (France), and parts of Switzerland.

■ **When** The day before Ash Wednesday — the last Tuesday before Lent.

■ **What happens** Families gather together for a feast and many areas have processions to welcome in the springtime. Honoured members of a town dress up as the carnival prince and peasant. Everyone else dresses up in anything from clown costumes to witches or even fruit!

■ **What it's celebrating** It's a time of celebration before the self-denial of Lent. It also goes back to pre-Christian times when it was a way to drive out the evil spirits of winter and encourage spring and good crops.

DAY OF THE DEAD

■ **Where** Mexico

■ **When** 1st and 2nd November

■ **What happens** People build altars in their homes, covered with photos and possessions of their dead relatives to guide the loved one home.

■ **What it's celebrating** Relatives who have died, but still live on in the memory. People believe that on the Day of the Dead it is easier for souls of the departed to visit the living.

WINTER CARNIVAL QUEBEC

■ **Where** Quebec City, Canada

■ **When** Last weekend of January until mid February.

■ **What happens** It's the largest winter carnival in the world. People get together to enjoy night parades, concerts, dogsled rides, and snow sculpture competitions.

■ **What it's celebrating** It's a rowdy get-together to eat, drink, and have fun before Lent begins.

THANKSGIVING

■ **Where** USA

■ **When** 4th Thursday of November

■ **What happens** Families gather together for a feast and traditionally eat turkey, stuffing, and pumpkin pie.

■ **What it's celebrating** Thanksgiving Day is a holiday in the USA. People celebrate the successful harvest early European settlers of the country experienced in 1621. The settlers were taught by Native American Indians to share of the natural abundance of the Earth by caring for crops, hunting, and fishing.

▲ FIRST THANKSGIVING *The Indians joining in the feast with New England pilgrims.*

CHRISTMAS

■ **Where** North America, Europe, Australasia and by Christians around the world.

■ **When** 25th December

■ **What happens** Families get together to go to church, give each other presents, and to eat traditional foods such as roast turkey, and panettone.

■ **What it's celebrating** The birth of Jesus Christ.

Panettone

HALLOWEEN

■ **Where** USA, Canada, and across Europe.

■ **When** 31st October

■ **What happens** Children go "trick or treating" often dressed up as witches or skeletons. People carve faces in pumpkins and light a candle in them.

■ **What it's celebrating** Halloween was based on pagan customs when Celtic people lit bonfires before winter, but it has come to mean the evening before the Christian festival of All Saints Day.

World art

Art tells us an enormous amount about the history and culture of people. We can tell what people did in everyday life and what they wore through their art. We can learn about their religious beliefs, their sports, and their skills.

📷 **TAKE A PICTURE**

Australian aboriginal art dates back many thousands of years, and contemporary pieces are popular. The art is connected to the sacred belief in Dreamtime. The painting above is a modern mural on an urban wall.

ANCIENT ART

A huge amount of art has been found in tombs of the Pharaohs that were built in ancient Egypt. They give us an incredible window into how people lived up to 4,000 years ago.

The art of the Aztecs

In the 15th century the Aztecs created a short-lived empire that was destroyed soon after the Spanish invasion of 1519. They produced jewellery in gold, jade, and turquoise, as well as ceramics and textiles with angular, geometric patterns.

Cave galleries

A series of famous Palaeolithic paintings in the Altamira cave near Santillana del Mar, northern Spain were developed over some 20,000 years, as descendents added to them.

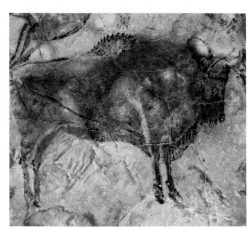

Terracotta army

In 1974, one of the most extraordinary pieces of art ever found was discovered by farmers. It was a huge army of Chinese warriors made out of terracotta pottery. In time, archaeologists found more than 8,000 life-size statues guarding the tomb of the first emperor of China, Qin Shi Huang, who ruled from 221–210 BCE. Some of the warriors even have horses.

▶ ANCIENT SCULPTURE
Ancient Greek sculpture heavily influenced Roman art. This Roman marble sculpture, The Disc Thrower, was based on an original Greek bronze sculpture.

◀ AFRICAN SCULPTURE
African art covers a wealth of styles and techniques used by the many different cultures. Sculptures of the human figure vary across the continent.

Art imitating life

The ancient Greeks were interested in ideals – statues that showed a perfect body. The ancient Romans were influenced by Greek art, but they were more interested in portraiture: statues that looked like a particular person, especially someone famous. They believed that having a good image of somebody's face kept its ghost happy.

Sculpture

Sculpture has been around since prehistoric people carved shapes into rock. While early peoples sculpted religious decorations and icons, the ancient Greeks made life-like statues.

Religious art

Many pieces of art depict religious scenes. They might present religious figures from history, or religious symbols and traditions. The artists often used gold leaf (thin sheets of gold) and rich reds.

RUSSIAN ICONS
Icons are images or representations of a religious figure. They are mainly painted in the symbolic style of Byzantine art.

SOUTH ASIAN ART
Thangkas *(embroidered banners)* and mandalas *(diagrams) are often used for meditation. They have detailed patterns to convey spiritual ideas.*

TAKE A LOOK: COLOURS FROM NATURE

Before we could buy paints, people had to make colours from nature. They often used crushed rocks, minerals, plants, or insects. They mixed the powder or juice with egg yolk or animal fat to make paint. Over the centuries, artists have found their perfect colour in all sorts of strange ways.

White – sourced from chalk
Black – sourced from charcoal
Golden Indian yellow – made from the urine of cows that had been fed mango leaves
Deep red – sometimes made from the crushed and dried bodies of female scale insects (*Dactylopius coccus*)
Green – made from the juice of parsley flowers
Brown – made from the inner bark of the oak tree (*Quercus tinctoria*)
Dark violet – made from crushed elderberries
Dark brown – created from the ink of a small squid called a cuttlefish (*sepia officinalis*)

Modern art

Four Ballerinas on the Stage
by Edgar Degas

Modern art is difficult to describe because these days "anything goes", from a beautiful oil painting to wrapping a building up in fabric or making a picture out of elephant dung. Some specific styles have emerged and many of these were controversial at the time.

IMPRESSIONISM

In the 1870s, a group of artists broke away from painting religious or historical subjects and instead painted everyday scenes in a new style. These impressionists often painted outdoors, aiming to capture the impression of light and create a snapshot of real life. The group included Édouard Manet, Claude Monet, and Edgar Degas.

◀ THE TECHNIQUE
Short brushstrokes of pure colour produced a sketchy, patchy, spontaneous painting that suggests a fleeting moment in time.

POINTILLISM Georges Seurat invented a technique called pointillism. He used tiny dots of pure colour which, when standing back, seem to merge to make new colours. This is known as optical mixing.

◀ THE TECHNIQUE *From a distance, this lady's hat looks red. But it is actually made up of red, green, yellow, and blue dots.*

Sunday Afternoon on the Island of La Grande Jatte
by Georges Seurat

TIMELINE OF MODERN ART

1860s–1890s	1880s–1905	1880s	1880s–1890	1907–1920s
Impressionism began in France when artists tried to capture a fleeting moment. 	Post impressionist artists, including Paul Gauguin, Paul Cézanne, and Vincent Van Gogh, painted vibrant, bold, and often personal pictures.	Pointillism is a form of art where paintings are made up of dots of colour.	The work of Expressionist artists including Edvard Munch conveyed people's feelings, such as joy or sorrow.	Cubism is a form of art that shows several different views of an object at once.

166

CUBISM

Pablo Picasso, one of the most famous modern artists, experimented with space by breaking pictures up into distorted and weird shapes. *Three Musicians* looks like a muddled-up picture but the instruments the musicians are playing can be seen. This style is called Cubism. It shows a scene from several different points of view all at once.

Three Musicians by Pablo Picasso

POP ART

A new popular culture emerged with television, pop music, and film in the 1950s and 1960s. Pop Art became the new movement and artists made simple, brightly coloured prints of popular images, such as soup cans and film stars, that could be printed again and again.

▲ *In the 60s, Andy Warhol celebrated popular figures with colourful screen-print portraits. This one is Marilyn Monroe – he produced similar images of Elizabeth Taylor, Elvis Presley, and Jackie Kennedy.*

ART TODAY

These days artists are experimenting as much as ever, pushing the boundaries, and finding new techniques. New Media artists use people's possessions, and record people's emotions and reactions using the new digital technologies.

◀ NEW MEDIA *David Hockney has taken many photographs and stuck them together to make a bigger picture.*

▲ INSTALLATIONS *Tracey Emin transported the beach hut where she met her boyfriend to an art gallery.*

1910–1950	1920s	1950s–1960s	1970s–MODERN DAY
Abstract art distorts the shape and colour of subjects. Jackson Pollock made pictures by splashing paint over a canvas on the floor.	Surrealist artists including Salvador Dali and René Magritte began to paint in a dream-like style. This is Magritte's 1964 self-portrait *The Son of Man*.	Pop art uses ideas and images from popular culture, such as food packaging, comics, or famous people.	Modern art experiments with new media. Dressed in suits, Gilbert and George Del used themselves in their art as "living sculptures".

Writing and printing

Imagine a life without books, newspapers, comics, magazines, menus, letters, and emails – it would be a very different place. Writing gives us news, entertains us, and more importantly documents history, and teaches and spreads ideas. Printing allows one person's ideas to be communicated to millions of people at the same time.

ANCIENT WRITING

The earliest form of writing didn't use letters, but pictograms – symbols that each represent a single word or sound. Some of the earliest writings are from Ancient Egypt. Known as hieroglyphics, these pictograms have been traced back 5,000 years. Nearby, in Mesopotamia, people started to keep accounts about taxes and crops using cuneiform script on clay tablets.

▼ *Cuneiform script was carved into wet clay using a blunt reed. Pictograms became simplified into wedge-shaped markings.*

◀ *Hieroglyphics on the Temple of Hathor, Egypt.*

Methods of writing

Modern pens are very different to the original methods of writing, such as reeds for carving clay, or a quill (bird feather) dipped in ink for writing on animal hide. The Romans used lead pencils 2,000 years ago, but the graphite pencils we use today were invented in England in the 1500s. But some traditions remain: Japanese script is still written with a brush and ink.

TAKE A LOOK: WRITTEN LANGUAGE

There are about 6,800 different languages spoken in the world today and many of them have their own letters or characters when written down. Although there are many localized styles of writing in the world, there are five main types that dominate.

▶ CYRILLIC *is used by many Slav people (eastern Europe), such as Russians. It is thought to have evolved from the older Greek script.*

◀ THE ARABIC ALPHABET *just uses consonants, vowels are indicated by signs above or below the consonants. Arabic is read from right to left.*

▲ CHINESE *is one of the oldest written texts in the world. It uses pictograms called characters.*

▲ LATIN *writing evolved about 2,600 years ago. It is the most widely-used alphabet in the world.*

▲ BENGALI *script is syllabic – rather than letters, it has symbols for consonants and vowels.*

PRINTING

The Chinese first invented printing by blocks in the 7th century. A word or whole page was carved onto a wooden block, which was dipped in ink and printed onto cloth. The block could be dipped and printed again and again, but each print had to be done by hand.

▲ BAD MOVE *In 1045, Chinese printer Pi Sheng invented movable type. Each block was carved with a character, and blocks could be rearranged to make new pages. But with thousands of characters, it didn't really work.*

WOW!

Every day, millions of newspapers are printed all over the world. Japanese newspaper The *Yomiuri Shimbun* has the highest circulation in the world, with an estimated 10 million readers each day.

◄ THE GUTENBERG PRESS
Four hundred years after Pi Sheng, in 1455 Johannes Gutenberg of Germany invented the mechanical printing press, which used metal movable type. For the first time in Europe, books could be mass-produced, with the Christian Bible being one of the first.

How do presses work?

Like the earliest hand printing, presses use blocks carved in relief – with reversed, raised letters that print the right way round. Letter blocks, called "type", are set into a frame and covered in ink, and the paper is pressed down on top.

BESTSELLERS

The most popular books in the world are known as bestsellers.

■ The biggest seller of all time is the Christian Bible at an estimated 6 billion copies. It has been translated into 2,000 languages.

■ Mao Zedong's *Quotations from Chairman Mao* sold some 900 million copies.

■ The seven *Harry Potter* books by JK Rowling have sold more than 500 million copies worldwide.

■ *Le Petit Prince (The Little Prince)* by Antoine de Saint-Exupéry has sold more than 80 million copies.

■ Beatrix Potter's *The Tale of Peter Rabbit* has sold 45 million copies worldwide.

Colour printing

How many colours can you see on this page? Technically, there are just four: cyan (C), magenta (M), yellow (Y), and black (K). As the paper runs through the CMYK printing rollers, a certain amount of each coloured ink is printed onto the paper. At the end of the run, the layers of ink have built up to produce thousands of different shades.

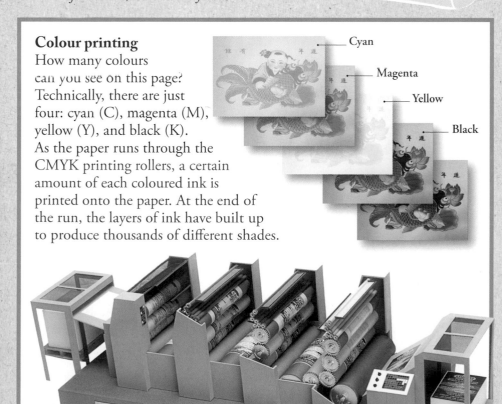

Cyan

Magenta

Yellow

Black

Education

It's an essential part of culture to pass on knowledge to the next generation. In most countries, this knowledge is taught in school. What you learn in the classroom and beyond gives you the skills that you will need for the future. Without education, you would not be able to read this book.

▲ SCHOOL UNIFORM *Many schools around the world have surprisingly similar uniforms. Some schools have unusual extras as part of their uniform – children who live near the Sakurajima volcano in Japan have to wear hardhats to school because the volcano hurls rocks daily onto the nearby town.*

IN SCHOOL

Children have been going to school for thousands of years. Archaeologists discovered a school building in the ancient city of Ur (in modern-day Iraq) – a city that died out 2,500 years ago. School hasn't changed very much since then. Across the world, children still sit together in classes to be taught lessons by a teacher.

TELL ME MORE...

Millions of children around the world cannot go to school. This is especially true in poor parts of the world, where there are places without schools and teachers. Some families can't afford to pay for schooling, so children have to work or are kept at home to help.

TAKE A PICTURE

Pens and books are taken for granted in most schools – but in the developing world, there might not even be one book per class.

A CLASS APART
Not all schools have the same facilities. While computers are used in many British schools, this primary school in Senegal, Africa, has no electricity.

What's on the timetable? Right now, somewhere across the other side of the world, a child is being taught literacy, maths, and sport, just like you. But children from different countries may learn things specific to their culture in their school. For example, some boys in Mongolia attend monastery schools to learn to be Buddhist monks. They also study nature, medicine, and art.

▲ HAKA *Students in New Zealand learn an important traditional Maori dance, the Haka.*

Homeschool Lots of children around the world are taught at home by their parents or tutors. Around 1 million children in America are home-schooled, but in some countries, such as Brazil, Germany, and Hong Kong, it's illegal not to go to a formal school. Hundreds of children in remote, rural parts of Australia live so far away from the nearest school, it is impossible for them to go to class. Instead, they learn through *The School of the Air*, making online or radio contact with a teacher.

▲ SCHOOL OF THE AIR *A pupil is guided through an online lesson at home.*

TAKE A LOOK: TEACHING TRADITIONS

Community education is especially important when it comes to passing

▲ WEAVING *A Marsh Arab mother teaches her girls a skill they will use to make clothes and rugs, and earn money.*

down cultural traditions, and most of this is done outside of school.

▲ HERDING *A Nenet boy spends nine months a year at boarding school, and three months at home learning reindeer herding.*

Always learning Education isn't just about sums and spelling: you learn many other things in school, possibly without even realizing it. When you play sport, you are learning how to stay healthy, how to be part of a team and how to compete. When you study history, geography, and religion, you learn about people and the different ways of life around the world. And when you interact with your classmates and teachers, you learn how to develop relationships.

▲ PLAYING SPORT *These children aren't just learning the rules of football, but also how to stay fit and healthy.*

What happens next? Have you ever thought about what you would like to do once you leave school? Some careers need a degree and professional qualifications, such as architects and lawyers. Practical careers, such as mechanics and hairdressing, might offer apprenticeships – "on the job" training where you work with (and so learn from) someone who is already doing that job.

It doesn't stop here! Education shouldn't finish just because you've reached the end of school. Going to college or university improves your chances of getting a job, and as you get older it's important to keep your brain active to stay healthy. Lots of people attend evening classes to brush up on old skills or learn entirely new ones.

WOW!

One out of every seven people in the world cannot read. If people can't read, write, or do maths, it will affect their whole lives. But education can help people escape poverty: children who go to school get better jobs when they are older, live longer, and are healthier.

Music

Everyone enjoys music in some form, whether they choose to play an instrument, or sing, or simply listen. Music brings people together at all sorts of events.

▲ THE FIRST MUSIC *We know that music has been played and enjoyed for thousands of years because ancient drawings have been found showing musical instruments.*

NOTATION

The most common way to write music today is the five-line notation using dots, symbols, and abbreviations. It is based on a system used by Roman Catholic monks in the 10th century. When you learn a musical instrument, you learn to read music at the same time.

Pitch is how high or low a note sounds. Notes are grouped into sets of eight, known as an octave and written on five lines called a stave.

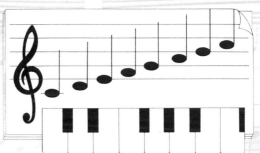

The "clef" shows what notes are on the stave. This is the treble clef.

The "key signature" shows which key the music is in.

The speed of the music, or "tempo", is often written in Italian. "Allegro" means "quickly".

The "rest" shows where the musician should pause.

All music is divided into equal measures, called "bars", each of which has the same number of beats.

The shape of each note tells the musician how long to play it.

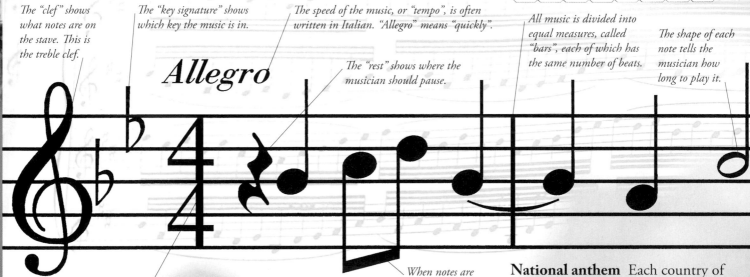

The "time signature" shows the musician the number of beats to a bar.

Dynamic markings indicate how loud to play the music. "mf" means moderately loud.

When notes are next to each other their hooks are sometimes joined together.

National anthem Each country of the world has its own cultural song, called their national anthem. They are often sung at important national occasions, including sporting events.

TELL ME MORE...

When musicians in an orchestra perform together, they need to make sure they play their notes at the right time. The conductor is the organiser of the orchestra who directs using visible gestures.

▶ THE SOUTH AFRICAN *national anthem includes five of the eleven official national languages including Africaans, English, and isiZulu.*

◄ FOLK MUSIC
A country or an indigenous people often have their own style of music and dance, known as folk music.

▲ RELIGIOUS MUSIC
Music is used a lot in religious worship around the world, whether in song, like this Christian choir singer, or using instruments like these Buddhist monks.

MUSIC STYLES

Music changes all the time, reflecting how each new generation feels and reacts to an ever-changing world.

- **Classical music** is a general term for music written to be performed in a concert hall. Often it is composed for an orchestra, for a choir, or for opera.

- **R&B** or rhythm and blues was originally performed by African-Americans in the 1940s. It was a mixture of religious gospel music and blues (slow melancholy songs). R&B has evolved over the decades into soul and funk-influenced pop music.

- **Jazz** originated in the early 20th century in America. It was a blend of African slave music played with European instruments. The saxophone, trumpet, and double bass are three of the key sounds in jazz bands.

- **Rock'n'roll** In the 1940s and 50s in America a whole new sound emerged with bands using electric guitars, bass guitars, and drums. This was known as rock'n'roll.

- **Rock music** emerged in the 1960s and includes lots of different styles from punk rock to heavy metal.

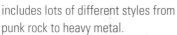

- **Reggae** originated in Jamaica in the 1960s. Reggae has a slow rhythmic style and is often associated with the Rastafarian religion.

- **Country music** is a blend of traditional music from the southern states of America and rock'n'roll. It is one of the biggest-selling styles of music today.

- **Dance** The dawn of the computer age and highly-developed synthesized sound led to a new sound designed to fill dance floors. DJs mixing music using turntables live on the dancefloor have become big stars in themselves.

- **Pop music**, or popular music, is not a particular style of music, but music that is made popular by people buying it, playing it on the radio, or paying to see it performed live. Pop music is designed to sell and do well in pop charts.

SOUND OF THE PEOPLE

A type of music can often be unique to the culture of a nation or people.

- **The didgeridoo**, an Aboriginal instrument from Australia, is considered to be one of the oldest wind instruments in the world. It is often used in Aboriginal ceremonies.

- **The sitar**, a stringed instrument, is the best-known of all Indian sounds. It has extra strings that lie beneath the main strings that vibrate to give it its shimmery sound.

- **The djembe drum** is a goblet-shaped wooden drum covered in a skin that is played by hand. The drum originated in west Africa and is still an important part of the culture in many west African countries. The rhythmic beat is often used in dance.

The orchestra

An orchestra is a collection of about 100 musicians that play different instruments which are grouped into strings, woodwind, brass, and percussion. Each instrument plays a different part to make one piece of music.

WOODWIND

■ Woodwind instruments make sound when air blown into them vibrates. Players can alter the sound by covering holes with their fingers, or pushing down on metal "keys" that cover holes the fingers cannot reach. The clarinet is a woodwind instrument and there are more than 12 types of clarinet, though not all are still in use. The one shown here is a bass clarinet, which produces a deep, mellow sound.

FAMOUS COMPOSER

Antonio Vivaldi (1678–1741) was born and raised in the Republic of Venice. He composed music in the Baroque style. His most well known piece is *The Four Seasons,* in which he tried to capture the atmosphere of each season.

PERCUSSION

■ Percussion instruments are hit, banged, scraped, or shaken. When you bang a percussion instrument, such as a drum, its surface vibrates, making the air inside ring with sound. This sound adds a beat or drama to a piece of music. Cymbals also vibrate to produce sound — they are clashed together in a swinging, brushing movement during the climax in orchestral music.

CONDUCTOR

■ A koy figurc in most orchestras, the conductor directs the musicians using hand and arm gestures.

TAKE A LOOK: SHEET MUSIC

Each member of an orchestra has their music written down in front of them as sheet music. The modern five-line written notation, widespread by the seventeenth century, was developed from a system of dots used by Roman Catholic monks in the tenth century.

▲ EARLY MUSIC NOTATION
This piece of music is the original score for Beethoven's Moonlight Sonata, *finished in 1801.*

BRASS

■ Brass instruments are long tubes that open into a bell shape at one end. To play them, the musician blows into the mouthpiece. Long tubes, such as that on a trombone, sound deep. Shorter tubes, such as that on a horn, sound higher. As well as air, lots of liquid is blown in. This is let out through the spit valve.

STRINGS

■ String instruments are played by plucking or running a bow across the strings. The double bass shown here is the deepest member of the string family. The thickest string produces the lowest note.

Let's perform

Everyone enjoys the spectacle of a show, be it a play, an opera, a film or a dance. What these performing arts have in common is that they communicate between people, and reflect their time and their culture.

DANCE

Everywhere in the world, people love to dance. A dance can be a performance, part of a religious ritual, or something to do for fun. Most dances happen in time to music or a beat.

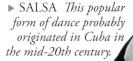

▶ SALSA *This popular form of dance probably originated in Cuba in the mid-20th century.*

Street dance is any dance that people have created for themselves, instead of being formally invented. Types of street dance include break-dancing and tango.

Religious dance *Bharatanatyam* is a Hindu dance performed by women. It is the national dance of India. The steps are incredibly precise – skilled dancers flow from pose to pose with complex movements of the feet, hands, arms, neck, head, and even the eyes!

Ballet requires great strength, skill, and grace, and it involves very specific and formal positions and movements. Classical ballets like *Swan Lake*, and *Giselle* feature only these traditions, while modern ballets (right) are often much freer and more expressive.

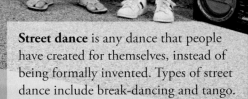

Tribal dance is important in many traditional cultures. Dances are usually performed to the rhythm of drums and there are special dances for all kinds of occasions – weddings, funerals, harvests, hunts, religious ceremonies, and even to prepare for war.

THEATRE

People have been taking to the stage for thousands of years, performing everything from comic and tragic plays to pantomimes, operas, and musicals. The oldest plays were performed in ancient Greece and included song and dance as well as acting. Some of their outdoor theatres still stand today.

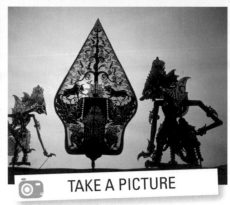

📷 **TAKE A PICTURE**

Shadow plays use puppets and clever lighting behind a fabric screen. The traditional shadow theatre of Indonesia, Wayang Kulit, is thought to be more than 800 years old.

◄ THE LION KING *is a musical play based on the animated feature film by Walt Disney.*

MOVING PICTURES

In 1895, the Lumière brothers astounded audiences with the first "movies", and cinema has been a popular form of entertainment ever since. Movies are made up of a sequence of still images, which create the impression of movement when they are shown in rapid succession.

WOW!

An average Hollywood feature film is just over 100 minutes long and uses 3000 m (10,000 feet) of tape, wound onto five double reels.

HOLLYWOOD is a part of the city of Los Angeles, USA, but the word is often used to mean the whole American film industry. Hollywood movies are watched all over the world, sometimes with subtitles or "dubbed" into other languages.

Asian martial arts movies made the names of stars like Bruce Lee. They are famous for elaborate stunts and fight scenes, and increasingly for special effects.

Bollywood is the name used to describe the film industry, which is based in Mumbai (Bombay), India. Bollywood films are produced in the Hindi language at a rate of about 1,000 a year. They usually include extravagant musical scenes.

177

Sport

Sport is good for health, but perhaps more importantly many sports are team events, and bring people together for competitive fun. After all, everyone likes to win!

BALL GAMES

Football is a typical team sport where 11 players try to kick the ball into their opponents' goal.

▲ FOOTBALL *is arguably the most popular sport in the world. People all over the world play it in schools and parks, on the streets, or wherever they can. Billions of people watch the Football World Cup held every four years, and for many countries football has become part of their culture. Football fans are fiercely loyal to their local or national teams.*

■ **Tennis matches** are played either as singles, between two players, or doubles, between four players.

■ **Cricket** is played by people in more than 100 countries. The best teams play in international test matches.

■ **Table tennis** or ping-pong became an Olympic sport in 1988. It is popular around the world, with an estimated 300 million players.

■ **American football** is different to European football and uses a ball with pointed ends. Players wear protective padding, and are allowed to carry the ball to make passes.

■ **Rugby** is played with an oval ball between teams of 15 players.

▲ GOLF *is played using a club to knock a small ball into a hole in as few shots as possible.*

▲ VOLLEYBALL *is played between two teams of six players over a net. It was invented in the 1890s.*

CONTACT SPORTS

■ **Fencing** contestants use lightweight blunt-tipped swords to hit target areas on their opponent's body.

■ **Wrestling** dates back thousands of years. It is a form of hand to hand combat.

◀ BOXING *is a tough sport, demanding huge upper body strength. Boxers wear padded gloves.*

▶ KARATE *is a Japanese martial art. It uses moves such as punching, kicking, and knee and elbow strikes.*

■ **Judo** first appeared in Japan in the 1800s, but developed from far earlier techniques.

■ **Kung Fu Taolu** is China's national sport, where it is known as "wushu".

▶ SUMO WRESTLING *was once part of the ancient Samurai warriors training and is the traditional and ritualistic combat sport of Japan. Each contestant tries to wrestle the other to the ground or out of a 4.55 m (15 ft) diameter circle.*

EXTREME SPORTS

▲ SKYDIVING *Skydivers usually leap from a small plane and freefall before opening a parachute to enable safe landing. Worldwide, there are more than 450 skydiving drop zones. Instead of a plane, some skydivers have jumped from helicopters or hot-air balloon baskets.*

- **Surfing** Surfers ride lightweight boards just ahead of a breaking ocean wave.
- **Ski jumping** involves skiing down a steep hill, leaping, and landing safely.
- **Hang gliders** use a triangular-shaped wing to glide through the air. They can stay up for many hours by finding rising air columns.
- **Bungee jumping** sees people leap from a high spot and freefall to be saved by a strong elastic rope secured to their ankles.

◄ EXTREME CLIMBERS *climb ice and rock faces that appear impossible.*

◄ BMX *is bicycle motocross. It involves spectacular jumps and hair-raising tricks.*

RACES

- **Drag racing** is the fastest land-based sport. It originated in the US and takes place between two highly charged dragster cars.
- **Speed skaters** can reach speeds of 65 km/h (40 mph).
- **Horse racing** with powerful thoroughbred horses may be over flat ground or over jumps.
- **Yachts** of all sizes are used for competitive racing.

▲ FORMULA ONE (F1) *Grand Prix races are fast and exciting.*

▶ ROAD CYCLISTS *may cover huge distances in a race such as the Tour de France.*

▲ HURDLE RACES *are a major part of any athletic event. Competitors race over 10 hurdles spaced over a set distance. The sprint course is 100 m (328 ft) for women and 110 m (360 ft) for men. A longer course takes place over 400 m (1,300 ft), but with the same number of hurdles. Many schools enjoy hurdle races.*

OLYMPIC GAMES

The Olympic Games is the most important sporting event in the world. Every country is invited to take part – athletes from 204 countries took part in the London Olympics in 2012. Winners receive a gold medal.

The original Olympic Games were first recorded in 776 BCE and were held in Olympia, Greece. The first modern-day Olympics were held in Athens in 1896. As a reminder of its origins, an Olympic torch of fire is carried from Olympia to the Games by a series of relay runners. It's used to light an Olympic flame in the stadium.

▶ ICE HOCKEY *is just one of more than 300 Olympic sports.*

Architecture

Architecture is the design of buildings and other structures, such as bridges. An architect's job is to make sure a building is well built, and safe and pleasant to use. It also has to be suitable for its purpose – theatres need room for a stage and dressing rooms, for example. Architects also try to make buildings look interesting and inspiring.

GETTING STARTED

Before designing a building, architects need to know what the building is for, where it is to be built, and how much money can be spent on it. They then work out what the building will be made from, and the position and measurement of every wall, door, and window, which they record in great detail on drawings called plans. Sometimes they make a scale model of the building too.

CHANGES IN STYLE

Every period of history is marked by its own style of architecture. This reflects changes in taste and fashion, and new building techniques and materials. Most cities are a mixture of old and new buildings that show many different styles.

▲ ANTONI GAUDI *was a Spanish architect with a distinctive style. His most famous work is the Sagrada Familia, the unfinished cathedral in Barcelona.*

▲ STILT HOUSES *Some people who live along coasts and rivers build their houses on stilts to avoid flooding.*

▶ BAMBOO HOUSES *The Gamo people of Ethiopia make houses from split bamboo, which is woven and thatched.*

Ideal homes People live in buildings that are suitable for the environment they live in. Often they use local materials, such as wood and stone, or clay made into bricks. Some are even built into rocky hillsides or caves. The Inuit of the Arctic make temporary shelters from ice because there is nothing else to build with.

TIMELINE OF ARCHITECTURE

ANCIENT EGYPT
2590–2500 BCE
Pyramids of stone erected in the Nile valley as tombs for kings.

ANCIENT GREEKS
700–44 BCE
Ancient Greeks built temples with specific proportions, known as the classical style.

ANCIENT ROME
200 BCE–500 CE
The Romans used concrete to construct many large buildings and structures.

BYZANTINE
330–1453
Byzantine buildings are characterized by rounded domes on square bases, and arches supported by columns.

GOTHIC
1100–1500
Grand buildings of the medieval period feature pointed arches, ribbed vaulting, and flying buttresses to support high walls.

GLASS BUILDINGS

Traditional building materials include wood, stone, and brick, but many modern buildings make use of large amounts of glass. Although glass is fragile, new construction techniques involving steel or reinforced concrete frames have allowed architects to build light yet strong buildings.

Glass pyramid, Paris

Modern designs Computers enable architects to design buildings that would not have been possible before. They can quickly work out if a shape can be built, and even allow the architect to walk around a virtual building.

TAKE A LOOK: DESIGN STYLES

Some structures are instantly recognizable because of their design. Every major city has a number of famous buildings, but each has a different style according to the period in which it was built.

▲ TAJ MAHAL *This marble building is one of the finest examples of 17th-century Indian architecture.*

▲ PALACE OF WESTMINSTER *When the original palace burned down in 1834 it was rebuilt in the Gothic style.*

▲ NATIONAL GALLERY, CANADA *The gallery is a striking modern structure of glass and granite.*

▼ THE DESIGN *of the Guggenheim Museum in the Spanish port of Bilbao is meant to resemble a ship.*

BAROQUE

1650–1750
The very grand, ornate style of Baroque design takes hold in Italy, France, and Spain.

SKYSCRAPERS

1890
The first skyscrapers are built in Chicago, USA, following the invention of the elevator.

ORGANIC ARCHITECTURE

1900–1940s
Organic architecture, with its curved shapes inspired by nature, is promoted by American architect, Frank Lloyd Wright.

Sydney Opera House

BAUHAUS

1919–1933
The German Bauhaus school created designs based on clean lines, cubic shapes, and flat roofs.

ECO-LIVING

1980s onwards
Houses are built to be more energy efficient and use environmentally friendly materials.

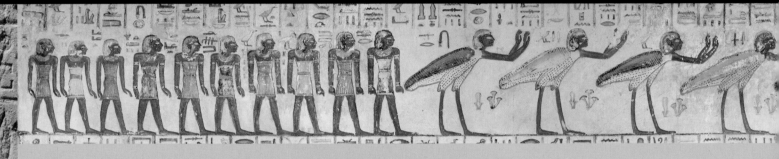

HISTORY AND POLITICS

- About one million years ago, early people began to spread out across the continents.

- Around 3000 BCE, Egypt became the first super-state.

- By 117 CE, the Roman Empire stretched across western Europe and into Asia.

- China has the oldest continuous known civilization, lasting at least 4,000 years.

- In 622, Muhammad established the Islamic state in the Arabian Peninsula.

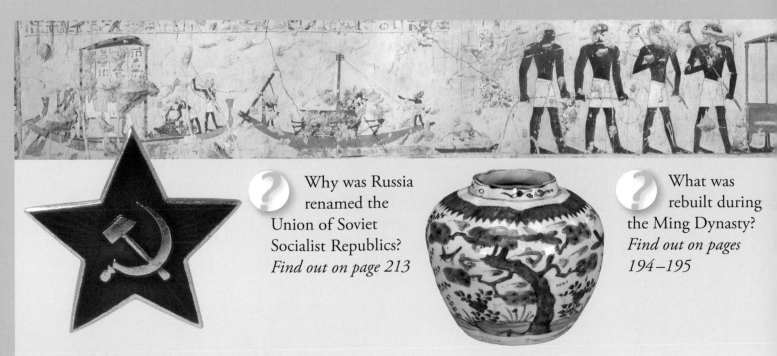

Why was Russia renamed the Union of Soviet Socialist Republics? *Find out on page 213*

What was rebuilt during the Ming Dynasty? *Find out on pages 194–195*

Definition: **History and Politics** is the study of the lives of people and the activity of governments and rulers in the past from written records.

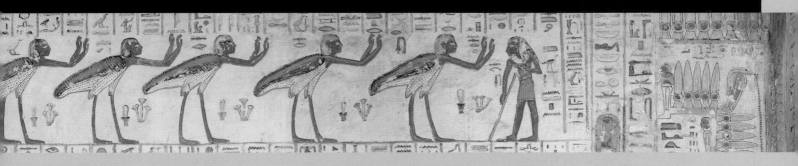

- The United States Declaration of Independence was signed on 4th July, 1776.

- By the 1900s, Great Britain's empire covered one-quarter of Earth's land surface.

- World War I ended at 11 am on the 11th day of the 11th month, 1918.

- In August, 1945, atomic bombs were dropped on two cities in Japan, ending WWII.

- The United Nations was founded in 1945, seeking to achieve world peace.

? When did Mecca become the centre of Islam? *Find out on pages 196–197*

? Which areas of the world are often in the news? *Find out on pages 214–215*

Tales from the past

History is the study of things that have happened in the past. This can be anything from the earliest people to events of the last few years. Rather like detectives searching for clues, historians look at evidence from the past known as primary sources.

- **What is the object made from?:** The artefact shows the materials available and the skills of the craftsmen.

- **Who would have used the object?:** The artefact may give clues about the status of people in society.

- **What was the object used for?:** Historians may be able to work out what the culture and the way of life for the people was like from the artefact.

Digging for clues The work of archaeologists help historians to know more about early people. During their excavations of a site, archaeologists uncover and study early buildings and find and examine artefacts – objects made by people from the past.

Bronze age pendant

10th century BCE statue from the Middle East

Ancient Greek vase

▼ MAYAN RUINS *The Maya civilization of central America was successful between 200 – 900 CE. Archaeologists have found many steep-sided pyramids with steps leading up to a temple where human sacrifices took place.*

Archaeology site After doing an aerial and surface survey of the area, the archaeologists begin excavating the site, removing the earth layer by layer and recording any discoveries.

TAKE A LOOK: WRITTEN SOURCES

Since ancient times, official records of births, marriages, and deaths, census results, and tax records have been kept.

▲ DOMESDAY BOOK *In 1086, King William I of England commissioned a survey of every estate and village in the country.*

Many eyewitness accounts and inscriptions have recorded important events and the lives of famous people.

▲ SOLDIER'S JOURNAL *The diary of a US infantry soldier tells of his life during the American civil war (1861–65).*

Other sources are the diaries and personal letters of ordinary people living through extraordinary events.

▲ ANNE FRANK'S DIARY *Between 1942 and 1944, a young Dutch Jewish girl wrote a diary while in a secret annex, hiding from the German Gestapo.*

▼ AT WORK AND PLAY
Photographs show the way of life and the changes in clothing styles and in technology, tools, and machines.

Caterpillar tractor used in France in the 1920s

Old photographs Since the mid-1800s, photography has become increasingly popular. Photos provide a visual source to historians studying the lives of people. Since recorded sound was developed, historians can also study oral accounts of people talking about their lives and reactions to events.

Early 1900s folding roll-film camera

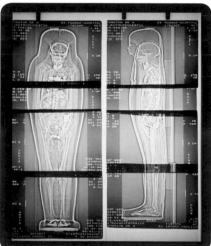

An x-ray of an Egyptian mummy

New technology Advances in technology have provided historians with loads more information about artefacts. Radio-carbon dating, x-rays, and thermal scans can reveal previously unknown details.

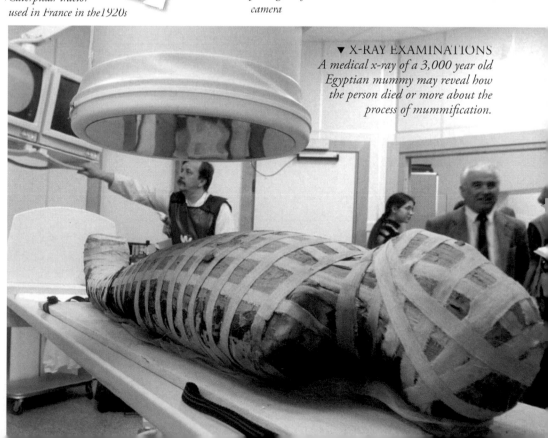

▼ X-RAY EXAMINATIONS
A medical x-ray of a 3,000 year old Egyptian mummy may reveal how the person died or more about the process of mummification.

Early people

From the limited fossil records, historians can only make suggestions at the possible origins of humans. There were many different hominids – "ape-men" that walked upright – but over five million years all but one became extinct. Only the successful *Homo sapiens* survived to roam the Earth.

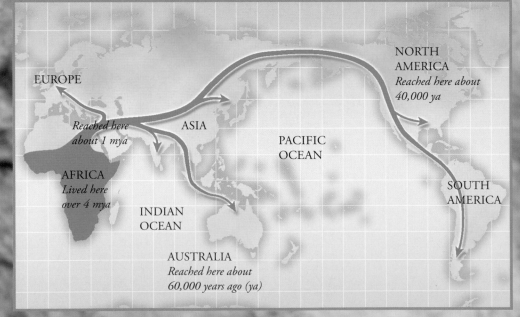

EUROPE

Reached here about 1 mya

ASIA

NORTH AMERICA
Reached here about 40,000 ya

PACIFIC OCEAN

AFRICA
Lived here over 4 mya

INDIAN OCEAN

SOUTH AMERICA

AUSTRALIA
Reached here about 60,000 years ago (ya)

OUT OF THE FORESTS

Many historians think that more than five million years ago (mya), ape-like creatures moved out of the forests of Africa to live on open ground. To survive, they learned to stand and walk upright to see further and move quickly, leaving their hands free to carry possessions and learn new skills. About one mya, early people migrated out of Africa and spread out across the continents.

TIMELINE OF HOMINIDS

AUSTRALOPITHECUS AFARENSIS

Dated: over 4 mya Fossils found in Africa with very low forehead and projecting face.

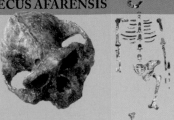

HOMO HABILIS

Dated: 2.3–1.6 mya Tools found with fossil remains that had large skulls.

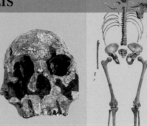

HOMO ERECTUS

Dated: 1.8 mya–300,000 ya Fossils in Africa, Europe, and Asia found with long, low skulls and large molar teeth.

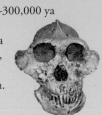

186

WHO'S WHO?

- **Lucy:** A female skeleton aged 25 years found in Ethiopia and estimated to have lived 3.2 mya. She was about 107 cm (3 ft 6 in) tall.
- **Nutcracker man:** Teeth and skull fragments found in Tanzania of a hominid estimated to have lived 2 mya. With the biggest, flattest cheek and thickest teeth enamel of any hominid, he ate only nuts and seeds.
- **Peking man:** One of 40 individuals found at a site in China and estimated to have lived 500,000–300,000 ya.
- **Old man:** A 30-40 year old skeleton with severe arthritis found in France. Estimated to have lived 50,000 ya, he would have had an average height of 168 cm (5 ft 6 in).

▶ PEKING MAN
Historians have found evidence that the Peking man and his companions would have lived in caves, made tools, and used fire to keep warm and cook food.

TELL ME MORE...

As the early people moved northwards, they had to cope with a colder climate and survive the ice ages. Clothes were first made from animal skins, but later people discovered how to spin and weave wool.

TAKE A LOOK: STONE AGE

- **Paleolithic period:** People moved around following the herds and used clubs and sharpened stones to hunt.
- **Mesolithic period:** Hunters made bows and arrows and the gatherers made baskets for collecting fruits and nuts. People continued to move around.
- **Neolithic period:** People became food producers so were able to have a more settled lifestyle. They made wooden agricultural tools and developed new crafts, such as pottery.

▼ FIRST TOOLS *Pieces of flint were shaped by chipping away flakes, leaving a sharp edge.*

Pebble hammer for shaping flint

▶ GATHERERS' TOOLS
Flakes of flint were attached to wooden handles. These tools were used to dig up edible roots and cut wood for fires.

A spark was made by hitting an iron stone against a flint.

Bark for collecting fruits and nuts

◀ HUNTERS' TOOLS
The metal tips of the arrows were dipped in poison made from beetle larvae.

Feathers

▶ CARVINGS
Animal bones were skilfully carved to show pictures and to make small sculptures.

Carving of a mammoth

HOMO NEANDERTHALENSIS

Dated: 250,000–30,000 ya
Fossils found in Europe and Middle East with protruding jaw, receding forehead, and weak chin.

HOMO SAPIENS

Dated: 100,000 ya to present
Found all over the world, these skulls have a rising forehead, prominent chin, and light bone structure and can fit a large brain.

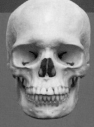

Ancient Egypt

From about 6,000 years ago, cities began to appear along the banks of large rivers. The civilizations in Egypt and Mesopotamia (now Iraq) were the earliest. Around 3000 BCE, Egypt was unified to become the first super-state under the rule of a pharaoh (king).

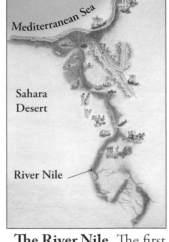

The River Nile The first ancient Egyptians were able to establish farming communities in this otherwise desert landscape all thanks to the river Nile. Annual flooding kept the land either side of the river fertile and watered the crops.

Tombs for the pharaohs
Vast, towering tombs were built by the pharaohs for their journey to the afterlife to become a god. The largest pyramid of Pharaoh Khufu (reign 2589-66 BCE) took about 20 years to build and was made from over two million limestone blocks.

Inside, passages led to burial chambers where the pharaoh was buried with his belongings.

One of the smaller pyramids for Khufu's wives

PYRAMIDS AT GIZA

The pyramids at Giza near Cairo, Egypt, were built over 4,000 years ago. The Great Pyramid is the only surviving monument of the Seven Wonders of the Ancient World.

EGYPTIAN GODS AND GODDESSES

■ **Many gods and goddesses:** The ancient Egyptians believed that each of their deities had a particular role to play in keeping Egypt successful.

■ **A living god:** The first pharaohs were thought to be a living version of the god Horus – a hawk-headed god of the sky that protected the pharaohs.

■ **Mural paintings:** Images of the deities meeting a pharaoh in the afterlife were painted on the walls of the pharaohs' tombs.

Anubis   Isis   Osiris

▼ GOLDEN MASK
The preserved body, or mummy, of Tutankhamun was discovered with a magnificent golden face mask on its head.

WHO'S WHO?

■ **Hatshepsut:** (reign 1473-58 BCE) This successful queen assumed the role of a pharaoh in place of her young stepson.

■ **Tutankhamun:** (reign 1333-23 BCE) This boy pharaoh's splendid tomb was discovered in 1922.

■ **Rameses II:** (reign 1279-13 BCE) His long reign was a period of peace and prosperity in Egypt.

■ **Cleopatra VII:** (reign 51-30 BCE) This last pharaoh of ancient Egypt was known for her great beauty and love affairs with the Romans Julius Caesar and Mark Antony.

Egyptian social pyramid The pharaoh at the top controlled all land, people, and possessions, and the vizier, his most trusted advisor, oversaw all the pharaoh's plans. The peasants at the bottom worked in the fields producing the crops collected as taxes to feed everyone, but during the flood season joined the craftsmen, working on building projects.

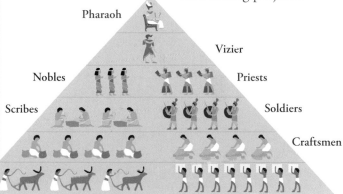

Pharaoh

Vizier

Nobles   Priests

Scribes   Soldiers

Craftsmen

Peasants (about 80 per cent of the population)

TAKE A LOOK: ANCIENT EGYPTIAN ARTEFACTS

Historians have been able to discover much about the lives of ancient Egyptians from the markings, possessions, and records found.

▲ ANKH *Hieroglyphic symbol meaning "life" often shown being held by gods and pharaohs.*

▲ SCARAB DUNG BEETLE *Sacred symbol meaning "rebirth", relating to the god Khepri, who pushed the Sun across the sky.*

▲ PAPYRUS *The inner pith of this tall plant that grew along the Nile was used to make paper.*

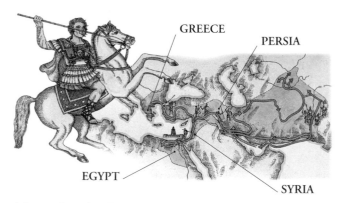

GREECE

PERSIA

EGYPT

SYRIA

Alexander the Great's empire
King Alexander III (356-323 BCE), who ruled over the Greek city-states from 336 BCE, led a 12-year-long military campaign, enlarging the ancient Greek empire. He conquered the Persian empire, Syria, and Egypt, and continued east as far as India.

Greeks *and...*

The ancient Greeks had one of the most advanced ancient civilizations. Historians know much about them from their writings, artefacts, and the influence of their culture on other nations.

▼ PARTHENON *A huge statue of Athena, the city's goddess, stood inside this large temple – the most important building on the acropolis.*

GREEK POLITICS

- The Greeks formed a collection of independent city-states.
- When a city needed to expand, they set up a new colony city around the Mediterranean Sea.
- The Greeks invented the democratic system in which people voted for their leader. However, only free men could vote.

ATHEN'S ACROPOLIS
The best-known acropolis was built in the city-state of Athens.

The propylaia was the gateway to the acropolis.

AN ACROPOLIS

- **Site:** An acropolis is an area of a city sited on high ground as a home for the city's god.

- **Buildings:** The main public and religious buildings were built on the acropolis.

- **Date:** The buildings seen today on the acropolis in Athens were mostly built in the mid-5th century BCE.

TIMELINE

1250 BCE	492–449 BCE	431–404 BCE	334–323 BCE
The early Greeks and the people of Troy fought a legendary ten-year war.	After a 50-year war, the Greek city-states succeeded in defeating an invading Persian army.	The Peloponnesian War between the rival city-states of Athens and Sparta and their allies involved almost all the Greek world.	Alexander the Great expanded the Greek empire across Persia.

Romans

Starting out as a people from a small town ruled by a king in 753 BCE, the ambitious Romans ended up conquering a vast empire by impressive military power.

The Roman Empire By 117 CE, the Roman Empire stretched around the Mediterranean Sea, up through western Europe to Britain and across into Asia. In the 3rd century, the empire was divided between two emperors for better control.

▼ THE ROMAN FORUM
At the centre of every Roman city was an open space surrounded by the main temples and public buildings. People gathered here to do business.

TELL ME MORE...

The Roman Republic, formed in 509 BCE, was governed by a senate, but senators came from wealthy families and only Roman citizens could vote. Later, the Empire was ruled by unelected emperors.

TAKE A PICTURE

Aqueducts, such as the Pont du Gard in France, are just one example of the Romans' great engineering feats across their empire.

148 BCE	58–50 BCE	27 BCE	476 CE
At the end of the fourth Macedonian War, the Roman Republic finally defeated the ancient Greeks.	Julius Caesar, the military leader of the Roman Republic, conquered Gaul in western Europe.	Augustus changed the Roman Republic to an Empire and became the first emperor of Rome.	Attacks from barbarians caused the Western Roman Empire to collapse.

Medieval period

The word "medieval" means "the middle ages", and covers a period of more than a thousand years between the fall of the Roman Empire (5th century) to the Renaissance (16th century). During this time, Europe was all about who owned land – and so held the power.

The feudal system In many parts of Europe, society was organized into a class system with the king at the top, who owned all the land. Barons and bishops were below him, then the lesser lords (knights), and finally the peasants.

📷 **TAKE A PICTURE**

On Christmas Day, 800 CE, Charlemagne (742–814) was crowned Holy Roman Emperor by Pope Leo III. Charlemagne was an important leader, establishing central government and schools in monasteries, spreading Christianity, and paving the way for modern Europe.

▲ BUILT FOR DEFENCE *In an age when land meant power, it was important to protect what you had. Cities, based around the lord's castle, were fortified with walls and a moat.*

1 *Raising the bridge and closing the **gates** slowed down invaders.*

2 *No large city was complete without a **cathedral**.*

3 *A lord could see enemy advances from his hill-top **castle** towers.*

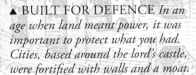

◀ CRESTS *Each guild had a coat of arms. This one belongs to the Merchant Adventurers of the City of York. These cloth traders funded ships for importing and exporting goods worldwide.*

Power in numbers It wasn't just the noblemen who had power and influence. Craftsmen formed guilds to protect their businesses, making sure they had high wages and no competition. The guilds built grand halls (such as the London Guildhall, left) and influenced the day-to-day life of a city. But guild masters often used the guilds to increase their own wealth, rather than look after their members.

Fighting for control Europe in the Middle Ages looked different to today. For example, modern-day Spain was divided into four separate kingdoms, and parts of France came under the rule of different kings and princes – including the English crown. Wars were not uncommon as kings sent (and often accompanied) armies into battle to take control of new land. The longest war was between England and France.

▶ THE HUNDRED YEARS' WAR *This series of battles between England and France actually lasted 116 years, from 1337 to 1453.*

TAKE A LOOK: TIMES OF CHANGE

While warfare shaped the physical boundaries of countries during the Middle Ages, there were many other events that changed Europe at that time.

▲ WEAPONS OF WAR
Kings often fought alongside their knights in major battles over control of land.

▲ BLACK DEATH
In the 1340s, the Great Plague killed one-third of the population of Europe.

▲ THE NEW WORLD
Explorers such as Polo and Columbus opened up trade routes across the world.

THE REFORMATION

■ During the Middle Ages, the Catholic Church, with the pope at its head, was very powerful throughout Europe.

■ But not everybody was happy with the Church's power and influence. The opponents called themselves Protestants.

■ In 1517, German monk Martin Luther spoke out about corruption of Church officials. Ulrich Zwingli in Switzerland and John Calvin in France proposed similar ideas for reforming the Church.

■ New, Protestant churches were set up in northern Europe, ending the total power of the Catholics in Europe.

China's dynasties

CHINA IN 221 BCE *united by the first emperor Qin Shi Huang.*

China can claim to have the oldest continuous known civilization, which has lasted at least 4,000 years. Since the first city-states along the Yellow River, China has expanded (and at times contracted) under the control of a succession of ruling monarchs until 1912. Periods of unity and disunity have shaped the country's politics and history.

WHO'S WHO?

- **Confucius** (551–479 BCE) Famous Chinese philosopher whose teachings have influenced China's society.
- **Qin Shi Huang** (ruled 221–210 BCE) Proclaimed himself first emperor of China after uniting the warring states.
- **Wu Zhao** (ruled 690–705) Only woman to rule as emperor and probably murdered many people to rise to power.
- **Hongwu Emperor** (ruled 1368–1398) Founder of the Ming dynasty after defeating the Mongols.
- **Pu Yi** (ruled 1908–1912) Last emperor of China, abdicated aged six years old.

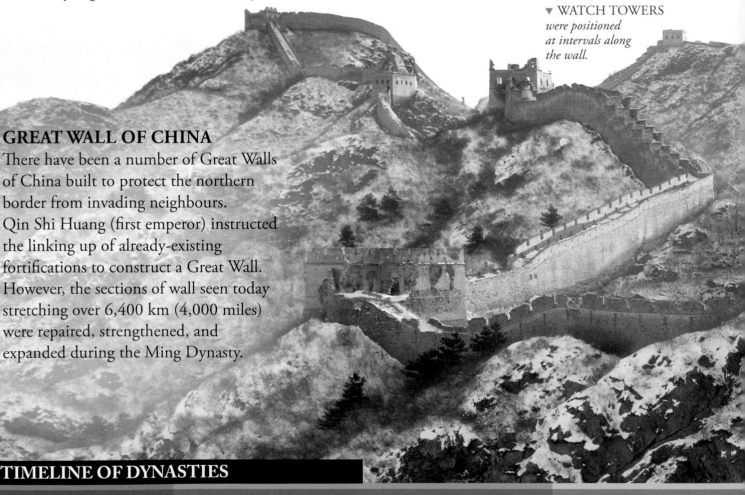

▼ WATCH TOWERS *were positioned at intervals along the wall.*

GREAT WALL OF CHINA

There have been a number of Great Walls of China built to protect the northern border from invading neighbours. Qin Shi Huang (first emperor) instructed the linking up of already-existing fortifications to construct a Great Wall. However, the sections of wall seen today stretching over 6,400 km (4,000 miles) were repaired, strengthened, and expanded during the Ming Dynasty.

TIMELINE OF DYNASTIES

DYNASTIES	221–206 BCE QIN	206 BCE–220 CE HAN	265–420 JIN
Much of Chinese history can be split into time periods of the dynasties, or royal families. Each dynasty brought its own changes to the country.	A short-lived dynasty during which the traditional beliefs of Confucius were forbidden and his books burned. 	The Silk Road – an important trading route – was established from China to the Mediterranean Sea.	Paper and ink became more popular and calligraphers perfected their writing style. 

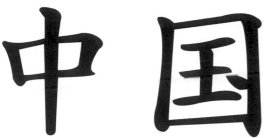

中国

Middle kingdom *Zhōngguó* (pronounced jung-gwo) means "Middle Kingdom". The name was first used by the rulers of the ancient Zhou dynasty (1050–771 BCE), who believed their country was the "centre of civilization". Throughout China's history, *Zhōngguó* has had different meanings and caused conflict between dynasties. Only since 1911 has it officially been used for the country's name.

Forbidden City In 1420, the Ming emperor and his household moved to a vast imperial palace in the capital, Beijing. Court officials and members of the imperial family were allowed inside, but only the emperor had unlimited access to all of the buildings.

▼ 980 BUILDINGS *survive enclosed by a 7.9 m (26 ft) high city wall.*

▲ COSTLY PROJECT *Millions of soldiers, prisoners, and local people were enlisted to build the Great Wall and many thousands died during the construction.*

TAKE A PICTURE

Qin Shi Huang (first emperor) ordered that thousands of life-size clay warriors, horses, and chariots, known as the terracotta army, were to be made to guard his tomb and help him rule his empire in his afterlife (👁 p165)

618–907 TANG	**1271–1368 YUAN**	**1368–1644 MING**	**1644–1912 QING**
Women were given many of the same rights as men and the educated Wu Zhao became China's only Empress.	Gunpowder, invented earlier by the Chinese, was developed to be used in powerful explosive cannons.	Production increased of the very popular blue-and-white porcelain with painted scenes.	Court officials wore robes with a dragon motif within the Universe, symbolizing the emperor as the "Son of Heaven".

Islamic golden age

In the 7th century, Muhammad established the Islamic state in the Arabian Peninsula. In the centuries after his death, the Islamic empire expanded rapidly, spreading the faith and laws of Islam based on his teachings.

MECCA

Muhammad was born in Mecca (now in Saudi Arabia). After being forced out of the city due to his teachings, he returned eight years later with his army to take control and establish the city as the centre of the faith of Islam.

◄ PROPHET OF ISLAM
At the age of 40, Muhammad had the first of many revelations about the word of God. His teachings were to become intertwined with the politics and social aspects of an Islamic state. His name is shown here in stylized form.

TAKE A LOOK: ISLAMIC ARTEFACTS

The Islamic civilization had a distinctive style in art, crafts, and architecture, and made great advances in mathematics, astronomy, and medicines.

▲ ISLAMIC ART
Calligraphy and mosaics of glazed tiles were used to decorate buildings.

▲ ASTROLABE *They perfected this instrument for calculating a person's position by using the Sun and stars.*

▲ OTTOMAN VASE
Flowers and large leaves were widely used as decorative patterns.

TIMELINE OF ISLAMIC EMPIRE

622–632 MUHAMMAD	661–750 UMAYYAD DYNASTY	750–1258 ABBASID DYNASTY
Muhammad took control of Mecca and established the Islamic civilization.	The caliphs of the Umayyad family expanded the Islamic Empire (shown in green).	Baghdad was made the Islamic capital and the city became the world's centre of trade, learning, and culture.

EUROPE
■ Baghdad
■ Mecca
AFRICA

Silver and copper basin

WHO'S WHO?

- **Muhammad** (570–632) He was the founder of the Islam religion and the first Muslim political leader.
- **Ali ibn Abi** (599–661) He was the son-in-law of Muhammad, who became the first Imam in 656.
- **Harun al-Rashid** (766–809) The fifth Abbasid caliph, who was the subject of the stories *The Thousand and One Nights*, also called *The Arabian Nights*.
- **Saladin** (1137–1193) A Muslim sultan (governor) of Egypt, Syria, Yemen, and Palestine, who captured Jerusalem and defeated the crusaders in 1187.

Minarets are the highest points in the mosque. Traditionally a muezzin calls everyone to prayer from the minaret.

The Grand Mosque in Mecca

▼ KAABA *According to Islamic tradition, this cube-shaped building in Mecca is said to be the house of God. Muslims (followers of Islam) are expected to visit it at least once in their lifetime.*

▲ QIBLAH *Muhammad instructed Muslims to pray five times a day, facing the direction, or qiblah, of the Kaaba in Mecca. This instrument was used to work out the direction (qiblah).*

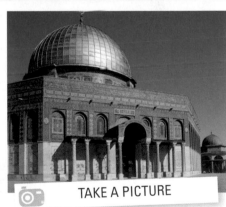

TAKE A PICTURE

The Dome of the Rock shrine in Jerusalem was completed in 691 and is the oldest existing Islamic building in the world.

1258 RISE OF THE SULTANS

Mongol invaders captured Baghdad and converted to Islam, while local rulers, called sultans, governed Egypt, Syria, and Palestine.

1369–1506 TIMURID EMPIRE

Timur, a Turkic-Mongol warrior, conquered the Islamic lands and one of his descendants founded the Mughal Empire in northern India.

1516–1924 OTTOMAN EMPIRE

The Ottoman Turks ruled over the Islamic state and expanded their empire into eastern Europe (shown in green).

Aztecs

At the end of the 1100s, a tribe of hunters and gatherers from northern Mexico migrated south and, during the 1200s, settled as farmers on the islands of Lake Texcoco in the Valley of central Mexico.

Tenochtitlán
Around 1325, the Aztecs began building their vast capital city, Tenochtitlán, in the centre of Lake Texcoco. Several causeways linked the island-city to the mainland. In the centre was a complex of religious buildings surrounded by palaces, warrior schools, and a ball court for playing a game called ulama.

The Great Temple

Map of empires
At the height of their empires, the Aztecs ruled over about six million people in central and southern Mexico, and the Incas ruled over 12 million people living along the Pacific coast and in the Andes mountains.

Atlantic Ocean

Pacific Ocean

South America

■ Aztecs
■ Incas

1300s CULTURES ESTABLISHED
The Aztec and Inca tribes create settlements and increase in population.

Incas

A tribe of farmers led by their king, Manco Cápac, settled in Cuzco in the highlands of Peru during the 1100s. Like the Aztecs, they were later to form a strong and powerful warrior-nation.

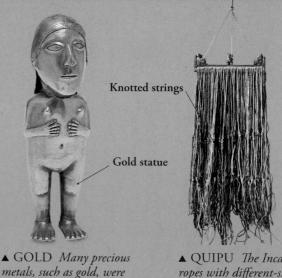

Knotted strings

Gold statue

FAST FACTS

■ Inca kings were called cápac.
■ The Inca language was quechua and the Aztec language was nahuatl.
■ Both civilizations worshipped many gods and performed human sacrifices.
■ The Incas traded with goods and services and the Aztecs traded with cacao beans and goods.

▲ MANCO CÁPAC
First ruler of the Incas

▲ GOLD *Many precious metals, such as gold, were found in South America and metalworking was a popular craft.*

▲ QUIPU *The Incas used ropes with different-sized knots to record information about their expanding empire.*

◄ CACAO *A bitter-tasting chocolate drink was made using the beans of the cacao plant.*

Pod

Beans

▲ MASK OF A GOD
*Mosaic made from
turquoise gems*

Montezuma I

WHO'S WHO?

■ **Acamapichtli** (reign 1376–96) A member of the ruling family of a neighbouring state who became the first king of the Aztecs.

■ **Montezuma I** (reign 1440–69) This ambitious king greatly expanded the Aztec empire through trade and conquest.

■ **Montezuma II** (reign 1502–20) The Aztec empire reached its largest size during his reign and then the Spanish conquest began.

■ **Hernán Cortés** (1485–1547) Spanish adventurer who overthrew the Aztec empire in 1521 and claimed Mexico as land belonging to the Spanish crown.

▲ SACRIFICIAL KNIFE
Aztec priests cut out the still-beating hearts from prisoners as a sacrifice to their gods.

Empire building The Aztecs became rich and powerful because they were extremely successful at growing crops. They became a nation of feared warriors as their large, conquering army could be fed. Merchants could trade goods with distant lands, creating wealth for the Aztecs.

Cortés arrives

Spanish conquest
Hernán Cortés was welcomed as an honoured guest by Montezuma II to Tenochtitlán in 1519 as was the custom of the Aztecs. However, Cortés arrested the king and two years later destroyed the city and the Aztec empire.

1400s
EMPIRES EXPANDED
The Aztecs and Incas extend their control over other tribes and gain more land.

1500s
CIVILIZATIONS CONQUERED
The Aztec and Inca empires are destroyed by the arrival of Spanish adventurers.

◀ MACHU PICCHU
Mountain city built by Cápac Yupanqui.

Inca conquests
Cápac Yupanqui (reign 1438–71) began the expansion of the Inca empire. A vast network of roads were built to link their territory.

▶ LLAMAS *were valued for their wool, their meat, and for carrying goods along the roads.*

Francisco Pizarro
In search of gold and other precious metals in South America, the Spanish adventurer Pizarro met the Incas. In 1533, he took control of Cuzco and claimed the land for Spain.

TELL ME MORE...

Despite having only a small army, Pizarro was able to seize the Inca ruler Atahuallpa after he refused to accept Christianity and the rule of Spain on 16 November 1532.

Pizarro meets Atahuallpa

Colonial America

By the early 1600s, more and more Europeans were sailing across the Atlantic Ocean to establish colonies in the eastern areas of North America. Over the next 170 years these colonies grew.

Reconstruction of the *Mayflower.*

▶ POCAHONTAS
As a young girl, Pocahontas helped to make peace between the Jamestown settlers and her native American tribe.

TELL ME MORE...

In November, 1620, a group of Pilgrims from England on board the *Mayflower* arrived in North America after a gruelling 66-day journey. They founded Plymouth in Massachussetts.

The Plymouth settlers

The *Mayflower* pilgrims had come to the "New World" so they could worship freely without persecution. Their new life was tough and half of the group died from disease or starvation during the first winter. However, most of the local native Americans were welcoming and showed them suitable crops to grow.

WOW!

The Thanksgiving festival now celebrated in November in the US, has its origins from the first Thanksgiving feast held in the autumn of 1621 by the pilgrims and native Americans to celebrate their first good harvest.

TIMELINE OF COLONIAL AMERICA

1607

The Jamestown settlement in Virginia was the first permanent English settlement in North America.

1608

Quebec City is founded by the French along the Saint Lawrence River.

1620

The *Mayflower* pilgrims establish a settlement at Plymouth, Massachusetts.

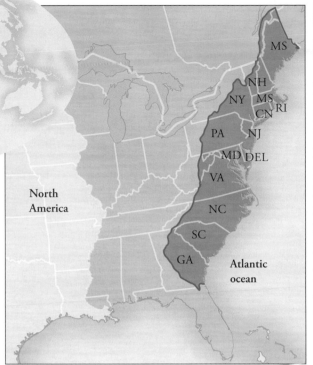

COLONIAL AMERICA

■	The original 13 colonies
■	Other British territories

MS	Massachussetts
NH	New Hampshire
RI	Rhode Island
CN	Conneticut
NY	New York
NJ	New Jersey
PA	Pennsylvania
MD	Maryland
DEL	Delaware
VA	Virginia
NC	North Carolina
SC	South Carolina
GA	Georgia

The British colonies By 1733, there were 13 colonies loyal to Britain along the east coast of North America. In 1763, the French surrendered their land to the British. In the 1760s, Britain began to tax the American colonists but their authority over the New World was starting to weaken as the colonists no longer needed their protection.

TAKE A PICTURE

The historic area of Williamsburg, which became Virginia's capital in 1698, has been restored and recreates colonial times.

▶ DECLARATION *On 4th July, 1776, the Congress of the American colonies issued a Declaration of Independence, signed by representatives of all 13 colonies. The united colonies were free, independent states.*

American revolution In the 1770s, the American colonists began to rebel against British rule and were especially angered by the heavy tax on tea in 1773. Between 1775 and 1783, the colonists fought the British army and won. The British were forced to recognize their new independent country – the United States of America.

1663	1763	1773	1775–1783
Companies were established to trade goods, such as fur skins and tobacco, with Europe.	The French surrendered their colonies to Britain, expanding the area the British controlled.	The Boston tea party was a protest by some American colonists angered by their high taxes to the British.	The American revolution was when the 13 colonies rebelled against the British and won independence.

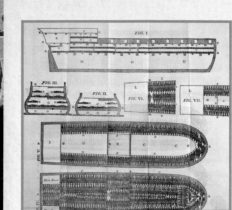

▲ *BROOKS* SLAVE SHIP *This ship was designed to carry around 450 slaves, but more than 600 were often packed in, chained together.*

The slave trade

Slavery has been a feature of many societies, such as ancient Egypt and Rome. But it was the Atlantic slave trade that made slavery a worldwide issue. It had its roots in the Portuguese transportation of workers from Africa to Madeira, in 1470. By the time slavery was abolished 400 years later, around 12 million slaves had been taken from Africa to the New World.

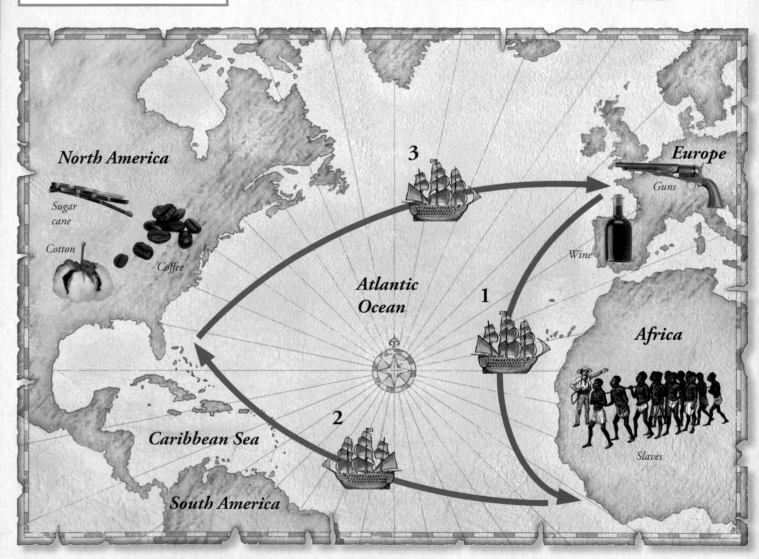

North America

Sugar cane

Cotton

Coffee

3

Europe

Guns

Wine

Atlantic Ocean

1

Africa

Caribbean Sea

2

Slaves

South America

THE TRIANGULAR TRADE

The slave trade was all about money. European traders exported goods to Africa, then used the ships to pick up a new cargo: people. They were taken to work on plantations in southern North America, South America, and Caribbean islands.

1 EUROPE TO AFRICA *The Europeans traded copper, iron, cloth, wine, glassware, and guns with African landlords for people.*

2 AFRICA TO AMERICAS *"The Middle Passage" People were snatched from villages and fields and marched to the coast to board slave ships.*

3 AMERICAS TO EUROPE *Sugar, rice, cotton, coffee, tobacco, and rum from the plantations were brought back to Europe.*

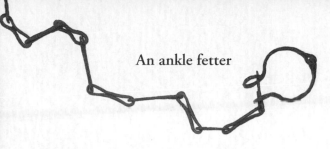
An ankle fetter

SLAVES FOR SALE

On arrival in the New World, slaves were taken to markets, where they were sold by auction to plantation owners. The slaves were branded – burned with hot irons – with the mark of their new owner. Men, women, boys, and girls were all put up for sale.

▲ NO ESCAPE *From the moment they were first seized in Africa, slaves were forced to wear shackles such as neck collars and ankle fetters. They were chained together so that they could not escape.*

◀ IN THE FIELDS *Slaves were made to pick crops such as cotton.*

Forced labour Slaves were taken to work on the plantations set up by European settlers. Life was brutal, with long hours, poor food rations, no wages, and frequent beatings. Children born to slaves became slaves themselves and belonged to the plantation owner, who could send them away from their families to work on another plantation.

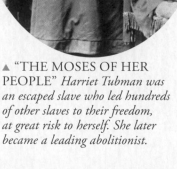

▲ "THE MOSES OF HER PEOPLE" *Harriet Tubman was an escaped slave who led hundreds of other slaves to their freedom, at great risk to herself. She later became a leading abolitionist.*

FROM SLAVERY TO CIVIL WAR

Confederate general

By the late 18th century, people were campaigning for the end of slavery.

■ **The Abolition of Slave Trade Act** was passed in Britain in 1807, outlawing the slave trade, but slavery itself didn't end in the British Empire until 1833, and in the USA until 1865.

■ Abolition was one of the main causes of the **American Civil War** (1861–1865), as the Southern Confederate "slave states" did not want to end slavery – but the Northern Unionist states did.

■ **Abraham Lincoln** was one of the key anti-slavery figures in the USA. When the Confederates declared war, he began freeing slaves.

Unionist soldier

The age of empire

Since the 1600s, European countries had steadily gained land and influence over countries around the world. From the mid-1800s, they competed against each other to control new trade markets, increasing the size of their empires and becoming wealthy.

USA

North America
Many people from Europe emigrated to the USA or Canada to escape bad conditions at home, such as the potato famine in Ireland. The arrival of these new settlers led to the exploration of remote inland areas and a route across the whole continent.

TELL ME MORE...

In 1805, Meriwether Lewis and William Clark were the first American explorers to find a route through the Rocky Mountains to reach the western territories of America. Other explorers, traders, and settlers followed afterwards.

IMPORTS AND EXPORTS

European countries imported raw materials from their empires and exported manufactured goods back to their colonies.

North America

Europe

▶ RAILWAYS
A vast network of tracks were laid across countries and continents for the transporting of goods by rail.

Africa

Coffee

Sugar cane

Gold

South America

Cocoa

▶ SOUTH AMERICA
During the 1800s, many of the countries in South America became independent. Only the British, French, and Dutch had colonies with big plantations.

▶ SOUTH AFRICA *The discovery of diamonds in the mid-1800s transformed a poor colony into a much desired one and sparked conflicts in the area.*

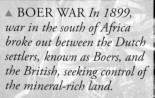

▲ BOER WAR *In 1899, war in the south of Africa broke out between the Dutch settlers, known as Boers, and the British, seeking control of the mineral-rich land.*

Africa
The "scramble for Africa" began in the 1870s when European countries competed against each other to gain control of land on this continent. Explorers had found raw materials such as gold and diamonds, and there was land and people available for setting up plantations.

Russia

China

This map shows the borders and empires in 1900.

Empire-builders

The main European colonial powers were Great Britain, France, the Netherlands, and Portugal. By the end of the 19th century, Great Britain's empire covered one-quarter of Earth's land surface.

- Britain
- France
- Spain
- Portugal
- Italy
- Netherlands
- Germany
- Ottoman Empire

INDEPENDENCE

The Commonwealth Games

After World War II, many colonies started campaigning to become independent countries. During the 1940s and 1960s, most gained independence although the transition for some countries, such as India, caused violence. Many nations still have links to their colonial power. The Commonwealth is an organization of 53 states that were once part of the British Empire.

India

By 1900, Britain ruled the whole of India. Many British administrators and traders with their families lived there, enjoying the privileged colonial lifestyle. Owners of tea plantations became rich while the local workers lived in poverty.

▼ EGYPT
The Suez Canal opened in 1869 allowing an easier and quicker access route to India.

Suez Canal

Tea

India

🔍 TAKE A LOOK: TRADE

Access to raw materials was very important to the growing industrial countries. It was simpler and more profitable to own the country where these came from rather than negotiate with the local rulers. Colonies also provided cheap labour for the mines and the plantations.

Cotton   Rubber

Ivory

► MALAYSIA
The British government set up very profitable tin mines and rubber plantations.

Tin

Coffee

Gold

Gold

Australia

Gold

► INDONESIA
After the success of the Dutch East India trading company in the 17th and 18th century, the Dutch government took control and set up big plantations to grow crops such as coffee and spices.

▲ AUSTRALIA
The discovery of gold in the town of Victoria in the 1850s led to a gold rush. The European population grew very quickly.

Australia

The British used convicts to establish their first colonies in Australia. Free settlers began to arrive in 1793. The native aborigines were pushed off their land by the new settlers and forced into the Outback – an inhospitable, unfertile area that the settlers did not want.

◄ THE FIRST FLEET *In 1788, British navy ships transported convicts to Botany Bay in Australia.*

Industrial Revolution

Between 1750 and 1850, the development of power-driven machines transformed the lives of people first in Britain and then other European countries and the United States. This period is known as the Industrial Revolution.

Burning the coal to produce steam to power the machines produced choking smoke.

Child labour Children as young as six years old worked in the factories, until 1833 when under-nines were banned. They worked up to 12 or 14 hours a day with few breaks. Sometimes, they were injured or even killed by the machinery.

WOW!

Before the revolution, most people worked as farmers in the fields. Spinning and weaving were done at home. The invention of machines changed this. Thousands of workers seeking more pay moved into the towns to work in the newly-built factories, which housed these big machines.

▲ FACTORIES *From the 1790s, steam power replaced the previously water-powered machines. Inside the factories, the noise of the machines was deafening. Outside, the towns were dirty and unhealthy places.*

TIMELINE OF INDUSTRIAL INVENTIONS

1712

Thomas Newcomen built the first commercially successful steam engine. It was used to pump water out of mines.

1764

James Hargreaves invented the spinning jenny – a mechanized spinning wheel that could spin eight threads at once.

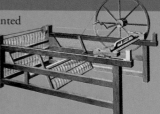

1779

Samuel Crompton's water-powered, spinning "mule" was bought by many factory owners.

TELL ME MORE...

The Industrial Revolution caused much unrest especially from the skilled textiles workers angered by the introduction of looms that could be used by unskilled workers for low wages, forcing them out of a job. One group, known as the Luddites, destroyed the machines in cotton and woollen mills.

Cotton gin The USA became the world's leading cotton producer thanks to the invention of the cotton gin by Eli Whitney. This machine could quickly separate the cotton fibres from the seeds, which had previously taken ages by hand.

WHO'S WHO?

■ **James Watt** (1736-1819) A Scottish engineer who made improvements to the steam engine in 1769 so that machines could be powered without water.

■ **Eli Whitney** (1765-1825) An American inventor who designed the cotton gin whilst staying on a plantation in the southern states.

■ **Francis Cabot Lowell** (1775-1817) An American merchant who established the first textile mill in the United States.

■ **George Stephenson** (1781-1848) An English engineer who built the first public railway line in the world.

■ **Isambard Kingdom Brunel** (1806-1859) A British engineer who designed many tunnels, bridges, railway lines, and ships.

TAKE A PICTURE

Canals were built to transport the heavy loads to and from the factories. The boat lifts on the Canal du Centre, Wallonia in Belgium show the amazing engineering feats of this age.

Railway mania In 1804, Richard Trevithick added wheels to his steam engine so that it could run along tracks. Within thirty years, a network of railways for transporting raw materials, goods, and people by steam locomotives was constructed. Travelling around was now much quicker.

1785
Textile-making could be done much faster by **Edmund Cartwright's** power loom.

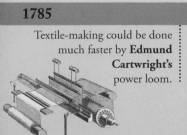

1793
Cotton could be produced much faster with **Eli Whitney's** cotton gin.

1801
Joseph-Marie Jacquard's loom was the first machine to be controlled by punched cards – an idea later used in computing.

1830
The world's first all-steam passenger railway opened in Britain.

World War I

At the beginning of the 1900s, military and political tensions existed between some of the countries of Europe. The assassination of the heir to the Austria-Hungary throne was the spark needed to fire up a war that involved the world.

MILITARY TRANSPORT

■ **Aircraft:** Biplanes and triplanes were used to fly over enemy lines to observe their movements and take photographs.
■ **Vehicles:** Horse-drawn vehicles were gradually replaced by mechanical ones to transport men and supplies to and from the front line.
■ **Tanks:** The first tanks used in 1916 were not very reliable but a year later they were leading the way across to the enemy trenches, shielding the troops.
■ **Warships:** Fleets of warships were used to protect supply ships from attacks by the German U-boats.

German triplane

Horse-drawn ambulance

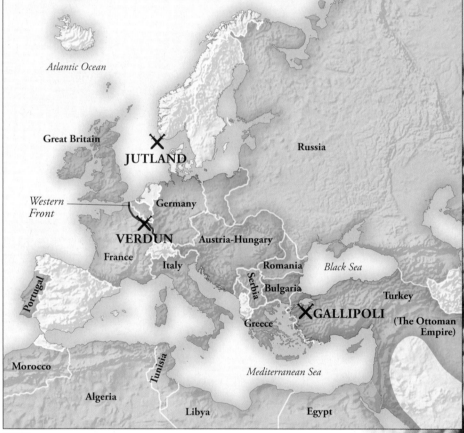

Allied powers

Central powers

Neutral nations

✗ Key battle sites

World at war Although most of the fighting took place in Europe, there was also fighting in the Middle East, in Africa, and in the German colonies in China and the Pacific Ocean.

TIMELINE OF WORLD WAR I

1914

The assassination of Archduke Francis Ferdinand on 28 June, 1914 caused Austria-Hungary to declare war on Serbia. European countries took sides and by August The Great War had begun.

1915

The German's zeppelins made frequent night-time bombing raids over British cities.

THE FRONT LINE

By the end of 1914, a network of trenches zig-zagged from the Belgian coast to the Swiss border, forming the Western Front. From these positions, the Allied troops tried to push back the advancing German army, but neither side made much progress. Under fire from machine guns, the strip of land between each other's trenches was impossible to cross.

▶ CROSSING NO-MAN'S LAND
Most attempts to advance occurred at dawn or dusk.

Trenchcoat

Gas attack
A deadly chlorine gas was used for the first time in the battle for the Belgium town of Ypres in 1915.

TAKE A PICTURE

More than half of the 65 million men who fought in the war were killed or injured and about 6.6 million civilians also died.

1916
The naval battle of Jutland was the largest fought in history.

1917
The USA joined the Allies, angered by the German U-boat attacks on shipping in the Atlantic Ocean.

1918
At 11 am on the 11th day of the 11th month (November), an armistice (cease-fire) took place. A peace treaty was later signed.

World War II

The peace treaty signed at the end of World War I (the Treaty of Versailles in 1919) forced Germany to give up much of its land and wealth, and restricted the size of its army. Twenty years later, the Nazi Party in Germany had rebuilt the nation and their leader Adolf Hitler was determined to rule Europe.

Adolf Hitler

Adolf Hitler (1889-1945) Born in Austria, Hitler became an influential politician in Germany. After being appointed chancellor in 1933, Hitler created a one-party state and made himself an all-powerful dictator.

Destruction Bombing raids by the Allied and Axis powers caused huge destruction across Europe, USSR, and east Asia. The raids were intended to target strategic buildings, such as airfields, factories, ports, and railways but often homes were destroyed, killing civilians or forcing them to evacuate (leave the area).

FAST FACTS

■ The leaders of Britain (Winston Churchill), the Soviet Union (Josef Stalin), and the USA (Franklin Roosevelt) met twice during the war to discuss strategies.
■ Resistant groups of people from German-occupied countries helped the Allies by spying and acts of sabotage.

▲ GAS MASK *Countries feared that gas would be used by the enemy so many people were issued with gas masks. They were never needed.*

TIMELINE OF WORLD WAR II

1939
On 1 September, German forces invaded Poland. Britain and France declared war on Germany.
210

1940
Between June and October, 1940, the German air force battled the British air force in the skies above Britain.

1941
On 7 December, Japan attacked the US naval base at Pearl Harbour in Hawaii. The US entered the war.

1942
In August, the Germans began the six-month-long battle for Stalingrad in the Soviet Union.

THE WORLD AT WAR

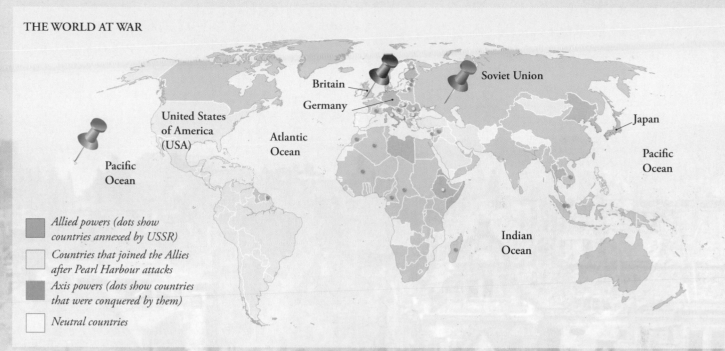

Britain
Germany
Soviet Union
United States of America (USA)
Atlantic Ocean
Japan
Pacific Ocean
Pacific Ocean
Indian Ocean

Allied powers (dots show countries annexed by USSR)

Countries that joined the Allies after Pearl Harbour attacks

Axis powers (dots show countries that were conquered by them)

Neutral countries

Main players Until mid-1941, the two sides were the Axis (Germany, Italy, and some east European countries) and the Allies (Britain, France, and countries in their empires). Nations around the world became involved when Germany invaded the Soviet Union and Japan's attacks began.

BATTLE OF BRITAIN *After conquering France in June 1940, Germany planned to take over Britain. The British air force was targeted first but the German air force was unable to defeat them.*

STALINGRAD *Germany invaded the Soviet Union in 1941. There was huge loss of life on both sides especially in the battle for Stalingrad in the south. In 1943, the weakened German army surrendered.*

PEARL HARBOUR *The unexpected attack by the Japanese air force on the US naval base in Hawaii destroyed 19 ships and killed 2,403 soldiers. The USA immediately declared war on the Axis powers.*

▼ THE CAMPS *Auschwitz in Poland was one of eight concentration camps that had gas chambers.*

THE COLD WAR

The Holocaust The Nazi party was very anti-Semitic (against Jews). They forced Jews to wear badges with a yellow star and from 1942 sent them to concentration camps. Many millions of Jews died from illness, starvation, and in gas chambers.

TAKE A PICTURE

After the war, relations between the Soviet Union and USA became very tense. Eastern and western Europe were separated. The collapse of the Berlin Wall, Germany, in 1989 became a symbolic end to this Cold War.

1943
In May, the Axis army in North Africa finally surrendered to the Allies.

1944
On 6 June (D-day), Allied forces invaded the beaches of Normandy, France, and began to push back the Axis forces.

1945
In May, Germany surrendered but the war continued in east Asia. Japan surrendered only after atomic bombs were dropped on two cities in August.

Revolution!

World history has been marked by episodes when a sudden uprising of people driven by hardship has overthrown those in power. An alternative political system has been established in the hope for a better life.

REVOLUTIONARY LEADERS

- **Vladimir Lenin** (1870-1924) was leader of the Bolshevik Social Democratic Workers' party and first head of the Soviet state.
- **Mohandas Ghandi** (1869-1958) is considered the father of India.
- **Mao Zedong** (1893-1976) was a Chinese communist leader and the founder of the People's Republic of China.
- **Fidel Castro** (1926-) has been president of Cuba since 1949 and is the world's longest serving leader.

The Year of Revolution A wave of unrest spread across many European countries in 1848. With many starving and unemployed, the demonstrators wanted more rights and a greater say in how their countries were governed. Although the revolts fizzled out, they were the sparks for later political reforms.

▼ *In March, a peaceful demonstration in Vienna, Austria, turned violent.*

1789
"LIBERTY, EQUALITY, FRATERNITY!"
Despite France facing severe food and money shortages, King Louis XVI and his wife Queen Marie-Antoinette enjoyed a luxurious lifestyle.

1799

1848
"WORKERS OF ALL LANDS, UNITE!"
In 1848, a German political writer, Karl Marx, published his thoughts on communism.

The storming of the Bastille
On 14th July, 1789, the starving people of Paris rioted when they heard rumours that King Louis XVI had ordered the army to suppress the commoners and wanted to raise taxes.

▼ LOUIS XVI
Executed in 1793

▼ *Napoleon wrote about 33,000 letters.*

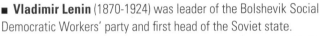

The French Revolution
After the death of Louis XVI, the country became a republic but there was a reign of terror with thousands of people executed at the guillotine. In 1799, the army eventually gained control under the dictatorship of its general, Napoleon Bonaparte.

▶ NAPOLEONIC WARS *Napoleon crowned himself Emperor of the First French Empire in 1804 and led successful military campaigns across Europe.*

India's peaceful revolution The political figure Mohandas Ghandi returned to India in 1914. He began a gradual campaign of urging Indians to boycott the British-run courts and schools and resign from government positions. In 1930, Ghandi led a 386 km (240 mile) march protesting against the tax on salt.

The Indian spiritual and political leader, Mohandas Ghandi, in 1947 – the year India finally won independence from the British.

Cuban revolution The revolutionary Fidel Castro led a small band of rebels and peasants in their two-year fight against the large army of the dictator Fulgencio Batista. When Castro took power in January, 1959, he made many reforms, improving Cubans' healthcare and education.

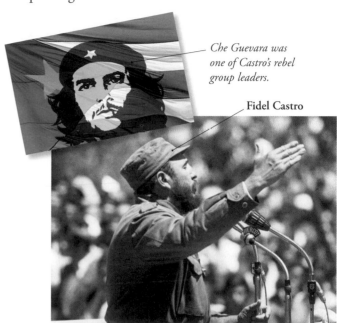

Che Guevara was one of Castro's rebel group leaders.

Fidel Castro

1914-47

"BE THE CHANGE YOU WANT TO SEE IN THE WORLD."
Ghandi encouraged resistance through non-violent civil disobedience.

1917

1956-58

"SMASH THE OLD WORLD, ESTABLISH A NEW WORLD."
Young people in China formed the Red Guards to promote Mao's message.

1966-76

▲ *Workers and mutinied soldiers marched on the streets of Petrograd (St. Petersburg).*

The two revolutions Stirred up by the Bolshevik socialist party, the starving and war-weary Russians demonstrated against the unpopular Tsar (king) Nicholas II in February, 1917, who then abdicated. In October, led by Vladimir Lenin, the Bolsheviks overthrew the government to form the first communist state.

▲ HAMMER AND SICKLE BADGE
In 1922, Russia was renamed the Union of Soviet Socialist Republics (USSR). Their symbol represented the unity of the workers and peasants.

China's cultural revolution In 1966, the leader of the Chinese Communist Party, Mao Zedong, launched a campaign to make China a classless society. Millions of educated and privileged people were forced into manual labour to be "re-educated" and many thousands were killed.

▼ *Everyone had to read and carry around a copy of Mao's "Little Red Book".*

Chairman Mao reimposed his control

无产阶级文化大革命全面胜利万岁

In the news

Every day, history is being made. Events affecting people's lives and altering the politics of nations around the world are reported in the newspapers, or on the television and the internet.

FAST FACTS

■ On 11 September, 2001, terrorists linked with a group called Al-Qaeda attacked buildings in the USA. These 9/11 attacks have led to a "War on Terror" against Muslim militants.

■ Founded in 1945, the United Nations is an international organization that seeks to achieve world peace.

BREAK UP OF THE USSR

In 1991, the Union of Soviet Socialist Republics (USSR) was broken up and some areas became independent countries. Since then other areas have wanted independence, sometimes causing unrest.

PROTEST *In 2008, people protested during the conflict between Russia and the independent state of Georgia.*

Russia, or the Russian Federation, became the largest of the new countries, continuing as a communist state. Rebel fighters from the Chechen Republic, or Chechnya, have taken hostages in an attempt to get independence from Russia. In 2008, Russia and Georgia were fighting over the control of the areas of Abkhazia and South Ossetia.

▲ CHECHNYA JOBS
Around 50 per cent of the population of Chechnya are unemployed. The dangerous work of climbing on to unstable ruins to collect construction material is one of the few ways to make some money.

CONFLICT IN AFGHANISTAN

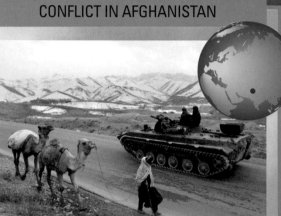

The Taliban is an Islamic movement that ruled Afghanistan from 1996-2001. After the 9/11 attacks (see fast facts), Al-Qaeda leaders were believed to be sheltering in Afghanistan and this led to the country being attacked by the USA and its allies. They overthrew the Taliban government, but Taliban troops have continued to fight against the new government of Afghanistan and against the US and allied troops who are still stationed there.

▲ GULF OIL FIELD
The states around the Gulf have become super rich due to the oil revenue. The 483-km (300-mile) long oil field in Saudi Arabia is the world's largest.

ISRAEL AND PALESTINE

After World War II, the state of Israel was created as a home for Jewish people. The Palestinians also have claims to the land. Since then there have been wars between Israel and its Arab neighbours and in more recent years many suicide bombings and other attacks between Israel and Palestinians.

The West Bank and the Gaza Strip are the two unconnected regions of the Palestinian territories. A network of fences, trenches, and high concrete walls have been constructed as a barrier around the West Bank and the Gaza Strip.

▲ BREACHING THE WALLS
The Palestinians in the Gaza Strip have made a number of attempts to cross into Egypt, seeking food and supplies.

THE GULF REGION

The region around the Persian Gulf – a large bay that extends from the Indian Ocean – is the world's largest source of crude oil. Any conflict in the region is an immediate threat to oil supplies around the world. Other countries are quick to intervene to safeguard the stability of the region and their own oil supplies.

The 2003 Gulf War

In 2003, the world was concerned that Iraq might be making dangerous biological and chemical weapons. A US-led multinational force rapidly defeated the Iraqi army and the authoritarian president was replaced by a new elected government.

Coalition troops continued to be stationed in Iraq to support the democratic process and the rebuilding of the country.

CENTRAL AND EAST AFRICA

Fighting between rebel groups and government forces in some countries in central and east Africa have forced many thousands of refugees to flee their homes. The area is also prone to environmental disasters, such as droughts or floods, causing food and water shortages.

Refugees living in vast camps rely on food aid supplied by charitable organizations.

📷 TAKE A PICTURE

In 2011 an extraordinary series of popular uprisings occured in North Africa and the Middle East. The overthrow of decades-old authoritarian regimes transformed the whole region, in events that became known as the "Arab Spring".

What is a government?

A government is a small group of people who make laws and decisions about how their country is run. They raise money from everyone in taxes and decide how this money is to be spent, such as on hospitals, schools, the army, prisons, and the building of new roads.

ONE-PARTY STATE

In some countries, only one political party is allowed to exist; all others are banned. When there is an election, the one party decides who the candidates will be and the voters only get to approve that choice.

▶ REPUBLIC OF CUBA
The Cuban Communist Party is the only recognized political party.

MONARCHY

Many countries, like the UK, have a king or queen that acts as head of state but does not govern the country. However, there are a few countries where the monarch still holds all the power and governs the country. These "absolute monarchs" are not elected, but when they die power passes to their son or daughter.

▲ KINGDOM OF BRUNEI
The Sultan of Brunei has absolute power.

WHO'S WHO?

■ **President** A head of state of a republic with either extensive powers (as in the USA) or limited powers (as in Germany).

■ **Prime minister** The head of government in a parliamentary democracy.

■ **Dictator** A ruler who has absolute power.

■ **Monarchy** The hereditary rule of a single person. An absolute monarch has unchecked powers, while a constitutional monarch has limited powers.

■ **Opposition** The parties that are not in a government and may disagree with the governing party.

■ **Senate** The upper house of a legislative assembly (as in the USA).

■ **Cabinet** A group of ministers or others that advises a head of government.

■ **Representative** A person who is elected to represent the public in making laws.

MILITARY RULE

In some countries, if the government is weak or unpopular, the army seize power and form a military government. The country is governed by a military junta – a group of senior military officers, often with one particular general in control.

◀ THE UNION OF MYANMAR
In 1962, a military coup overthrew the Burmese government and since then a general has taken the position as head of state. All the cabinet roles are held by military officers. Ethnic struggles between the Government (junta), the Karen National Union, and the Mong Tai Army have continued.

NON DEMOCRATIC

MULTI-PARTY DEMOCRACY

▲ **THE CANDIDATES**
In an election, candidates may be nominated by different political parties. The person who gets the most votes is elected and the party with the most elected candidates forms the government.

SYSTEMS OF GOVERNMENT

A constitution is a written document or unwritten code that establishes the structure and rules of the political organization of a country. Constitutional democracies may take the form of republics as in France and the USA or constitutional monarchy as in the UK and Spain. The country may have a presidential system (USA), a parliamentary system (UK), or a semi-presidential system (France).

▼ **PROTESTS**
If people disagree with a bill, they will often organize protests to try to make their government take notice or change it.

TAKE A LOOK: VOTING IN ELECTIONS

In a democracy, all adults are allowed to vote. On election day, they are given a piece of paper with the names of the candidates on it, and they show which one they want to vote for by putting a cross or a number next to the candidate's name. The voters post their voting slips into a locked ballot box. Afterwards, the votes are counted and the candidate with the most votes is elected.

TYPES OF DEMOCRATIC GOVERNMENTS:

United Kingdom (UK) constitutional monarchy

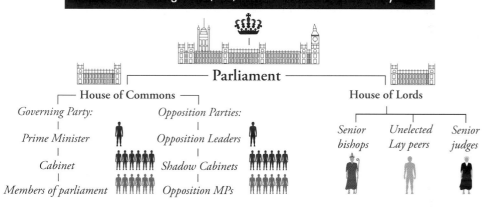

▲ **UNITED KINGDOM (UK)** *The monarch acts as head of state, but the parliament is responsible for making and changing the laws in the UK, which is done with the majority approval of both the House of Commons and the House of Lords.*

United States of America (USA) constitution

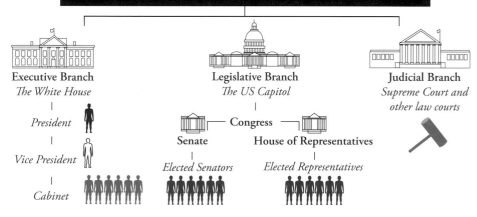

▲ **UNITED STATES OF AMERICA (USA)** *The USA is the oldest constitutional republic and has three separate branches. The executive branch carries out the instructions of congress, the legislative branch creates and changes laws, and the judicial branch manages the system of justice.*

DEMOCRATIC

SCIENCE

- The word science comes from the Latin *scientia*, meaning knowledge.

- Scientific ideas were recorded by the philosopher Aristotle about 2,350 years ago.

- Sound waves with a frequency of 20,000 Hz or more are known as ultrasound.

- The Universe is about 13.7 billion years old, and is expanding at an increasing rate.

- The Earth's core is a solid iron sphere surrounded by a deep layer of molten iron.

? How does a nutcracker crush a walnut? *Find out on page 233*

? What is terminal velocity and how does it affect a skydiver? *Find out on pages 234–235*

Definition: **Science** helps us understand the workings of the Universe and everything in it. We increase our knowledge by observing, experimenting, and testing theories.

- Einstein's famous equation $E=mc^2$ explains that energy and matter are the same thing.

- The Earth's climate is changing as a result of carbon dioxide produced by human activity.

- The instructions to make you are carried on about 25,000 genes in the DNA of your cells.

- In 1514 Copernicus was the first to show that the Earth moves around the Sun.

- Sound travels at a speed of 1,190 km/h (740 mph) through dry air that is 0°C (32°F).

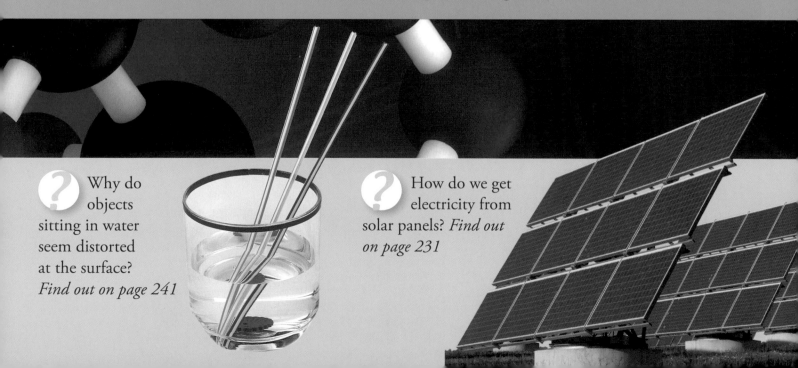

? Why do objects sitting in water seem distorted at the surface? *Find out on page 241*

? How do we get electricity from solar panels? *Find out on page 231*

What is science?

Science is the search for knowledge about the world and the way it works. Unlike other ways of explaining how the world works, science is based on experiments that test theories (ideas).

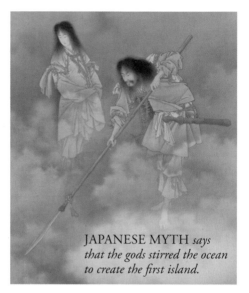

JAPANESE MYTH *says that the gods stirred the ocean to create the first island.*

BEFORE SCIENCE

In the past, people relied on ancient stories to explain such things as how life began, why the Sun appears to cross the sky, what lies beyond the oceans, and so on. These stories often came from religious books or from scholars who dreamed up imaginative ideas without checking them. Because the stories were never tested, there were hundreds of different versions, and every culture had a different version of the truth.

TAKE A LOOK: COPERNICUS

■ One of the greatest ever scientific theories was put forward by Polish astronomer Nicolaus Copernicus in 1507. His idea was that Earth travels around the Sun rather than vice versa. At first, people thought this was daft because the Sun moves across the sky each day, as though it's going round Earth. But Copernicus discovered that this is an illusion caused by Earth spinning round.

▲ COPERNICAN WORLD SYSTEM
Pictures like this showed the Sun at the centre of the Universe for the first time.

How does science work?

Science began when people started to check their ideas about the world. One of the first people to do this was an English doctor named William Gilbert (1544–1603). He carried out many experiments on magnetism and eventually proved that Earth is like a giant magnet.

◄ OLD MARINERS COMPASS *Gilbert showed that compasses point north because of Earth's magnetism.*

Testing theories

Scientists begin with an idea or "theory". Imagine you have a cold but get better after drinking orange juice. You might form a theory that orange cures colds. To test this, you could give orange to people with colds. If they get better faster than people who don't drink orange, the theory is strengthened.

Orange juice

Proving theories

Although scientists can prove that a bad theory is wrong, they can never prove that a good theory is absolutely right. Even if a theory seems correct, someone could always do a new experiment in the future and prove it wrong. So theories always remain theories.

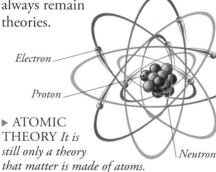

Electron

Proton

▶ ATOMIC THEORY *It is still only a theory that matter is made of atoms.*

Neutron

TIMELINE OF SCIENCE

c.350 BCE	1543	1665	1687	1730–1880
Aristotle is often called the first scientist. His ideas helped lay the foundations of modern sciences such as physics, chemistry, and biology.	**Andreas Vesalius** was a Belgian who wrote a seven-volume book about the human body.	**Robert Hooke** was an English scientist. He used an early microscope to show that cells are the building blocks of all living things.	**Isaac Newton** was a British scientist. He set out new ideas about motion and gravity.	Many scientists built on one another's work to understand electricity and turn it into a useful source of power.

THE SCIENCES

Since science began more than 2,000 years ago, our knowledge of the world has increased enormously. Science has led to many discoveries that have transformed society, such as cures for diseases. It's also led to amazing new inventions, such as telephones, televisions, space rockets, and computers. These practical spin-offs of science are called technologies.

Medicine

Medicine is the science of healing illnesses. In the past, people believed that diseases were a punishment for bad behaviour. Scientists now know that most diseases are caused by microscopic organisms, inherited genes, or faults with a person's immune system.

Chemistry

All substances are made of chemicals, from your hair and teeth to the air around you and the paper in this book. Chemists investigate how atoms join together in different ways to form molecules, or how molecules break apart and recombine to form new substances.

Biology

Biology is the scientific study of living things. Its many branches are devoted to different kinds of life, including botany (the study of plants) and zoology (the study of animals). The most important idea in biology is the theory of evolution by natural selection, which explains how living things came to exist in their current form.

▶ FOSSIL
Preserved remains of living things helped scientists to understand evolution.

Physics

Physicists investigate energy and movement. They study the tiniest particles of matter that make up atoms, and things that aren't made of matter at all, such as time, light, gravity, and space. The work of physicists led to the discovery of radio waves, which gave us television and mobile phone technology.

Geology

Geology is the study of Earth and its interior. Geologists study how rocks form from chemicals called minerals and how they break down or change into new types of rock. Geologists also look at processes that happen deep underground in Earth's interior. These processes cause earthquakes and volcanoes, and continually re-shape our planet's surface over long periods of time.

Astronomy

Planet Earth is a tiny speck of matter in a vast universe of planets, stars, galaxies, and colossal areas of empty space. Astronomy is the study of this gigantic realm beyond our own planet. Thanks to rocket technology, astronomers can now study space at first hand.

1869	1890–1956	1905–1915	1953	1989
Dmitri Mendeleyev was a Russian chemist. He laid the foundations of modern chemistry when he wrote the Periodic Table.	Scientists developed the atomic theory. They knew how atoms are put together and how they break apart.	**Albert Einstein's** theories of relativity changed physics with new ideas about space, time, light, and gravity.	**Francis Crick** and **James Watson** unravelled the structure of DNA, the genetic code inside living things.	**Tim Berners-Lee** invented the World Wide Web, a new way of sharing information.

Mighty atoms

Everything is made up of atoms. These incredibly small particles are the building blocks of all matter, from the rocks that make up our Earth, and the animals, plants, and other creatures that live on it, to the planets and stars in distant galaxies.

INSIDE ATOMS

Atoms may be small, but they contain even smaller particles. Protons and neutrons cluster together in the nucleus at the centre of the atom. Electrons move in a cloud that surrounds the nucleus. Strong electrical forces hold these small particles together inside atoms.

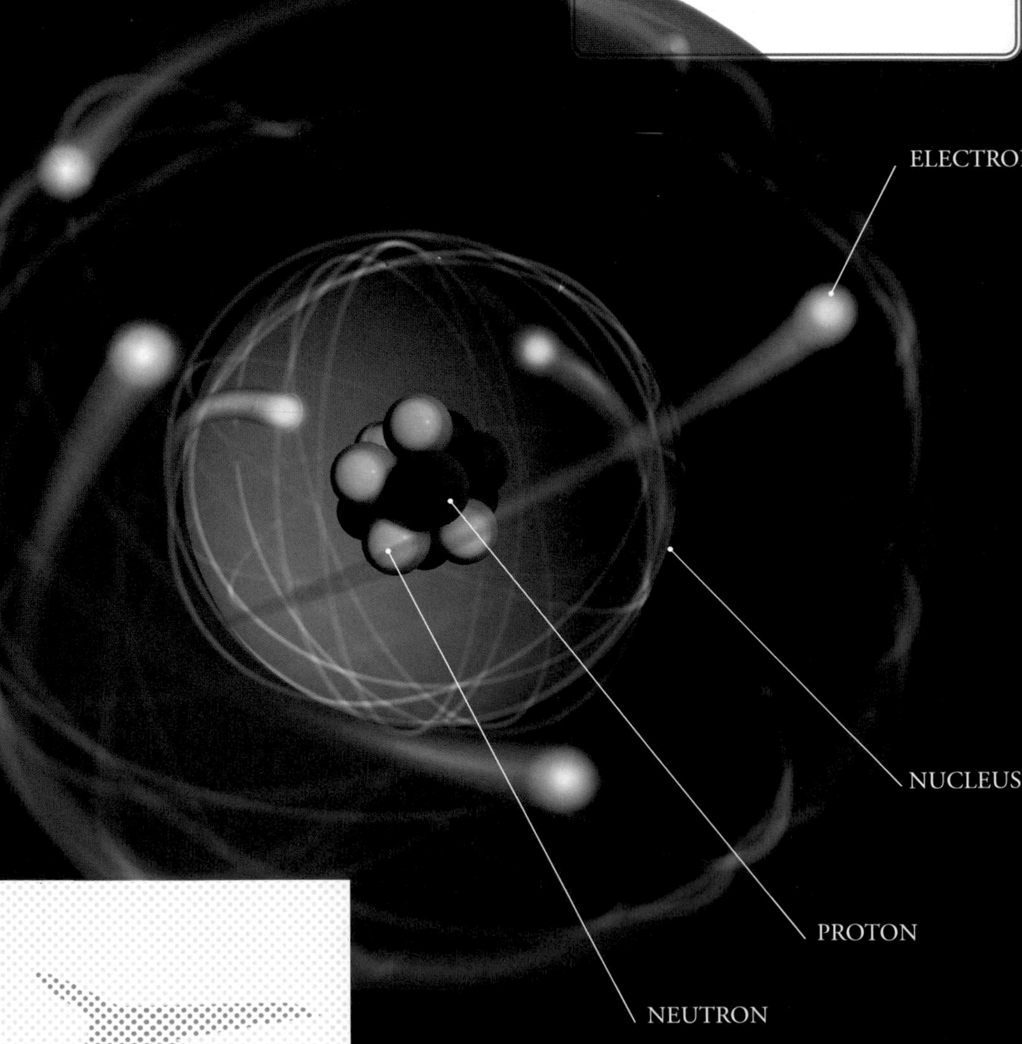

▼ ATOMS *Just as the images on a computer monitor consist of tiny dots of light called pixels, objects in the real world are made of tiny dots of matter called atoms.*

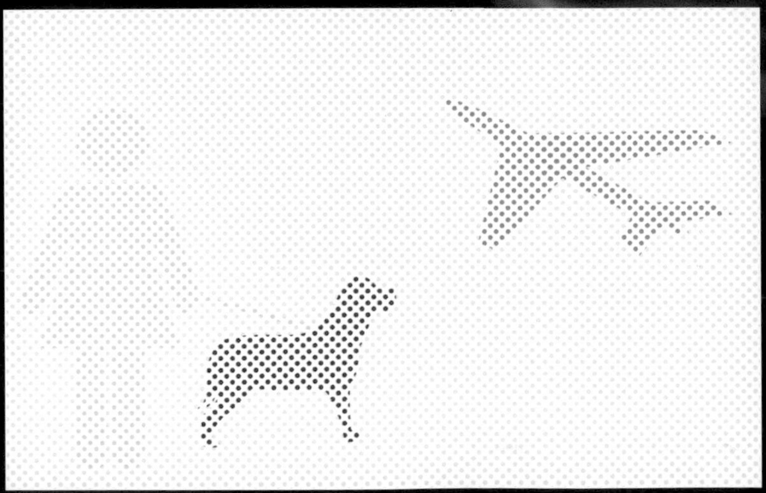

ELECTRON

NUCLEUS

PROTON

NEUTRON

LOOKING AT ATOMS

Atoms are too small to see. In fact they are much smaller than the wavelengths of visible light, so a microscope is not much use either. Instead, scientists "see" atoms by taking pictures of the electric fields around these tiny particles.

Glucose
$C_6H_{12}O_6$

- Also known as dextrose
- First isolated from raisins in 1747 by Andreas Margaff

Plants make this simple sugar using the energy in sunlight. Animals eat these plants and other animals and then use the glucose in them as a source of energy to stay alive.

Alcohol
C_2H_6O

- Also known as ethanol
- Formed by the action of yeast on natural sugars.

The word *alcohol* is the common name for ethanol, which is the type of alcohol found in beer, wine, and spirits. In concentrated form it kills germs. Doctors and nurses use it to clean the skin before an injection.

Water
H_2O

- Covers around 70 per cent of Earth's surface
- Essential for life

Without water, life on Earth could not survive. This simple molecule makes up around 70 per cent of the human body. Water is the only molecule that exists on Earth in three different forms – as a solid (ice), a gas (water vapour), and liquid (water).

Vitamin B₇
$C_{10}H_{16}N_2O_3S$

- Also known as biotin or vitamin H
- First isolated in 1941 by Vincent Du Vigneaud

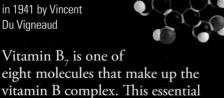

Vitamin B_7 is one of eight molecules that make up the vitamin B complex. This essential vitamin is vital for cell growth. Sources include liver, brewer's yeast, and dairy products.

Vitamin D
$C_{28}H_{44}O$

- Also known as cholecalciferol
- First isolated in 1922 by Edward Mellanby

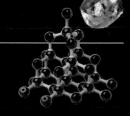

Vitamin D is essential for building strong bones. This molecule is made in the body when the skin is exposed to sunlight. Other sources include cereals and fatty fish.

Diamond
C

- Hardest known substance in nature
- Highly prized as a gemstone for jewellery

Diamond is a rare form of carbon in which each carbon atom bonds with four other carbon atoms to form a tightly packed crystal structure. Diamonds are very hard so they are used to make the tips of drills.

MOLECULES Atoms stick together to form bigger particles called molecules. The force that holds them together is called a chemical bond. Atoms form chemical bonds by donating or sharing electrons with other atoms.

▼ EACH DROP OF WATER
below is made up of three atoms – one oxygen atom (light blue) and two smaller hydrogen atoms (white)

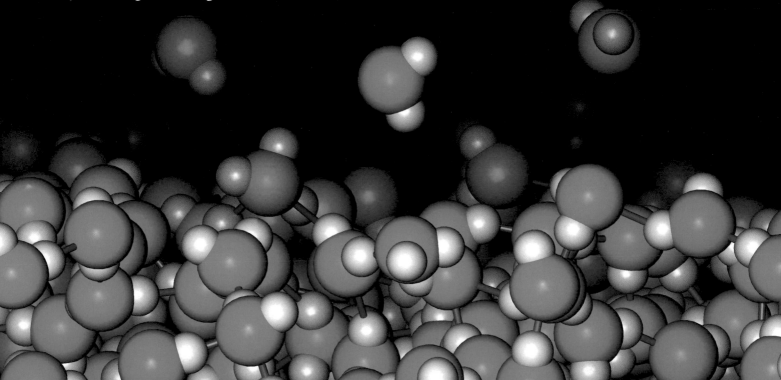

Solid, liquid, or gas?

Almost everything in the world exists in one of three states of matter. Solids keep a fixed shape, liquids have no fixed shape but fill the container in which they are held, and gases float around in space with no fixed shape or volume.

▲ SOLID *The atoms or molecules in a solid are packed tightly together.*

SOLID STATE

The atoms or molecules in a solid substance are held together by electrical forces. They are arranged in a repeating pattern called a crystal lattice – similar to the way apples or oranges stack together in a grocery store. This makes the solid dense and hard.

▲ LIQUID *The atoms or molecules in a liquid are packed less tightly than those of a solid.*

SOLID TO LIQUID *If you heat up an ice cube to its melting point, the solid ice gradually turns into liquid water. Ice melts at 0°C (32°F).*

Melting

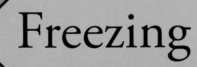

Freezing

LIQUID TO SOLID *When the molecules in liquid water lose energy, they freeze and turn into solid ice. Water freezes at 0°C (32°F).*

Carbon crystals A diamond is made up of many carbon atoms, which line up to form a crystal. The arrangement is so perfect that the carbon atoms are held very tightly. This makes diamond the hardest substance found in nature.

CHANGING STATES

If you heat a solid enough, the atoms or molecules from which it is made get enough energy to break apart and slide over each other. The solid melts and changes from the solid state into the liquid state. Heat the liquid further, and it boils, changing into the gaseous state.

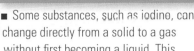

INTO THIN AIR

- Some substances, such as iodine, can change directly from a solid to a gas without first becoming a liquid. This is called sublimation.
- At room temperature, dry ice (frozen carbon dioxide) sublimes to become carbon dioxide gas.

LIQUID STATE

The atoms or molecules in a liquid substance can slide over each other, so a liquid can be poured into a container. But the electrical forces between the atoms or molecules in a liquid stop them from pulling apart.

▲ GAS *The atoms or molecules in a gas are held so loosely that they fly away into space.*

GASEOUS STATE

The electrical forces between the atoms and molecules in a gaseous substance have broken down completely, so they will fill the container in which they are held. Gases cannot be poured like liquids, and many, but not all, are invisible.

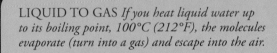

LIQUID TO GAS *If you heat liquid water up to its boiling point, 100°C (212°F), the molecules evaporate (turn into a gas) and escape into the air.*

Evaporation

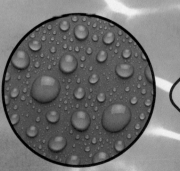

Condensation

GAS TO LIQUID *When water vapour in the air loses energy, the molecules stick together and become liquid water.*

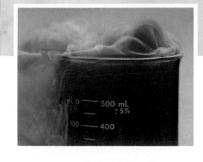

Liquid metal At room temperature, nearly all metals are solids. But there is one exception – mercury. Mercury has a melting point of –38°C (–36.4°F), so it stays liquid – even if you put it in a freezer.

Heating up Solid aluminium reacts with liquid bromine to give solid aluminium bromide. The reaction produces a lot of heat, and the excess bromine boils. This produces brown fumes of bromine gas.

Mixing chemicals

A few common substances are made of just one chemical, such as pure water or pure salt. Most of the things that we come across every day, however, are combinations of several chemicals.

COMPOUNDS

Many substances undergo changes when they are mixed together. The chemical bonds that bind the molecules to each other break apart and then recombine to form new substances called compounds.

▲ OIL AND WATER *never combine because their molecules repel each other.*

▲ WASHING LIQUID *is a mixture of soap, water, and other chemicals.*

MIXTURES

Some substances do not react when they are added together because they cannot form chemical bonds. These are called mixtures. Mixtures can easily be separated again because the original substances do not change.

TAKE A LOOK

Mixtures are made of different elements or molecules. During mixing, some of the substances may become harder to see. In coarse mixtures you can usually spot each substance. Suspensions may look like a single liquid, but eventually they separate out. Solutions are the most thoroughly mixed – it is often difficult to tell there is more than one substance.

▲ COARSE MIXTURE *In some mixtures the particles are large enough to be seen and separated easily. Gravel is a coarse mixture.*

▲ SUSPENSION *When small soil particles are mixed with water they form a suspension. Eventually the heavier solids will sink to the bottom.*

▲ COLLOID *These are like suspensions, but the particles do not sink to the bottom. In milk, tiny droplets of fat float in a watery solution.*

▲ SOLUTION *When one substance dissolves in another it is called a solution. Seawater is a solution of salt and water; air is a solution of gases.*

SEPARATING MIXTURES AND COMPOUNDS

It is much easier to separate a mixture than a compound. Mixtures can be separated using physical methods, such as evaporation, filtration, flotation, or distillation. Separating compounds may require several steps before you get the substance you want, including mixing with other chemicals, heating, and filtering.

◀ CHROMATOGRAPHY
This is used to identify coloured substances in a mixture. A drop of the mixture is placed onto chromatography paper and solvent is then dripped onto it. As the solvent travels across the paper, the different substances travel across the paper at different speeds. Scientists can then work out what each substance is by the distance it has travelled.

▼ PANNING FOR GOLD
Gold prospectors separate grains of gold from river gravel by swirling the gravel around in a shallow pan. The heavier gold sinks to the bottom and can be picked out.

▲ ALLOY *This is a solid solution in which one metal has dissolved in another. Alloys are often tougher and more durable than the original metals.*

CHEMICAL REACTIONS

When the atoms of two or more substances rearrange themselves to form a new compound, we say that a chemical reaction has taken place. Most chemical reactions are irreversible – you cannot turn a cake back into eggs and flour. Some reactions can be reversed but may need heat or pressure to change back.

▲ IRON *can be prevented from rusting by coating it with a less reactive metal, such as zinc (left).*

Reversible reaction When iron is exposed to air or water it starts to react. The metal reacts with oxygen, which turns the iron into the reddish brown iron oxides we call rust. However, if you were to heat the iron oxides in a blast furnace they would change back into iron and oxygen.

Irreversible reaction Burning wood causes irreversible changes. The carbon atoms in the wood react with oxygen in the air to form ash, smoke, and carbon dioxide. The wood also loses energy as heat and light. Even if you put all these things together in a test tube they would not change back into wood. Another irreversible change happens when food starts to rot. Tiny micro-organisms feed on the food and turn it into new substances. This process is called decomposition.

It's elementary

An element is a pure substance that cannot be broken down into simpler chemicals. An element is made of only one type of atom. So, the element hydrogen is made only of hydrogen atoms, and gold of gold atoms.

WHERE DO ELEMENTS COME FROM?

Most scientists believe that much of the hydrogen and some of the helium in the Universe were formed in the "big bang" that formed the Universe. Hydrogen has the smallest and simplest atoms, and helium has the next smallest.

THE PERIODIC TABLE

Scientists recognize 117 different elements, which have been organized into a chart known as the periodic table. This table was first devised in 1869 by Russian chemist Dmitry Mendeleyev, who organized elements with similar properties into groups. The elements are arranged by the size of their atoms.

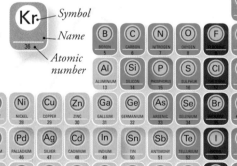

Every element has a one- or two-letter symbol. For example, Kr is the symbol for the element Krypton. Scientists use these symbols to write down the chemical formulae for molecules and chemical reactions.

Kr — Symbol
— Name
36 — Atomic number

Metals are on the left-hand side and centre of the periodic table. On the right-hand side are gases and non-metal solids.

Compounds

Most chemicals are not pure elements, but compounds. A compound is a chemical made up of two or more different elements that are chemically combined.

Water is a compound made of two hydrogen atoms and one oxygen atom.

RADIOACTIVE DECAY

Some elements are made of atoms so large, they spontaneously break apart. This is called radioactive decay, and the subatomic particles (smaller than atoms) and energy released by it can be dangerous. Each radioactive element has a half life, the time it takes for half of its atoms to break apart.

Gold
Aurum

- **Group** Transition metals
- **Discovery date** Unknown (prehistoric times)
- **Melting point** 1,064°C (1,947°F)
- **Boiling point** 2,856°C (5,173°F)

Gold gets people excited. It has been prized and valued since prehistoric times, and turned into many crowns, idols, and crosses over the centuries. Gold never loses its shine and is easy to melt and mould. It is measured in carats – pure gold is 24 carats.

Iron
Ferrum

- **Group** Transition metals
- **Discovery date** Unknown (prehistoric times)
- **Melting point** 1,538°C (2,800°F)
- **Boiling point** 2,862°C (5,182°F)

Iron is a versatile and abundant metal. We use it to build bridges and make machines and cutlery. Iron is vital to your well-being. It gives red blood cells their colour, and helps to carry oxygen around your body. The centre of the Earth is made of iron.

Helium
Helium

- **Group** Noble gases
- **Discovery date** 1868
- **Melting point** - 272°C (- 458°F)
- **Boiling point** - 269°C (- 452°F)

Helium is the second most abundant element in the Universe, after hydrogen. It was discovered in space, before we found it on Earth. It weighs very little and is used to make things float, such as airships and balloons. It is also used in liquid form as a coolant in big scientific computers.

Mercury

- **Group** Transition metals
- **Discovery date** Pre-1500 BCE
- **Melting point** - 39°C (- 38°F)
- **Boiling point** 356°C (674°F)

Mercury is poisonous, although in ancient times it was thought to have healing and life-giving properties. Early chemists (alchemists) once thought it held the secret to making gold. At room temperature mercury is a liquid.

Carbon
Carbo

- **Group** Non-metals
- **Discovery date** Unknown (prehistoric times)
- **Melting point** diamonds 3,852°C (6,917°F) sublimes 4,800°C (8,672°F)

Carbon is vital to all living things and on Earth it is frequently exchanged between the air, living things, and the soil, in a never-ending cycle. Carbon atoms can join together to make coal and diamonds, as well as with other elements to make more than 10 million compounds.

Uranium
Uranium

- **Group** Actinides
- **Discovery date** 1789
- **Melting point** 1,132°C (2,070°F)
- **Boiling point** 4,131°C (7,468°F)

Uranium is a naturally occuring radioactive metal and was named after the planet Uranus. It is refined and used in industry, nuclear power stations, and warfare. In the 1940s it was used to make the atomic bomb "Little Boy" that was dropped on Hiroshima in 1945.

Calcium
Calcis

- **Group** Alkaline-earth metals
- **Discovery date** Pre-100 CE
- **Melting point** 842°C (1,548°F)
- **Boiling point** 1,484°C (2,703°F)

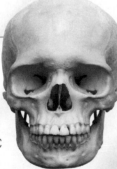

Calcium is the most abundant metal found in living organisms and is vital for many cellular reactions. It is also a key component of bones and shells, giving them strength. Calcium is also found in milk, chalk, and seaweeds.

Phosphorus
Lucifer

- **Group** Non-metals
- **Discovery date** 1669, by German chemist Hennig Brand
- **Melting point** 44°C (111°F)
- **Boiling point** 277°C (531°F)

This fiery element is very reactive and so isn't found naturally on Earth. Phosphorus is used to make matches, fertilizers, and some weapons. It is also a component of DNA, and helps to make energy in your body.

WHO'S WHO?

- **Robert Boyle** (1627–1691) was a British scientist who laid the foundation for modern chemistry and proposed the idea of elements.
- **Henry Cavendish** (1731–1810) was the first scientist to prove water was not an element, but a compound.
- **Joseph Priestley** (1733–1804) was a clergyman and scientist. He discovered several gases including oxygen.
- **Alfred Bernhard Nobel** (1833–1896) was an explosives scientist. He created dynamite and founded the five Nobel prizes.
- **Marie Curie** (1867–1934) was famed for her work on radioactivity, and discovered polonium and radium.

Energy

Energy is the power behind our world. Although you can't see it, you can't do much without it. Whenever things move, light up, change shape, get hotter or colder, or make noises, energy is involved.

Freewheeling turns potential energy into kinetic energy.

STORED ENERGY

You can do two things with energy: store it or use it. It takes lots of energy to ride a bike up a hill, but that energy doesn't disappear. It's stored by your body and by your bike in a form called potential energy. You use this stored energy when you race back down without pedalling. The potential energy you stored is then converted into kinetic energy (movement energy).

TYPES OF ENERGY

Energy exists in many different forms. Almost everything we do involves changing energy from one form into another. When we're "using" energy, we're actually converting it into another form.

Kinetic
The energy moving things have. Racing cars have lots of kinetic energy.

Light
A kind of kinetic energy carried by invisible waves of electricity and magnetism.

Electromagnetic
Electromagnetic energy is also carried by radio waves, X-rays, and microwaves.

Heat
Hot things have energy because their atoms or molecules move more quickly.

Electrical
Electricity is a convenient form of energy that can be carried along wires.

Nuclear
Atoms can release energy from their nucleus (central core).

Gravitational
Falling things, like this waterfall, release potential energy stored using gravity.

CHANGING ENERGY

Heat sensitive photograph There's a fixed amount of energy in our Universe. We can't make any more or use any up. All we can do is change energy to other forms. When a car brakes, its kinetic energy doesn't vanish. It changes to heat in the brakes and wheels (glowing in this heat-sensitive photograph).

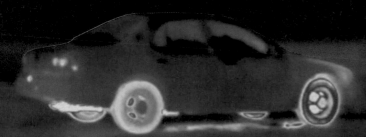

RENEWABLE ENERGY

Earth has limited amounts of fossil fuels, such as oil, coal, and gas. Once we've used them, there will be no more. There are unlimited amounts of renewable energy. This includes energy from the Sun, the wind, and the oceans. We can go on using renewable energy forever.

ENERGY SOURCES

Most of the energy people now use (80-90 per cent) comes from fossil fuels. The rest comes from renewable energy and nuclear power.

▼ TURBINES *(water wheels) behind these channels generate electricity when water flows past them.*

Hydroelectric power
Energy from moving rivers and seas

- **Percentage of current energy use** 6 per cent
- **Reserves left** Unlimited

Rivers flow from mountains and hills down to the sea. This means they release stored potential energy. Hydroelectric power stations capture this energy to make electricity.

Fossil fuels
Energy from coal, oil, and gas

- **Percentage of current energy use** Oil 38 per cent, coal 25 per cent, gas 23 per cent
- **Reserves left** Oil 40 years, gas 100 years, coal 250 years

Although bad for the environment, fossil fuels are still the world's main energy source. Coal is cheap to make electricity, gas is easy to pipe to homes, and oil is convenient for powering vehicles.

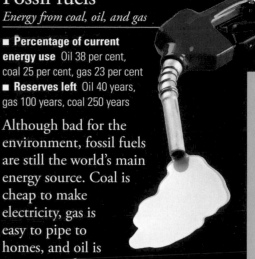

Geothermal power
Energy from Earth's internal heat

- **Percentage of current energy use** Less than 1 per cent
- **Reserves left** Unlimited

Deep inside, Earth is hot molten rock. Some of this heat is released when volcanoes erupt. Geothermal energy means using Earth's inner heat to generate hot water and electricity.

Biofuels
Energy made using living plants and animals

- **Percentage of current energy use** 4 per cent
- **Reserves left** Unlimited

Growing plants and animals store energy we can use in the future. We can grow crops to make oil or make electricity by burning animal waste such as chicken manure. Energy made this way is called biofuel.

Solar energy
Energy made from the Sun's light or heat

- **Percentage of current energy use** Less than 1 per cent **Reserves left** Unlimited

Almost all the energy on Earth originally comes from the Sun. We can tap the Sun's energy directly to make electricity. Solar panels like these turn sunlight into electricity.

Wave power
Energy from the oceans and tides

- **Percentage of current energy use** Less than 1 per cent **Reserves left** Unlimited

Wind moving over the oceans stores energy in waves. Waves have kinetic energy (because they move) and potential energy (because they're above the normal sea surface). We can use the energy in breaking waves and shifting tides to generate electricity.

Nuclear power
Energy made from atomic reactions

- **Percentage of current energy use** 6 per cent
- **Reserves left** Raw uranium, 80 years

Atoms are made of tiny particles held together by energy. Large atoms can release this energy by splitting apart. Small atoms can release energy by joining together. Most nuclear power stations make electricity by splitting apart large uranium atoms.

Wind power
Energy from air currents moving across Earth

- **Percentage of current energy use** Less than 1 per cent **Reserves left** Unlimited

Wind turbines work like propellers in reverse. As their rotors spin in the wind, they turn small generators inside and make electricity.

Feel the force

Forces are at work all the time, pulling you down to the ground, stopping you from slipping over, and pushing you one way and then the next. Forces act on everything, from the tiny nuclei inside atoms to the planets and stars that make up the Universe.

PULLING AND PUSHING

A force is a push or a pull. For example, your hand applies a pulling or pushing force to open and close a door. Forces act on all objects all of the time. They make them move or change their speed or direction.

Your hand applies a pushing force on a toy car to make it move.

HIDDEN FORCES Usually you must touch an object to push or pull on it. But some forces act on things without touching them. For example, this magnet pulls on these paperclips with a magnetic force.

A boxer's fist lands a powerful blow on a punch bag.

Action and reaction
When the boxer punches the punch bag, his or her fist applies a force to move it. But the punch bag applies an equal but opposite force on the boxer's fist to slow it down.

232

SCIENCE

FRICTION FORCES
Roll a ball along the ground and eventually it will come to a standstill. Friction acts on the ball to slow it down. Try to push a heavy box along the floor. Friction provides grip, making it hard to get the box moving.

Disc brakes create friction on the brake disc to slow the car.

INERTIA
When there are no forces acting on an object, it will either stay still or keep moving in a straight line at the same speed. This is called "inertia". In practice, friction usually slows down a moving object.

◀ RUNAWAY TROLLEY! *When you let go of a shopping trolley it carries on moving under its own inertia.*

WHO'S WHO?

■ **Aristotle** (c. 384–322 BCE) The ancient Greeks were the first to study forces. Aristotle came up with theories about how forces make objects move.

■ **Archimedes** (c. 287–212 BCE) built war machines with levers to strengthen forces.

■ **Galileo Galilei** (1564–1642) The Italian scientist studied forces by rolling different balls down ramps and shooting cannonballs through the air.

■ **Sir Isaac Newton** (1642–1727) The English scientist came up with three laws of motion to explain how forces affect the motions of objects.

LOTS OF LEVERS

▶ YOUR FINGERS *grip the chopsticks at the pivot point. This reduces your gripping force but magnifies your finger movements.*

Fulcrum

MAGNIFYING FORCES
People use machines to magnify forces. Machines called levers move around a fixed point called a fulcrum. Most levers magnify forces, but they act over a shorter distance than the force you put in. Simple levers include chopsticks, a pair of pliers, and a nutcracker.

Fulcrum

▶ PLIERS *convert the weak force of your hand on one side of the lever into a stronger gripping force on the other side of the lever.*

Fulcrum

▶ A NUTCRACKER *crushes a walnut by turning the weak force of your hand into a stronger force nearer the fulcrum.*

BALANCED FORCES
When two or more forces act on an object, they combine to produce a single "net force". In some cases, the forces combine to make a larger net force. In other cases, the forces work against each other, resulting in a weaker net force. Sometimes the two forces cancel each other out completely.

◀ TUG-OF-WAR *If both teams pull on a rope with the same force, the net force is zero and nobody moves.*

Gravity

Gravity is the force of attraction that pulls things together. On Earth, we experience it as the force that pulls us down onto the surface of the planet. In the Universe, gravity is the force that pulls planets in orbit around stars.

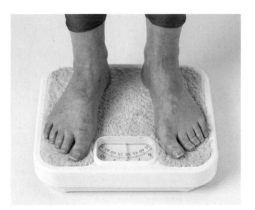

WEAK OR STRONG?

Gravity may seem impressive, but it is actually the weakest known force in the Universe. It takes objects the size of planets and stars to produce a noticeable effect. The Sun's gravity is strong enough to hold all the planets of the solar system in orbit around it.

Weight and mass

Weighing scales measure the pulling force that Earth's gravity exerts on your body. Gravity exerts more pulling force on a body with greater mass. So the scales would register a bigger weight for a person with greater mass.

GRAVITY AT WORK

Take up skydiving and you will soon feel the full effects of gravity at work. When you jump out of a plane, gravity makes your body accelerate towards the ground. At the same time, air rubs against your body, creating friction, or drag, which works against gravity. Eventually the two forces balance, and you stop accelerating – you have reached "terminal velocity".

According to legend, Galileo dropped balls of different weight from the Leaning Tower of Pisa to show they hit the ground at the same time.

Gravity and Galileo

The first scientist to study gravity seriously was an Italian called Galileo Galilei (1564–1642). He did lots of experiments and concluded that in the absence of air resistance all falling objects would accelerate downward at the same rate. It is the air resistance, called drag, that allows some objects to reach the ground more slowly than others.

▲ TERMINAL VELOCITY *The highest velocity reached by skydivers with an unopened parachute is about 200 km/h (125 mph). Opening a parachute slows the skydiver down by increasing drag.*

NEWTON

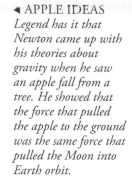

▼ SCIENCE GENIUS
Sir Isaac Newton was the first person to figure out that the force of gravity keeps the Moon trapped in orbit around the Earth.

◀ APPLE IDEAS
Legend has it that Newton came up with his theories about gravity when he saw an apple fall from a tree. He showed that the force that pulled the apple to the ground was the same force that pulled the Moon into Earth orbit.

EINSTEIN

▼ WARP FACTOR *Albert Einstein came up with another theory to explain gravity. He suggested that a big mass, such as a planet, warps space and time in the same way as a heavy ball resting on a rubber sheet.*

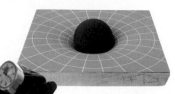

The warping effect creates the force of gravity.

▼ RELATIVE SUCCESS
Einstein came up with his theory in 1916. A few years later, astronomers showed he was right, when light from a distant star was shown to bend as it passed the Sun.

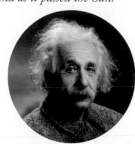

Centre of gravity
Gravity pulls down on an object through a point called the centre of gravity. An object will tip over if the centre of gravity is too high or moves outside the base of the object. All-terrain vehicles have a very low centre of gravity so they can drive up and down steep slopes.

Vomit Comet Astronauts appear to float weightlessly in an aircraft as the plane follows the path that an object in free fall would take. In fact, the astronauts and the aircraft are accelerating at the same rate, but there is no contact between them. The plane is nicknamed the "Vomit Comet" because it makes some astronauts feel sick.

EXPLODING STARS
Stars are powered by nuclear reactions. In the core of the Sun, hydrogen atoms combine to form helium, releasing extreme heat. When the Sun runs out of hydrogen in its core, the core will collapse. The collapse of the core of a larger star might release enough energy that the star is seen as a supernova. The outer parts of the star are blown into space.

Neutron
Proton
Electron

Charge carriers Atoms contain particles that carry electrical charge. Protons are found in the nucleus and carry a positive charge. Neutrons are also found in the nucleus, but are uncharged. Electrons orbit around the nucleus.

Electricity

Everything in the Universe is made up of atoms that we can't see. Each atom has particles that transport an electric charge. Electricity powers items we use every day, from lights to computers. It is carried to our homes by a series of cables and power stations.

CHARGED CLOUDS

Lightning strikes when static electricity builds up in a storm cloud. Negative charge collects at the bottom of the cloud, while positive charge builds up near the top. Eventually the negative charge shoots down to the ground in a bolt of lightning.

Static electricity The build up of static electricity can make your hair stand on end. If you touch the metal dome of a Van de Graaf generator, positive charge transfers to your body, including your hair. The hairs repel each other, making them stand on end.

TELL ME MORE...

Static electricity can be very handy if you are a farmer. Crop spraying delivers pesticide as a spray of fine droplets. The spray is given an electric charge so that the droplets repel each other and spread out over the crops.

BATTERIES
provide power

PAPER CLIP
acts as a switch

BULBS
light up

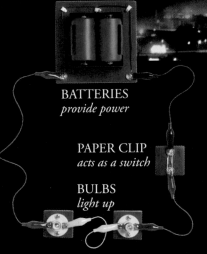

Current electricity
Electrons can flow through metals and other conductors. This flow of electrical charge is called current electricity, and it can be used to light up our homes and power electrical devices such as microwaves and televisions.

NERVES

The nerves inside your body work like electric wires. They carry messages between the brain and different parts of your body in the form of electric signals.

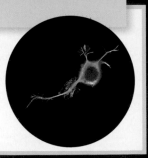

Magnetism

Whenever there is electricity, there is magnetism. This mysterious, invisible force draws some metal objects together or pushes them apart.

WHAT CAUSES MAGNETISM?

The same moving electrons that create electricity also create magnetism. This force acts through an invisible magnetic field. You can see this field of force if you scatter some iron filings around a bar magnet.

Natural magnet Earth is a giant natural magnet whose magnetic field makes compass needles point towards the magnetic North Pole. Earth's magnetic field extends thousands of kilometres into space, forming a vast area known as the magnetosphere.

Compass aligns with the magnetic field of the bar magnet

▲ LIKE POLES REPEL
Magnets have north and south poles. If you push the same poles together they repel each other.

▲ UNLIKE POLES ATTRACT
Push opposite poles together and a powerful force of attraction will snap the magnets together.

MAGNETIC NORTH POLE   MAGNETIC SOUTH POLE

Electromagnetism Magnetism and electricity are united by the force of electromagnetism. If you move a magnet next to a wire, electricity flows through the wire. Similarly, whenever electrons flow through a wire, they create a magnetic field around the wire.

◄ ELECTRICITY *flowing through the loops of electric wire inside an electromagnet generate a powerful magnetic field to lift scrap metal.*

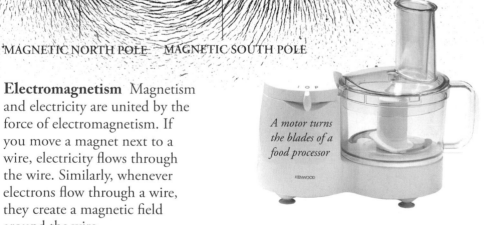

A motor turns the blades of a food processor

Moving motor Electrons flowing through a wire coil can make a magnet move in and out of the coil. Electrical energy changes into kinetic energy. This is how an electric motor works. Electric motors power devices ranging from computers to kitchen appliances.

Science of sound

Sound is a form of energy. It passes through air, water, and solid objects as invisible waves. We can hear sound because the waves make the delicate skin of our eardrums vibrate. The vibrations are converted to nerve signals in our brains.

Good vibrations Objects can give out sound energy when they vibrate. This vibrating guitar string causes molecules of air to bump into each other. The collisions between molecules spread like ripples in a pool, carrying the sound outwards in all directions.

▶ TUNING FORKS *vibrate at a particular frequency, so it always gives out sound at the same pitch.*

WOW!

Sound waves travel through air at about 1,190 km/h (740 mph). This is slower than light waves, which is why we hear the sound of a distant jet aircraft or explosion after we see it. Sound travels faster under water, about 5,000 km/h (3,125 mph), though the exact speed varies with temperature.

▼ PEAKS AND TROUGHS *The height, or "amplitude", of peaks and troughs in a sound wave dictates loudness.*

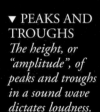

——— *Peak*

——— *Trough*

SOUND WAVES

We can't see sound waves, but we can get a good idea how they work by watching the way a wave travels along a glowing string. The end of the string is vibrated by a machine called an oscillator.

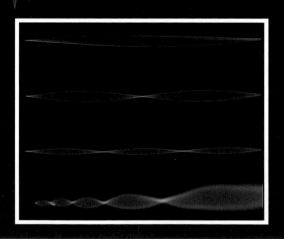

◀ FREQUENCY 0.5 HERTZ *The string is vibrating with a long wavelength.*

◀ FREQUENCY 1 HZ *Vibrations in double time give shorter wavelengths.*

◀ FREQUENCY 1.5 HZ *At this higher frequency the wavelength shortens again.*

◀ FREQUENCY 2.5 HZ *High frequency sound waves make high-pitched sounds.*

🔍 TAKE A LOOK: DECIBEL SCALE

We measure the loudness of sound using the Decibel scale. This is what mathematicians call a "log scale", meaning the quietest sounds measure 0 dB, a sound ten times louder is 10 dB, a sound 100 times louder is 20 dB, and a sound 1,000 times louder is 30 dB.

▲ 0 dB
The tiny sound of a finger brushing skin.

▲ 15 dB
A whispered conversation.

▲ 60 dB
A normal speaking voice.

▲ 90 dB
The sound of a high-speed train passing by.

Seeing with sound Sound waves bounce off objects in the same way light waves do. Dolphins and bats are able to use these echoes to picture objects around them. With the aid of computer-imaging software that converts sound waves into pictures, we can do the same.

Echolocation
Seeing with sound

Bat calls The echolocation calls produced by bats are loud but so high pitched that most people cannot hear them at all. Bats have incredibly sharp hearing and use faint echoes from nearby surfaces to pinpoint prey or detect obstacles.

◄ FIRST PHOTO
Advanced ultrasound scanners can produce amazingly detailed images such as this unborn baby.

◄ ULTRASOUND SCANNERS
send out high-pitched waves and pick up the echoes to create an image.

Sonogram
A sound diagram

PITCH AND TONE

The way we hear a sound depends on the shape of the sound waves. The spacing of waves affects the frequency or pitch of the sound. Closely packed waves indicate high pitch, while stretched out waves are low-pitched. A clear-toned sound like a bell creates smooth waves, while harsh tones such as drumbeats make jagged-looking waves.

The "sonic shock" caused by a supersonic aircraft causes water in the atmosphere to condense, forming a visible cone, or collar, of vapour.

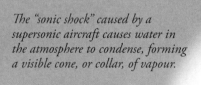

▲ 100 dB
The blast of a car horn.

▲ 110 dB
The sound of a thunderstorm overhead.

▲ 120 dB
The roar of a jet aircraft taking off.

Breaking the sound barrier
When a supersonic aircraft breaks the speed of sound, it overtakes its own sound waves, pushing them closer together to create a "sonic boom". A whipcrack is a type of sonic boom, caused when the whip tip breaks the sound barrier.

Light fantastic

Energy takes many forms. Light is one we are familiar with because our eyes are specially adapted to detect it. However seeing light is one thing – understanding it is more tricky.

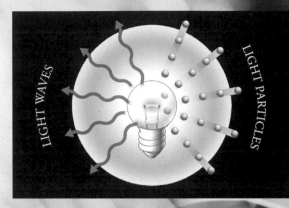

LIGHT WAVES

LIGHT PARTICLES

HOW DOES LIGHT TRAVEL?
Puzzlingly, light behaves as though it is made of both waves and particles. Like waves, light can be reflected and refracted, and its wavelength can be measured. Other types of wave need something (a "medium"), to ripple through, but light can travel across a vacuum.

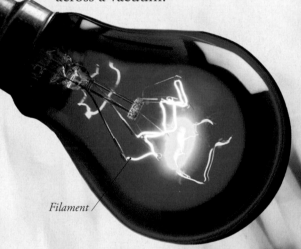

Filament

Where does light come from?
Atoms that are excited by a collision return to their normal state by emitting light energy. The atoms in a heated lightbulb filament shed their excess energy by flinging out tiny packets of light called photons, causing the filament to glow.

Shadows
Light travels in a straight line, and cannot bend round obstacles. The space behind an obstacle looks dark because the only light reaching it is that reflected from other objects nearby.

THE SPEED OF LIGHT

- Light is the fastest moving thing in the Universe. It travels across empty space at the unimaginable speed of 300,000 km/second (186,411 miles/second).
- One light year is the distance light can travel in one year. This is about 9.5 trillion km (5.9 trillion miles). Light years are used to measure colossal distances across space. The Sun is a mere 499 light seconds away.
- Albert Einstein worked out that if there was a way to travel at close to light speed, time would slow down and you would age more slowly.

▼ ALL A BLUR
Fast-moving objects appear blurred because light travels much faster than our brain takes to interpret what we are seeing.

SCIENCE

240

REFLECTION When light strikes an object, some of it is bounced back or "reflected". The angle of reflection is always the same as the angle at which the light hits the surface, so on a smooth surface we see a perfect reflection, or mirror image. If the surface is curved or uneven, the image is distorted.

The break in the straws is an illusion caused by refraction.

REFRACTION When light crosses the boundary between two media with different densities (such as air and water), it bends, or "refracts". This is why objects standing in water appear distorted at the surface. If you try to touch a coin or pebble in a bucket of water, it will not be exactly where your eyes tell you it is.

Lenses A lens is a transparent object with curved surfaces that refract light in a predictable way. An object close behind a bulging or "convex" lens will appear magnified while one seen through a dished or "concave" lens will appear reduced in size. Telescopes, microscopes, and spectacles all use lenses.

▶ IMPERFECT *eyesight can be corrected with artificial lenses.*

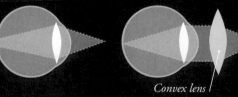

Concave lens

◀ SHORT SIGHT *is when the eye focuses an image too far forward. It is corrected with a concave lens.*

Convex lens

◀ LONG SIGHT *causes the image to focus too far back, so the retina only detects a blur. It is fixed with a convex lens.*

FIREWORKS
The atoms of different materials emit light of different colours or wavelengths. Firework makers use this to create wonderful displays.

Heat haze
Refraction can happen when light passes through air of mixed density. Cool air over hot ground contains layers of variable density, and light passing through the layers is bent, causing a shimmering heat haze. In extreme cases the effect results in a "mirage" – a watery-looking reflection of the sky.

Spectrum

The Universe is full of electro-magnetic radiation, which travels in waves. Our eyes see a small range of these waves as visible light, but we can also detect the effects of other radiation types.

WOW!

To remember the colours of the visible spectrum in order, memorise this phrase: "Richard Of York Gave Battle In Vain", for Red, Orange, Yellow, Green, Blue, Indigo, and Violet.

RAINBOWS We see rainbows when white light is refracted as it passes through different media, such as drops of water or thin layers of oil. Sunlight passing through rain or mist from a fountain creates rainbows, and we see them produced by solid materials such as crystal or perspex.

Prism

White light contains a mixture of visible wavelengths.

When waves strike the surface of a different medium at an angle, they are bent by an amount that differs slightly for different wavelengths. The bending is known as "refraction".

Because short wavelengths refract more than long ones, the different wavelengths of the spectrum are separated by the prism.

THE ELECTROMAGNETIC SPECTRUM

The visible spectrum is a small part of a much larger spectrum of energy waves. We have found technological uses for most types of electromagnetic radiation.

The wavelengths of different types of electromagnetic radiation range from shorter than an atom to millions of kilometres (miles) long.

WAVELENGTH

GAMMA RAYS	X-RAYS	ULTRAVIOLET (UV)	VISIBLE RAYS

Gamma radiation is immensely powerful. In large quantities it damages our cells and DNA.

X-rays pass through our bodies. We can use them to take pictures of our insides.

Ultraviolet rays damage our cells. Sunscreen or a suntan can help filter them out.

Visible light waves make the world a colourful place for us to experience and enjoy.

SEEING COLOUR

Colour vision Objects appear coloured to our eyes because their surfaces reflect some wavelengths of light but not others. Plants have chemicals called pigments that colour their fruits and flowers, making them attractive to the animals that disperse their pollen and seeds. Most fruit-eating animals see in colour.

A tomato absorbs green and blue light and reflects red.

Lemons reflect red and green light, which we see as yellow.

Blackberries absorb all colours of light, reflecting very little.

Green peppers reflect green light and absorb red and blue.

Adding colour

Televisions produce hundreds of colours by mixing red, green, and blue light in different quantities. Blending these three primary wavelengths to create new colours is known as colour addition.

You see green light because the ink used here absorbs all other colour wavelengths.

Subtracting colour

Paints create colours by absorbing light rather then emitting it. Mixing the primary paint colours of magenta, yellow, and cyan creates new colours by reducing the range of wavelengths that are reflected. This is called colour subtraction.

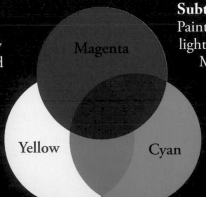

Magenta

Yellow   Cyan

Unstoppable waves

Electromagnetic radiation is everywhere. Visible light is bouncing off this page, allowing you to see the words and pictures printed in different colours. But other kinds of electromagnetic wave are passing straight through the pages and through your body without you even noticing.

▲ COLOUR PRINTING
The microscopic dots used in colour printing come in four colours, but blend to create the illusion of thousands more (👁 p168–169).

INFRARED (IR)

Warm objects emit IR radiation. IR cameras see heat as white or red. Cool objects appear blue.

MICROWAVE

Microwaves make certain molecules move very fast and give out lots of heat energy.

RADIO WAVES

Data, sound, and pictures can be transmitted as radio waves. Devices such as telephones,

radio, and TV sets convert the waves back into images and sound for us to see and hear.

Evolution

Over long periods of time, all species of organism slowly change. This gradual change, called evolution, is driven by the process of natural selection. This process allows organisms that are best suited to their environment to survive and reproduce.

The father of evolution
The English naturalist Charles Darwin first proposed the theory of evolution after studying hundreds of different animals, plants, and fossils. He realized that many species were related and had a common ancestor. Modern DNA testing is now proving that his theory was correct.

NATURAL SELECTION

Darwin observed that most animals and plants produce more offspring than survive to become adults. He realized that nature was selecting those with the characteristics best adapted to their surroundings, allowing them to pass on their characteristics to future generations.

ARTIFICIAL SELECTION

In the wild, species evolve by natural selection. However, humans have been helping evolution by choosing animals and plants with desirable characteristics and breeding them to produce sheep with more wool, cows that give more milk, and crops that have better yields. This process is called artificial selection.

Domestic dogs All dogs are descended from wolves. Over time, humans selectively bred them for things like hunting or herding ability, speed, and size, so that we now have hundreds of different species.

Broccoli (flowers)

Cauliflower (flowers)

Grey wolf

Wild cabbage

These dogs have all got a little bit of wolf in them.

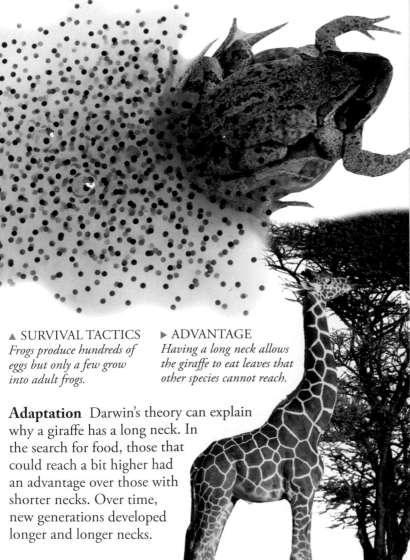

▲ SURVIVAL TACTICS
Frogs produce hundreds of eggs but only a few grow into adult frogs.

▶ ADVANTAGE
Having a long neck allows the giraffe to eat leaves that other species cannot reach.

Adaptation Darwin's theory can explain why a giraffe has a long neck. In the search for food, those that could reach a bit higher had an advantage over those with shorter necks. Over time, new generations developed longer and longer necks.

THE FOSSIL RECORD

Fossils show that life on Earth has changed throughout its history. Each major layer of rock contains species that are slightly different to those below or on top of it. Although it is not easy to find fossils that show every change in a species, this bird-like Archaeopteryx (right) is a clear example that birds evolved from feathered dinosaurs.

Family trees Scientists trace evolution by examining fossils and seeing where they fit on the family tree. Many elephant fossils have been found that show how these animals developed tusks and a long trunk, but not all are direct ancestors of modern elephants.

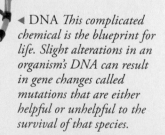

Phiomia

Asian elephant

Moeritherium

Gomphotherium

Deinotherium

Brussels sprouts (large buds)

Red cabbage (leaves)

Green cabbage (leaves)

Cabbages These vegetables may look different but they are all descended from the wild cabbage. Brussels sprouts, cabbages, cauliflowers, and broccoli have been bred for their leaves, flowers, or buds.

EVOLUTION AND GENES

Organisms use DNA to pass on their characteristics to the next generation. DNA is divided up into sections called genes. Every gene is a code for a particular characteristic, such as hair, feathers, skin, or scales.

Woodpecker finch

Medium ground finch

Vegetarian finch

Warbler finch

New species When Darwin visited the Galápagos Islands, he noticed that all the finches looked like a species on the mainland but had different beaks. He realized that all these new species had evolved from the same parents, but their beaks had changed to suit the food sources on each island.

◄ DNA *This complicated chemical is the blueprint for life. Slight alterations in an organism's DNA can result in gene changes called mutations that are either helpful or unhelpful to the survival of that species.*

HOW LIFE BEGAN

It remains a mystery how life began. Earth was so hot that life began in the oceans, perhaps around vents in the ocean floor (right). Simple molecules began to copy themselves, then formed into cells and colonies, and finally, complicated organisms.

Genes *and* DNA

WOW!

There are about 30,000 genes in the human genetic code. Some appear just once and others repeat many times. About 99 per cent of human genes are identical to chimpanzee genes. Even more amazingly, you share about 75 per cent of your genes with a dog!

Unless you are an identical twin, your body is built according to a unique set of biological instructions, your own genetic code. These instructions, or genes, are present in all cells and are passed from parent to offspring.

DNA FOR DUMMIES

Genes are made of a substance called Deoxyribose Nucleic Acid, or DNA. DNA is a very long molecule, found packed up tight in the chromosomes in the nucleus of every cell.

▶ DNA *is made up of two chains, linked down the middle by molecules called bases, which always pair up the same way. The order of the bases spells out the genetic code.*

DNA

Nucleus

Cell membrane

Chromosomes

▲ CHROMOSOMES *Human beings normally have 46 chromosomes in every cell, except gametes (egg and sperm cells), which have just 23.*

▲ CELL *All living things are made of cells. When cells divide, the nucleus divides too, and the genetic message is duplicated in each new cell.*

IN THE GENES

If a person inherits two different genes from their parents, often one will dominate the other. For example, the gene for brown eyes overrides the one for blue eyes.

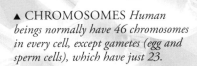

TIMELINE OF MEDICINE

1859

Charles Darwin's book *Origin of Species* outlines the importance of inherited traits in evolution.

1860

Gregor Mendel's experiments on pea plants prove the existence of genes.

1869

Friedrich Miescher extracts DNA from cells. He calls it "nuclein".

1953

James Watson and **Francis Crick** discover the structure of **DNA** and show how it can copy itself.

TAKE A LOOK: GENOME

■ A genome is the entire genetic code inside an organism. The first genetic code to be sequenced in full was that of a virus known as bacteriophage phi X174, in 1975. In 1984, the first bacterial genome was sequenced, and in 1990 scientists began to sequence the human genome. The project took 13 years to complete. They found that the genes were padded out by sequences of "junk DNA", which had no obvious function. The human genome contains about three billion base pairs and codes for roughly the same amount of data that can be fitted on one CD.

▲ THE CHROMOSOMES *in this preparation have been treated to make a particular gene glow green.*

FACTFILE

■ Scientists can "cut and paste" genes from one species into another to create useful characteristics. The genetically altered organism is described as "transgenic". Transgenic bacteria are used to produce useful drugs, and transgenic mice are used to research cures for many diseases.

▲ GLOW FOR IT *These mice were given a jellyfish gene to make them glow in the dark.*

GM crops Genes can be transferred into plants to create transgenic, or "genetically modified" (GM) crops. GM technology has been used to produce rice enriched with vitamins, sweetcorn and cabbages which produce their own insecticides, and soybeans that survive being treated with weedkillers that kill all other plants.

▲ CHEMICAL CURE *In the future GM crops should reduce the need to treat fields and orchards with chemicals that may harm the environment.*

▲ CYSTIC FIBROSIS *is caused by a mutation in a gene controlling the production of sweat and mucus.*

Genetic diseases Some genes contain errors which cause them to malfunction. These faulty genes can cause diseases such as cystic fibrosis and sickle cell anaemia. Most disease genes are "recessive", like the gene for blue eyes, meaning the disease only develops if a child inherits a faulty copy from both parents.

Cloning means using DNA from an organism to create an identical new individual, or clone. Some clones occur naturally – many plants and some simple animals reproduce by cloning, and identical twins are clones. Artificial cloning can be used to grow new organs for transplant patients.

▶ DESIGNER BABY *Would you pick and choose which genes to pass on to your children?*

1961	1970	1990	1996	2003
Marshall Nirenberg deciphers the genetic code hidden in the order of the bases.	**Frederick Sanger** begins sequencing DNA.	Doctors use gene therapy for the first time, treating a four-year old girl suffering from an immune disorder.	The first experimentally cloned mammal, Dolly the sheep, is born.	The completed sequence of the **human genome** is published.

Forensic science

Forensic science helps the police fight crime. Most people think of murder investigations when they talk about forensics, but forensic scientists deal with a range of crimes. Some are computer specialists who trace "cybercriminals" on the Internet, for example, while others are art experts who identify forgeries.

CRIME SCENE DO NOT ENTER CRIME SCENE

CRIME SCENE
Crime scene investigators collect the evidence at a crime scene. They look for any clues that might secure a conviction, from bloodstains and body fluids to fibres and footprints. Crime scene investigators photograph all the evidence and then take it back to the crime lab for further analysis.

Post mortem After any suspicious death, a doctor called a pathologist will do a post mortem. This involves cutting open the body to find out the cause and time of death. If the corpse has been dead for a long time, the time of death can be established by studying the kinds of insects present.

◄ CRIME SCENE
Forensic scientists seal a body inside a body bag. The corpse will be stored at a mortuary until the post mortem.

DEAD-BODY TIMELINE

3–36 hours	0+ hours	0–24 hours	50–365 days
Rigor mortis There is a chemical change in the muscles that makes a corpse stiffen up. This starts about three hours after death and lasts about 36 hours.	**Bacterial decay** Bacteria start to break down the body. In warm, moist conditions, the soft, fleshy parts rot very quickly.	**Insect invasion** Insects such as flies lay eggs inside the body. When the larvae hatch, they start to feed on the rotting remains.	**Bare bones** All that is left of the dead body are the hard parts such as the skull, teeth, and bones.

FINGERPRINT FEATURES

If you look at your fingertips, you will notice they are covered in tiny ridges. The ridges form distinct patterns of arches, loops, and whorls. No two people have been found to have the same prints (not even identical twins) so they can be used for identification.

Double loop   Whorl   Arch

DNA fingerprinting

Everyone has a unique DNA sequence (except for identical twins). Forensic scientists can turn a DNA sample into a fingerprint by breaking the DNA into small fragments and then making these spread through a sheet of gel to form a series of bands.

DO NOT ENTER CRIME SCENE DO NOT ENTER

Leaving prints

Criminals leave prints on everything they touch. Prints left in blood stains show up clearly. Other visible marks can be left on soft materials such as soap. Latent prints are made by natural skin oils. These prints show up when forensic scientists dust the crime scene.

Dusting brush

▶ DUSTING FOR PRINTS *A forensic scientist dusts a window to reveal a set of prints hidden on the glass.*

Digital data

Long gone are the days of using ink to record fingerprints on paper. Instead, the police use electronic scanners to record the prints digitally. The police store the prints on a database, which can then be used to match the prints found at crimes scenes. A new development is iris scanning, which looks at the coloured tissue around the pupil.

▶ FINGER SCAN *A scanner records the pattern of arches, loops, and whorls that make up a fingerprint.*

▼ IRIS SCANS *The scanner records the features of the iris, which is unique to each person.*

Cybercrime

Crime involving computers is on the increase. The crimes often involve people stealing credit-card details and pretending to be someone else. Computer experts are helping the police to track down these cybercriminals.

TAKE A LOOK: FACE FROM THE PAST

Forensic scientists have studied skeletal remains. They can help forensic artists to build up a 3D image of the face from the skull. Facial reconstruction is extremely important. It has helped the police solve crimes that happened decades ago. It also reveals what people from ancient civilizations looked like.

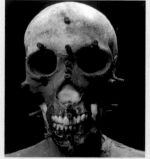

▲ DEPTH MARKERS *The artist makes a cast of the skull. Pegs act as depth markers for skin and muscles.*

▲ FACE SCULPTURE *The artist uses a modelling tool to build up the muscle layers with modelling clay.*

▲ SKIN DEEP *The artist adds a layer of clay to form the skin. The head is now fully reconstructed.*

TECHNOLOGY

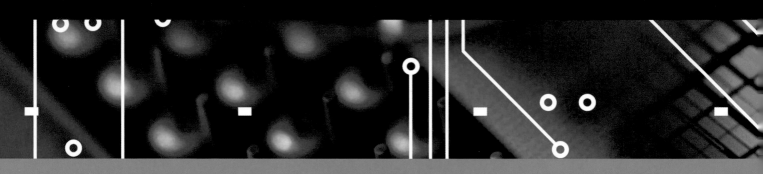

- Technology began about 3 million years ago when people invented the first tools.

- Computers work at least a million times faster than they did in the 1940s.

- A single DVD can store as many words as over 10,000 thick books.

- There are over 600 million cars on the planet – roughly one for every 11 people.

- A space rocket makes 10 times more power at lift-off than an aeroplane's jet engines.

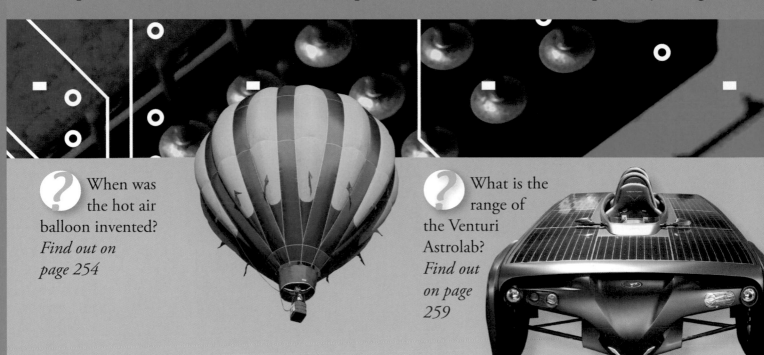

? When was the hot air balloon invented? *Find out on page 254*

? What is the range of the Venturi Astrolab? *Find out on page 259*

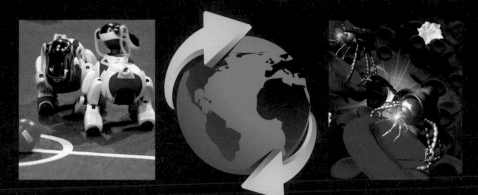

Definition: **Technology** solves practical problems to make our lives easier. It often uses science to find ways to improve things like medicines or communications.

- A vaccine for the measles has saved 7 million lives in developing countries since 1999.

- Fibre-optic cables send messages fast enough to go 5 times around the world in a second.

- Engineers have managed to fit more than 2 billion transistors on a single computer chip.

- The IBM computer firm has filed the most patents (invention ideas) for 15 years in a row.

- Over half the world's oil is used for transportation.

? How does a digital camera work? *Find out on pages 260–261*

? What is virtual snowboarding? *Find out on pages 264–265*

Inventions *and* discoveries

Since people began living in simple dwellings, inventions have been a part of technological development. From the first use of stone for tools to the worldwide dependence on computers, people are always finding something new.

◄ 3000 BCE
COTTON
Cotton fabrics were first made in the valley of the River Indus.

▲ 3500 BCE
ROAD
One of the first roads to be built was the Persian Royal Road in 3500 BCE. It was 2857 km (1785 miles).

◄ 7500 BCE
WHEAT AND BARLEY *have been used to feed people for thousands of years. It is thought that it was first grown in the Middle East.*

► 6000 BCE
DRUM
Drums have been used for thousands of years. The remains of drums as old as 6000 BCE have been found by archaeologists.

▲ 3500 BCE
BRICK
People started making strong, waterproof bricks by baking them in a kiln instead of just letting the mud they were moulded from dry in the Sun.

10,000 BCE	7500 BCE	5000 BCE

▲ 10,000 BCE
WHISTLE
Archaeologists have found whistles dating from 10,000 BCE. The whistle may well have been the first musical instrument.

▲ 7000 BCE
FIRE *Although fire has been used for millions of years, it was only nine thousand years ago when people discovered how to make it.*

▲ 4000 BCE
SCALES
Early scales were beam balances. A straight length of metal or wood was held from its centre, pans were hung from either end and an object was weighed in one pan against weights in the other pan.

▼ 3500 BC
WHEEL
Without the invention of the wheel we wouldn't be able to do lots things today. Early wheels were made from planks of wood and were used in Mesopotamia. They were most likely to have been developed by potters who desired to make completely rounded pots.

◄ 7000 BCE
CHISEL
About nine thousand years ago people started to make stone chisels. The chisel gave the user more control when carving soft materials, such as wood.

▲ 5000 BCE
PLOUGH *Seeds grow better in soil that has been prepared by a plough. Early ploughs were pushed or pulled by people to prepare the ground.*

▲ 3500 BCE
POTTER'S WHEEL
Originally potters had to mould pots with their bare hands. With the invention of the potter's wheel pots were a lot easier to make.

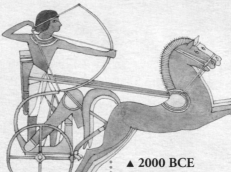

▼ 3000 BCE
RAMP
Around 3000 BCE people started to use a mechanical aid called a ramp to help with building work. Heavy stone blocks were easier to pull up a ramp than to lift straight up.

▲ 2500 BCE
ARCH
The first arches were built in Mesopotamia. The top of two walls were built until they met each other in the middle to form an arch.

▲ 2000 BCE
CHARIOT
Chariots were developed from oxcarts. Chariots were faster than carts as they only had two wheels and were much lighter.

▲ 1000 BCE
MAGNET
Magnets get their name from Magnesia, where they were first found in their mineral form (magnetite).

▲ 2500 BCE
INK
Ink was originally made from soot and glue. It came as a dry block, it had to be mixed with water.

▼ 700 BCE
SHADOW CLOCK
The ancient Egyptians were among the first to develop a clock. The Egyptian shadow clock had to be turned in the opposite direction halfway through the day. It had a straight scale to show hours of the day.

2500 BCE	2000 BCE

▲ 2900 BCE
DAM
The earliest dam was built by the Egyptians. They built a mound to act as a dam to stop the city of Memphis from flooding.

▼ 2500 BCE
MIRROR
Early mirrors were discs of polished bronze or copper. The first glass mirrors came nearly 4,000 years later.

▲ 2000 BCE
LOCK
The ancient Egyptians invented locks that were made from a piece of wood and pins. Most of the locks we use today are based on the concept of the original locks.

▲ 2500 BCE
WELDING
Welding was first used to join pieces of metal together to make jewellery.

▲ 1700 BCE
RUNNING WATER
Minoans in Crete were the first to build drains and pipes so they could have running water in the palace of Knossos.

◄ 3000 BCE
CANDLE
Candlesticks dating from 3000 BCE have been found in Egypt and Crete. Candles are made from putting thin cords in liquid wax.

ΑΒΓΔΕΖΗΘ
ΙΚΛΜΝΞΟΠ
ΡΣΤΥΦΧΨΩ

◄ 900 BCE
ALPHABET WITH VOWELS AND CONSONANTS
The Greeks adapted the ancient Palestinian alphabet (with symbols for consonants) and made their own which included vowels and consonants.

The golden age of invention and discovery came in the last two hundred years. New scientific theories helped people invent things that changed the world.

▲ **1280**
SPECTACLES
English scientist Roger Bacon came up with the idea of using a magnifying glass as a reading aid. In 1301, two Italian inventors took it a step further by inventing spectacles.

▼ **1565**
PENCIL
Conrad Gesner of Switzerland is credited with inventing the pencil but may only have been writing about an existing invention.

▼ **1800**
ELECTRICITY
The Italian scientists Luigi Galvani and Alessandro Volta invented the first device to give a continuous flow of electricity.

▲ **1700s**
INDUSTRIAL REVOLUTION
Jobs moved from farms into factories, where new machines greatly increased production.

▼ **1876**
TELEPHONE
Alexander Graham Bell holds the patent for the telephone. He was the first to make it successful, but there is evidence that others, such as Antonio Muecci, invented it first.

◄ **1878**
LIGHT BULB
Thomas Edison and Joseph Swan came up with the idea of the electric light bulb independently. No need for candles and gas lamps – life would be much easier for everyone.

1500 CE	1800 CE

▼ **1455**
PRINTING PRESS
Johannes Gutenberg's invention allowed multiple copies of books to be printed, making them available for everyone to read.

▲ **1608**
TELESCOPE
Hans Lippershey is generally credited with inventing the first telescope, but Galileo was the first person to use it for astronomy.

▼ **1868** TYPEWRITER
Christopher Scholes and partners patented the typewriter. The American company Remington and Sons. took their invention into production in 1873.

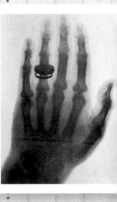

Movable type using metal letters made printing quick and cheap.

▲ **1783**
HOT-AIR BALLOON
The French Montgolfier brothers invented the first hot-air balloon, but they promised their father they would not fly it.

▼ **1827**
MATCHES
John Walker dipped a wooden stick in a mixture of chemicals and the first friction match came to light.

▲ **1895** X-RAY
Wilhelm Röntgen's discovery of X-rays earned him the first Nobel Prize for Physics in 1901.

◄ **1982**
CD
The first compact discs hit the stores in 1982. They have continued to be a popular way of storing data in digital form.

▲ **1903**
POWERED FLIGHT
The pioneers of powered flight were Orville and Wilbur Wright, who took to the skies in a plane known as the Wright Flyer. *Their historic flight over the sands of Kitty Hawk in North Carolina, USA, lasted only 12 seconds.*

▼ **1979**
MOBILE PHONE
The first commercial mobile phone was about the same size as a brick. It was developed and launched in Japan, but the idea had been around for more than 20 years.

▶ **2001**
MP3 PLAYERS
Apple launched its first portable MP3 player, called the iPod. Within two years, they were becoming integrated with mobile phones.

▼ **1928**
SLICED BREAD
When Otto Rohwedder invented a bread slicer, many bakers thought the idea was silly because the bread would go stale. Little did they know!

▲ **1977**
PERSONAL COMPUTERS
Our lives have been transformed by PCs. Almost every office, school and home in the developed world now includes PCs for everyone to use.

▲ **1983**
INTERNET
The Internet grew out of a network of computers that linked universities and the military across the United States. Today it is used for the World Wide Web, email, and much more.

▲ **2005**
E-READER
E-books, which are read on e-readers, are the digital equivalent of printed books. They are popular in Japan.

1900 CE

2000 CE

Penicillin mould

▼ **1957**
FIRST SPACE SATELLITE
The Soviet Union launched the first artificial satellite, Sputnik 1, on October 14. Within a month, they had launched a dog called Laika into space aboard Sputnik 2.

▲ **1982**
FIRST ARTIFICIAL HEART
A dentist from Seattle in the United States became the first person to be implanted with an artificial heart.

▶ **1997**
DOLLY THE SHEEP
Scientists at the Roslin Institute in Scotland cloned the first mammal and named her after country and western singer Dolly Parton.

▲ **1928**
ANTIBIOTICS
Sir Alexander Fleming discovered penicillin, but left it to others to turn it into a practical treatment that saved millions of lives.

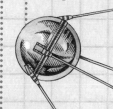

◄ **1938**
BALLPOINT PEN
A Hungarian named Laszlo Biro invented the ballpoint pen but World War II put back production until 1943.

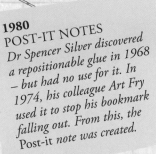

1980
POST-IT NOTES
Dr Spencer Silver discovered a repositionable glue in 1968 – but had no use for it. In 1974, his colleague Art Fry used it to stop his bookmark falling out. From this, the Post-it note was created.

▶▶ FAST FACTS ▶▶
- German-born U.S. scientist Albert Einstein started his career studying new inventions in a patent office in Switzerland.
- The first electric washing machine was invented by U.S. engineer Alva Fisher in 1907.
- Thomas Edison is credited with more than 1,000 new inventions during his life and is one of the most successful nventors of all time.

SLICE OF SURGERY

The image of a surgeon has changed from backstreet doctors to computer-controlled robot such as the da Vinci Surgical System, which can perform routine surgical procedures with precision.

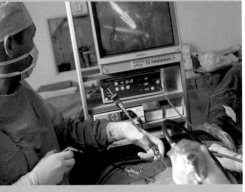

▲ THROUGH THE KEYHOLE *Surgeons use an endoscope to look inside a patient's body.*

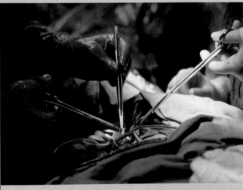

▲ PLASTIC FANTASTIC *Skin grafting is one of the most common procedures in plastic surgery.*

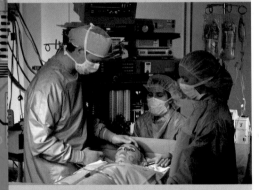

▲ HEART SURGERY *is now routine thanks to advances in technology.*

Modern medicine

Medicine has come a long way since the Greek philosopher Hippocrates laid the foundations for modern medicine nearly 2,500 years ago. Advances in all areas of medicine are now helping us live longer, healthier, and happier lives.

MEDICINE IN MINIATURE

Making things smaller allows doctors to see and do more. In the future, nanotechnology could revolutionize medicine with developments such as nanorobots.

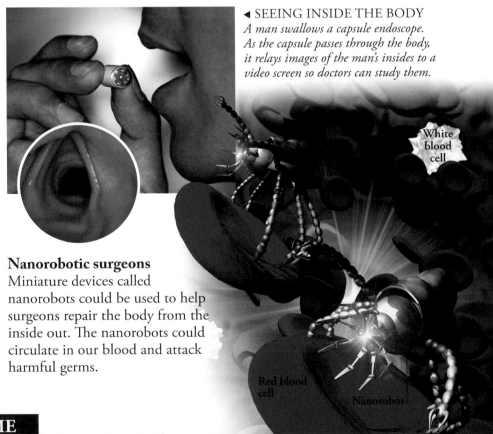

◀ SEEING INSIDE THE BODY
A man swallows a capsule endoscope. As the capsule passes through the body, it relays images of the man's insides to a video screen so doctors can study them.

White blood cell

Nanorobotic surgeons
Miniature devices called nanorobots could be used to help surgeons repair the body from the inside out. The nanorobots could circulate in our blood and attack harmful germs.

Red blood cell

Nanorobot

MEDICINE THROUGH TIME

6,500 BCE	1590 CE	1867 CE	1895 CE	1901 CE
Trepanation was a form of primitive surgery that involved drilling holes in the skull to release "evil spirits".	Dutch father and son Hans and Zacharius Jannsen invent the first microscope, and by doing so open up the invisible world of the cell.	Sterilization practices pioneered by Joseph Lister.	X-rays are discovered by Wilhelm Röntgen and later used to look inside the body without the need for invasive surgery.	Karl Landsteiner discovers the ABO human blood group system.

TAKE A LOOK: STEM CELLS

It is now possible to grow new tissues and organs from stem cells rather than wait for transplants. Stem cells are primitive cells that can divide and produce any type of cell in the body. The body will not reject tissues and organs grown from stem cells because they come from the patient's own body.

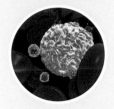

◀ STEM CELL
Doctors use stem cells taken from the body.

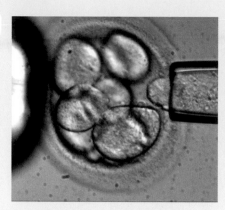

▲ EMBRYONIC STEM CELLS
In the laboratory, scientists isolate the stem cells from a developing embryo.

▲ SKIN FROM STEM CELLS
The stem cells are used to generate new skin for use in transplant surgery.

BODY REBUILDING

When the body cannot repair itself, doctors use technology to rebuild it. Advances include miniature retinal implants that can restore sight and prosthetic limbs under direct control of the brain.

◀ SPRINT CHAMP
Blake Leeper from the US is a sprinting champion with spring-loaded legs.

▶ MIND CONTROL
Former US marine Claudia Mitchell uses her brain to move her prosthetic arm.

WHO'S WHO?

■ **Hippocrates** (c. 460–c. 377 BCE) becomes the founding father of modern medicine. Hippocrates suggests that disease has natural causes rather than being a punishment from the gods.

■ **William Harvey** (1578–1657) studies the circulatory system and shows how the heart pumps blood around the body.

■ **Elizabeth Blackwell** (1821–1910) becomes the first woman to graduate with a medical degree from Geneva College in New York in 1849.

■ **Dr Crawford Long** (1815–1878) uses ether as an anaesthetic during surgery.

■ **Sir Alexander Fleming** (1881–1955) discovers penicillin. In 1940, Howard Walter Florey (1898–1968) and Ernst Chain (1906–1979) mass-produce penicillin as an antibiotic.

■ **John Heysham Gibbon Jr** (1903–1973) invents the first heart-lung machine in 1935. He performs the first open-heart surgery on a human in 1953.

■ **Christiaan Barnard** (1922–2001), South African surgeon, performs the first successful heart transplant in 1967.

1950 CE

Surgeons from Chicago, USA, perform the first successful organ transplant – the kidney of a woman named Ruth Tucker.

1957 CE

The first practical transistorized pacemaker was made by Earl Bakken.

1985 CE

For the first time, surgeons use a robotic assistant called PUMA 560 to help take a tissue sample from the brain.

1996 CE

Scientists clone the first mammal – Dolly the Sheep (died 2003).

2007 CE

Doctors make huge strides in stem cell research.

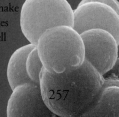

Electric cars

Most cars use petrol, made from oil, which causes pollution and adds to global warming. Oil supplies are running out, too. That's why car designers are turning to electric engines, which can use energy from cleaner sources.

▲ Open the bonnet of an electric car and you won't find a petrol engine. Instead, there's an electric motor (shown below in a cutaway).

HONDA FCX CLARITY

This might look like an ordinary car but it's powered in what could be a much cleaner way. In a normal car, the engine burns petrol, releases energy, and makes pollution. But in this car the fuel tank is replaced by a kind of battery called a hydrogen fuel cell. This takes hydrogen from a tank and oxygen from the air, reacts them together, and produces electricity. The only waste product is steam, so if the hydrogen comes from a clean source there is no pollution at all.

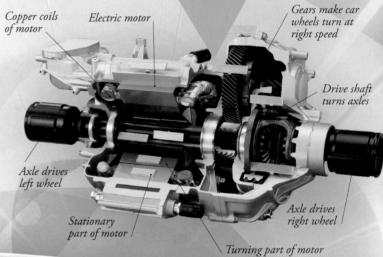

Copper coils of motor

Electric motor

Gears make car wheels turn at right speed

Drive shaft turns axles

Axle drives left wheel

Axle drives right wheel

Stationary part of motor

Turning part of motor

TAKE A LOOK: HOW IT WORKS

1 The **hydrogen tank** stores enough fuel to power the car for 450 km (280 miles).

2 The **fuel cell** chemically reacts hydrogen from the tank with oxygen from the air to make electricity.

3 The **rechargeable battery** stores energy released when the car brakes and helps the fuel cell power the car.

4 The **power drive unit** works like a gearbox. It makes more electricity flow from the battery to the motor.

5 The **electric motor** is light and compact and turns the front wheels to drive the car along.

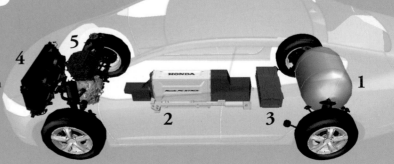

Suzuki Pixy
Three-wheeled, low-speed city car

- **Top speed** Less than 30 km/h (20 mph)
- **Range** 30 km (20 miles)
- **Made in** Japan

Suzuki have created a single-seater electric pod that is great for short journeys. Two of the Pixy pods can sit in a fuel-cell coach that recharges them as it moves. The larger coach can go on longer journeys.

Microcab
Useful for short journeys

- **Top speed** 64 km/h (40 mph)
- **Range** 80–160 km (50–100 miles)
- **Made in** United Kingdom

Fuel cell cars are being used as taxis in Birmingham, England. They are incredibly light and can travel for 160 km (100 miles) before they need to stop and refuel.

The life car
Stylish and speedy fuel-cell sports car

- **Top speed** 140 km/h (85 mph)
- **Range** 320 km (200 miles)
- **Made in** United Kingdom

Built from lightweight aluminium, this Morgan uses five times less energy than an ordinary steel-bodied car. It speeds from 0 to 100km/h (0 to 60mph) in 7 seconds!

Venturi Astrolab
High-performance car powered by sunlight

- **Top speed** 120 km/h (75 mph)
- **Range** 110 km (60 miles)
- **Made in** France

This solar car has no engine or fuel cell. Instead, it's covered in solar panels with lenses on top. These capture sunlight, turn it into electricity, and store it in batteries.

WOW!
Few electric cars are 100 per cent eco-friendly, because their batteries have to be charged using electricity. Most electricity still comes from power stations burning dirty fuels. These make pollution and add to global warming.

Tesla roadster
Fast, quiet, and less polluting

- **Top speed** 210 km/h (130 mph)
- **Range** 400 km (250 miles)
- **Made in** USA

The Tesla is designed for people who love ordinary cars but want them to be environmentally friendly as well. Its powerful electric motor can accelerate almost as fast as a petrol-driven Ferrari!

▶ TESLA ROADSTER
The Tesla's rear wheels are powered by an electric motor and batteries at the back.

Batteries

Electric motor

Air cooling pipe

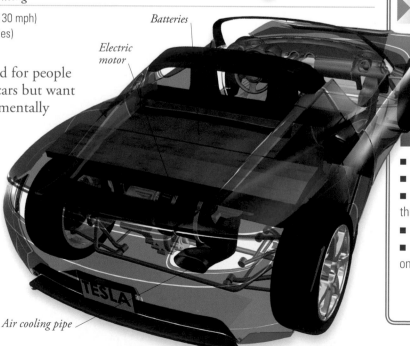

▶▶▶ **TESLA ROADSTER** ▶▶▶

- 100 per cent electric.
- Powered by 6831 laptop batteries.
- The lithium-ion battery pack takes three and a half hours to charge.
- Burns no oil.
- Accelerates to 100 km/h (0–60mph) in only four seconds.

Through a lens

Cameras are everywhere. Mobile phones often include one, they are used in security systems, in space exploration, medical equipment, and in speed cameras. Cameras are devices that capture still or moving images.

▶ MEMORY CARDS *can store thousands of digital images.*

GOING DIGITAL

Digital cameras are similar to film cameras except that they store the images on a memory card. Their lenses focus the image onto an electronic sensor (CCD or CMOS) that converts the light into electrical charges. The charges are measured to give digital values. Computer chips process the data to construct the image which is then stored on a memory card.

The digital screen lets the user check and review images.

A control dial allows the photographer to have control over settings.

An inbuilt flash provides light when it is too dark to take a photo.

A circuit board processes information from the sensor into a digital format.

FinePix

Autofocus system makes sure an image is clear.

TAKE A LOOK: SENSOR

A digital camera requires a sensor in order to work. A shutter allows light to pass through the lens to a sensor. The sensor is a grid of millions of pixels.

Each pixel measures the amount of light that hits it through a green, blue, or red filter.

The measurements are changed into digital information which is used to make the final digital image.

TIMELINE OF CAMERAS

TENTH CENTURY
The concept of a camera obscura is credited to Abu Ali Al-Hasan. It works by light passing through a hole and hitting a surface, where it forms an upside-down image. In later models mirrors were used to reflect the image so that it appeared the right way up.

1500s–1800s
Artists used more developed camera obscuras to trace images of scenes onto paper. The invention of the camera obscura led to the development of modern day cameras.

1840s
Simple photographic cameras were in use by the 1840s and were little more than a wooden box with a hole cut to hold a lens. Images were recorded on a glass or metal plate.

1880s
Photographic film was made in the 1880s. It was made from a strip of plastic coated with crystals of a silver compound. Cameras were developed to include an automatic shutter mechanism allowing the right amount of light in the lens.

FACTFILE

Movie cameras are similar to still-image cameras except that the film runs continually. Each frame of film captures a slightly different image so that when the frames are run back through a projector you get the illusion of continuous movement. Movie cameras can also record sound at the same time.

Professional studio cameras are used in television. They split the light into red, green, and blue and detect each colour separately, which gives a better quality image. The pictures are sent to a separate recorder. Most studio cameras are mounted on special trolleys, but they can also be attached to moving vehicles.

Video cameras and camcorders These initially used analogue and then digital tape to record and store information. Now they use optical discs or memory cards. Camcorders are mainly used for home movies. Over the years they have become smaller and lighter and can be carried in one hand.

▼ INSTANT PRINTS
Polaroid cameras take pictures that develop themselves, producing a photo a minute or so after it has been taken.

Technology (side tab)

Lenses can be changed over to obtain a required effect. Wide angle lenses, as the name suggests, are used to take wide shots.

Filters control the light coming through the lens.

WOW!

The first CCTV (closed-circuit television) camera that was installed in the UK was in 1949. It was put in Guy's Hospital, London. There are approximately 20 million CCTV cameras in the world.

Light needs to travel through the lens in order to capture an image.

1920s
Small cameras with interchangeable lenses were developed in the 1920s. This allowed photographers to take a wider range of photographs.

1970s
Cameras were made with automatic exposure and electronic autofocus in the 1970s.

1990s
The technology for digital cameras was invented in the 1970s and it was developed in the 1980s, but it wasn't until the 1990s that digital cameras came into popular use.

Global village

Technology is helping to bring our planet together. People on the other side of the world live up to 20,000 km (12,500 miles) away, but you can email or phone them in seconds. Hundreds of millions of computers in more than 200 countries are now connected into a giant network called the Internet.

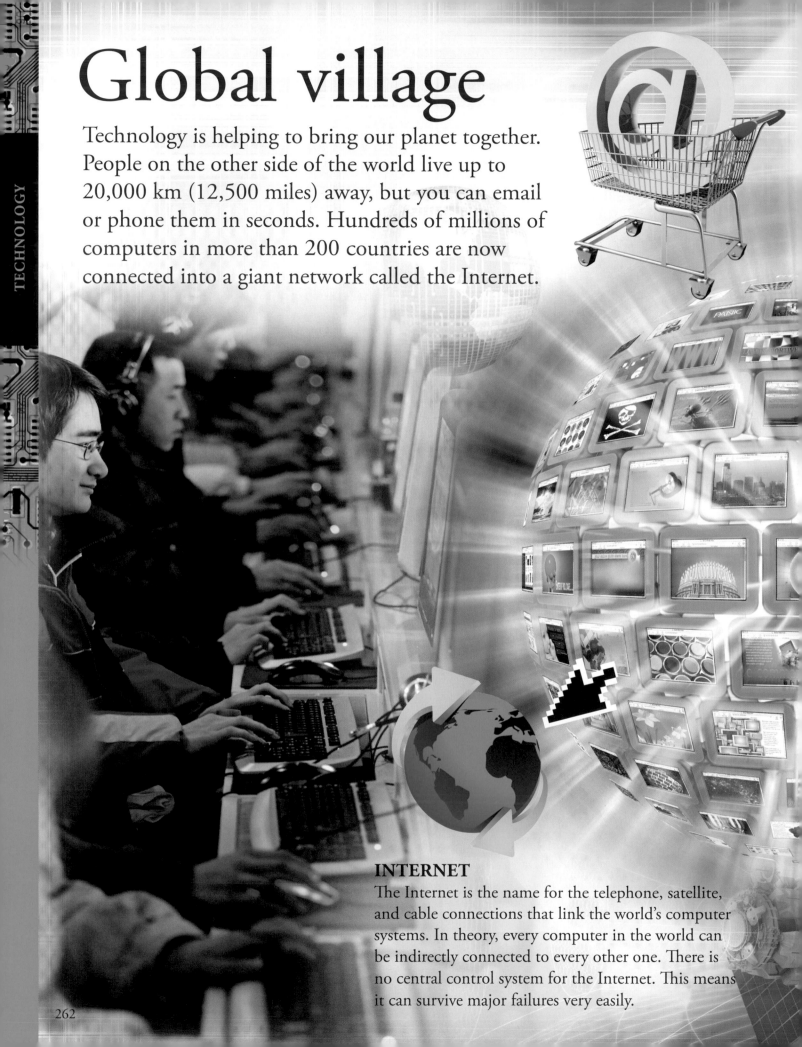

INTERNET

The Internet is the name for the telephone, satellite, and cable connections that link the world's computer systems. In theory, every computer in the world can be indirectly connected to every other one. There is no central control system for the Internet. This means it can survive major failures very easily.

ELECTRONIC MAIL

Electronic mail (email) is a way of sending written messages between computers. Invented in 1971, it has now become one of the world's favourite forms of communication – especially for work. No-one really knows, but it's thought somewhere between 100 and 500 billion emails are sent worldwide each day.

WOW!

The World Wide Web is like a huge library you can use over the Internet. It has around 200 million separate websites containing well over 20 billion text pages, photographs, and music and sound files.

MOBILE PHONES

Ordinary phones are fixed in place because they have to be connected with wires. Mobile phones can go anywhere because they send signals with radio waves. There are more than three billion mobile phones in the world. They've proved a big hit in developing countries where traditional telephone networks cost too much to build.

NEWS

When letters were the fastest way to communicate, it could take months for news to go round the world. Now, with satellite and Internet technology, you can watch events happening live. Using a website, you can even set up your own personal newspaper called a blog.

BRINGING PEOPLE TOGETHER

The Internet has created new ways for people to connect. Social networking websites, where people make friends and share interests, are very popular. A website called Facebook has over 150 million members worldwide. If it were a country, it would be one of the ten biggest nations on Earth.

Is this real?

Virtual reality (VR) uses computers to create the illusion of being in a completely different environment. VR stimulates the senses with artificial sights and sounds, tricking the brain into thinking the experience is real.

◀ INTERACT
A woman wears VR glasses and uses a wand to interact with a virtual world.

WOW!

VR systems allow a user to see virtual objects, but some enable a sense of touch too. A user wears a special pair of gloves that have small inflatable bladders inside them, which allows the person to actually feel virtual objects.

▲ VR GAMES
Virtual reality recreates the sensation of snowboarding.

HAVING FUN WITH VR

In most VR systems, headsets or glasses project the image of the virtual world in front of the user's eyes. People interact with the virtual world using devices such as joysticks, tracking balls, control wands, voice-recognition software, data gloves, and treadmills.

VIRTUSPHERE

The "VirtuSphere" is a ball that moves on rollers, so the user can walk on an unlimited amount of space. The user wears a wireless headset to track movement and create a picture of the virtual world.

◀ USING VR *The VirtuSphere has many uses, ranging from military training to virtual tours of museums.*

INDUSTRIAL DESIGN

Architects, manufacturers, and designers use VR to test new products or building designs. Testing in the virtual world eliminates any problems before actual work is carried out.

▶ WALK IN THE PARK
An architect uses VR to look at a proposed design for a new park.

TRAINING DOCTORS AND SOLDIERS

The military uses virtual reality to simulate dangerous battle scenes without putting the lives of any soldiers at risk. And in hospitals, trainee surgeons practice virtual surgery on computer screens without harming live patients.

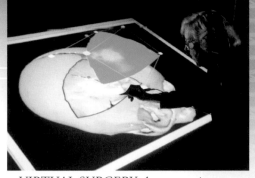

▲ VIRTUAL SURGERY *A surgeon views a VR image of a patient's head prior to surgery.*

▲ WAR GAMES *A soldier fights on the virtual battlefield to train for real combat.*

FLIGHT SIMULATION

Pilots train in flight simulators — one of the earliest forms of virtual reality. The pilot sits inside a life-size replica of a cockpit and views computer-generated images of the outside world. The controls of the simulator respond in the same way as those of a real aircraft.

◄ FLIGHT SIMULATOR *Using VR, a pilot can learn to fly without putting lives in danger.*

SPACE EXPLORATION

The American space agency NASA used virtual reality to help with the design of a Mars rover vehicle before it sent the latest rovers, *Spirit, Opportunity*, and *Curiosity*, to the surface of Mars. Astronauts also use VR to prepare for space missions.

◄ MARS ROVER *An engineer uses virtual reality to help understand the problems of navigation on the rocky surface of the red planet.*

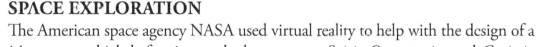

Robotics

Robots are machines that can do the sort of jobs that people do but never get tired or bored. Some robots work in dangerous places. Others have artificial intelligence, making them clever enough to solve problems and learn from experience.

ROBOTIC SURGERY

Surgeons use robots to do operations that would be too difficult for human control. They study the operation site on a TV screen and guide the robot by remote control.

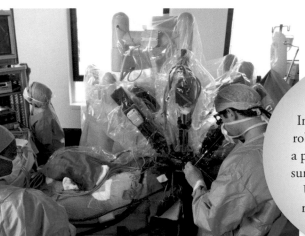

◄ DA VINCI *is a surgical robot used to perform complex surgical procedures.*

WOW!

In 2001, surgeons used robotic surgery to remove a patient's gallbladder. The surgeons were based in the United States, but the robot and patient were in France.

TAKE A LOOK: FACIAL EXPRESSIONS

Engineers at the Massachusetts Institute of Technology in the United States developed a robot called Kismet.

The robot copies human expressions by moving parts of its "face" and can learn by talking and interacting with people.

▲ HAPPY *Kismet can simulate human emotions such as happiness by copying the smiles of people it talks to.*

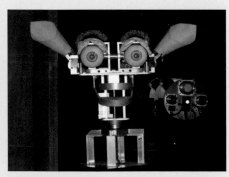

▲ SURPRISE *The robot can learn from experience but will appear "surprised" in unusual situations.*

Space exploration

- **Name** Mars Exploration Rover
- **Cost** US $820 million

In 2003, NASA deployed two robotic vehicles called rovers to explore the surface of Mars. The robots work in conditions that are far too difficult for human astronauts.

Spy plane

- **Name** MQ-1 Predator Drone
- **Cost** US $4 million

The Predator Drone is an unpiloted aerial vehicle used for surveillance. It is controlled, via a satellite link, by a pilot on the ground and is equipped with two Hellfire missiles.

Bomb disposal

- **Name** Remotec HD-1
- **Cost** Around US $110,000

This robotic bomb disposal unit is equipped with a colour camera and a telescopic arm and pincer to disarm explosive devices such as land mines without risking lives.

Industrial robots

- **First used** 1960s
- **Cost** Varies according to use

Industrial robots such as those used in car assembly lines are computer-controlled machines that do the same jobs over and over again. They are fast and accurate and do not get tired like human workers do.

Domestic robots

- **Name** Robomow
- **Cost** About US $1,600

Some robots are designed to take the hard work out of domestic chores such as mowing the lawn. Robomow is a robotic lawn mower that uses sensors to avoid trees and other hazards in its path.

TELL ME MORE...

The Roomba robotic vacuum cleaner was introduced by the US company iRobot in 2002. It works by sensing obstacles such as furniture and walls and avoiding them.

ROBOTIC ANIMALS

In the 2000s, Sony developed a robotic dog called AIBO, shown above playing football in the 2004 RoboCup football event. AIBO is a complex robot that can see and hear and has a sense of balance and touch. The robot moves and behaves almost like a real dog, for example, by chasing a ball. Sony no longer makes AIBO because the company did not sell enough to make a profit.

267

Nanotechnology

The word *nanotechnology* describes the development of devices on the scale of atoms. Scientists hope to use this new technology to produce some amazing inventions, from nanorobots used in surgery to nanomaterials that could take people to the Moon.

▼ MICRO-MECHANICS *Scientists have already made machine parts on the scale of micrometres (millionths of a metre). The parts are shown below next to a fly's leg to show how small they are.*

Fly's leg

WHAT'S IN A NAME?

The word *nano* means one-billionth. So there are one billion nanometres in one metre (3 feet). Nanotechnology is the study of devices that are billionths of a metre (3 feet) in size. To give you an idea of exactly how small that is, one nanometre would be 100,000 times smaller than the width of a human hair.

▶ ROTATING PARTS
Individual carbon and hydrogen atoms arranged in a circle could form the bearings for rotating parts in a nanomachine.

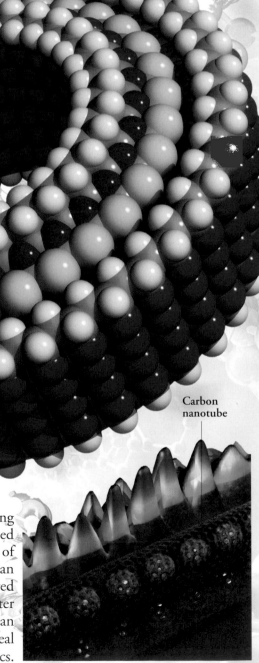

Carbon nanotube

NANOFACTS

■ By weight, carbon nanotubes are more expensive than diamond or gold.

■ In the future, nanotechnology may be used to assemble individual molecules into the parts for electronic devices such as laptops and mobile phones.

■ Other electronic devices using nanosized parts include flexible digital screens and sensors that may detect chemicals in the air.

■ Scientists hope to build nanosensors to weigh molecules as small and as light as a strand of deoxyribonucleic acid (DNA).

■ Nanotechnology is being used to make "smart drugs" that target individual cancer cells and kill specific germs.

Nanomaterials Scientists are getting very excited about structures called carbon nanotubes. These tiny tubes of carbon atoms are stronger than diamond and extremely long compared with their width. They are better conductors of electricity than metal, which makes them ideal for future electronics.

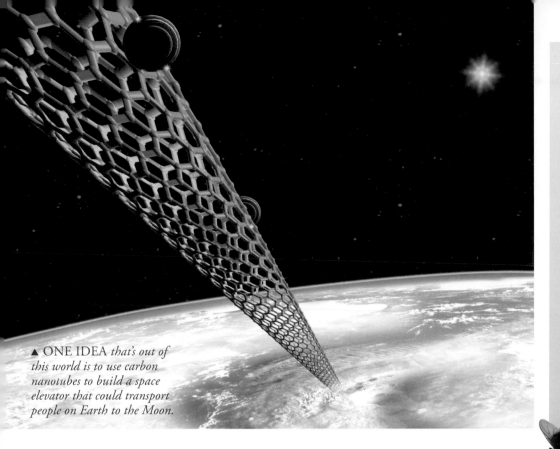

WOW!

Scientists are looking at the possibility of using **strong nanomaterials** to build very tall skyscrapers. Carbon nanotubes are one possibility. The carbon atoms in these tiny tubes form hexagon shapes, making them extremely strong and lightweight. Engineers could use the carbon nanotubes as the supporting structures for the skyscrapers.

▲ ONE IDEA *that's out of this world is to use carbon nanotubes to build a space elevator that could transport people on Earth to the Moon.*

NANOTECHNOLOGY IN ACTION

Scientists have already made tiny electric motors, gears, and springs that are just a few hundred nanometres across. In the future, they hope to connect these miniature parts to make nanomachines and nanorobots. These devices could be used to help surgeons repair the human body from the inside or they could circulate in our blood and attack harmful germs.

▶ A ROBOT FLY *is similar in size to a real fly, but the electronic components inside the robot fly are nanometres across.*

Common fly   Robotic fly

Everyday nanotechnology While the future uses of nanotechnology may lie with hi-tech industries such as electronics and robotics, this emerging technology has already found uses in many everyday items, ranging from clothing and paints to cosmetics and health-care products.

Robotic ants Scientists are using micro-robotic ants to study the behaviour of real ants. Nanotechnology helps in the manufacture of the tiny electronic circuits that control the movement of the robots.

◀ NANOPARTICLES *in sunscreen ensure even coverage and do not leave white marks on the skin.*

◀ A WATER-REPELLENT *fabric is covered with a layer of nanoparticles. The water forms a near-perfect sphere as it touches the waterproof layer and rolls away from the fabric. The droplets collect dirt as they roll over the surface and so they clean the fabric, too.*

THE HUMAN BODY

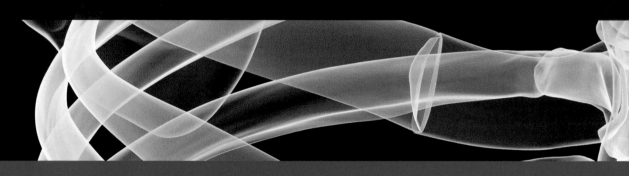

- At rest, a child's heart beats about 85 times a minute.

- The left lung is slightly smaller than the right lung.

- A human being takes about 23,000 breaths each day.

- There are about three million pain sensors in a human body. Most are in the skin.

- Your ears will grow about 6.55 mm (¼ in) in 30 years.

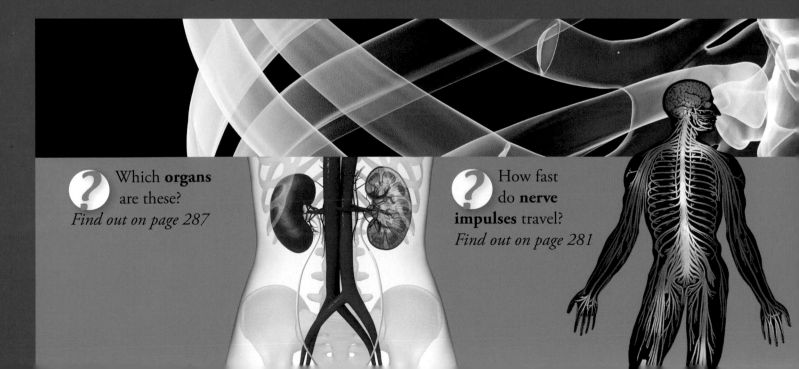

Which **organs** are these?
Find out on page 287

How fast do **nerve impulses** travel?
Find out on page 281

  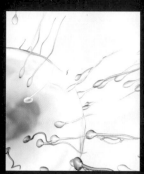

Definition: The **human body** is an amazing machine. Humans are mammals, who breathe air and eat plants and animals to nourish their bodies and provide energy.

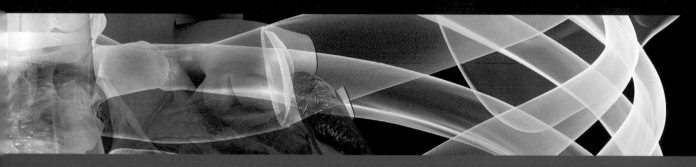

- You blink more than 9,000 times a day.

- In most places, your skin is about 2 mm (1/16 in) thick.

- In a fingernail-sized patch of skin, there can be up to 600 sweat glands.

- On average, a human body contains enough iron to make a nail 2.5 cm (1 in) long.

- A drop of blood contains around 5 million red blood cells.

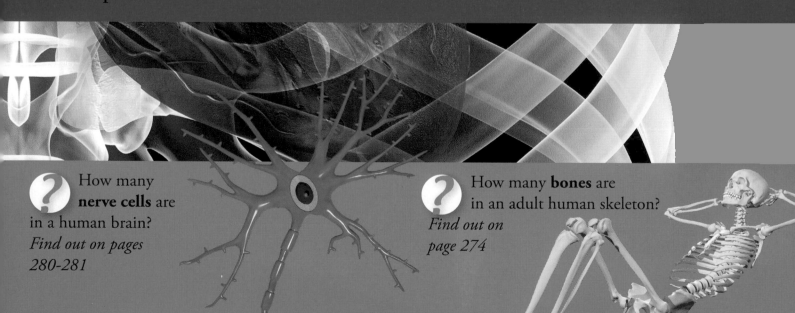

How many **nerve cells** are in a human brain? *Find out on pages 280-281*

How many **bones** are in an adult human skeleton? *Find out on page 274*

Your body

Six billion human beings share planet Earth. Each is unique. But we all share certain characteristics, notably our basic body systems, from our circulatory to our respiratory system. Body systems are made up of groups of tissues and organs that work together.

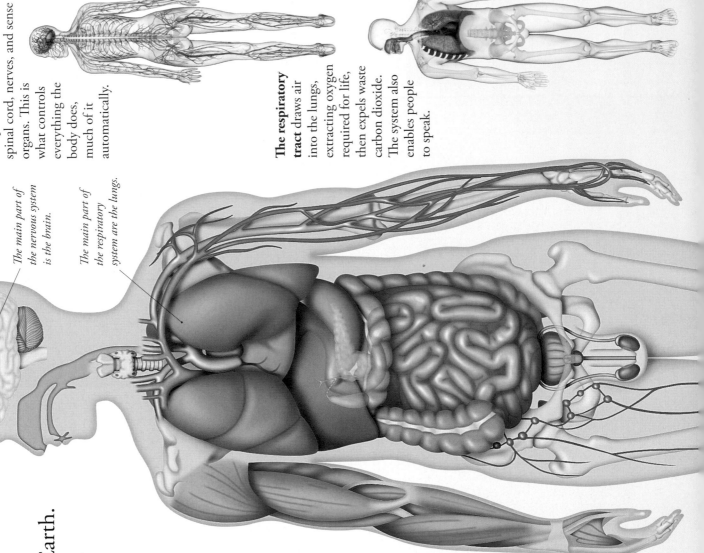

The nervous system is composed of the brain, the spinal cord, nerves, and sense organs. This is what controls everything the body does, much of it automatically.

The respiratory tract draws air into the lungs, extracting oxygen required for life, then expels waste carbon dioxide. The system also enables people to speak.

The main part of the nervous system is the brain.

The main part of the respiratory system are the lungs.

SKIN, HAIR, AND NAILS

Our skin, hair, and nails form a protective covering and together form a body system called the integumentary system. Your hair and nails grow through your skin, which is the body's largest organ. Dead skin cells are constantly shed from the surface of the skin.

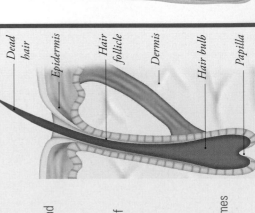

Dead hair
Epidermis
Hair follicle
Dermis
Hair bulb
Papilla

FAST FACTS
■ Human hair will grow between 6 mm (¼ inch) and 8 mm (⅓ inch) every four weeks.
■ On average, a person sheds about 0.5 kg (1 lb) of dead skin cells each year.
■ An adult human's skin weighs approximately 5 kg (11 lb).
■ Skin is waterproof.
■ Fingernails grow four times faster than toenails.

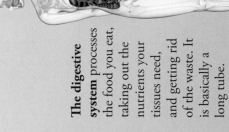

The skeletan system is the moveable skeleton that provides a frame for your body and which protects your internal organs. An adult has 206 bones.

There are about 10 body systems, but it's difficult to state an exact figure as the muscular system and skeletal system are sometimes combined and referred to as one system.

Skin covers your body. It contains hair follicles, nerve endings, sweat glands, and tiny blood vessels called capillaries.

The digestive system processes the food you eat, taking out the nutrients your tissues need, and getting rid of the waste. It is basically a long tube.

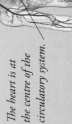

The heart is at the centre of the circulatory system.

The cardiovascular or circulatory system pumps blood around your body. Blood transports oxygen and other vital substances to your organs and tissues and then removes waste products.

Each of the body's systems has its own job to do. If all are functioning properly, they will work together to ensure the body's overall health.

The muscular system is made up of muscles attached to bones by tendons, smooth muscles in your organs, and heart muscle. Muscles need a regular blood supply to bring them the oxygen and energy they require to work efficiently.

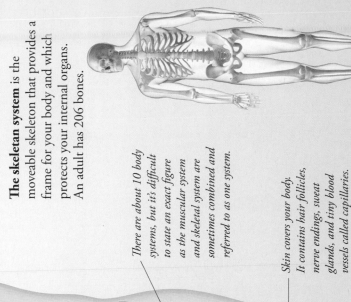

TAKE A LOOK: CELLS

Every living thing begins life as a single cell. Your body is made up of millions of cells so small that, on their own, they can only be seen under a microscope. Cells group together to form tissues, which in turn make up our organs.

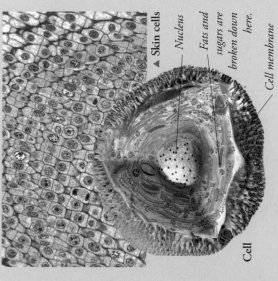

▲ **Skin cells**

Nucleus

Fats and sugars are broken down here.

Cell membrane

Cell

- Epithelial cells form a protective outer layer to the human body.

- Fat cells are blob shaped. They get larger as the body stores more fat.

- Nerve cells transfer electrical signals around the body to and from the brain.

- Smooth muscle cells are found in the intestine.

- Photo receptor cells are found in the eyes.

Bones

Your bones form a framework for your body called a skeleton. If you did not have a skeleton your body would flop all over the place. Bones also protect your soft internal organs (such as your heart) and work with muscles to make you move.

Pieces of the skull

Your skull is not made up of one bone, but of a large number of bones. The pieces of the upper skull lock together to form an incredibly strong casing for your brain, while fourteen bones form your facial bones. The shape of your facial bones and their muscles determines what you look like.

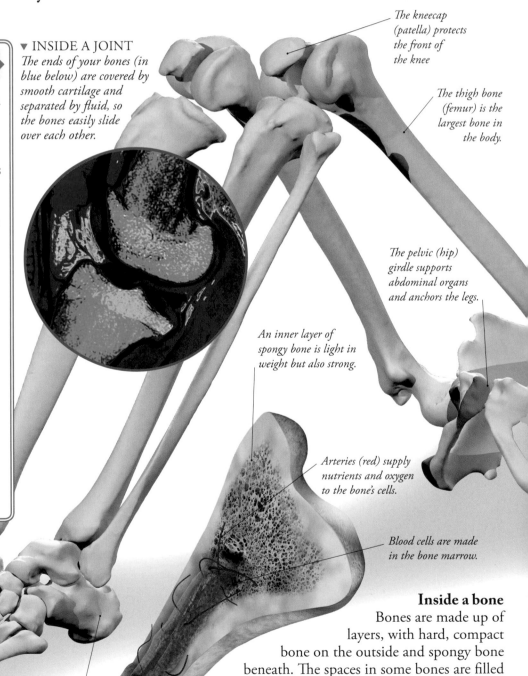

The kneecap (patella) protects the front of the knee

The thigh bone (femur) is the largest bone in the body.

The pelvic (hip) girdle supports abdominal organs and anchors the legs.

An inner layer of spongy bone is light in weight but also strong.

Arteries (red) supply nutrients and oxygen to the bone's cells.

Blood cells are made in the bone marrow.

The heel (calcaneus) is a short bone.

▶▶ FAST FACTS ▶▶

- There are 206 bones in the human body.
- Compared to a steel bar of the same weight, bone is six times stronger.
- Your largest bone is your femur. Your smallest bone is the stirrup bone, which is in your ear. It's no larger than a grain of rice.
- About eighty bones make up the human skull, backbone, and ribs.
- You need calcium in your diet to make your bones hard.
- You have the same number of neck bones as a giraffe: seven.
- A baby's skeleton is largely formed of cartilage (the stuff that makes your nose bendy).
- The thigh bone (femur) is the longest bone in your body. It is about a quarter of your height.
- More than a quarter of your bones are in your hands.

▼ INSIDE A JOINT
The ends of your bones (in blue below) are covered by smooth cartilage and separated by fluid, so the bones easily slide over each other.

Inside a bone

Bones are made up of layers, with hard, compact bone on the outside and spongy bone beneath. The spaces in some bones are filled with jelly-like bone marrow. Bone marrow stores fat and also produces new blood cells.

BONES AND JOINTS

Bones are living tissue that contain blood vessels, nerves, and cells. They are strong, but light, and if they get broken, they can heal themselves. You can bend and move your body because you have lots of joints. These are where two bones meet and move over each other.

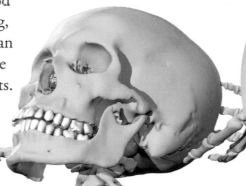

Ulna

Radius

Collar bone (clavicle)

Upper arm bone (humerus)

Breastbone (sternum)

Ribs help you breathe. They also protect the heart and lungs.

Spine or backbone (vertebral column). This is the body's central support.

Shoulder blade (scapula)

WOW!

There are four main types of bones: long (such as the thigh bones), short (such as the heel bones), flat (shoulder bones), and irregular (such as your vertebrae). There are also small, round bones with a funny name: sesamoid (such as the kneecap).

TAKE A LOOK: X-RAYS

If you have a broken bone, an x-ray allows your doctor to see what is happening beneath the skin.

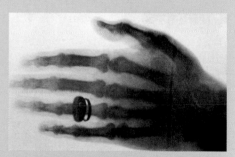

THE FIRST X-RAY *was taken in 1895 by German physicist Wilhelm Röntgen. He took an x-ray of his wife's hand that clearly showed the shadows of the bones and the lighter shadowing caused by the soft tissues.*

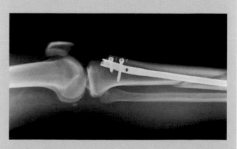

PINNING A BONE *A bone can heal itself if broken, but after an especially bad break a surgeon may put a metal pin along the bone to hold it rigid while it mends. A fracture can take up to eight weeks to heal.*

TYPES OF JOINT

Some joints (such as your elbows) allow you to bend in one direction. Others (such as your shoulders) allow circular movement.
- Saddle joints are found at the base of your thumbs.
- Ball-and-socket joints are found in your shoulder.
- Hinge joints are found in your knees.
- There's a pivot joint at the top of your spine.
- Gliding joints are found in the ankles and wrists.

    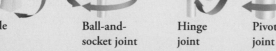

| Saddle joint | Ball-and-socket joint | Hinge joint | Pivot joint | Gliding or plane joint |

275

Mighty muscles

Muscles are tissues that move parts of the body by contracting, or getting shorter. You have around 650 skeletal muscles layered over your skeleton and these make up about half of your weight. They are attached to bones by stringy tendons.

TYPES OF MUSCLES

There are three types of muscle: skeletal muscles move bones when you want them to. Most muscle is skeletal muscle. Cardiac muscle keeps the heart beating. Smooth muscle is found inside hollow organs such as the digestive tract. You can't control the actions of smooth muscle – they are automatic.

This large, powerful muscle, the gluteus maximus, *straightens the hip when you walk, run, stand up, or climb a hill.*

HOW MUSCLES WORK

Skeletal muscles get shorter and fatter when working – they stretch when relaxed. They work because your brain tells them to. If you want to reach out to grab something, your brain tells your arm muscles to work. The muscles shorten, pulling the arm bones. Muscles work in pairs, because they work by pulling. So in your arm, your biceps works to bend your arm and your triceps straightens it.

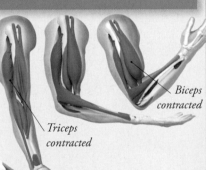

Biceps contracted

Triceps contracted

Muscles cover the skeleton and give the body its shape.

The calf muscle (gastrocnemius) *bends your foot downwards when you point your toes.*

The extensor digitorum longus *straightens your toes and helps to lift the foot up when you walk.*

WOW!

Muscles need oxygen to make energy. If starved of oxygen, perhaps during a burst of activity, they produce energy without it and a waste product called lactic acid builds up in the muscle cells. This can cause painful muscle cramps.

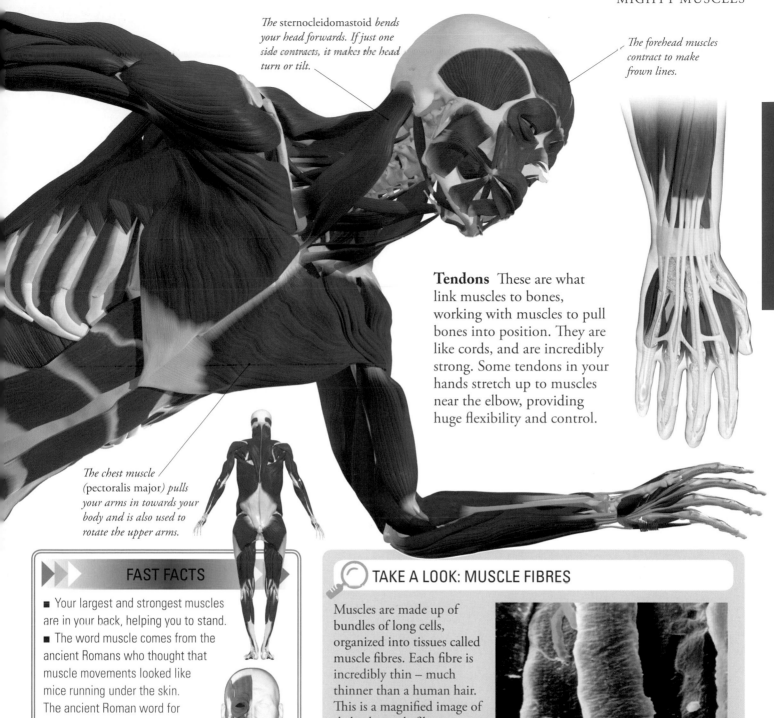

The sternocleidomastoid bends your head forwards. If just one side contracts, it makes the head turn or tilt.

The forehead muscles contract to make frown lines.

Tendons These are what link muscles to bones, working with muscles to pull bones into position. They are like cords, and are incredibly strong. Some tendons in your hands stretch up to muscles near the elbow, providing huge flexibility and control.

The chest muscle (pectoralis major) pulls your arms in towards your body and is also used to rotate the upper arms.

FAST FACTS

■ Your largest and strongest muscles are in your back, helping you to stand.

■ The word muscle comes from the ancient Romans who thought that muscle movements looked like mice running under the skin. The ancient Roman word for mouse was musculus.

■ Surprisingly, you use more muscles to smile than you use to frown! It takes 12 muscles to smile and 11 to frown.

■ The first drawings of human muscles were published in 1543 by Belgian scholar Andreas Vesalius in his book On the Structure of the Human Body.

■ Your tongue is made up of muscles.

TAKE A LOOK: MUSCLE FIBRES

Muscles are made up of bundles of long cells, organized into tissues called muscle fibres. Each fibre is incredibly thin – much thinner than a human hair. This is a magnified image of skeletal muscle fibres.

◄ INSIDE EACH MUSCLE FIBRE *are long threads of protein. This image has been magnified almost 400 times.*

Blood flow

Think of your arteries and veins as a road network for your body. Blood flows through this network, just as lorries move along roads, carrying and delivering the essentials that your cells need, and removing waste products. Your arteries and veins are your body's transport, or circulatory, system.

It takes a blood cell about one minute to circulate your body.

The heart pumps blood along a network of blood vessels.

The femoral artery supplies blood to the thigh.

An adult body contains about 5 litres (8¾ pints) of blood.

WHAT BLOOD DOES

Blood delivers oxygen, water, and nutrients to your body's organs and takes away waste carbon dioxide. It also takes white blood cells to where they are needed, to fight infection, and clots to stop bleeding and form a seal to repair damage if you cut yourself. There's more? Yes! It allows you to maintain a steady body temperature.

BLOOD GROUPS

Blood is not all the same. There are four different groups, and each group is given a letter. You might be type A, B, AB, or O. AB is the rarest. If a person has to have a blood transfusion, they have to receive the same blood group.

BLOOD CIRCULATION

Blood is pumped around the body by the heart, which is the hardest working muscle in the body. It follows a figure-of-eight route. The shorter loop (green arrows) takes blood from the heart to the lungs and back. The longer loop (yellow arrows) takes blood to other parts of the body, then returns it to the heart.

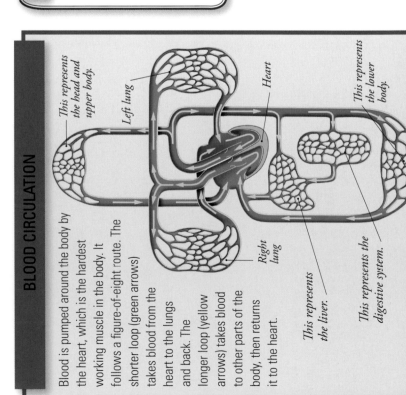

This represents the head and upper body.

Left lung

Heart

This represents the lower body.

Right lung

This represents the liver.

This represents the digestive system.

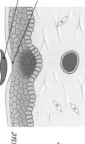

This is the body's longest vein. Blood flows through it from the foot and lower leg on its journey back to the heart.

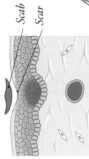

▲ BODY CIRCULATION Stretched out, your blood vessels would reach 150,000 km (93,000 miles). That's about four times around Earth.

What goes into blood?

Blood is made up of red blood cells, white blood cells, platelets, and plasma. Plasma is mostly water but also carries dissolved proteins, glucose, minerals, hormones, and carbon dioxide.

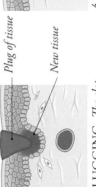

Plasma (about 50–55%)

White blood cells and platelets (about 1–2%)

Red blood cells (about 40–45%)

Blood clots

If you fall over and cut your knee, the cut area scabs over and heals. This happens in a series of steps, as shown below.

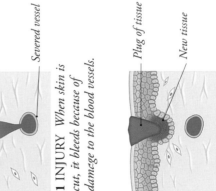

Injury site

Severed vessel

1 INJURY When skin is cut, it bleeds because of damage to the blood vessels.

Blood clot

2 CLOTTING Platelets stick together and a blood clot begins to form.

Plug of tissue

New tissue

3 PLUGGING The clot forms a plug that stops blood leaking out.

Scab

Scar

4 SCABBING The plug hardens to form a protective scab, which eventually falls off.

Your heart
and how it works

- **Beats per day** Approx 100,000
- **Average weight** Male: 300 g (10½ oz) Female: 200 g (9 oz)
- **Length** 12 cm (5 in)
- **Width** 9 cm (3½ in)

The muscular human heart is about the size of a fist. It pumps blood around your body, which takes oxygen to the cells, and removes waste. A heart has four chambers, two lower ventricles, and two upper atria. If your heart stops, no other part of your body can work.

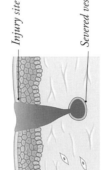

Pulmonary valve

Superior vena cava

Aorta

Pulmonary artery

Right atrium

Right ventricle

Thick cardiac muscle

TAKE A LOOK: BLOOD VESSELS

There are three types of blood vessels: arteries, veins, and capillaries. Blood begins its journey around the body in a large artery, called the aorta. Arteries have thicker walls than other vessels because the blood flow is at higher pressure.

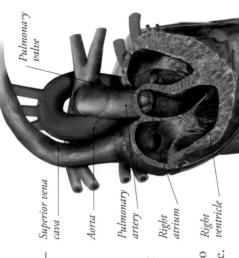

▲ ARTERIES carry oxygen-rich blood away from your heart. They have thicker walls than veins or capillaries.

▲ VEINS carry oxygen-poor blood to your heart. Many veins have valves to stop the blood running backwards.

▲ CAPILLARIES are microscopic, with walls just one cell thick. They link your arteries to your veins.

Think! Act!

Your brain is a complex organ. It's a bit like a big computer but more adaptable. It controls all you do. It makes you think. It allows you to learn. It stores your memories. It makes you who you are.

WHAT IS YOUR BRAIN?

Your brain is a collection of about a hundred billion nerve cells called neurons. These are linked to each other and they share and pass information all day and all night throughout your life.

Message transfer Messages constantly arrive in your brain from your body, sent in the form of electrical signals along nerves. Your brain processes those messages and sends out instructions telling your body what to do.

WOW!

Your brain has a joke centre, which allows you to understand why a joke is funny. This means that some people with damage to the front of their brains, (particularly on the right-hand side) just don't find jokes funny. Given a joke with a choice of different punchlines they can't tell which is the funny one.

CENTRAL NERVOUS SYSTEM (CNS)

A bundle of nerves called the spinal cord runs from the brain down your back, protected inside a column of bones, the backbone. The brain and spinal cord form your central nervous system.

The central nervous system allows you to make voluntary actions such as eating, reading, and walking, as well as controlling many actions itself. For example, you aren't aware of the muscles working in your stomach – they work automatically.

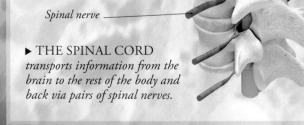

Cross-section of spinal cord

Spinal nerve

▶ THE SPINAL CORD *transports information from the brain to the rest of the body and back via pairs of spinal nerves.*

▶ FITTING TOGETHER *This model shows how the brain, spinal cord, and eyes link up.*

The spinal cord is as thick as your little finger.

Neurons are thin cells that carry electrical signals called nerve impulses. A neuron has a cell body, with short, spreading projections called dendrites. An axon connects to other neurons.

The axon, a nerve fibre, takes electrical impulses away from the cell body to other neurons.

The nucleus of the cell controls the cell's activity.

Cell body

Dendrites pick up nerve signals.

BRAIN CELL OR NEURON

The nervous system is made up of the CNS and the peripheral nervous system, which consists of nerves that branch to the rest of your body. It's hard working and fast; a nerve impulse travels from the big toe to the spinal cord in one hundredth of a second.

▶ HARD HAT
The human brain is soft and squidgy so it is protected in a bony case called the skull.

*The **thalamus** passes messages between the brain and spinal cord.*

*The heavily folded **cerebrum** is the largest part of your brain.*

The cerebral cortex is the surface of the cerebrum.

Parts of the brain
The main regions of the brain are the cerebellum, the brain stem, and the cerebrum. The cerebrum is responsible for many complex everyday activities, from eating to speaking.

*The **cerebellum** deals with movement.*

*The **hypothalamus** plays a part in thirst, hunger, and temperature control.*

*The **brain stem** works at the same level when you're asleep and awake.*

YOUR BRAIN

Sight, hearing, speaking and thinking are controlled in different areas of the cerebrum. Hearing uses an area linked to the ears' nerves. Sight involves a small area linked to the eyes' nerves. Thinking and speaking use large areas of the brain. Heat scans show the different areas.

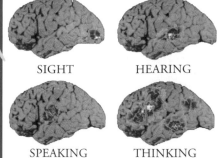

SIGHT HEARING

SPEAKING THINKING

Sensing the world

Humans have five senses: sight, hearing, touch, smell, and taste. Your senses tell you about the world around you. They work because billions of nerve cells flash messages to your brain, which interprets the messages and tells you what you are sensing, whether good or bad.

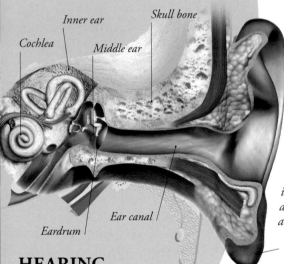

Inner ear

Skull bone

Cochlea

Middle ear

◄ INSIDE THE EAR
Your ear is made up of three main parts – the ear (auditory) canal, the middle ear, and the inner ear.

BALANCE TOO!
Your ear helps you to balance. Hair cells in the inner ear tell your brain about your body's position and movements.

Eardrum

Ear canal

Outer ear

HEARING

Sounds are made up of vibrations, which are funnelled inside the ear by the outer ear. Soundwaves first travel down the ear canal and vibrate the eardrum. These vibrations reach the cochlea. From here, messages pass to the brain, which interprets the vibrations as the sounds we recognize.

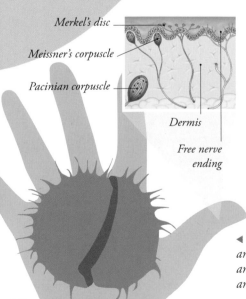

Merkel's disc

Meissner's corpuscle

Pacinian corpuscle

Dermis

Free nerve ending

TOUCH

You have about three million pain sensors, and most of these are in your skin. Your fingertips are particularly sensitive. You also have touch receptors that detect light touch, pressure, vibration, heat, and cold.

◄ TOUCH SENSATIONS *Skin layers are full of touch receptors. Some receptors are contained in a capsule while others are free nerve endings.*

SIGHT

The eye works like a camera. Light from an image passes through the cornea, is adjusted by the lens behind it, and forms an upside-down image on the retina at the back of the eye. This is translated by the brain.

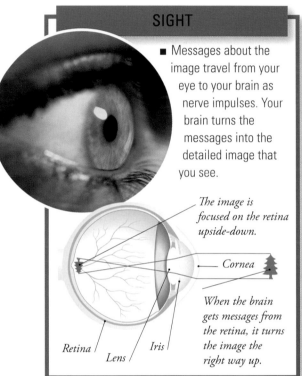

SIGHT

■ Messages about the image travel from your eye to your brain as nerve impulses. Your brain turns the messages into the detailed image that you see.

The image is focused on the retina upside-down.

Cornea

When the brain gets messages from the retina, it turns the image the right way up.

Retina

Lens

Iris

TAKE A LOOK: IRIS

Your eye will react differently depending on how bright light shining into it is. How it reacts is controlled by the iris, a ring of muscle.

Iris

Pupil

Dim light

▶ IRIS AND PUPIL
The coloured part of your eye, called the iris, has a hole in the middle called the pupil. In bright light, the pupil shrinks to prevent too much light getting into your eye. In dim light, the pupil expands to allow more light into your eye.

Bright light

SMELL

Your nose can recognize up to 10,000 different smells. Receptors high up in the nasal cavity pick up smell molecules in the air that you breathe in and send signals to your brain. If your brain hasn't come across the smell before, it will remember it so that you recognize it next time.

TELL ME MORE...

■ Smell and taste work together. The flavour of food depends more on smell than taste. This is why it's difficult to taste food if you have a blocked nose.

■ Your senses of smell and taste protect you. If you smell smoke it warns you of fire. You can smell if food has gone off. Poisonous food often tastes bitter to make sure you spit it out.

TASTE

It is now thought to be a myth that you can taste particular flavours at different places on your tongue. We have five basic tastes: sweet, sour, salty, bitter, and umami (a savoury taste), and these can usually be picked up all over your tongue.

The gustatory cortex is the taste centre for analysing tastes.

Smells are sorted by the olfactory bulb in the nose.

Taste sensors are found on the surface of the tongue and in the lining of the mouth.

▲ SENSE ORGANS *This view inside the head shows the position of the smell and taste organs. They send nerve messages to the brain.*

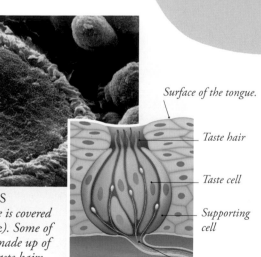

▲ TASTE RECEPTORS
The surface of your tongue is covered with tiny bumps (papillae). Some of these contain taste buds, made up of taste cells that have tiny taste hairs. These hairs detect chemicals in food, and your brain tells you the flavour.

Surface of the tongue.

Taste hair

Taste cell

Supporting cell

Diagram of taste bud

Nerve fibre

▶▶▶ FAST FACTS ▶▶

■ Children have around 10,000 taste buds, but the number of taste buds declines with age.
■ People who can't smell are called "anosmic".
■ If you only had one eye from birth, the world would look two-dimensional.
■ There are 100 touch receptors in each of your fingertips.
■ Girls usually have more taste buds than boys.
■ The sense of smell is thought to be 20,000 times more powerful than the sense of taste.

Take a breath

You need to breathe constantly to take in oxygen. You do this by breathing in air, which is taken down your windpipe and into your lungs, where the oxygen is removed and enters the blood. At the same time, carbon dioxide passes into the lungs.

What happens inside your lungs?

Inside each lung, air tubes called bronchi get smaller and smaller, becoming bronchioles. Each bronchiole ends in clusters of small, stretchy air sacs called alveoli. This is known as the bronchial tree, because it resembles an upside-down tree.

Windpipe (trachea)

Left bronchus

Each of the branching networks ends in a bronchiole, which leads into groups of alveoli.

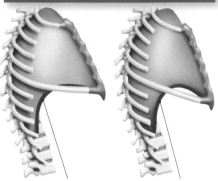

Diaphragm moves down as we inhale.

Diaphragm moves up as we exhale.

Breathing is helped by your ribs moving up and out. A dome-shaped muscle called the diaphragm also helps the process. It flattens a little, to increase the size of your chest cavity when you breathe in.

Terminal bronchiole

Capillary

Diagram shows groups of alveoli.

▲ ALVEOLI *Oxygen passes through the walls of the alveoli into capillaries, thin-walled blood vessels (👁 p279-280).*

▲ BRONCHIOLI *This greatly magnified image shows the end of a bronchiole (in blue) surrounded by a group of alveoli. There are more than 300 million alveoli in each lung.*

 TAKE A LOOK: CHEST SECTION

Your left lung is smaller than your right lung to allow room for the heart, which is positioned towards the left side of the chest cavity. The heart's position can be seen in a scanned cross-section of the chest, taken from above.

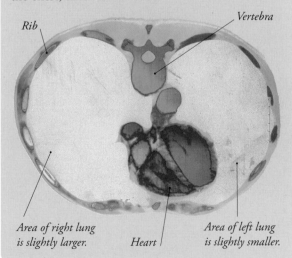

Rib

Vertebra

Area of right lung is slightly larger.

Heart

Area of left lung is slightly smaller.

FAST FACTS

- Flattened out, a pair of lungs would cover a tennis court.
- An average person takes about 12 to 15 breaths a minute when at rest. After physical activity they take in about 60 breaths a minute.
- The trachea is about 11 cm (4 in) in length.
- Your lungs act like giant sponges. They take in air instead of water.
- Each minute around 5–6 litres (1⅓–1½ gallons) of air pass into and out of your lungs.

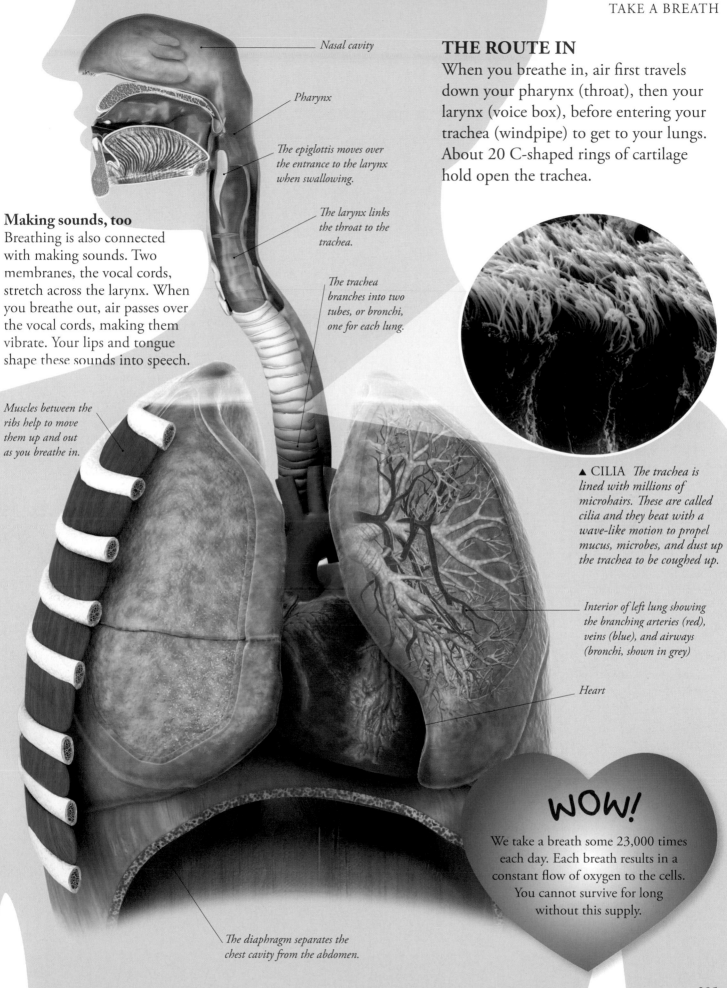

Nasal cavity

Pharynx

The epiglottis moves over
the entrance to the larynx
when swallowing.

The larynx links
the throat to the
trachea.

The trachea
branches into two
tubes, or bronchi,
one for each lung.

THE ROUTE IN

When you breathe in, air first travels
down your pharynx (throat), then your
larynx (voice box), before entering your
trachea (windpipe) to get to your lungs.
About 20 C-shaped rings of cartilage
hold open the trachea.

Making sounds, too

Breathing is also connected
with making sounds. Two
membranes, the vocal cords,
stretch across the larynx. When
you breathe out, air passes over
the vocal cords, making them
vibrate. Your lips and tongue
shape these sounds into speech.

Muscles between the
ribs help to move
them up and out
as you breathe in.

▲ CILIA The trachea is
lined with millions of
microhairs. These are called
cilia and they beat with a
wave-like motion to propel
mucus, microbes, and dust up
the trachea to be coughed up.

Interior of left lung showing
the branching arteries (red),
veins (blue), and airways
(bronchi, shown in grey)

Heart

WOW!

We take a breath some 23,000 times
each day. Each breath results in a
constant flow of oxygen to the cells.
You cannot survive for long
without this supply.

The diaphragm separates the
chest cavity from the abdomen.

Food flow

We eat to refuel our bodies. We need fuel from food to provide energy, as well as for growth and repair. Digestion is the process by which the food we eat is broken down to extract the nutrients we need. Waste matter is then passed out of the body.

Salivary glands
Saliva is produced by glands in the mouth. It makes food slippery and begins the process of digestion. About 1.5 litres (2½ pints) of saliva is secreted into the mouth each day.

TAKE A MOUTHFUL
Digestion begins with ingestion when you take in and chew food, mixing it with saliva to make it easier to swallow. Swallowing moves the food into the oesophagus, from where it goes into the stomach.

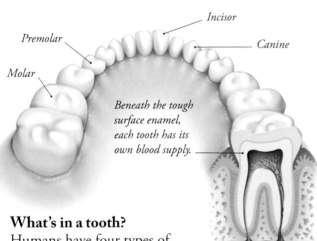

Incisor

Premolar

Canine

Molar

Beneath the tough surface enamel, each tooth has its own blood supply.

What's in a tooth?
Humans have four types of teeth: chisel-shaped incisors cut, while pointed canines tear. The flatter premolars and molars crush and grind. These are the largest teeth.

Down it goes
Once food has been chewed, it is swallowed as a ball called a bolus. It is prevented from entering the larynx and trachea by the epiglottis, a flap of cartilage.

THE STOMACH AND HOW IT WORKS

Three muscle layers enable the stomach to twist into different shapes.

When food arrives your stomach stretches to store it.

Acid and food are churned together.

Oblique

Longitudinal   Circular

Churned food is passed into the small intestine.

■ **Inside the stomach** Food enters your stomach about eight seconds after you swallow. It is mixed with acids (called gastric juice) and churned into a semi liquid. Up to 3 litres (5 pints) of gastric juices are made in the stomach every day.

▲ A GOOD CHURNING
A meal spends up to four hours in your stomach before being passed slowly on into the small intestine.

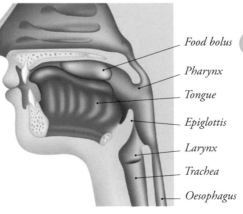

Food bolus

Pharynx

Tongue

Epiglottis

Larynx

Trachea

Oesophagus

▲ CHEWING FOOD *The bolus of food is about to be swallowed. The epiglottis is in its usual position.*

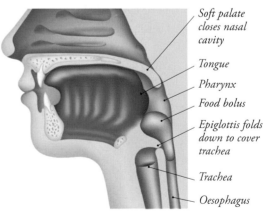

Soft palate closes nasal cavity

Tongue

Pharynx

Food bolus

Epiglottis folds down to cover trachea

Trachea

Oesophagus

▲ SWALLOWING FOOD *On swallowing, the epiglottis moves down to close entry to the trachea.*

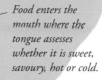

Food enters the mouth where the tongue assesses whether it is sweet, savoury, hot or cold.

Food is swallowed and passes into the oesophagus. It is moved by muscle contractions called peristalsis.

BEYOND THE STOMACH

After leaving the stomach, food enters the small intestine. This is where nutrients are absorbed from the food for use by your body. Material that isn't digested passes into the large intestine where it's turned into faeces.

WOW!

Why does your stomach "growl" when empty? If you are hungry, your stomach receives signals from the brain to begin digestion. The muscles begin to work and acid is mixed in the stomach without food. This produces vibrations we hear as growls.

Inbuilt protection
The stomach wall is deeply folded and pitted. Mucus is constantly secreted to prevent the stomach's acids from digesting itself.

Gastric pit

Mucus

The large intestine is where the last nutrients are extracted together with water. Undigested material is combined with other waste products and moved on to the rectum before passing out of the body.

The pancreas constantly releases digestive juices into the small intestine.

The liver is thought to have more than 250 different functions. Among these, it processes nutrients, removing what your body needs. It also stores glucose (which gives you energy) and breaks down harmful substances.

The gall bladder stores bile, a digestive juice. Bile is used to break down fats.

The large intestine is wider than the small intestine.

The small intestine is a long tangled tube that produces many different enzymes to digest food. The tube is covered inside with tiny, finger-like projections called villi. These increase the intestine's surface area for the absorption of nutrients.

FASTFACTS

- The stomach can store about 1.5 litres (2½ pints) of food.
- A meal takes 18-30 hours to pass through the human body.
- The small intestine is about 5 m (17 ft) in length.
- The large intestine is about 1.5 m (5 ft) in length.
- The liver, the body's largest internal organ, produces about 1 litre (2 pints) of bile a day.
- The large intestine contains millions of bacteria.

SOLID OR LIQUID
Solid food takes longer to break down, which means that a meal stays in the stomach for much longer than a drink, which may pass through in minutes.

The start of life

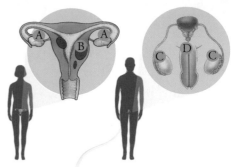

Human life begins after a sperm fertilizes an egg and the egg develops in the uterus (the womb). A fertilized human egg takes about nine months to grow into a baby ready for birth. In the uterus, the foetus depends on the placenta (the tissue that links the mother's and foetus's blood) for all its needs.

▲ REPRODUCTIVE ORGANS
Women have two ovaries (A), where eggs, or ova, are stored, and a uterus (B), where a baby is nourished and grows until birth. Men have two testes (C), where sperm are made. They also have a penis (D) through which the sperm travel to get to the eggs.

FERTILIZATION

Millions of sperm swim towards the egg, propelled forward by flexible tails, but usually only one will fertilize it. On contact, the sperm and egg merge to create a single cell – the fertilized egg. The cell then begins to divide.

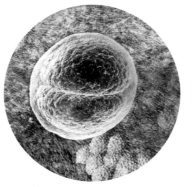
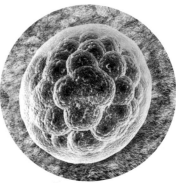

1 WITHIN 36 HOURS *the fertilized egg has divided into two cells. Twelve hours later it has divided into four cells, and so on.*

2 THREE TO FOUR DAYS *after fertilization, there is a cluster of 16 to 32 cells. The cluster enters the uterus.*

Each sperm has a rounded head and a long tail.

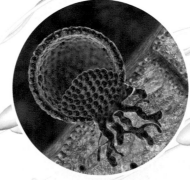
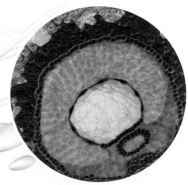

3 ABOUT SIX DAYS *after fertilization, the cell cluster forms a hollow cavity. It attaches itself to the lining of the uterus with root-like growths.*

4 ABOUT EIGHT DAYS *after fertilization, an embryo begins to form. New cells will form tissues and organs as a baby develops.*

After an egg is fertilized it begins to form a barrier to other sperm.

ULTRASOUND SCAN

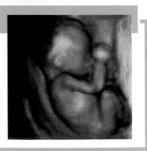

■ This is a scan of a foetus inside the womb, taken between four and six months into pregnancy. It was produced using sound waves to form a picture, which was then turned into a three-dimensional (3-D) image. 3-D scans first appeared in 1987.

GROWING EMBRYO

Cells continue to divide as the embryo develops. They become specialized, with the head, brain, body and heart taking shape first, followed by the arms (initially as buds) and lastly the legs. From eight weeks after fertilization, the baby is known as a foetus.

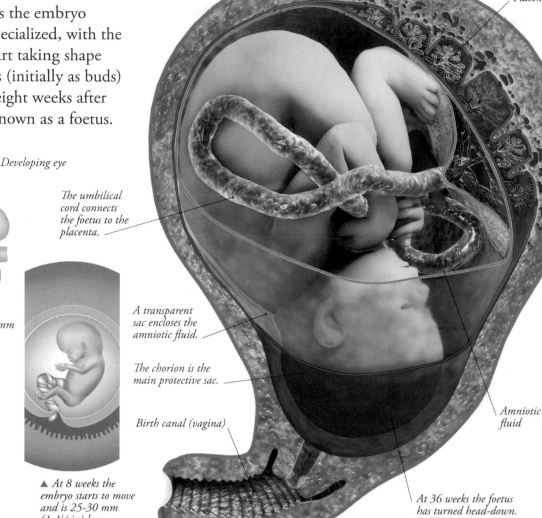

Placenta

The umbilical cord connects the foetus to the placenta.

A transparent sac encloses the amniotic fluid.

The chorion is the main protective sac.

Birth canal (vagina)

Amniotic fluid

At 36 weeks the foetus has turned head-down. It fills the uterus.

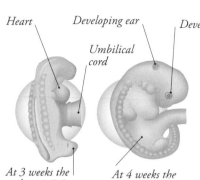

Heart

Developing ear

Developing eye

Umbilical cord

At 3 weeks the embryo is 2-3 mm (³⁄₅₀-⁵⁄₅₀ in) long.

At 4 weeks the embryo is 4-5 mm (¹⁄₅ in) long.

Growing embryo Three weeks after fertilization, the embryo is smaller than a pea and looks a bit like a tadpole. At eight weeks, the embryo looks more human, but is only the size of a strawberry. The foetus is fully developed at 24 weeks. The last stage of development is growth.

▲ At 8 weeks the embryo starts to move and is 25-30 mm (1-1⅕ in) long.

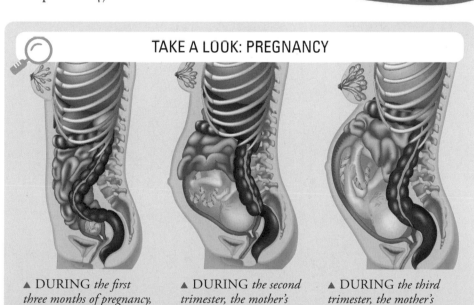

TAKE A LOOK: PREGNANCY

▲ DURING *the first three months of pregnancy, called the first trimester, the mother's breasts become larger. Many pregnant women feel sick around this time.*

▲ DURING *the second trimester, the mother's breasts continue to enlarge, her heart rate increases, and her enlarging womb shows as the foetus grows inside.*

▲ DURING *the third trimester, the mother's intestines and organs are pushed up. She may feel tired, have back pain, and get breathless when walking about.*

Newborn babies adapt quickly to life in the outside world. The umbilical cord, by which it was attached to its mother during pregnancy, is cut. The baby takes its first breaths, forcing its circulation to start working.

TELL ME MORE...

Run and jump, eat a varied diet, and drink lots of water. All these things will help your body to stay as healthy as it can.

Stay healthy

You have just one body for life, so it makes sense to look after it. Giving your body the best chance you can means it will work better for you. That begins with a healthy, mixed diet.

EAT A RAINBOW

Foods can be divided into groups, such as grains and cereals and meat and fish. It is good to eat a range of foods every day, and choose from all the major food groups, eating more of some and less of others (for example, you should eat more fruit than meat or fish). Thinking of food groups as a rainbow of colours can help to separate foods into these groups.

OIL/SUGAR *Small quantities of oil are needed in the diet. A good source is oily fish, such as salmon. Try to limit sugar.*

MEAT, FISH, BEANS, AND LENTILS *provide protein for growth and repair, as well as vitamins and minerals.*

DAIRY *products, such as cheeses and yoghurts, are a rich source of calcium, which helps your bones and teeth.*

FRUIT *is a source of vitamins, water, and fibre, as well as natural sugars.*

VEGETABLES *are rich in fibre and in the vitamins and minerals our bodies need for growth and repair.*

GRAINS *Bread, rice, and pasta, as well as potatoes, are largely carbohydrate, the body's main source of energy.*

HEALTH PROBLEMS

It's not always easy for somebody to stay well. There may not be access to clean drinking water, or food may be restricted. Malnutrition is a serious problem in some parts of the world, which is when somebody doesn't have enough of one or more of the food groups. But if your immune system is working well, it will act to protect your body from illness, fighting off the viruses and bacteria that may cause you harm.

KIDNEYS

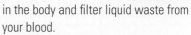

- Your two kidneys are at the back of your abdomen.
- The kidneys control the amount of fluid in the body and filter liquid waste from your blood.
- Filtered waste is removed to the bladder and then expelled as urine.

WHAT MAKES US SICK?

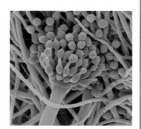

- **Bacteria** are single-celled organisms. Most are harmless, but certain bacteria invade our bodies to cause illness. Tuberculosis is caused by bacteria.

- **Viruses** are far smaller than bacteria. They attack our cells from the inside, taking them over. Colds and flus are the result of a viral infection.

- **Fungi** usually cause infection on the skin's surface, like dandruff, but other fungi can cause serious illness inside the body by damaging the cells.

White blood cells These cells fight bacteria and viruses that might make you sick. Some produce antibodies that work to kill germs. Babies are born with antibodies they inherit from their mother, but they begin to develop their own as they grow.

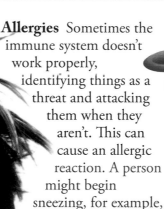

Red blood cell

White blood cell

Allergies Sometimes the immune system doesn't work properly, identifying things as a threat and attacking them when they aren't. This can cause an allergic reaction. A person might begin sneezing, for example, when in contact with pollen or dust.

HOW TO STAY HEALTHY

- Vitamins and minerals are found in many foods, and are essential to general body health.

- Exercise helps strengthen the heart, lungs, and muscles. It also helps to keep the body supple.

- Water is needed for all of the body's processes to function properly. Dehydrated cells will not perform at their best.

- Good hygiene helps to keep germs away. Brushing teeth helps combat tooth decay by cleaning teeth of the bacteria that cause it.

◀ HAYFEVER
Increasing numbers of people around the world are suffering from allergies, such as hayfever. Hayfever is an allergic response to plant pollen. This can be worse at particular times of year, when the pollen count is high.

Glossary

Alveoli Tiny sacs in the lungs through which oxygen and carbon dioxide pass to and from the blood.

Altitude Height above sea level.

Amphibian Cold-blooded vertebrate such as a frog or newt.

Apprenticeship Working under a skilled craftsperson to learn a trade.

Artefact Object made by human workmanship.

Arteries Blood vessels that carry oxygen-rich blood away from the heart.

Artificial intelligence A branch of science that aims to create intelligent machines.

Astrolabe An ancient instrument used to calculate the position of stars in the sky.

Atmosphere The mass of air that surrounds the Earth.

Atoll A ring of coral reef surrounding a central lagoon.

Bacteria Single-celled micro-organisms that can be helpful or harmful.

Big bang The cosmic explosion that created the universe billions of years ago.

Biodiversity The range of different organisms that live in a particular area.

Biofuel Any fuel made from biological matter, such as plants or animal waste.

Biome Any of Earth's major ecosystems with a particular climate and vegetation.

Black hole A collapsed star in which the pull of gravity is so strong that not even light can escape it.

Calligraphy The art of decorative writing.

Camouflage A colour or pattern on an organism's body that allows it to blend in with its surroundings.

Canopy The uppermost leafy layer of a tree or forest.

Canyon A deep, narrow valley with steep sides.

Capillaries Tiny blood vessels that connect arteries to veins.

Carnivore An animal that eats only meat.

Cells The building blocks of almost all living organisms.

Ceramic Any object made from clay and hardened by heat.

Chlorophyll The green pigment in plants that helps them absorb sunlight for photosynthesis.

Chromosomes Packages of DNA found inside the nucleus of most cells.

Colloid A suspension of fine particles dispersed in a liquid.

Colony A group of organisms that live together.

Condensation The change of state from a gas to a liquid or a liquid to a solid.

Continent One of several large landmasses on Earth.

Climate The average weather conditions over a long period of time.

Cloning The process of producing genetically identical animals or plants.

Communism A political theory based on the common ownership of property.

Crystal A solid in which the atoms or molecules from which it is made are lined up in a regular pattern.

Cubism A style of art that shows a scene from several different points of view all at once.

Deities Gods and goddesses.

Democracy A system of government in which people elect their leaders.

Diaphragm A sheet of muscle that separates the lungs from the stomach.

Dictator A ruler who has absolute power.

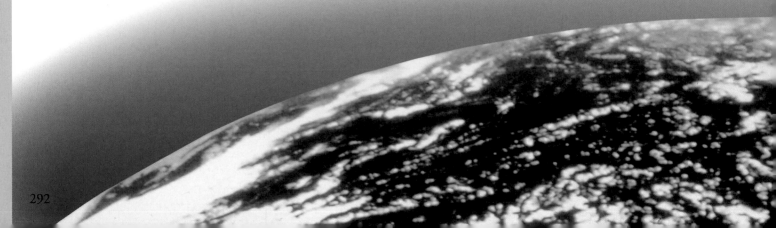

Distillation Purifying a liquid by boiling it and then collecting the vapour.

DNA Deoxyribonucleic acid, the molecule that contains the blueprint for life.

Echolocation Seeing objects with sound by bouncing sound waves off them and detecting the reflections.

Ecosystem The community of organisms living in a particular area.

Elytra The hard forewings of beetles, earwigs, and some bugs.

Embryo Organism in the earliest stage of its development.

Epiphyte A plant that grows on another plant without damaging it.

Evaporate To change from a liquid to a gas.

Evolution The gradual development of living things over a long period of time.

Exoskeleton An external skeleton that supports and protects an animal's body.

Extinct No longer existing on Earth.

Famine Severe shortage of food, causing widespread hunger.

Fertilization When male and female sex cells unite to form an embryo.

Filtration The process of separating liquids from solids using a filter.

Foetus The developing young of an animal before it is born.

Fossil fuels Fuels formed from the remains of animals and plants that lived millions of years ago.

Friction The force that opposes movement.

Fuel cell A device like a battery that generates electricity from fuel and oxygen.

Fungi A large group of organisms, including mushrooms and yeasts, that feed by breaking down the bodies of other organisms.

Galaxies Groups of dust, gases, and stars that fill the universe.

Genes Stretches of DNA that contain the code needed to build a particular protein.

Genome The entire genetic make-up of an organism.

Gills Feathery structures on the bodies of amphibians and fish through which oxygen is absorbed from the water.

Gourd A large, fleshy fruit with a hard skin.

Gravity The force that pulls objects together.

Greenhouse gases Gases in Earth's atmosphere that trap heat from the Sun and warm the planet.

Habitat The place in which an animal or plant lives in nature.

Herbivore An animal that eats only plants.

Hominids The family of primates to which humans belong.

Impressionism A 19th-century style of art characterized by highly finished pieces of art that reflected the artist's response to what they saw.

Inertia The tendency of an object to remain at rest or in constant motion unless a force is applied to it.

Invertebrate An animal without a backbone.

Joints The meeting point of bones.

Keratin Tough protein found in animals' hair, nails, claws, hooves, horns, feathers, and scales.

Lagoon An enclosed body of water cut off from the sea by a reef or other landform.

Lava Molten rock flowing on the surface of Earth.

Magma Molten rock flowing under the surface of Earth.

Mammals Warm-blooded, furry animals that feed their young with milk.

Mantle Thick rocky layer of Earth between the crust and the core.

Marsupial A mammal that rears its young in a pouch or fold of skin, usually on its front.

Matter Anything that has mass and takes up space.

Meditation The process of emptyng the mind of thoughts allowing the body to relax.

Metamorphosis A change in body form shown in animals such as insects and amphibians as they grow into adults.

Microchip The part of a computer made from silicon on which electronic circuits are etched.

Migration Moving from one place to another according to the seasons, usually to find food or to breed.

Mineral Solid material found in nature, usually as a crystal.

Mirage Optical illusion in which hot air distorts the reflection of an object.

Monarchy A ruling system in which a king or queen is the head of a country but does not necessarily govern it.

Mosaic An image created by using small pieces of coloured glass or stone.

Nanotubes A sheet of carbon atoms rolled up into a tube with a diameter of 1 or 2 nanometres.

National anthem The official song sung in celebration of a particular country.

Nebula A gas cloud in space from which stars are born.

Neurons Nerve cells.

Nutrients Substances your body needs to live and grow.

Omnivore An animal that eats all kinds of food, both plant and meat.

Opera A dramatic work set to music.

Orchestra A group of musicians playing different types of instruments, from string and brass to woodwind and percussion.

Organism An individual member of a species.

Ozone Colourless gas that forms a layer in Earth's atmosphere, absorbing some of the harmful ultraviolet radiation in sunlight.

Parasite An organism that lives on another organism and feeds off it.

Peat A rich type of soil formed from plants and their decaying remains.

Periodic table A table that organizes all the known elements in order of increasing atomic number.

Peristalsis The muscle contraction in the walls of the oesophagus and intestines that help us swallow and digest food.

Persecution The harrassment of an individual or group because of their race or beliefs.

Pharaoh The title given to the ancient kings of Egypt.

Photosynthesis The process by which plants make their own food using the energy from sunlight.

Phylum The biggest division within a kingdom of living things. A phylum is further divided into classes, orders, families, genera, and species.

Phytoplankton Tiny plants and algae that drift in the ocean and form a source of food for larger marine animals.

Pigment A substance that colours other materials.

Pilgrim Someone who travels to a sacred place as an act of religious devotion.

Pixel A tiny piece of information that makes up an image on a screen.

Pointillism A painting style that uses small dots of colour.

Pollinators Animals that carry pollen from one flower to another.

Pollutants Any substance that contaminates the environment.

Post mortem The medical examination of a dead body to establish the cause of death.

Poverty Not having enough money to take care of basic needs such as food and clothing.

Predator An animal that hunts other animals.

Prey An animal that is hunted by other animals.

Prophet A person who receives divinely inspired revelations.

Prosthetics The branch of medicine that deals with the manufacture of artificial body parts.

Pupating A stage in an insect's life cycle when the larva breaks down inside a pupa and transforms into an adult.

Reflection When light bounces off a surface and then travels in a different direction.

Refraction When light bends as it travels from one substance to another.

Refugee A person who flees his or her own country to escape danger.

Reptiles Group of cold-blooded vertebrates that breathe air using lungs, such as snakes and lizards.

Reservoir A large artificial lake used to store water.

Rodents Mammals with large incisors used to gnaw hard substances.

Ruminate To regurgitate food and chew it again – sometimes called "chewing the cud".

Savanna Tropical grassland with distinct wet and dry seasons.

Scavengers Organisms that feed on the remains of dead organisms.

Shaman A religious leader in some tribes who is thought to have the power to heal people.

Species A group of similar organisms that can breed and produce fertile offspring.

Spores The reproductive structures of some plants and fungi.

Stem cell A type of cell that can multiply and develop into different types of cells.

Sublimation When a solid changes directly into a gas (or gas into solid) without first becoming a liquid.

Succulent A plant such as a cactus that has fleshy tissue to conserve water.

Sultan The ruler of a Muslim country.

Supernova The bright explosion that occurs as a star collapses.

Tendons The strips of fibrous tissue that connect muscles to bones.

Textiles Cloth or fabric produced by weaving or knitting.

Tissues Collections of cells that work together to do the same job.

Transgenic A genetically modified organism that contains a gene from another species.

Transpiration The loss of water by evaporation from plant leaves and stems.

Tricolour A flag with three coloured stripes.

Tsunami A large wave created by a volcano or earthquake, usually under the surface of the ocean.

Veins Blood vessels that carry oxygen-poor blood back to the heart.

Velocity Speed in a given direction.

Venom poisonous liquid produced by some animals, such as snakes and spiders.

Vertebrate An animal with a backbone.

Viruses Tiny particles that take over cells and reproduce inside them.

Viscosity The "thickness" of a fluid.

Vizier A high-ranking official in a Muslim government.

Index

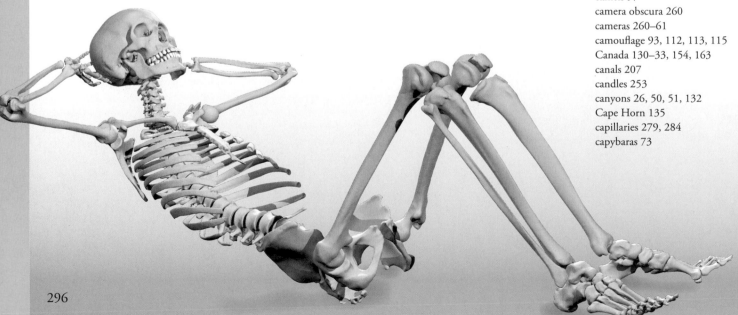

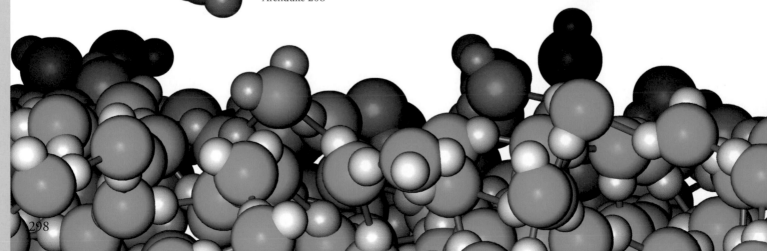

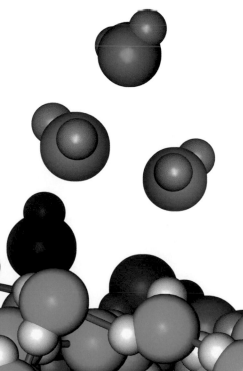

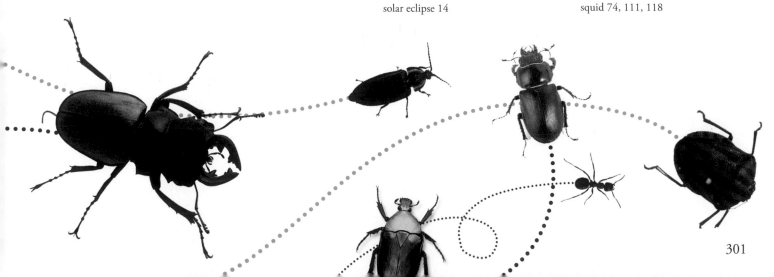

Acknowledgements

The publisher would like to thank the following for their kind permission to reproduce their photographs:

(Key: a-above; b-below/bottom; c-centre; f-far; l-left; r-right; t-top)

akg-images: 208br, 210tl, 253crb; RIA Nowosti 213bl; **Alamy Images:** Bryan & Cherry Alexander 130crb, 149tl, 171tr; Arco Images 91ca, 99tc; ARCO Images GmbH 51br, 124t, 142bl, 151br; Arco Images GmbH / Wittek, R. 93fbr; Olivier Asselin 170cb; avatra images 112cla; B.A.E. Inc 52cr; Bill Bachmann 151cr, 171bl; Stephen Barnes / Religion 159cb; Stephen Bisgrove 145cl; Blickwinkel 32t, 98bc, 115br, 115cla, 117cl; Steve Bloom Images 94l; Oote Boe Photography 185c; BrazilPhotos.com 134cb; Scott Camazine 91cl; Steve Cavalier 108cl; Chris Cheadle 45bl, 132tl; Classic Image 197bc; David Coleman 181bc; Derek Croucher 37tc; David Noble Photography 127tr, 145cr, 148tc; David R. Frazier Photolibrary, Inc. 87br; Danita Delimont 136tr; David Dent 29bl, 44b; Redmond Durrell 109bc; Chad Ehlers 29tc, 31tr, 52cra; Elvele Images Ltd 107cr, 107cra; Eye Ubiquitous 63c; David Fleetham 109br, Free Agents Limited 177tr; Tim Gainey 91tl; Geophoto / Natalia Chervyakova / Imagebroker 119bl; Mike Goldwater 149tc; Tim Graham 133tc; Sally & Richard Greenhill 171br; David Gregs 126-154 (sidebar); Robert Harding Picture Library 3ca, 38clb, 38tr, 136b; Martin Harvey 141tr; Shaun Higson 165tl; Bert Hoferichter 181tr; Holmes Garden Photos 193tc; Horizon International Images Limited 38t, 52tr; Peter Horree 180cl; Chris Howes / Wild Places Photography 140tr; IGG Digital Graphic Productions GmbH 176bc; Image Register 052 235cr; Image Source Pink 176cl; Image Source Pink / IS752 157bc; imagebroker 141tl, 196cl; Images and Stories 180c; Images of Africa Photobank 29tr, 39tr, 127tl, 140b, 140cr; Interfoto Pressbildagentur 134b, 137ca, 196t, 196-197, 253bl; Interfoto Pressebildagentur 168-169 (background); J L Images 132-133b; Huw Jones 167cl; Juniors Bildarchiv 113tc; Juniors Bildarchiv / F349 93crb; Jupiterimages 39cr, 52ftr; Anthony Kay / Flight 52crb; Steven J. Kazlowski 96bl; Georgios Kollidas 253br; Karl Kost 149cr; H Lansdown 121cr; Leslie Garland Picture Library 45bc; Mark Lewis 151t; Tony Lilley 145br; The London Art Archive 145bc; Suzanne Long 164tr; Lou-Foto 168fcra; Dirk V Mallinckrodt 91c; Mary Evans Picture Libray 207c, 207crb; Medical-on-line 256cb; Mettafoto 260t; Mira 49bl; Mirrorpix 171tl; Jeff Morgan 172br; NASA 49tl; Nature Picture Library 173cl; Ron Niebrugge 97tl; North Wind Picture Archives 192-193b, 199br, 200br, 201bc, 206c, 244t; Michael Patrick O'Neill 134cr; Edward Parker 113c; pbpgalleries 173tl; David Pearson 149br; Photos 12 261tl; PHOTOTAKE Inc 266tl; Pictures Colour Library 173bl; Chuck Place 126bl, 132cl; Print Collector 197bl, 199cra, 208bl, 209bl; Rolf Richardson 177t; Jeff Rotman 112cra; Allen Russell 133c; Andre Seale 134c; Alex Segre 145tr; Dmitry Shubin 214c; Stefan Sollfors 113bl; Norbert Speicher 268c; Keren Su / China Span 148b; John Sundlof 217bl; Liba Taylor 289br; Travelshots.com 46fclb; Martyn Vickery 193tl; View Stock 253ca; Visual & Written SL 72r; Visual&Written SL 112br; Visum Foto GmbH 144b; David Wall 208cl; John Warburton-Lee Photography 180crb; Richard Wareham Fotografie 1ftr, 3c, 133cl; Wasabi 177cb; WidStock 43cr; World History Archive 204tl; Worldspec / NASA 126-127; **Ancient Art & Architecture Collection:** C M Dixon 187tl; **Anglo Australian Observatory:** 7tr, 13bc, 13br; **Ardea:** Steve Downer 96tl; Kenneth W. Fink 97cr; **The Bridgeman Art Library:** 190br; Capitol Collection, Washington, USA 201c; Look and Learn 191t, 207t, 252clb; Museum of Fine Arts, Boston, Massachusetts, USA, William Sturgis Bigelow Collection 220tl; Private Collection 188cl; Private Collection / © Michael Graham-Stewart 202tl; **Bryan and Cherry Alexander Photography:** 161cl; **Carnegie Observatories - Giant Magellan Telescope :** Giant Magellan Telescope 21br; **Corbis:** 174cla, 211bl, 211cl, 259tl; Alinari Archives 165bl; Theo Allofs 49, 63br; The Andy Warhol Foundation for the Visual Arts 167tr; ANSA / ANSA 257tr; H. Armstrong Roberts 221br; Art on File 79br; The Art Archive 191bc, 192tl, 212t; Anthony Bannister / Gallo Images 108bl; Dave Bartruff 213crb; Bettmann 2cr, 3br, 24bc, 34c, 163bl, 169cla, 193bc, 200cr, 203bl, 203cl, 204bl, 206br, 206t, 207bc, 209t, 210bc, 210br, 213tr, 221bl, 246bl, 254cl, 254crb, 257bl, 275cr; Stefano Bianchetti 220tr; Jonathan Blair 19b; Blend Images 162tr; Gary Braasch 81bc; Tom Brakefield 84cl, 85cb, 98t; Brand X / Southern Stock 269bl; Brand X / Triolo Productions / Burke 117crb; Bojan Brecelj 203tr; Andrew Brookes 228-229; Brunei Information / epa 216cb; Burstein Collection 253cb; Car Culture 79crb; Angelo Cavalli / Zefa 160c (background); CDC / PHIL 93br; Ron Chapple 52ca; Christie's Images 3ftr, 212br; Christie's Images / © ADAGP, Paris and DACS, London 2009 167bc; Ralph A. Clevenger 109tr; W. Cody 167bl; Construction Photography 42b; Gianni Dagli Orti 165c, 189bc; Fridmar Damm 71tr, 89bc, 145bl; Tim Davis / Davis Lynn Wildlife 97tc; Deborah Betz Collection 221bc; P. Deliss/Godong 294-295; Sebastien Desarmaux/Godong 162cra; DLILLC 120b; DLILLC / Davis Lynn Wildlife 4-5, 97cra; Doc-stock 111 (Leech); Edifice 253clb; EPA 1fbl, 54br, 55cr, 162br, 162ca, 162cr, 185br; Frederic Soltan 37t; Michael Freeman 185tl; Stephen Frink 111 (Clams), 121br, 122-123t; Jose Fuste Raga 148tl, 180bl, 181c; The Gallery Collection 166bl, 166cl, 166t, 191br, 212clb; David Gard / Star Ledger 172-173; John Gillmoure 162-163; Lynn Goldsmith 156-157; Frank Greenaway 120tl; Martin Harvey 119tc, 120-121ca; Lindsay Hebberd 157cla; Lindsay Herbberd 163cl; Historical Picture Archive 164c; Jack Hollingsworth 129t; Julie Houck 122bl; Carol Hughes 111br; Hulton Collection 211cb; Richard Hutchings 170bl; Image 100 241tr; Image Source 233cl; Simon Jarratt 243bc; JJamArt 164bl; Sylwia Kapuscinski 176bl; Kevin Schafer 1bl, 3 (Parthenon), 73cl, 105cl, 121t, 183tr, 190clb; Matthias Kulka 290-291b, 291tc; Frans Lanting 2br, 59ftr, 66-67t, 73br, 81clb, 81tr, 84ca, 84cra; Danny Lehman 58bc, 163tc; Charles & Josette Lenars 198tr; James Leynse 249crb; Massimo Listri 168fbr; Gerd Ludwig 85bc; Alen MacWeeney 165crb; David Madison 179c; Lawrence Manning 232c; James Marshall 136c; Robert Matheson 292-293; Buddy Mays 97tr; Mary Ann McDonald 94cr; Momatiuk-Eastcott 82-83; Moodboard 163clb, 249fbr; Arthur Morris 3ftl, 106t, 107tr; Kevin R. Morris 162cl; NASA 52bl; David A. Northcott 101cl; Richard T Nowitz 163cr, 200bl, 201cl; Tim Pannell 178tl; Paul A. Souders 3tr, 57tc, 64t, 73bc, 173clb, 219tl, 236cl; Douglas Pearson 157ca, 181tc; Philadelphia Museum of Art / © Succession Picasso/DACS 2009 167tl; Michael Pole 87; Radius Images 163br; Enzo & Paolo Ragazzini 184b; Roger Ressmeyer 21cl, 24crb, 158br, 170tr, 221cl, 265b; Reuters 5tc, 21c, 25c, 44t, 162bc, 172bl, 205tr, 209cr, 239fbr, 253tl, 255br, 266tr; Reuters / Rafael Perez 216ca; Neil C. Robinson 224clb; Roger Ressmeyer / NASA 26cl; Jenny E. Ross 4tr, 95bl; Pete Saloutos 256cl; Jacques Sarrat / Sygma 174-175; Alan Schein 239bl; Phil Schermeister 61cl; Herb Schmitz 120 121; Denis Scott 18; Denis Scott / Comet 92bl; Smithsonian Institution 198c; Joseph Sohm / Visions of America 201cra; Ted Soqui 255ca; Stapleton Collection 252t; George Steinmetz 264br; STScI/NASA 6-7; Jim Sugar 45c; Sygma 84cla, 134clb, 173cra, 255cb; Sygma / (c) Tracey Emin, courtesy White Cube (London) 167crb; Ramin Talaie 25crb; Paul Thompson / Ecoscene 161br; Penny Tweedie 3bl, 161cr, 171tc; Underwood & Underwood 181bl, 205cr; Vanni Archive 181tl; Steven Vidler 177bl; Visuals Unlimited 284cr, 291ca, 291tl; Werner Forman 198cr, 199tl; Michele Westmorland 121cl; Nick Wheeler 163tr; Ralph White 245br; Steve Wilkings 4tl, 50; Douglas P. Wilson / Frank Lane Picture Agency 123bc; Keith Wood 43bl; Lawson Wood 110fcl (Sponges); Michael S Yashamita 35c; Zefa 84bl, 224bc, 242t; Jim Zuckerman 273bl; **F. Deschandol & Ph. Sabine:** 117bc, 117br; **DK Images:** Roger Bridgman 260cl; British Library 168bc, 168br, 212bc; British Library Board 168fbl; British Museum 172t, 184cr, 184crb, 184tr, 199tr; Geoff Dann / Jeremy Hunt - modelmaker 280br, 281cl; Courtesy of the Egyptian Museum, Cairo 189cl; ESA - ESTEC 25fbr; Rowan Greenwood 5tl, 161cla; Imperial War Museum 210c; Simon James 191bl; Jamie Marshall 63tr, 161ca, 183tl, 213tc; Judith Miller / Ancient Art 168tc; Judith Miller / Sloan's 182bc, 195br; Judith Miller / Wallis and Wallis 195fbr; Courtesy of The Museum of London 187cr; Museum of the Order of St John, London 168bl; NASA 25bl, 25clb, 25tc; National Maritime Museum, London 183bl, 196cb; National Museum of Kenya 186br; Courtesy of the Natural History Museum, London 39bc, 40 (Limestone), 40 (Pegmatite), 40 (Siltstone), 40 (Tillite), 41, 41 (Agate), 41 (Calcite), 41 (Lapis lazuli), 41 (Magnetite), 41 (Quartz), 41 (Sulfur), 68br, 69c, 104cr, 116cr, 186bc, 186fbl, 187tc, 224br, 245, 245 (Gomphotherium), 245 (Moeritherium); Stephen Oliver 47br; Oxford University Museum of Natural History 40 (Peridotite); Courtesy of Sam Tree of Keygrove Marketing Ltd 249cla; Courtesy of The Science Museum, London 38c, 40 (Obsidian), 40 (Pumice), 169fcra, 220bl; St Mungo, Glasgow Museums 159fcr; Courtesy of the U.S. Army Heritage and Education Center - Military History Institute 185tc, 202cra; Courtesy of The American Museum of Natural History 187c; Courtesy of the University Museum of Archaeology and Anthropology, Cambridge 187crb; Wilberforce House Museum, Hull City Council 203tl; Jerry Young 61cr, 102c, 117ftr, 138c; **David Doubilet:** 74c; **ESA:** 21t; **FLPA:** Ingo Arndt / Minden Pictures 116tl; Nigel Cattlin 116bl, 116crb; R. Dirscherl 103cra; Michael & Patricia Fogden / Minden 79bl; Mitsuaki Iwago / Minden Pictures 95ca; Heidi & Hans-Juergen Koch 102cr; Gerard Lacz 99tl; Chris Newbert / Minden 109cr; Norbert Wu / Minden Pictures 106cl, 302-303; Pete Oxford 102cl; Schauhuber/Imagebroker 117fbr; Mark Sisson 113br; Jan Vermeer / Minden Pictures 106br; Tom Vezo / Minden Pictures 112cl; Albert Visage 120c; Tony Wharton 121bl; Shin Yoshino 84clb; **Courtesy of Friendly Robotics:** 267cr; **R Gendler:** 1ftl, 11bl; **Getty Images:** 55br, 115c, 136bl, 167br, 180tl, 185tr, 214tr, 215tr, 247bc, 257c, 257cl; Peter Adams 137br; AFP 141bl, 157fcla, 159fbr, 173bc, 173tr, 183br, 211cr, 215br, 215cl, 215cr, 247c, 251tc, 255cra, 267l; AFP Photo / Jamie Mcdonald / Pool 179cb; Doug Allan 149bc; William Albert Allard 127br, 149tr; Theo Allofs 65cl, 151bc; Altrendo 62c; Tito Atchaa 238bc; Rob Atkins 230 (skyline sunset); Aurora / Ian Shive 110cr (coral); Aurora / Jurgen Freund 92tr; Aurora / Sean Davey 103bc; Paul Avis 239bc; Axiom Photographic Agency 183tc, 199clb; Daryl Balfour 140tc, 244bl; Jim Ballard 12; John W Banagan 2cra, 45r, 238fbr; Anthony Bannister 65tc; Tancredi J Bavosi 234bl; Walter Bibikow 231bl; Steve Bly 49tr; Steve Bonini 67tr; Philippe Bourseiller 77fbr; John Bracegirdle 67cr; Per Breiehagen 130b; The Bridgeman Art Library 133cr, 165tr, 189br, 193br, 196br, 196cr, 212bl, 252crb; The Bridgeman Art Library / Anton Agelo Bonifazi 159t; The Bridgeman Art Library / German School 3cb, 159ftr, 169tc; The Bridgeman Art Library / Italian School 158b (background); The Bridgeman Art Library / Ludwig van Beethoven 175ftr; Jan Bruggeman 240-241; Frank & Joyce Burek 75bc; JH Pete Carmichael 110cr (Tarantula); Luis Castaneda Inc 111bc; Angelo Cavalli 63tc, 137bl; Paul Chesley 81cla; China Span / Keren Su 169cb; John Coletti 69br; Jeffrey Coolidge 80bl, 230 (plugs), 232t, 243br; Gary Cornhouse 262tr; Livia Corona 137tr; Daniel J. Cox 59fbl, 69cr; DEA / G. Cozzi Cozzi 140tl; Derek Croucher 101tc; Mark Daffey 73bl; Stefano Dal Pozzolo - Vatican Pool 159fcla; Geoff Dann 165cl; Peter David 75br; De Agostini Picture Library 3fbl, 39cra, 182-183c, 189t, 190c; Digital Vision 52-53, 59bc, 59bl, 60cr, 200cl, 204cr, 205cb, 217tr, 230 (radio), 238br, 240r, 242bl; Digital Vision / Rob Melnychuk 158bl; DigitalGlobe 35br, 35crb;